Riches for All

Riches for All

The California Gold Rush and the World

Edited by
Kenneth N. Owens

University of Nebraska Press
Lincoln and London

A variation of chapter 10 appeared as "The Last Fandango"
in *Roaring Camp: The Social World of the California Gold Rush*
by Susan Lee Johnson. Copyright by Susan Lee Johnson.
Used by permission of W. W. Norton & Company, Inc.
Library of Congress Cataloging-in-Publication Data
Riches for all: the California Gold Rush and the world / edited
by Kenneth N. Owens.
     p. cm.
Includes bibliographical references and index.
ISBN 0-8032-3570-4 (cl.: alk. paper) – ISBN 0-8032-8617-1 (pbk. : alk. paper)
1. California–Gold discoveries–Social aspects.   2. California–Ethnic
relations.   3. California–Social conditions–19th century.
4. Minorities–California–Social conditions–19th century.
5. Immigrants–California–Social conditions–19th century.
6. Frontier and pioneer life–California.   I. Owens, Kenneth N.
F865.O94 2002
979.4'04—dc21
2002022323

To the memory of Rodman W. Paul

Contents

Preface

These essays are the work of scholars who have undertaken to reassess and reevaluate select aspects of California gold rush history. Some contributors are relatively young historians; others have spent a great many years researching, writing, and teaching about the American West. Included are a few who have not previously written about California or the gold rush era. But in preparation for this assignment, all have devoted time and energy to considering the California gold rush in ways pertinent to their own areas of interest and expertise. All have examined substantial bodies of documentary sources, and all have considered interpretive points that might perhaps be overlooked by specialists who limit their study only to the gold rush period in the Golden State.

The essays have their source in a series of public lectures, the Gold Rush Sesquicentennial Lectures, presented in 1998–1999 in Sacramento, California's state capital and the premier boom city of the gold country 150 years earlier. The opening lecture in the series, Malcolm Rohrbough's account of the international rush to northern California, was a feature of the 1998 annual meeting of the Western History Association, at Sacramento's Hyatt Regency Hotel. The remaining fourteen lectures alternated between town and gown venues, either in the student union on the campus of California State University, Sacramento, in the Secretary of State's auditorium in the California State Archives near the state capitol, or in the main branch of the Sacramento Public Library. From first to last, the lectures attracted substantial and enthusiastic audiences, quick to express their appreciation alike to locally based lecturers and to those who came as visiting scholars, some from considerable distances.

The designated agenda for each lecturer, and so for their essays, was to consider the California gold rush as a world event with reference to their own area of special expertise. Amid a general atmosphere of filiopietistic self-congratulation that characterized much of the state's Gold-Rush-to-Statehood Sesquicentennial ballyhoo between 1998 and 2000, this theme, the gold rush as a world event, provided a useful measure of analytical distance. More to the point, it emphasized the need for historians and their public to remain aware of larger contexts when examining local developments, especially developments of such undisputed significance as the Sutter's mill gold discovery and the subsequent worldwide rush into northern California.[1] As readers will see, the lecturer-essayists exercised free rein in determining how to develop this theme in accord with their own interests, but the results demonstrate substantial intellectual coherence, if not an exact interpretive consistency. In a broad sense, the lectures and the essays in this volume, considered together, provide a state-of-the art representation of scholarly views about more than the gold rush itself. They reveal current convictions about the nature of Western history and its meanings, and about many of the concerns important to Western historians as the field continued its conceptual growth at the end of the twentieth century.

The California gold rush was not simply a spontaneous response to news about the presence of gold in the streams and dry gravels of northern California's Mother Lode region, as writers of an earlier age tended to depict it. We view it now as a complex cultural creation, running its course in a setting of psychic, social, and material conditions unique to the time and place, yet exerting influences that extend far beyond the gold country and that can still be observed in our own time. Neither this volume nor any other will provide an all-inclusive history of this remarkably intricate, complicated, endlessly fascinating historical episode. At best, we can approach the whole as industrious placer miners approached the gold-bearing gravels they claimed, by working one bucketful, one drift, one topic at a time.

With unlimited funding resources and a younger, more energetic, per-haps more foolhardy planner and manager, the lecture series and this collection of essays might well have been extended by another dozen or more contributions. Missing here, for example, are discussions both of California's environmental history and the state's wayward political evolu-tion during the gold rush era. Likewise absent are discussions focused on the immigration process, transportation history, gold rush art and literature, and the robust growth of the California economy, which first gave the American nation a strong commercial position on the eastern edge of the Pacific rim. All these and still other topics received consideration at an early, wildly visionary point in planning, but ultimately reality intervened, shaping the project to the dimensions seen here.[2]

This volume, readers should know, does not exactly replicate the lecture series. Beyond the expected editorial emendations that authors made to their lectures for publication, circumstances brought about other changes. Two lecturers found themselves unable to commit to essay versions of their presentations. One essay, Charlene Porsild's gem treating California's influence on the Klondike gold rush a half-century later, was a late addition, prepared for this volume after the end of the lecture series. Also written especially for this work are the editor's two introductory essays. The first is a review of historians' treatment of the California gold rush, intended to provide a thematic context for this work. The second is a review of fundamentals in northern California geography and history that should assist readers who are not already familiar with the local scene and the lore related to the region's one best-known, most abundantly mythologized event.

The success of the lecture series depended on support from diverse sources. Partial funding came from the California Council for the Humanities directed by James Quay and from the University Affairs Office of California State University, Sacramento, through the efforts of csus vice-president Robert Jones. After a promising start, the series nearly became a casualty in the unfortunate collapse of fund-raising efforts by the state government's Gold-Rush-to-Statehood Sesquicentennial Commission. At a critical point, Laura Bekeart Dietz, a member of the Sesquicentennial Foundation board who is rightfully proud of her family heritage from the gold rush period in Coloma, volunteered a generous personal donation that enabled the series to survive. The California Studies Program at csus, headed by Timothy Comstock, provided a last, substantial, very necessary contribution that allowed the series to conclude without red ink on the ledger. Along with these benefactions, the series had the advantage of cost sharing and nonfunding support from the Western History Association, the California State Archives, the office of California Secretary of State Bill Jones, the Sacramento Public Library, and the History Department of csus.

No one who has studied the California gold rush in any detail will need an explanation of this volume's dedication to Rodman W. Paul. With the publication of his work *California Gold: The Beginning of Mining in the Far West* in 1947, Rod Paul became the gold rush's preeminent historian. Based on his Harvard Ph.D. dissertation, this work about the beginning of Western mining inaugurated the modern study of the California gold rush. More broadly, Paul expertly instructed all of us about the importance of this event in the wider world, first in *California Gold*, then in works that examined the mining rushes that spread from California northward and eastward and that provided much of the impetus for later phases of settlement and society building in western America. For anyone who has become engaged with the so-called New Western history over the past few decades, it is well to recall that Rod Paul was one of the first and certainly the best of our teachers. As a writer, a lecturer, and a gentle, kind, astute guide for other historians during his years at the Huntington Library, he put our profession forever in his debt. The Gold Rush Sesquicentennial Lectures and this collection of essays have been from the first intended as a tribute, heartfelt, to the memory of this fine historian and peerless individual.

Kenneth N. Owens

Notes

1. But perhaps not undoubted by everyone. The late Matt Sugarman, for many years the chief ranger at the James Marshall Gold Discovery State Park in Coloma, related with wonder his experience when he nominated Marshall's gold discovery site to the National Register of Historic Places, only to have a National Register staff member in the nation's capital tell him that the 1848 gold discovery did not have the requisite level of significance in American history.

2. For a demonstration of the possible proliferation of topics regarding the California gold rush, one need only examine the outstanding four-volume series prepared under the general editorship of Richard Orsi as special editions of *California History* and published also as separate volumes by the University of California Press. Specific citations to these volumes will be found in the historiographical review that comprises the first chapter of the present work.

Riches for All

Introduction

Kenneth N. Owens

The California Gold Rush in History

During the early months of 1848 stories began to spread through California about gold discoveries at John Sutter's Coloma mill site and further discoveries at the Mormon diggings lower down the American River. Soon these stories were reaching port cities worldwide, moving along the seaways that carried ships from San Francisco Bay, the epicenter of a growing California gold mania. The earliest reports from those at the scene were factual narratives, the tone awed but unembellished.[1] Within a year a cadre of writers—journalists, guidebook authors, and imaginative fabulists—began fashioning a compelling image of the rush, its potential rewards, and the society of gold seekers that it was calling into existence: partly fact, partly exuberant fantasy, partly a literary invention that reflected attitudes and images already fixed in Anglo-American culture. The flow of publications about California continued throughout the 1850s, including the first appearance of journals and memoirs by those who returned from the Pacific Coast to homes in the eastern states. Before 1860, according to the exhaustive, magisterial bibliographical guide prepared by Gary Kurutz of the California State Library, an amazing total of 285 books and pamphlets about gold rush California and the routes to the gold fields had appeared in print.[2]

Among these publications were a dozen or so that achieved best-selling status, going through successive editions, with a few being translated into the major western European languages.[3] In them we find the earliest composite narrative of gold rush history as a distinct and unique episode in American and world development.[4] Their predominant genre is the travel narrative. The authors write as visitors to a strange land, describing the country and its inhabitants for the benefit of curious, comfortable stay-at-homes or prospective tourists. San Francisco, the seaport metropolis that was the usual point of arrival and departure for literary sojourners, became for them a privileged locale; their accounts featured prominently the observable life of its streets, saloons and gambling halls, banking houses, restaurants, commercial exchanges—all the public places that visitors might see. Sacramento, Stockton, and other newly created interior cities were secondary exhibits on the literary tours of these authors. The placer diggings had less sustained interest for most of them, at least in part because food and accommodations in the mining camps frequently failed to meet the authors' minimal standards. And while they all described the methods and the evident toil of placer mining, only two—E. Gould Buffum and Alonzo Delano—had actually dug deep, experiencing firsthand the travails and trials of a placer miner's life.[5]

In keeping with the literary techniques of the travel narrative, these writers customarily incorporated a brief sketch of California before 1848 and an abbreviated version of the start of the gold excitement. This was history at its most elementary level, based on little or nothing more than randomly gathered common knowledge, often ill-informed or misunderstood. The greater value of the earliest gold rush accounts can be found in the eyewitness descriptions the authors sketched with vivid coloration. Along with depictions of mining methods and detailed stories about the hardships of travel, they all offered detailed accounts of the dress and behavior they believed typical of the diverse ethnic groups they found in California, especially California Indian peoples and immigrants from southern China and Latin American countries. Their works described fires and fleas, frequently reported on episodes of lynch law and vigilante activities, and discussed at length the social dislocations and adjustments that resulted from the great rarity of respectable women in California's gold rush society. Uniformly, they strove for a humorous, engaging style, filling their pages with stories that would reveal wryly comical aspects of the gold rush experience. Sketchy, anecdotal, picturesque, funny, their literary efforts embodied a wealth of detail that emphasized in particular the novel, the exotic, and the romantically appealing features of the California gold rush experience.[6]

Widely accessible, this body of material later became familiar to researchers seeking authentic firsthand sources about California society during the early period of the gold excitement. The information and attitudes conveyed by these comparatively few accounts have thus gained a second and third life, into the present. Too often accepted without critical analysis, they have perpetually reinforced a reading of gold rush history first designed to enlighten, titillate, and amuse early Victorian readers.

Within a few years, as literary historian Michael Kowalewski has observed, a second generation of authors began shaping a mythic, sentimentalized version of California's gold rush era that gained far greater attention than the work of their predecessors.[7] The most prominent figures in this grouping were Bret Harte and Mark Twain; their literary fellows included Joaquin Miller, Charles Warren Stoddard, Ina Coolbrith, and Prentice Mulford. From their pens came a collective pseudohistory of California life during the gold rush years, embodied in tales that alternated between burlesque comedy and maudlin, syrupy Victorian sentimentality.[8] Turning from the travel narrative mode, they sought to gain fortune and fame by supplying invented fables of the past, bogus as history and counterfeit in emotional nuances. Harte, Twain, and their compatriots supplied a stock of stereotypes that soon became hackneyed, trite figures: the innocent and naive greenhorn, the grizzled old prospector, the public-spirited gambler, the harlot with the heart of gold. They made their mythical gold rush a stage setting for simple morality plays that the literate Anglo-American public and its cultural authorities, reading them at a distance, might accept as representations of the original—and that have figured prominently ever since in imaginative depictions of gold rush events. The immense popularity of these stories in the eastern United States and abroad can be read as a testimony to their authors' shrewdness in divining and exploiting the tastes of their mostly middle-class, urban audience and their skills in satisfying those tastes.

A more authentic, fact-based history of the gold rush era made its appearance in California during the last decades of the nineteenth century, prompted by a cultural sensibility that sought to record the experience and commemorate the achievements of a generation rapidly disappearing from the scene. Most prominent among those who shaped California's emerging historical consciousness was Hubert Howe Bancroft, a successful San Francisco businessman with New England antecedents. His monumental thirty-nine volume *History of the Pacific States*, cooperatively written by Bancroft and a staff headed by Henry L. Oak, appeared between 1881 and 1890; it included eleven volumes dealing entirely with California, among them one—titled *California Inter Pocula*—about the gold rush, another more broadly chronicling the gold rush era in California history, and two more that concentrated on vigilante episodes and miners' courts.[9] Rivaling

Bancroft's accomplishment was the work of Theodore H. Hittell, whose four-volume *History of California* appeared between 1885 and 1897. The third volume in this work mainly focused on the gold rush and northern California's growth during the gold rush period.[10]

As though in response to the literary imaginings of Harte and Twain, both Bancroft and Hittell took great care to put before the world a full, accurate record of the major events and trends that marked these years. They found their sources principally in published accounts; both relied heavily on California's pioneer newspapers as well as the growing supply of printed journals and memoirs. Bancroft was the more assiduous chronicler of events. He had begun his tremendously ambitious project by collecting an imposing historical library that included a trove of personal manuscripts. He added to his collections by gathering an outstanding archive of oral histories. He also sprinkled his chapters liberally with classical allusions, side by side with undocumented stories of mining adventures and other colorful episodes. Frequently he editorialized, displaying a battery of Yankee Republican attitudes that extended to social, political, and racial matters.

Hittell, who has remained less well known than Bancroft, was a gold rush era pioneer from the upper Midwest, German in family background, who had achieved great professional and financial success as a San Francisco civil lawyer and author of legal treatises. The first two volumes of his California history reflected a long, careful study of the surviving archives of the Spanish and Mexican periods, especially the land records. Hittell's third volume, published in 1897, provides an account of the gold rush period that is more precise in statement and less highly colored than Bancroft's comparable work. While his social attitudes were scarcely more liberal than Bancroft's, his prose was more measured, his evidence more carefully marshaled, and his judgments delivered with greater care.

More limited in scope but more expansive in interpretation was a third work from this same period: Josiah Royce's *California from the Conquest in 1846 to the Second Vigilance Committee in San Francisco: A Study of American Character* (Boston: Houghton Mifflin, 1886). A California native who had recently accepted a position in the Philosophy department at Harvard University, Royce composed this work as part of the popular American Commonwealth series.[11] Although the author made extensive use of the documentary resources of Bancroft's library and other primary sources, the volume is less a history than an extended interpretive essay on social morality and public virtue during the years 1846–1857. His account of the gold rush forms a relatively small part of the work. Unfortunately for this account, he relied substantially on a volume supposedly written by one J. Tyrwhitt

Brooks, *Four Months among the Gold-Finders in Alta California*, a plausible but entirely bogus diary actually composed by Henry Vizetelly, who had never been to California, first published in London and New York in 1849.[12] Royce found a more reliable authority in Charles H. Shinn's *Mining Camps: A Study in American Frontier Government* (New York: Charles Scribner's Sons, 1885), which portrayed the extralegal proceedings of mining camp justice as a shining chapter in the history of responsible government. Royce, however, reached more critical conclusions than did Shinn about the inconsistent, sometimes unjust, and often cruel proceedings of miners' courts. Altogether, Royce presented the gold rush period as an era of forced social evolution that ultimately taught not a historical but rather a lofty philosophical lesson: "the sacredness of a true public spirit," as he expressed it, "and the great law that people who forget the divine order of things have to learn thereof anew someday, in anxiety and in pain."[13]

Royce's volume not inexplicably faded rapidly from consideration, but for half a century the works of Bancroft and Hittell remained the essential body of historical authority on the flush times of the early 1850s in California. Additional firsthand accounts by the score came into print, a few benefiting from the efforts of scholarly editors.[14] Better known than any other California figure of the time, John Sutter became the subject of three biographical studies.[15] But broad scholarly reexamination of the California gold rush era and its historical importance waited until the centennial years, when two new works came to share the preeminent place occupied so long by Bancroft and Hittell: Rodman W. Paul's *California Gold: The Beginning of Mining in the Far West* (Cambridge: Harvard University Press, 1947) and John Walton Caughey's *Gold is the Cornerstone* (Berkeley: University of California Press, 1948).

Paul did not ignore earlier historians, yet his was a work of striking originality, describing the developments that made California preeminent in the history of mining in the American West. Based on extensive research into mining's technical literature and an array of newspapers and mining journals, as well as firsthand accounts from those familiar with scenes in the early mining camps, *California Gold* successfully placed North America's first major gold rush into a context that emphasized its national and international significance. The study had its origins in Paul's Harvard doctoral dissertation, completed under the supervision of Frederick Merk. Although substantially completed by 1942, the book's progress to publication was interrupted by the Second World War. Consequently, it reached print just as public attention began to be spurred by the upcoming centennial of gold discovery in California, an event that helped assure the book a properly appreciative reception.

While Paul's *California Gold* explained in substantial detail the state's key role in the history of the American mining industry, taking the story into the mid-1870s, Caughey's *Gold is the Cornerstone* reemphasized the central importance of the first mining rush in the creation of modern California and its strikingly multiethnic social order. Already a well-known historian, a member of the UCLA history faculty with an outstanding publication record and great literary skill, Caughey designed his book as a comprehensive popular account of the California gold rush. The volume, as Caughey stated in the preface, was a pioneer effort to deal broadly with the subject; it included well-crafted chapters on the routes of travel to the gold fields, the local business enterprises stimulated by gold rush population growth, and the transit of religion, education, journalism, and theatrical entertainment to California, along with early displays of a distinctive California literature. For the development of mining, Caughey relied substantially on Paul's newly published study. In this and other respects, the book did an excellent job of presenting to a wide audience an accurate, entertaining summary based on the best published sources for the gold rush era, primary and secondary, that had appeared prior to the centennial observances.

During the decades following California's gold rush centennial, the continued dynamic growth of the state's economy and its population brought renewed attention to state history, especially the history of the gold rush era. Social and cultural changes throughout the nation at the same time swelled university enrollments while promoting academic and scholarly research careers for a new, vastly enlarged generation of graduate students. As part of a popular upsurge of interest in Western Americana, publications related to the gold rush period in California found willing buyers. A good many excellent gold rush journals, reminiscences, and collections of letters came into print for the first time, along with new editions of some classic accounts.[16] Meanwhile, the growth in original scholarship was reflected in the booklists of commercial publishers and university presses that by the 1990s had brought out an impressive number of research studies. Taken together, these publications amply demonstrated the complexity and diversity of California's gold rush history.

Among these works are biographical studies of figures prominent at the start of the gold rush. John Sutter has become the subject of two modern scholarly studies, with another on the way.[17] James Marshall now has a full-scale biography, likely the only one that will ever be needed.[18] Thomas O.

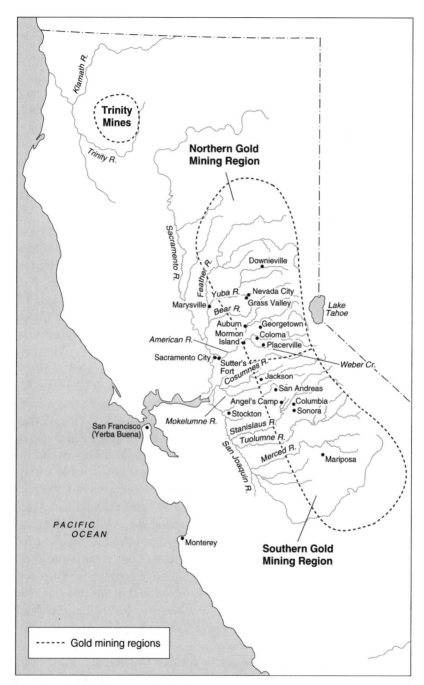

Northern California during the Gold Rush

Larkin, the American consul at Monterey, has received the attention of a pair of scholars whose work builds on the superbly edited ten-volume set of *The Larkin Papers*.[19] An edition of Henry William Bigler's California journal, supplemented by his interpretive recollections, forms a significant addition to the scant primary sources dealing with the events of the Coloma gold discovery and its immediate consequences.[20] Samuel Brannan, a particularly contentious figure in 1848 and 1849, has also recently become the subject of an exceptionally well researched biographical study.[21]

Building on an extensive body of documentary sources, modern accounts of the overland and sea journeys have greatly increased our understanding of travel to the California gold fields. The central and southern overland routes to the gold fields have all received detailed attention.[22] The most engaging account of the overland journey is J. S. Holliday's extremely successful work, *The World Rushed In: The California Gold Rush Experience* (New York: Simon & Schuster, 1981), centered on the 1849 diary and letters of William Swain. The sea routes to California, for years a relatively neglected research topic, have at last received a fully developed treatment in James P. Delgado's comprehensive book, *To California By Sea: A Maritime History of the California Gold Rush* (Columbia: University of South Carolina Press, 1990).

Prominent in modern scholarship are studies of distinctive groups— identified by race, ethnicity, gender, or national origin—that previously had been objects of comment but not the subjects of historical investigation. New historical accounts of northern California's Native peoples, frequently the casualties of white American aggression, have added greatly to our knowledge of racial conflict, accommodation to conquest, and the enduring consequences of forced cultural change.[23] Leonard Pitt's study of the Hispanic Californios after the American conquest and Rudolph Lapp's treatment of African Americans in the California gold rush, both based on doctoral dissertations, were pioneering works.[24] Our knowledge of Hispanic community histories following the American conquest has been greatly extended by additional local studies.[25] Few comparable works have appeared on black Californians, but the large population of Chinese gold seekers who arrived in the 1850s has received scholarly attention.[26] In addition, we now have fine accounts, narrative and documentary, of Jews, Chilenos, French, and Australians in the California gold fields.[27]

Alongside the subjects of these works, gold rush women have become a topic of renewed investigation during the past two decades. The famous series of letters by "Dame Shirley," Louise A. K. S. Clappe, heads a relatively short list of women's accounts, some available in recent editions.[28] JoAnn

Levy's highly entertaining volume, *They Saw the Elephant: Women in the California Gold Rush* (Hamden CT: Archon Books, 1990), offers an inclusive survey of female participation in the California excitement.[29] The history of prostitution during the gold rush era has received particular attention in two modern works focused on San Francisco, one of which considers exclusively the Chinese women engaged in this profession.[30] In addition, Albert L. Hurtado's *Intimate Frontiers: Sex, Gender, and Culture in Old California* (Albuquerque: University of New Mexico Press, 1999), though brief in its treatment of the gold rush era, recasts the analysis of gender-related issues in ways certain to prompt further research and discussion.

The Golden State's gold rush sesquicentennial, begun with a series of ceremonial observances in 1998, arrived at a time of intense interest in social and cultural themes among specialists in California and western American history. This realm of professional concern is strongly apparent in Malcolm J. Rohrbough's outstanding publication, *Days of Gold: The California Gold Rush and the American Nation* (Berkeley: University of California Press, 1997). In his wide-ranging study, Rohrbough concentrates on the gold rush's impact on individual lives, both in California and in the places from which the gold seekers came and to which a great many would return. Making use of manuscript diaries, collections of private letters, and local newspaper accounts not previously exploited by researchers, Rohrbough has assembled a social history that portrays a society substantially influenced but not deeply changed by the gold rush experience.[31] But, as he describes in his concluding chapter, some of the young, adventurous gold seekers of 1849 would recall and even attempt to recapture the bold spirit of their California years with pride and self-satisfaction to the end of their lives.

A different interpretation is set forth in an intriguing, theoretically rich, strongly revisionist work by Brian Roberts, *American Alchemy: The California Gold Rush and Middle-Class Culture* (Chapel Hill: University of North Carolina Press, 2000). Using many of the same sources as Rohrbough, Roberts presents a social history of a particular category of forty-niners—male gold seekers from the northeastern region of the United States—that is grounded on paradox. In the lives of these men, he contends, the California gold rush should be read as a rebellion against constricting middle-class behaviors, carried out by middle-class individuals at a time when their society was actively redefining class-based values and standards. Despite other differences, Roberts agrees with Rohrbough on the need to place within the gold rush story the women who stayed behind. As mothers, sisters, wives, daughters, or fiancées and sweethearts, countless women found their lives and often their social situation radically altered by the absence of men significant to them, whether that absence was brief, prolonged, or permanent.

Like virtually all the studies that have preceded them, these recent works about the California gold rush are influenced by an inherent cultural and social bias in the most accessible source materials. Their necessary dependence on written sources leads historians first and foremost to documents reflecting the dominant literary tradition of mid–nineteenth century America, the New England literary tradition. Men and women from New England and its cultural hinterlands—particularly upstate New York, western Pennsylvania, and the upper Midwest—tended more frequently to write letters, keep journals and diaries, and set down reminiscences than their fellow gold seekers from other countries and other parts of the United States. The so-called New England Renaissance in American letters during this period rested on a broad-based regional culture of literacy that made it almost second nature for ordinary people to put pen or pencil to paper, creating written records of their experiences.[32] The same cultural impulse also made it likely that such records would be preserved and that a substantial number of these accounts would, sooner or later, appear in print. With so many people of New England origins taking part in the California gold rush, our total universe of historical sources, published and unpublished, is thus exceptionally large, and it overrepresents the activities and attitudes of those—especially young men—raised within the wide range of New England cultural influences.[33]

In *American Alchemy*, Roberts deals with the problem of source bias in part by making the men and women of the northeastern seaboard the exclusive focus of his study, without implying that his sources represent the totality of human experience during the California gold rush. Moreover, Roberts explicitly treats the documentary records of the northeastern forty-niners as literary creations, observing that "the social reversal of eastern norms and behaviors" appears as a common literary formula in these works (11). For respectable white middle-class participants, Roberts concludes, the gold rush was a liberating experience that turned out not to be liberating at all, but rather an acting out of the theme of reversal; it represented the affirmation of a middle-class identity by men who found it invigorating—and an intrinsic part of their middle-class role—to deny at least temporarily their middle-class status. This playacting at social reversal, Roberts concludes, in time became encoded in ritualized gold rush reenactments that have been continued with little change to the present day.

Susan Lee Johnson's engaging volume, *Roaring Camp: The Social World*

and insights of historians who intend to enrich our understanding by adding new interpretive nuances to conventional state-centered, middle-class oriented versions of gold rush history. Certainly the gold rush years must be accorded cardinal importance in any appraisal of California's development. But the California gold rush was also, these essayists contend, in many different ways an event of worldwide significance, with influences and consequences that extended far beyond the state's borders. In history it has become commonplace to observe that context is everything. Here we are engaged in broadening and deepening the contexts that demand attention when we give thought to California's emergence to worldwide fame, economic power, and cultural influence. As the essays in this volume demonstrate, California's gold rush truly has many contexts and thus many histories.

California Gold Rush Fundamentals

Native-born northern Californians grow up in a popular culture saturated with references, direct and indirect, factual, semifactual, and wholly myth-ical, to the gold rush era and gold rush locales. From the primary grades onward, the children of this region are indoctrinated with a historical credo that the California gold rush was a unique and colorful experience that somehow shaped the region and imbued its people with special qualities. Fourth-grade lesson plans, local and regional museum exhibits, living history events, and public extravaganzas of many descriptions reinforce the message that the gold rush was the single most important episode in the area's history.[34] The popular culture provides its own adult education program, unplanned but ubiquitous, that perpetuates gold rush images as central icons for regional identity. Advertising adds to this lesson. Wells Fargo stagecoaches, for example, ride endlessly across California's TV screens to promote one of the state's largest banking enterprises—although historians and the bank's executives know full well that the Wells Fargo name never appeared on a stagecoach in California during the nineteenth century.

With no more than a smattering of fact for authentication, the gold rush of the imagination has today an active, vigorous life throughout the gold country and its environs. Everyone in northern California knows that the gold rush was exciting. Everyone hears over and over again that the gold rush became the foundation for the modern state. And, so a popular message adds, the gold rush spirit is still present in California, always on call to grab public attention and help us decide which candidate to vote for, how to entertain ourselves, or where to buy a new sport-utility vehicle that can carry us into the high country.

Along with the mythology and advertising gimmickry, northern Californians absorb a body of knowledge about their region's historical geography and local lore. Anyone who has lived here more than four days, to take a simple case, knows that the word "placer"—as in Placer County, Placerville, Placer Title Company, Placer Savings Bank, Placer Overhead Door Company, Placer Pizza Parlor, ad infinitum—is pronounced "plaa-sur," not "play-sir." Old timers, those who have remained a couple weeks or more, probably know that the term refers to an easily mined type of surface gold deposit, eroded free from its granite matrix, associated with the early boom period in northern California mining. The more alert soon learn also that Placerville is the county seat, not of Placer County, but of adjoining El Dorado County, which received its name from the Spanish American myth of a golden man who supposedly guarded the richest treasure in the Americas.

As an introduction to the essays that follow, readers from other areas may find it helpful to review in advance a few pertinent facts related to California's gold rush history. Northern Californians as well may appreciate an introductory summary that comes without a message to vote, bank, buy, or believe. This factual preamble provides fundamental information about the gold country's geography and geology and about the circumstances that set in motion the gold rush as a world event.

One hundred fifty miles inland from the Pacific Ocean's shoreline, the Sierra Nevada mountain range extends over four hundred miles north and south, defining the eastern boundary for most of northern and central California. The Sierra is an immense granite mass fractured and uplifted along its eastern edge, raised by ancient tectonic pressures, topped by ridges and peaks that form a virtually unbroken barrier to the passage of plants, animals, and peoples across its heights. The passage from the high arid deserts on the east side to the Sierra summit is abrupt; travelers headed across the Great Basin for California found themselves faced with high walls of snow-covered rock reaching ten thousand to twelve thousand feet above sea level, a baffling, often terrifying sight. Coming from the west, the transition from the floor of California's central valley into the Sierra is more gradual. From grassy foothills dotted with valley oak trees, the country rises by moderate grades through a landscape of digger pine and black oaks, into a yellow pine belt above three thousand feet. Travelers reach the Ponderosa pine belt above five thousand feet, with redwoods and Douglas fir still higher. Except in a few favored locations, the soils of this region are thin, composed in large part of gravels and easily eroded clays. But the heart of the Sierra Nevada's western slope is gold country, the Mother Lode region, a long belt of gold-bearing granite more extensive and richer in mineral than any comparable area on the world's surface.

The prevailing weather systems for northern California take form in the Pacific Ocean, carried from west to east across the region by high wind currents that tend to flow from the central and southern Pacific in spring and summer and from the Gulf of Alaska in the late fall and winter. The result is a strongly seasonal climate pattern, hot and dry during the summer months, relatively cold, wet, and stormy during the winter and early spring: a Mediterranean climate in the terminology of weather observers. From early May until late October or November in most years the region lacks any precipitation. Though the specific weather sequence is unpredictable, with cycles of drought and flooding alternating in irregular fashion, residents expect heavy rain and snow storms throughout the winter, anticipating a snowpack on the Sierra that will provide abundant runoff throughout the dry season. Snow on the Sierra is the most vital natural resource for life in the valley below, California's central valley, which today is the world's most extensive and richly productive area of prime agriculture.

Rain and snow melt flows into an intricate network of streams and rivers that lead downstream from the Sierra into the central valley. The northern Sierra is in the watershed of the Sacramento River, which runs southward 250 miles from headwaters in the Sierra Nevada and the Siskiyou Mountains. Along the way the Sacramento gathers in the waters of major tributaries, including the Pitt River, the Feather River, the Yuba River, and the American River. The southern Sierra is in the watershed of the San Joaquin River, which flows northward 350 miles from its southern Sierra Nevada headwaters, joined by the Merced, the Stanislaus, the Mokelumne, and the Cosumnes Rivers as its major tributaries. The two river systems meet and merge in the Sacramento–San Joaquin Delta, then wind through mazelike channels a short distance eastward to San Francisco Bay, the single outlet to the Pacific Ocean for all these inland streams.

During the runoff seasons, water tumbles and roars downhill all along the western slope of the Sierra. It cascades over rocks and through narrow canyons, overflows stream banks, widens through mountain meadows, then deepens and shapes natural levees as it reaches the soft soil overlay of the valley. All along the way moving water continues its eons-long work, cutting into the Sierra and moving it downstream piece by piece. Endlessly repeated episodes of freezing and thawing accelerate the erosion process, weathering and cracking the granite surface rock to make it more pervious to water's powerful action. Through successive geological epochs, this erosion process has exposed, shattered, and ground into gravel the gold-bearing granites of the Mother Lode. Coming from rock that is uniquely free of other mineral and chemical admixtures, the Sierra's placer gold is in constant motion, carried to temporary resting places nugget by nugget, flake by flake with the force of gravity and flowing water.[35]

The gold first located and first mined came from surface deposits, unalloyed flakes and larger pieces mixed in a matrix of gravel and heavy sand. These deposits could be easily discovered within the shallow streambeds, in gravel bars alongside larger rivers, or simply lodged in the crevices of river rocks. As recalled later by Henry Bigler, the first person after James Marshall to make a gold discovery on the South Fork of the American River, "I could see the yellow pieces lying as if they were looking at me saying, pick me up if you can."[36] Nowhere else on earth had geological processes created placer gold fields so extensive and so amazingly rich. By best estimate, more than $345 million in gold, calculated at contemporary value, came from the northern California Mother Lode between 1848 and 1854, the peak years of the gold rush.[37]

This gold was unique in the relative ease with which unskilled workers could capture it from nature. At first novice miners could succeed with the simplest technological contraptions—a gold pan or an Indian basket, a pick, a shovel, a hand-constructed rocker or sluice. Northern California's early gold seekers required no large capital investments, no fortunes to risk. They needed to invest only their time and their labor; they risked only their health and their lives.

California's gold was unique too in that it was free to the finder. Because of peculiar political and administrative circumstances in 1848, neither the federal government nor any other official agency would attempt to regulate, license, or tax the taking of it, or to claim a share from those who did take it. The U.S. Congress had formerly managed the nation's mineral lands by reserving these lands from public sale and leasing mining rights under the supervision of U.S. Army junior officers, a system applied mainly to the lead mining regions of Missouri, Illinois, and Wisconsin. Lax administration and local resistance to the enforcement of the leasing system led to its breakdown by the 1840s. Consequently, Congress abolished the system in 1846 and put nothing in its place, allowing lands known to contain mineral deposits to be sold by the General Land Office on the same basis as agricultural lands.[38]

As a further complication, federal administrative authority over California's public lands was not yet established when the gold rush began. The Treaty of Guadalupe Hidalgo brought an end to the war between the United States and Mexico just a week after James Marshall's discovery of gold on the South Fork of the American River. Under the terms of the treaty, the United States agreed to recognize all valid land titles under previous Spanish or Mexican land grants. U.S. law of long standing also required federal authorities to settle the aboriginal title claims of California's Native peoples before the customary process of federal land survey and sale could be carried out.

The nation's officials knew very little about California at the beginning of 1848, and any intent by either the Polk administration or Congress to move forward with these requirements in an orderly way was swept aside in the excitement and confusion that followed the gold discovery. Consideration of California's governmental situation, moreover, was further complicated and delayed by the rancorous sectional debate over the extension of black racial slavery, a debate raised by the Mexican War and only quieted temporarily in Congress with the Compromise of 1850. While the nation's representatives wrangled, California remained technically a conquered province under a makeshift form of military rule. In 1850 the military governor at Monterey encouraged local leaders to bypass established procedures, form a state constitution, and petition for direct admission to the federal union. Meanwhile no army commander dared send his troops close to the gold country for fear that every last recruit would desert and join the unnumbered thousands digging for wealth in the gold-bearing gravels and sands of the Sierra Nevada. Outside of Monterey and perhaps San Francisco, where small cadres of military and civilian officials dutifully carried out their assignments within a narrow territorial ambit, federal authority in any form remained largely illusory until well after statehood.[39]

In 1850 the first session of the state legislature took action to improvise rules regarding land rights that might serve in the absence of federal land law. The Possessory Act of 1850, amended in 1852, declared that duly constituted local law officers should protect any persons using public lands for grazing or farming purposes against interference with their peaceable possession. Exception was made, however, in the case of mineral-bearing lands. Miners, the state law established, had a usufruct right superior to farmers and stock raisers. It was not an act of trespass to enter on public lands already occupied and in use for agricultural purposes if the interloper intended to work deposits of gold or other precious metals. In addition, the state legislature in 1851 legitimized the locally constituted codes of the placer mining districts, requiring state courts in cases involving mining claims to recognize and shape their decisions according to the established customs, usages, and rules of the mining camps.[40] In time this privileged position for mining and miners received further validation when Congress, at long last, approved a very flawed measure that became the Mining Act of 1866.

Both geologically and politically, in short, the placer deposits of the Mother Lode region were ideal for opening poor peoples' gold mines. But until the gold discovery early in 1848, the Sierra Nevada's west slope was virtually unknown except to small resident communities of Native people. The Sacramento Valley in 1848 itself remained a thinly inhabited region. The valley's Native population had been sharply reduced by a devastating epidemic following the introduction of malaria a decade and a half earlier. European and American settlers were few, their numbers limited by the region's isolation and apparent lack of easily marketable resources. The first of these settlers was John Sutter, an ambitious, charismatic Swiss adventurer and would-be frontier magnate, who arrived in the valley in 1839 with the promise of a land grant from California's Mexican governor. Captain Sutter directed his small work force of Hawaiian and Native employees in constructing a fort near the American River a few miles above its confluence with the Sacramento. By 1847 Sutter's Fort was the center of commercial and social activities for a diverse population of frontier farmers, traders, stock raisers, and craft workers, including large numbers of Native laborers whose poorly paid services constituted the area's most vital economic asset.[41]

The circumstances that led to James Marshall's gold discovery, often glossed over or misunderstood, deserve explanation. In the spring of 1847 Captain Sutter decided to erect a water-powered sawmill at some suitable site in the Sierra with a good stream and an ample supply of yellow pine. The mill, he hoped, would supply lumber for his own building operations and bring him profits from sales to his neighbors. An exploring party sent out by Sutter identified the Coloma location, on the South Fork of the American River about forty miles upstream from Sutter's Fort, as the most likely spot for the mill. Marshall, a carpenter by trade who had come from New Jersey and who had earlier worked for Sutter, inspected the site, then in August 1847 entered into an agreement to become Sutter's partner in the project. Sutter would provide supplies, workers, and trade goods as wages for the Native laborers; Marshall, lacking capital, contributed expertise and direct supervision. The two men agreed to share the mill's anticipated profits on a fifty-fifty basis.[42]

The conclusion of the contract between Sutter and Marshall and the start of construction at the sawmill site waited until Sutter received a surprise proposition from a large, willing crew of discharged veterans from the

Mormon Battalion who came to Sutter's Fort anxious to find short-term employment. As described in the following essay, these men arrived at the fort in late August 1847 on their way from southern California to the Salt Lake region, where they expected to rejoin family and friends after more than a year's service in General Stephen W. Kearny's Army of the West. Short of animals, equipment, and supplies, many of the Latter-day Saints immediately sought out Sutter, who agreed to hire them for the Coloma sawmill project and his other new venture, a gristmill to be constructed on the American River a few miles above the fort. A small group of veterans at once started eastward across the Sierra, but at Truckee Meadows they received a message from Brigham Young, who had just reached the Salt Lake Valley at the head of the LDS pioneer colonizing expedition. Young directed those battalion members without dependent families to return to California and work until the following spring before heading to the newly designated Mormon Zion. About thirty more men returned to the fort, where they, too, offered to help build Sutter's two mills on the promise of future payment. The Mormon work force assured him the skilled, industrious hands that he needed for both projects. Sutter's agreement with the LDS veterans was a further critical link in the chain of events that placed James Marshall in the Coloma millrace in January 1848.

The sawmill site was in the home country of the Yalisumni band of Nisenan Indians, located well outside the boundaries of Sutter's Mexican land grant. After starting mill construction, in September Sutter and Marshall negotiated with the Yalisumnis a verbal contract that allowed them to occupy and use the land for twenty years. The Yalisumnis pledged to do no harm to the two partners' animals and to avoid setting afire the grass and brush near the mill. In return, Sutter agreed to pay the headmen of the Native community an annual allotment of $150 worth of clothing and farming utensils and to grind grain for the Yalisumnis. Eleven days after gold discovery, Sutter and Marshall put this lease on paper, getting the marks of the Yalisumni leaders to attest to the lease's validity and having it witnessed by two of the workmen at the mill. The document, termed an indenture, they predated to January 1, 1848. It described the supposed boundaries of the two partners' leased property, setting off a triangle of country estimated at ten or twelve square miles in extent. Without mentioning gold, they included in the document a statement of their right "to erect a Saw Mill . . . and to cultivate Such land as they may think proper and likewise open such Mines and work the Same as the aforesaid tract of land May Contain."[43] "In true Sutter style," Marshall's biographer remarks of the partners' claim, "it was expansive and fabulous."[44]

The partners' attempt to secure a title of sorts to the gold discovery site and the surrounding area did not have a favorable outcome. In late February, Sutter sent one of the construction crew, Charles W. Bennett, to Monterey with the written lease agreement, requesting the U.S. military governor of California, Colonel Richard B. Mason, to approve it. Along with the letter from Sutter, Bennett carried a sample of American River gold, and he did not hesitate to inform anyone who would listen about the surprising discovery at the mill site. After discussing the matter at length with Bennett and others, Colonel Mason had his adjutant, Lieutenant William Tecumseh Sherman, draft a reply to Sutter. The United States government, Mason very properly explained, does not recognize the right of Indians to sell or lease their lands to private individuals, and so he must refuse to sanction the supposed lease agreement. If subsequently, he added, the United States should properly extinguish the Indians' titles to any lands (the terminology referring to federal land cession treaty agreements), these lands would at once become part of the public domain, not subject to prior individual claims on the basis of Indian title.

Sutter and Marshall adopted one further tactic in their effort to establish legal title to Coloma property. Marshall and the Mormon workers surveyed and marked two individual preemption claims, following the customary procedures made possible by the federal Preemption Act of 1841. Marshall staked his claim to a settler's preemption of a quarter section of land (160 acres), downstream from the sawmill, that included the actual discovery site. Sutter claimed the adjacent quarter section just upstream. Despite Colonel Mason's rejection of the spurious Yalisumni treaty or contract, these claims would provide a substantial basis for Marshall and Sutter to assert their property rights at Coloma—rights that could be registered, traded, or sold—once the gold rush began.

These small local beginnings, as history frequently demonstrates, had wide consequences. At the mid-nineteenth century only an immense wealth in easily accessible placer gold, poor people's gold, could have set in motion the enormous voluntary migration that came to California from 1848 through the early 1850s. By 1855 this migration numbered at least a quarter million people, with perhaps another quarter million arriving by the end of the decade. One observation may encapsulate many of the consequences: The California gold rush set the world in motion on a scale previously unknown, in ways that broke the cake of custom and encouraged the growth of a bourgeois society, filled with the energetic and upwardly mobile from many different situations and places, but thoroughly middle class in their aspirations. John Sutter, James Marshall, the Mormon Battalion veterans, and everyone who came after them to hunt gold became participants, albeit unwittingly, in a process of social and cultural hybridization that reshaped the way that people lived and thought in northern California and, in time, at increasingly greater distances from the gold country.

Notes

1. Thomas O. Larkin, U.S. Consul at Monterey, wrote a report after his first visit to the gold regions for Secretary of State James Buchanan on June 28, 1848, which is reprinted in Rodman W. Paul, ed., *The California Gold Discovery: Sources, Documents, Accounts and Memoirs Relating to the Discovery of Gold at Sutter's Mill* (Georgetown CA: Talisman Press, 1967), 86–90. Acting Governor Mason set down a more detailed report on August 17, following his July tour of the mining sites on the American River and Weber Creek accompanied by his adjutant, William Tecumseh Sherman. This report, addressed to the Adjutant General in Washington DC, appears in the same volume, pages 90–100. A particularly well researched, well written summary account of the background and beginnings of the California gold rush appears in Mary Hill, *Gold: The California Story* (Berkeley: University of California Press, 1999).

2. Gary F. Kurutz, *The California Gold Rush: A Descriptive Bibliography of Books and Pamphlets Covering the Years 1848–1853* (San Francisco: Book Club of California, 1997). This magnificent work describes a total of 706 publications that appeared between 1848 and 1994, all dealing with California between 1848 and 1853, the peak period of the gold rush. My count of 285 publications before 1860 excludes articles of incorporation for various mining companies, but includes trail guides as well as those items describing California scenes and events. Among the more esoteric items, this outpouring of literary efforts included promotional guidebooks in Polish and Norwegian, as well as a great number in German, Dutch, and French. Another recently published bibliographical guide, indispensable for dedicated researchers, is Robert LeRoy Santos, *The Gold Rush of California: A Bibliography of Periodical Articles* (Denair CA: Alley-Cass, 1998).

3. These works include one or more publications each by J. D. Borthwick, Edwin Bryant, E. Gould Buffum, Alonzo Delano, T. J. Farnham, Hinton R. Helper, Theodore T. Johnson, Frank Marryat, and Bayard Taylor.

4. The literary invention of the gold rush is the focus for Michael Kowalewski's "Romancing the Gold Rush: The Literature of the California Frontier," in *Rooted in Barbarous Soil: People, Culture, and Community in Gold Rush California,* ed. Kevin Starr and Richard J. Orsi, a special issue of *California History* 74:2 (summer

2000): 204–25. See also Michael Kowalewski, ed., *Gold Rush: A Literary Exploration* (Berkeley: Heyday Books, 1997; and Kevin Starr, *Americans and the California Dream, 1850–1915* (New York: Oxford, 1973).

5. Buffum, who had come to California with the New York Volunteers, mined at the Weber Creek diggings. His account, *Six Months in the Gold Mines from a Journal of Three Years Residence in Upper and Lower California, 1847-8-9*, was first published in Philadelphia in 1850. Delano, who arrived in California overland from Illinois in 1849, mined along the Yuba River. His account, *Life on the Plains and among the Diggings*, appeared in 1854, published in Auburn, New York. Frank Marryat, an 1850 English visitor to California, described his adventures quartz mining in Tuolumne County in *Mountains and Molehills; Or Recollections of a Burnt Journal*, published in both New York and London in 1855.

6. James Joseph Ayers, *Gold and Sunshine: Reminiscences of Early California* (Boston: Gorham Press, 1922), quoted in Gary Kurutz, *The California Gold Rush*, 27.

7. Kowalewski, "Romancing the Gold Rush," 218.

8. The characterization of these works as pseudohistory appears in Starr, *Americans and the California Dream*, 49.

9. John Walton Caughey, *Hubert Howe Bancroft, Historian of the West* (Berkeley: University of California Press, 1946). An excellent brief essay on Bancroft appears in Starr, *Americans and the California Dream*, 115–19. The complaints of Bancroft's principal researcher and writer are aired in Henry Lebbeus Oak, *Literary Industries in a New Light* (San Francisco: N. J. Stone, 1893). Bancroft's operations are well described in Harry Clark, *A Venture in History: The Production, Publication, and Sale of the Works of Hubert Howe Bancroft* (Berkeley: University of California Press, 1973).

10. Robert W. Righter, "Theodore Henry Hittell: California Historian," *Southern California Quarterly* 48 (1966): 289–306.

11. The fullest study of Royce's career and thought is Robert V. Hine, *Josiah Royce: From Grass Valley to Harvard* (Norman: University of Oklahoma Press, 1992).

12. Kurutz, *The California Gold Rush*, 675–79. Vizetelly's book also appeared simultaneously in Dutch and German translations. Based on other publications and reports, it continued to be accepted as authentic until well into the twentieth century. As Kurutz relates, the spurious character of this publication was demonstrated at last in 1932.

13. Royce, *California*, ed. Robert G. Cleland (New York: Alfred A. Knopf, 1948), 366.

14. Particularly important examples include J. Goldsborough Bruff, *Gold Rush: The Journals, Drawings, and Other Papers of J. Goldsborough Bruff . . . April 2, 1849–July*

20, 1851, ed. Georgia Willis Read and Ruth Gaines, 2 vols. (New York: Columbia University Press, 1944); and Ernest de Massey, *A Frenchman in the Gold Rush: The Journal of Ernest de Massey, Argonaut of 1849*, trans. and ed. Marguerite Eyer Wilbur (San Francisco: California Historical Society, 1942).

15. The first significant biography of Sutter appeared in 1895, with a substantially enlarged version by the author published twelve years later: Thomas J. Schoonover, *The Life and Times of Gen'l. John A. Sutter* (Sacramento: D. Johnson & Co., 1895); idem, *The Life and Times of Gen. John A. Sutter*, rev. and exp. (Sacramento: Bullock-Carpenter Printing, 1907.). A popular biography and a lightly edited version of Sutter's Bancroft manuscript autobiography both saw print in the mid-1930s: Julian Dana, *Sutter of California, A Biography* (New York: Halcyon House, 1934); Erwin G. Gudde., ed., *Sutter's Own Story: The Life of General John Augustus Sutter and the History of New Helvetia in the Sacramento Valley* (New York: G. P. Putnam's Sons, 1936).

16. For example, Howard C. Gardiner, *In Pursuit of the Golden Dream: Reminiscences of San Francisco and the Northern and Southern Mines, 1849–1857*, ed. Dale L. Morgan (Soughton MA: Western Hemisphere, 1970); Peter Decker, *The Diaries of Peter Decker, Overland to California in 1849 and Life in the Mines, 1850–1851*, ed. Helen S. Giffen (Georgetown CA: Talisman Press, 1966); and, for the Sacramento region, William Robinson Grimshaw, *Grimshaw's Narrative, Being the Story of Life and Events in California during the Flush Times, Particularly the Years 1848–1850, Including a Biographical Sketch*, ed. J. R. K. Kantor (Sacramento: Sacramento Book Collectors Club, 1964).

17. Richard Dillon, *Fool's Gold: The Decline and Fall of Captain John Sutter of California* (New York: Coward-McCann, 1967. Reprint, Santa Cruz CA: Western Tanager Press, 1981); Kenneth N. Owens, ed., *John Sutter and a Wider West* (Lincoln: University of Nebraska Press, 1994). Albert Hurtado has a detailed comprehensive biography of Sutter in preparation.

18. Theressa Gay, *James W. Marshall, The Discoverer of California Gold: A Biography* (Georgetown CA: Talisman Press, 1967).

19. Harlan Hague and David J. Langum, *Thomas O. Larkin: A Life of Patriotism and Profit in Old California* (Norman: University of Oklahoma Press, 1990); George P. Hammond, ed., *The Larkin Papers: Personal, Business, and Official Correspondence of Thomas Oliver Larkin, Merchant and United States Consul in California*, 10 vols. (Berkeley: University of California Press, 1951–1964).

20. Henry William Bigler, *Bigler's Chronicle of the West: The Conquest of California, Discovery of Gold, and Mormon Settlement as Reflected in Henry William Bigler's Diaries*, ed. Erwin G. Gudde (Berkeley: University of California Press, 1962). Bigler's account was subsequently supplemented by Rodman Paul's documentary collection: *The California Gold Discovery: Sources, Documents, Accounts and Memoirs Relating to the Discovery of Gold at Sutter's Mill* (Georgetown CA: Talisman Press,

1966). The other critical eyewitness record is now available in print: David L. Bigler, ed., *The Gold Discovery Journal of Azariah Smith* (Salt Lake City: University of Utah Press, 1990).

21. Will Bagley, ed., *Scoundrel's Tale: The Samuel Brannan Papers* (Spokane WA: Arthur H. Clark Company, 1999).

22. John D. Unruh, *The Plains Across: The Overland Emigrants and the Trans-Mississippi West, 1840–1860* (Urbana: University of Illinois Press, 1979) places the central overland route in broad context. Gold rush travel on the central overland trail is summarized in George R. Steward *The California Trail, An Epic With Many Heroes* (New York: McGraw-Hill, 1962. Reprint, Lincoln: University of Nebraska Press, 1983). The trans-Sierra alternative used by a majority of the gold seekers in 1849 and 1850 is described in Kenneth N. Owens, "The Mormon-Carson Emigrant Trail in Western History," *Montana, The Magazine of Western History* 42 (winter 1992): 14–27. The development of all the trans-Sierra routes receives comprehensive treatment in Thomas Frederick Howard, *Sierra Crossing: First Roads to California* (Berkeley: University of California Press, 1998). For the history of southern trails, the place to begin is Patricia A. Etter, *To California on the Southern Route 1849: A History and Annotated Bibliography* (Spokane WA: Arthur H. Clark Company, 1999). Also particularly important are two works by Harlan Hague: *The Road to California: The Search for a Southern Overland Route, 1540–1848* (Glendale CA: Arthur H. Clark Company, 1978) and "The First California Trail: The Southern Route," *Overland Journal* 5 (winter 1987): 41–50. Texas connections are explored in Howard R. Lamar, *Texas Crossings: The Lone Star State and the American Far West, 1836–1986* (Austin: University of Texas Press, 1991).

23. The leading study is Albert L. Hurtado, *Indian Survival on the California Frontier* (New Haven: Yale University Press, 1988). Other pertinent works include George Harwood Phillips, *Indians and Indian Agents: The Origins of the Reservation System in California, 1849–1852* (Norman: University of Oklahoma Press, 1997); and James J. Rawls, *Indians of California, The Changing Image* (Norman: University of Oklahoma Press, 1984). Robert F. Heizer, ed., *The Destruction of the California Indians* (Santa Barbara CA: Peregrine Smith, 1974) brings together an extensive body of documents that illustrate the book's theme.

24. Leonard Pitt, *The Decline of the Californios: A Social History of Spanish-Speaking Californians, 1846–1890* (Berkeley: University of California Press, 1970); Rudolph Lapp, *Blacks in Gold Rush California* (New Haven: Yale University Press, 1977).

25. The most detailed are Albert Camarillo, *Chicanos in a Changing Society: From Mexican Pueblos to American Barrios in Santa Barbara and Southern California, 1848–1930* (Cambridge: Harvard University Press, 1979); Richard Griswold del Castillo, *The Los Angeles Barrio, 1850–1890* (Berkeley: University of California Press, 1979); and Douglas Monroy, *Thrown Among Strangers: The Making of Mexican*

Culture in Frontier California (Berkeley: University of California Press, 1990). Lisabeth Haas creatively explores the historical issues of community identity involving both Hispanic and California Native peoples in *Conquests and Historical Identities in California, 1769–1936* (Berkeley: University of California Press, 1995).

26. Gunther Barth, *Bitter Strength: A History of the Chinese in the United States, 1850–1870* (Cambridge: Harvard University Press, 1964) remains the most prominent work, but see also Roger Daniels, *Asian America: Chinese and Japanese in the United States since 1850* (Seattle: University of Washington Press, 1990); Sucheng Chan, *Asian Californians* (San Francisco: MTL/Boyd Fraser, 1991); and Thomas W. Chinn, Him Mark Lai, and Phil Choy, eds., *A History of the Chinese in California: A Syllabus* (San Francisco: Chinese Historical Society, 1969).

27. Jay Monaghan, *Chile, Peru, and the California Gold Rush of 1849* (Berkeley: University of California Press, 1973); George Edward Faugsted, *The Chilenos in the California Gold Rush* (San Francisco: R & E Research Associates, 1973); Edwin A. Beilharz and Carlos U. López, trans. and eds., *We Were Forty-Niners! Chilean Accounts of the California Gold Rush* (Pasadena CA: Ward Ritchie Press, 1976); Robert E. Levinson, *The Jews in the California Gold Rush* (New York: Ktav Publishing House, 1978); Jay Monaghan, *Australians and the Gold Rush: California and Down Under, 1849–1854* (Berkeley: University of California Press, 1966); Charles Bateson, *Gold Fleet for California: Forty-niners from Australia and New Zealand* (East Lansing: Michigan State University Press, 1964); Gilbert Chinard, *When the French Came to California* (San Francisco: California Historical Society, 1944).

28. Louise Amelia Knapp Smith Clappe, *The Shirley Letters,* (1922; reprint edited by Marlene Smith-Baranzini, Berkeley: Heyday Books, 1998); Eliza Woodson Burham Farnham, *California In-doors and Out* (New York: Dix Edwards, 1956; reprint, Nieuwkoop, Netherlands: De Graaf, 1972); Sarah Royce, *A Frontier Lady: Recollections of the Gold Rush and Early California*, ed. Ralph Henry Gabriel (New Haven: Yale University Press, 1932); Mary Jane Megquier, *Apron Full of Gold: The Letters of Mary Jane Megquier from San Francisco, 1849–1856* (San Marino CA: Huntington Library, 1949); Mary B. Ballou, *I Hear Hogs in My Kitchen: A Woman's View of the Gold Rush* (New Haven: Yale University Press for Frederick W. Beinecke, 1962). Less generally known is the charming volume of recollections by Luzena Stanley Wilson, *Forty-niner: Memories Recalled Years Later for Her Daughter, Correnah Wilson Wright* (Oakland CA: Mills College Eucalyptus Press, 1937). A recent collection is Susan G. Butruille, *Women's Voices from the Mother Lode: Tales from the California Gold Rush* (Boise: Tamarack Books, 1998).

29. In addition to Levy's book, interested students will want to see a popular work by Elizabeth Margo, *Taming the Forty-Niner* (New York: Rinehart, 1955), reissued with the title *Women of the Gold Rush* (New York: Indian Head Books, 1992).

30. Jacqueline Baker Barnhart, *The Fair but Frail: Prostitution in San Francisco,*

1849–1900 (Reno: University of Nevada Press, 1986); Benson Tong, *Unsubmissive Women: Chinese Prostitutes in Nineteenth-Century San Francisco* (Norman: University of Oklahoma Press, 1994). Anne M. Butler, *Daughters of Joy, Sisters of Misery: Prostitution in the American West, 1865–1890* (Urbana: University of Illinois Press, 1985) provides context. The story of prostitution in the major inland cities— Sacramento, Stockton, Marysville, and Placerville—awaits examination, but a few female entrepreneurs from these areas also appear in the pages of Marion S. Goldman's *Gold Diggers and Silver Miners: Prostitution and Social Life on the Comstock Lode* (Ann Arbor: University of Michigan Press, 1981).

31. Though not so fully documented, Paula Mitchell Marks's *Precious Dust: The American Gold Rush Era, 1848–1900* (New York: William Morrow, 1994) reaches conclusions similar to those found in Rohrbough's study. Also engaged with issues of class formation and social relationships during this period is David Goldman's *Gold-Seeking: Victoria and California in the 1850s* (Stanford: Stanford University Press, 1994).

32. A particularly strong variant of this Yankee writing tradition can be found within the Church of Jesus Christ of Latter-day Saints, the Mormon Church, whose leaders—mostly New-England born—urged members to keep journals or diaries of their experiences and to preserve the materials for church and family history. As a result, the LDS Church Archives at Salt Lake City is a repository extraordinarily rich in sources for many aspects of Western history, including the California gold rush.

33. The essential introduction to Yankee culture and its wide influence, as well as the other main strains of Anglo-American culture, is David Hackett Fischer, *Albion's Seed: Four British Folkways in America* (New York: Oxford University Press, 1989). Compared with the California gold rush, it is an apparent feature of later mining rushes in North America—particularly the Rocky Mountain rushes during the Civil War period—that a Yankee element was less evident, with a greater admixture both of southerners and of immigrant Irish from the start.

34. A notable exception was the state government's California Gold-Rush-to Statehood Sesquicentennial, started with great promotional enthusiasm in 1998, which fizzled to an embarrassing conclusion in 2000. The state legislature cut the commission's funding, and Gray Davis, the new Democratic governor, declined to endorse fund-raising initiatives by the chief administrator for sesquicentennial activities, Secretary of State Bill Jones (who appeared to be the top vote-getter in the Republican Party and Governor Davis's most likely future opponent in a reelection campaign). Administrators and politicians in Sacramento, moreover, were late to understand that a celebration of Anglo-American accomplishment as signified by traditional gold rush mythology has limited appeal in today's California, the most culturally and socially diverse state in the Union. As a regional event, furthermore,

the northern California gold rush has very little cultural resonance in the heavily populated southern part of the state. In the quest for a usable past, Los Angelenos are far more likely to dance with mariachi bands while recalling California's Hispanic origins than to sing rollicking songs about the days of '49.

35. Rodman W. Paul, *California Gold: The Beginning of Mining in the Far West* (Cambridge: Harvard University Press, 1947), 39–42, has a summary of Mother Lode geography and geology. More detailed treatments will be found in Rodman W. Paul, *Mining Frontiers of the Far West* (New York: Holt, Rinehart and Winston, 1963); and Mary Hill, *Gold: The California Story* (Berkeley: University of California Press, 1999), 94–113, 149–78.

36. Erwin G. Gudde, ed., *Bigler's Chronicle of the West: The Conquest of California, Discovery of Gold, and Mormon Settlement as Reflected in Henry William Bigler's Diaries* (Berkeley: University of California Press, 1962), 102.

37. Hill, *Gold*, table A4, 263, presents a comprehensive calculation of California's gold production, showing the estimated annual amounts in troy ounces, the dollar value at the time, and dollar values based on alternative gold prices. Regarding the basis for these figures, see Paul, *California Gold*, appendix A, 346–52. Paul's figures in contemporary dollar values are the same as those reported by Hill.

38. On the curious absence of any federal law governing mining at the start of the gold rush, consult Robert W. Swenson, "Legal Aspects of Mineral Resources Exploitation," in Paul W. Gates, *History of Public Land Law Development* (Washington DC: U.S. GPO, 1968), 699–716; and Carl J. Mayer and George A. Riley, *Public Domain, Private Dominion: A History of Public Mineral Policy in America* (San Francisco: Sierra Club Books, 1985), 34–50.

39. The best summary of these circumstances remains William Henry Ellison, *A Self-Governing Dominion: California, 1849–1860* (Berkeley: University of California Press, 1950).

40. Swenson, "Legal Aspects," 701–11. For the property rights issues that were at the heart of voluntary mining codes, see also Martin Ridge's essay "Disorder, Crime, and Punishment in the California Gold Rush" in this volume.

41. The most recent evaluations of John Sutter and his activities appear in Owens, ed., *John Sutter and A Wider West*. The standard biography remains Dillon, *Fool's Gold*.

42. No copy of the contract has survived. The details are known through John Bidwell's later descriptions, admirably reported in Gay, *James W. Marshall*, 132–33. In addition, as Gay states, the partners had a verbal understanding concerning the legal options for the mill's ownership after the end of the war between the United States and Mexico. If California remained a Mexican territory, Sutter, a citizen of

Mexico, should own the mill property, with Marshall retaining partnership rights in its operation. If California became part of the United States, Marshall should own the mill property and Sutter would have partnership rights.

43. Gay, *James W. Marshall*, 161–62, reproduces a manuscript copy of the lease agreement that is in the collections of the California Room, California State Library. The original presumably was burned with Sutter's papers in the fire that destroyed his Hock Farm home in June 1865. On the issue of Yalisumni identity and occupation of the Coloma site, see the discussion in note 23 in this volume's essay by Albert Hurtado, "Clouded Legacy: California Indians and the Gold Rush."

44. Gay, *James W. Marshall*, 163.

1

Gold-Rich Saints

Mormon Beginnings of the California Gold Rush

Kenneth N. Owens

In his later years James Marshall enjoyed a modest fame as the first person to discover placer gold in northern California.[1] John Sutter, Marshall's ambitious business partner in planning and building the sawmill at the Coloma discovery site, claimed even greater honor for his role in creating the gold rush—even though, he frequently lamented, his own fortunes were ruined as a result.[2] Yet in truth the events that led to the 1848 discovery and subsequently to the start of the California gold rush were not mainly shaped by Marshall and Sutter, but by others: mostly members of the Mormon Church, the Church of Jesus Christ of Latter-day Saints, who came to California for reasons closely connected with their religious beliefs and their sense of duty toward the LDS church authorities. By taking account of the Mormon beginnings of the California gold rush, a story often ignored, we gain fresh insight into the history of California during that pivotal era and, as well, into the early development of the LDS church community in the American West.

To fully understand the events of 1848 and 1849, we need to begin a few years earlier, at the Mormon headquarters city of Nauvoo, Illinois. In 1844, following the murder of church founder Joseph Smith and his brother Hyrum by a wrathful mob, Brigham Young assumed the leadership of a religious and social movement in deep crisis. Young and his closest advisers faced sharp factional dissension within the LDS community and continuing violent, mob-led attacks without. Threatened by Illinois state authorities, the Mormon leaders decided to abandon Nauvoo and seek, somewhere in the West (as Joseph Smith had once prophesied), a new location for the LDS Zion. They expected to find a gathering place, a homeland for all Mormons that would be situated safely beyond the Rocky Mountains—

then the western boundary of the United States—in a territory that could support the faithful until, as devout Mormons confidently believed, the Second Coming of Christ should bring an end to the present era. Along with the Bear Lake and Salt Lake valley regions in the Great Basin and possibly Texas or Oregon or Vancouver Island, California figured prominently in the short list of alternatives.[3]

By late August 1845, Brigham Young and his closest advisers in Nauvoo had decided to relocate their people at least temporarily to the Great Basin, though this decision did not become general knowledge among the church's rank and file for nearly a year. In New York City, meanwhile, Samuel Brannan, an energetic, extremely ambitious LDS lecturer, promoter, and newspaper editor, received encouragement from Young to establish a colony of LDS converts in northern California, an area that, like the Utah region, was still part of the Mexican republic. "I wish you together with your . . . paper and ten thousand of the brethren," Young wrote Brannan in September 1845, "were now in California at the Bay of San Francisco, and if you can clear yourself and go there do so and we will meet you there."[4]

Acting on Brigham Young's letter of counsel and the instructions of other church leaders, Brannan organized a colonizing expedition of 240 men, women, and children, the men well armed with rifles, pistols, and bowie knives, that sailed from New York harbor aboard the ship *Brooklyn* in early February 1846. Their goal, as Brannan described it to Young just prior to their departure, was to establish LDS primacy in California. With the aid of such figures as John Sutter and Lansford Hastings, Brannan stated, the Mormon colonists could win over the native Californians; and then, he declared, "no mistake the country is ours." As a result, he added, "we shall have a strong and ruling party in this country that will back us, politically and commercially." Showing his hazy knowledge of northern California's geography, Brannan promised that he would "select the most suitable spot on the Bay of Francisco for the location of a Commercial City," which he thought necessary to assure Mormon dominance.[5] Their ultimate goal, Brannan's colonists well understood, would be to prepare the way for successive groups of Mormon refugees who—as they had every reason to believe—would soon be coming to California.[6]

The *Brooklyn* put to sea coincidentally on the same day that the first contingent of Nauvoo Saints left Illinois, crossed the ice-covered Mississippi River, and headed westward, struggling along the frozen trails of Iowa toward a temporary haven near the Missouri River in the region centered on Council Bluffs.[7] While the evacuation from Nauvoo continued, Brannan and his colonists sailed around Cape Horn and into the Pacific, stopped briefly in Hawaii, and arrived in San Francisco Bay at the very end of July 1846, taking just over six months for the voyage.[8] But when the *Brooklyn* cleared Fort Point and came in view of the straggling little town of Yerba Buena, those aboard were surprised and dismayed to see a U.S. warship in the harbor and the Stars and Stripes waving from a flag post in the central plaza. "By God!" Brannan is supposed to have exclaimed, "There's that damned American flag."[9]

The situation in northern California now was quite different than when Brannan and Young had made their plans the previous fall. Two and a half months before the *Brooklyn*'s arrival, the Polk administration carried the nation into war against Mexico, fully determined to acquire California and New Mexico as part of the anticipated spoils of victory. While the Bear Flag irregulars and Captain John Charles Frémont's small military force campaigned about the country, news of the fighting in Mexico brought Commander John Montgomery and his ship, the U.S. frigate *Portsmouth*, into San Francisco Bay. Meeting no opposition, Montgomery, his sailors, and marines made themselves masters of the situation. They took formal possession of the customs house and the town on July 9, hoisted the American flag over the town square, and thus effectively preempted Brannan's grandiose plans for establishing a Mormon dominion on San Francisco Bay.[10]

Commander Montgomery apparently realized that Brannan's colonists could be important allies in shifting the local balance of power from the Hispanic Californios to the Anglo-Americans. He immediately sought to ensure a cordial relationship with Brannan and other prominent men among the *Brooklyn* group, visiting them aboard their ship, then hosting them at a conference aboard the *Portsmouth*. According to the description of one young woman among the colonists, Montgomery also sought to establish ties with the newcomers in a less formal, more socially amiable fashion. "The American officers," she wrote home to her family, "were so pleased to see so many immigrants . . . that they gave a festival at the tavern. Invited us all to attend. A great number attended[—]plenty of cakes and wines, music, and Spanish dancing." Her description ended on an intriguing cultural note: "I wish you could see them dance what they called a Spandango."[11]

For the next year or more, according to pioneer historian Hubert Howe Bancroft, under American rule Yerba Buena (renamed San Francisco in January 1847) became a virtual Mormon outpost on the Pacific. Despite growing differences between Brannan and other *Brooklyn* Saints over his management of the group's business affairs, many of the Mormons claimed land, put up tents and houses, and began building a Yankee-style trading town around the Mexican plaza, now called Portsmouth Square, while the American flag continued to wave in the bay breezes.

About thirty of the *Brooklyn* Saints also ventured inland, intending to start an agricultural colony and raise the crops—principally wheat and potatoes—they believed would be necessary when the Nauvoo Mormons under Brigham Young reached northern California. At a poorly chosen location in the San Joaquin delta, on the north bank of the Stanislaus River less than two miles upstream from its confluence with the San Joaquin, they selected a town site that they named New Hope and began plowing, planting, and building fences. Although it had a promising beginning, this venture ended in total failure in the late summer of 1847, when the combined effects of floods, mosquitoes and endemic malaria, and quarrels over Brannan's attempts to impose communal ownership drove away the last of the New Hope colonists.[12] Some returned to the bay area, while others gravitated north in search of employment, toward John Sutter's New Helvetia operation near the confluence of the Sacramento and the American Rivers. By the fall of 1847 they had become part of Sutter's work force, shortly before the discovery of gold changed everything.

At this point Sam Brannan still hoped to reclaim his authority over the *Brooklyn* colonists and restore his fortunes by bringing the church to California. In late April 1847, despite the deep snow that still covered the Sierra Nevada high country, he and two or three companions took the established trail route eastward—passing the grisly site of the Donner party remains—to find the migrating LDS "Camp of Israel" headed toward the Great Basin.[13] He met Brigham Young's advance expedition on June 30 at the crossing of the Green River. At once he entered into earnest and vigorous discussions with Young and his closest advisers, extolling the advantages of northern California as the site for the new Mormon Zion. A few days later Young sent him off to guide a party of Mormon Battalion veterans coming to join the pioneer camp from their winter quarters on the Arkansas River. Early on July 27, three days after Young's arrival in the Salt Lake Valley with the last wagons of the pioneer company, Brannan reappeared, then immediately joined Young and other church leaders on an exploring excursion to the Great Salt Lake.[14]

Late in the afternoon of the following day, July 28, Young assembled a general congregation of the Mormon pioneers at the site of the future Salt Lake City temple. Cutting off further controversy, the church president struck the ground with his cane and proclaimed that this would be the spot—a moment memorialized by a bronze statue of Young that now stands nearby, alongside Temple Square. Without a dissenting voice, though Brannan was looking on, the Saints passed a motion to "locate in this valley for the present, and lay out a city at this place."[15] According to one later report, Young turned to Brannan and declared "We have no business in San Francisco; the Gentiles will be there pretty soon."[16]

The heat of the argument between Young and Brannan is reflected in the recollection of another close witness to this scene. Wilford Woodruff remembered that Brannan saw at the Salt Lake City site only "desolation and barrenness, and tried with all the power he had to persuade President Young not to stop here, but to go on to California." It was then, as Woodruff recalled, that Young struck the soil with his cane and answered "No, sir; I am going to stop right here. I am going to build a city here. I am going to build a temple here, and I am going to build a country here."[17] His stubborn determination, all agree, was one of the great strengths of Brigham Young's leadership.

Disgruntled, but still hopeful that he might in time bring the church leaders to his way of thinking, Sam Brannan returned to northern California. By his own account years later, before leaving Salt Lake he denounced polygamy to Brigham Young and Heber Kimball, or told them at least that "Women are the mothers of great men & Nations, and should be looked up at instead of down."[18] But this statement, if he actually made it, by no means marked a break between Brannan and the church.

When Brannan departed, he carried with him a letter from Brigham Young addressed as an "epistle of the Council of Twelve Apostles of the Church of Jesus Christ of Latter-day Saints to the Saints in California." The letter appointed Brannan to be president of the church in California, though taking note that he had made mistakes—particularly in advocating and attempting to practice the common ownership of property. Along with a lengthy narrative of the church's tribulations and a description of the coming of the pioneers to Salt Lake, President Young took note of reports that some of the *Brooklyn* colonists at San Francisco had abandoned their obligations to the LDS community in pursuit of wealth. Here Young dictated words of advice that ring across the years: "Get rich, for the Lord designs that his should be the richest people on earth."[19] There can be little doubt, in the light of later events, that Elder Brannan took this message to heart. Was it these words that came to mind when Brannan first learned of the gold discovery on the American River? One must wonder, however, how carefully he read the rest of Young's letter: "Get your riches honestly, and close not your ears, neither tie up your purse strings against the cries of the widow, the fatherless, the poor, and especially of the household of the faith."

The gold discovery: For this part of the story we must shift attention from the *Brooklyn* Saints to the men of the Mormon Battalion—the Battalion Boys as they frequently called themselves—and return again to the year 1846. In mid-May President James Polk convinced Congress to declare war on Mexico. At this point, the Nauvoo refugees had found safety in temporary camps along the Missouri River, where they would remain, with growing numbers of sick and destitute, until spring of the following year. Early in June 1846, President Polk authorized the U.S. Army to enlist five hundred men from these LDS refugee camps as a special force, the Mormon Battalion. Led by their own company officers, these men would march with the Army of the West commanded by Colonel Stephen Watts Kearny to carry out the American conquest of New Mexico and the occupation of California.

Although President Polk's order did not offer the sort of assistance they had requested from the federal government, Brigham Young and his counselors welcomed the opportunity and urged able-bodied men to volunteer. Many of the Mormon refugees were suspicious of the U.S. authorities, and they feared for the well-being of their families if they left. But for the church leadership, the creation of the Mormon Battalion promised a much-needed infusion of cash, since each man would receive a clothing allowance of forty-two dollars, paid upon enlistment, in addition to his regular army pay of seven dollars a month. Brigham Young expected— too optimistically, as it turned out—that the volunteers would cheerfully turn over all their clothing funds to church officials to help fed impoverished families and outfit them for the move westward.

The march of the Mormon Battalion from Fort Leavenworth to Santa Fe, then onward across the Arizona desert to San Diego and Los Angeles, is an epic of endurance and fortitude. One of the longest infantry marches in history, carried out by poorly supplied recruits with no military back-ground, ragged, often hungry, many barefoot by the end of their ordeal, the battalion's expedition had important direct results for the future of California. Although the Battalion Boys fought no battles, they surveyed and constructed a wagon road from New Mexico across the Arizona desert to San Diego. With few changes their road became the main southern over-land route, the critical line of communication and immigration that helped end southern California's long-endured geographical isolation. Moreover, when they reached California in January 1847, rumors of renewed Mexican resistance were causing concern among U.S. military and naval officers. The battalion became briefly the largest military unit in California. Given supplies and a month's training in close-order drill, then posted at San Diego and Los Angeles, the LDS troops provided a margin of safety for U.S. authorities in securing southern California for the American nation.[20]

After months of garrison duty, the battalion veterans were discharged at Los Angeles in mid-July 1847. At once these men began efforts to locate the main body of the church, somewhere east of the Sierra Nevada according to the vague reports they had received. One contingent marched northward along the coast toward San Francisco. A second force of 160 men proceeded through the heat of the San Joaquin Valley during late July and August, heading toward Sutter's Fort and the Donner Pass route eastward across the Sierra Nevada, the only well-known trail connection with the Great Basin. While camped on the Mokelumne River in late August, this group heard from a messenger just arrived in California that the pioneers with Brigham Young and the council of twelve had reached Salt Lake, that the main body of Saints was expected there by the end of the summer, and that the Salt Lake Valley was where the church would stay.

With this news, the Mormon veterans moved northward to the American River, camped two miles from Sutter's Fort, and paused to consider their options. Many in the group, forty to sixty men according to the recollection of James S. Brown, appointed a committee to approach John Sutter and offer to work for him. Short of funds, they lacked provisions, equipment, and animals necessary for the trip across the Sierra, so they had decided to remain in northern California until the following year. "The committee," Brown later wrote, "informed Mr. Sutter that we had carpenters, blacksmiths, wheelwrights, millwrights, farmers and common laborers, and that we should want horses, cattle, and a general outfit for crossing the plains early the next summer, and if we could not get all money, we could and would take a part of our pay in the above mentioned stock and supplies." Sutter liked these conditions, Brown stated, "as he had an abundance of the above mentioned property . . . [while] the greatest obstacle that confronted him had been removed by the propositions that our committee had made to him."[21]

As Brown emphasized, this Mormon work force became an unexpected but most welcome boon for John Sutter. With his credit overextended and his ambitious empire-building plans already tumbling to ruin, Sutter gladly entered into an agreement with the Battalion Boys: skilled, honest, mostly sober, hard-working, and willing to accept his promise of food and lodging, reasonable pay, and wages in kind when their term of employment was over. Sutter could use these men for many tasks, but he wanted them for two main projects that he hoped would rescue his fortunes. At a site along the lower American River a few miles east of Sutter's Fort—approximately where the campus of California State University, Sacramento, now stands—he put to work thirty or more of the battalion veterans building a water-powered gristmill that would grind his wheat into flour. More famously, Sutter detailed another four or five of the veterans to go up into the mountains with his new partner, James Marshall, to construct a sawmill at the Coloma site, where the local Nisenan Indians would provide additional milling though untrained workers.

The rest of the LDS veterans paused only to have their horses shod at Sutter's Fort and then set out across the Sierra, cheered by the news from Salt Lake and anxious to rejoin their families and friends. At Truckee Meadows, just beyond Donner Pass, they met another party, fresh from Salt Lake, that carried a further message: Brigham Young counseled all battalion members with no dependent families to go back to California and work there until the following year. Provisions were scarce at Salt Lake, Young stated; Zion's pioneers had no food to spare for the unattached veterans. "It would be wisdom," his message continued, " . . . to return to California and go to work and fit themselves out with plenty of clothing, stock, provision, etc., and come up the next season to the valley."[22]

Ten years later, the Mormon community at Salt Lake City had survived its starving time. The Saints were prospering with the trade that came to them because of the overland traffic going to and coming back from California. At that time, in 1857, Brigham Young told a story about a man from Boston who had stopped in Salt Lake City on his way to the California gold diggings. This man listened to Young preach, then asked the church president if he knew where hell was. "I told him," Young declared, "I thought he was on the road to that very place; and when he crossed the Sierra Nevada mountains into the gold diggings in California, if he discovered that he had not found hell, to come back and let me know. As I have not heard from him," Young concluded, "I presume he found it."[23]

In 1847, however, before the gold rush began, the Mormon leader had a different view of California. Though not suitable as a permanent home for the LDS faithful, it could be a useful source of support for the infant colony he was building in the Great Basin. At his behest, at least thirty more of the Mormon veterans, as Azariah Smith recorded, "turned our course back to California to work and fit ourselves out ready for the Spring."[24] Of course, the place most of them went to find work was Sutter's Fort, where they joined their LDS compatriots and friends already engaged in John Sutter's New Helvetia enterprises.

Ironically, then, Brigham Young had sent all these men, the Battalion Boys, to John Sutter, and their presence set the stage for Marshall's gold discovery in January 1848, leading to the creation of that California society President Young later likened to hell. History is never simple; but in this case, the sequence is plain: No Mormon Battalion veterans, no sawmill at Coloma, and thus no gold discovery there in January 1848.

The events of January 1848 have been told and retold countless times, with most of the solid evidence coming from the journals kept by Mormon workers at the Coloma site and from their later reminiscences. One of these men, Henry W. Bigler, has special importance to our story. Thirty-three years old in 1848, Bigler was a native of West Virginia who had converted to Mormonism twelve years earlier. In the days following Marshall's discovery, he and his companions, with Marshall's approval, picked up additional small amounts of gold in the millrace. Captain Sutter came to Coloma to see the site for himself, then left after treating the workers to a celebratory drink and urging them to keep quiet about the find. But by mid-February 1848, three weeks after the original discovery, Henry Bigler found himself gripped by northern California's first authentic case of gold fever.

Although he continued working on the mill during the week, Bigler began devoting his weekends to the search for more gold at different places nearby, telling no one his purpose. We should not be too surprised that at first he remained alone in his quest; his Mormon comrades and other coworkers were not particularly interested in braving the cold American River's turbulent currents in midwinter, with snow on the ground, just for the unlikely chance of finding riches amid the rocks in the stream bed. "I seemed to be the only one in the crowd," Bigler later related, "that had gold badly on the brain."[25]

On Saturday, February 12, pretending that he was going duck hunting, he set out downstream to resume his search. His unskilled prospecting on this and the following day, Sunday the thirteenth, paid off well. Across the river and approximately one mile below the mill site, Bigler found color. He spotted gold particles on the exposed seams of rock and simply picked them up, grain-by-grain, with the point of his knife. Excited by the find, he wrote a letter to three of his closest friends who were working on Sutter's gristmill. He told them about the Coloma discovery but urged them to keep the whole matter to themselves unless they revealed it to someone who also could keep the secret—presumably any of their trusted associates among the Mormon Battalion veterans at Sutter's Fort. "Mr. Marshall," he explained, "did not want it known until further development."[26]

A little more than a week later, on Tuesday, February 22, Marshall allowed his crew a day off because of a snowfall, and Bigler returned to his downriver site. There, as he later wrote, "I could see the yellow pieces lying as if they were looking at me saying, pick me up if you can." Though already numbed with cold from wading across the river and quickly becoming stiff and cramped, he worked at the edge of the river until dark. Back at the Coloma camp that evening, Bigler showed the gold to his comrades, and they weighed out the proceeds. His day's effort, as they figured, returned "one ounce and a half of clean gold dust." In 1848 values, this amounted to more than twenty dollars, while John Sutter had promised to pay the men twenty-five dollars a month, plus keep—an amount considered a good California wage until that point.

The next Sunday, in warmer weather, four Mormon companions went with Bigler to his site, where they spent the day searching for gold, "frequently laying on our bellies," Bigler recalled, "scratching and hunting for it." The reward for their hard work was altogether about two ounces of gold, thirty dollars worth.[27]

While commemorating James Marshall's first chance discovery, we should also recognize and honor the significance of Henry Bigler's deliberate gold hunting. We do him mere justice to observe that his strike showed clearly that the gold in Sutter's Coloma millrace was not an isolated freak of nature. Before anyone else made the attempt, Bigler proved that placer gold was easy to locate and relatively easy to gather at more than one place in the riverbeds of the Sierra Nevada. Given his religious turn of mind, Bigler might well have reflected on his good fortune and the good fortune of his Mormon companions. Their success showed God to be ecumenical in the disposition of riches and not at all insistent on a pious observance of the Christian Sabbath—at least not in California.

Henry Bigler's contributions did not end there. A few of his Mormon Battalion comrades, drawn by Bigler's letter, soon came from Sutter's Fort to visit the Coloma sawmill. They were inspired by his success and educated by his experience. Prospecting on their own on March 2, two of these men—Sidney Willes and Wilford Hudson—found a still better paying site twenty miles downstream, near the junction of the South Fork and the Middle Fork of the American River, where John Sutter had no possible claim to ownership. They in turn reported their discovery to their LDS friends at Sutter's gristmill. Again with encouragement from Henry Bigler, who had gone briefly to Sutter's Fort for a meeting with his Mormon brethren, a few men moved upriver to this newest site to try their hand at gold mining, and others followed.[28] In mid-April seven Mormon Battalion veterans were steadily at work. Using Indian baskets to wash out the gold-bearing gravel, they were making a hundred dollars or more a day with their crude methods.[29] By the end of April, according to Azariah Smith, "men, women and children, from the Bay and other places in California, were flocking to the gold mine, by the dozens, and by wagon loads."[30] These diggings soon gained the name Mormon Island.

In early July, Colonel Richard Mason, California's military governor, arrived at the Mormon diggings on a tour of inspection. He found two or three hundred men hard at work under an intensely hot sun, living in canvas tents and brush arbors scattered thickly about the hillsides. They were washing gold, Mason reported, "some with tin pans, some with close-woven Indian baskets, but the greater part had a rude machine known as a cradle." Four men with a cradle, he stated, were averaging a hundred dollars a day. The gold they gathered, Mason added, was "in fine bright scales."[31]

The Mormon Island site, now submerged beneath the waters of Lake Folsom, became the principal mining location during the earliest phase of northern California's gold rush in 1848. In the latter part of May another two Mormon miners, battalion veterans Benjamin Hawkins and Marcus Shepherd, discovered an additional extremely rich placer site a short distance downstream and across the river, at a location later called Negro Bar. While John Sutter and James Marshall were still hoping to avoid publicity so they could monopolize the search for gold at Coloma, on land where they had no legal claim and where the gold deposits were comparatively less rich and abundant, it was at these diggings, Mormon Island and Negro Bar, that the gold-mining industry in western America truly got its start.[32]

Mormon Island also attracted Sam Brannan, who had spent the winter attempting to direct the LDS congregation in San Francisco while still locked in political and personal quarrels. He made a short visit to Sutter's Fort in early April, when the Battalion Boys told him about the diggings at Mormon Island, but not until May 4 did Brannan return and tour the site. At once he became convinced, as he later said, that "there was more gold [here] than all the people of California could take out in five years."[33] Brannan took with him a gold sample in a quinine bottle, stopped briefly to arrange construction of a warehouse and store at the embarcadero along the river front that would become the site of Sacramento, and quickly rode toward San Francisco. He arrived at the Bay City on May 10, stepped from the ferry onto the beach, and acted out that other most famous scene of the California gold rush: Holding his bottle of gold dust in one hand, swinging his hat in the other, Brannan moved along the street shouting "Gold! Gold! Gold! from the American River."[34] Two weeks earlier Edward Kemble, Brannan's close friend and his successor as editor of the *California Star* newspaper, had visited Coloma and reported that the rumors of rich gold deposits were only a hoax, a humbug. But Brannan's newer report, based on his experience at Mormon Island, convinced San Francisco and soon the world that the riches were real; and so, powered by the enthusiasm of this LDS entrepreneur, the wider rush to California's gold fields began.

On Colonel Mason's July tour of the mining regions, he was accompanied by his adjutant, Lieutenant William Tecumseh Sherman. According to Sherman's recollections, three hundred men were mining at Mormon Island; Sam Brannan was also there, collecting tithes for the church. When questioned by one of the Saints whether Brannan had a right to claim this levy, continues Sherman's account, Mason replied that "Brannan has a perfect right to collect the tax, if you Mormons are fools enough to pay it."[35] In fact, it was not a 10 percent tithe that Brannan claimed, but something more. On behalf of the original discoverers, Sidney Willes and Wilford Hudson, who had become his partners, he was managing the diggings by collecting a toll or rent of 30 percent on all gold mined—10 percent for Willes and 10 percent for Hudson by right of discovery, and 10 percent for Brannan as his collection fee. But the report appears accurate that with Mason and Sherman's visit, the payments ceased. Brannan then took his profits and moved to the new city of Sacramento to pursue his expanding business affairs. California's first millionaire, he would become as well the most prominent if not the first California Mormon to fall away from the faith.

The sudden, enormous, unexpected wealth coming from the gold diggings, along with the worldly temptations so prevalent in California's gold rush society, created something of a crisis of faith and practice for the California Mormons. Church leaders expected that adherence to the faith would mean hewing to high standards of personal conduct and mean also that the faithful would continue to support the church and its representatives generously, through tithing. In the middle of 1850, Amasa Lyman came from Salt Lake for the purpose of collecting overdue tithes. In July he reported to Brigham Young and the council that the "Brethren of wealth in San Francisco have paid little or no tithing. Mr. Samuel Brannan has paid nothing and now disclaims any connection or interest in the Church." Some San Francisco Mormons, largely among the *Brooklyn* Saints, Lyman observed, had lost the spirit, strayed from the paths of righteousness, and a few "have fallen into the path of the Gambler or the Drunkard." And while many recent immigrants from Salt Lake had remained true to the faith, lamented Brother Lyman, "To strike hands with a man haveing the spirit of God is a rare treat in California, and is like a fruitfull shower in a parched land."[36]

As a group, the Battalion Boys largely ignored the temptations that came with quick riches. Even as they succeeded with their mining in the spring and early summer of 1848, they kept in mind the purpose set forth by Brigham Young, expecting soon to take supplies and tools eastward across the Sierra Nevada and desert country to the struggling LDS community in the Salt Lake Valley. During an April meeting at Sutter's Fort, where Brannan also was present, these men reached agreement that they would leave in early June as soon as the snow melted enough to allow passage over the Sierra. The question of what route they might take brought considerable discussion. "It was further decided," Henry Bigler wrote, "that we send out a few men as pioneers before that time [June 1] to pioneer out a route across the Sierra Nevada, and if possible find a much nearer way than to go the Truckee route and thus shun crossing the very deep and rapid Truckee River twenty-seven times."[37] The group determined to make their way along the dividing ridge between the American River and Cosumnes River drainages and cross the mountain range somewhere near the headwaters of the American River's south fork. "As we had become accustomed to pioneer life," expedition member James S. Brown later recalled, "it was thought we could find a better route."[38]

Deep snows in the high mountain areas turned back a first exploration party in early May.[39] When they returned, these men broadcast the report that, as Addison Pratt recorded, "a road could be made acrost the Sierra Nevada Mountains at that point, and that the snow would be gone so that we could start by the first of June."[40] But the battalion veterans actually delayed their departure until early July. According to Henry Bigler, "The snow seemed to lie on the mountains a little longer than we expected; and the mines also became more attractive, so that our pioneers did not go out so soon to hunt a pass across the mountains as first expected."[41] Meanwhile, nearly all the Battalion Boys remained busy with gold mining at the Mormon Island and Negro Bar diggings. By June many of the battalion veterans had become gold-rich, according to their lights, the first successful fortune-seekers in the northern California gold fields.[42]

The opening of the Mormon-Carson Pass Emigrant Trail by some of the LDS veterans is also significant, since this route became the most heavily used branch of the California Trail during the early years of the gold rush.

While the story, replete with dramatic incident, has been told elsewhere, a few key features can be summarized here.[43] These first gold-rich Saints built the wagon road from west to east, the heaviest work being done by a party of forty-five men and one woman—Melissa Coray, a Mormon Battalion wife—in July and August 1848. The road-building expedition numbered seventeen wagons loaded with supplies, seeds, and tools intended for the Salt Lake colony, all pulled by docile, slow-moving oxen. Along with the wagons came a herd of at least 150 horses and a similar or larger number of cattle, tended by a few mounted herdsmen who had adopted the colorful vaquero costume of the Hispanic Californios.[44] Two more parties, numbering about twenty men and one woman, soon followed them with pack animals, while yet one more Mormon group with pack animals and about a dozen wagons took the same trail later in the season.[45]

Scouting the route was a challenging and, as it turned out, hazardous task. Three advance scouts, Daniel Browett, Ezrah H. Allen, and Henderson Cox, traveling alone with horses and heavily loaded mules, met their death at the hands of Indians. The site is named Tragedy Spring; there the remnants of a burial cairn put up by their comrades can still be seen.

Making a road for wagons was difficult, muscle-straining work, a task for experienced, callused hands and strong backs. The route took the party across snowfields in late July and led them down a steep one-mile pitch on the east side of Carson Pass that other travelers, coming from the east, would later call the Devil's Ladder. The most challenging task was to bring the wagons through the boulder-clogged seven-mile length of the canyon of the West Carson River that led from Hope Valley downstream to Carson Valley. With shovels and axes as their only equipment, the road builders chopped and moved logs, rolled away those rocks that they could manage, filled in the stream with smaller stones at places they planned to cross, and constructed two rude bridges of logs and rough-hewn timber. To get wagon space among the larger boulders, they piled fallen logs and brush against the rock faces, lighted fires, and let the heat shatter the rocks as far as it would penetrate. After shoveling away the rubble, they repeated the process until they gained enough room to wheel the wagons through.[46] Later gold rush immigrants would call this West Carson Canyon road the worst traveling on the whole length of the California Trail; yet they could find a passage for their wagons, and most took for granted that there was just clearance enough to navigate past the tightest canyon walls.

Their success in making the mountain crossing led the road-building expedition and the other Mormon parties that followed them in 1848 to recommend the new road to all westward-moving emigrants they met on the Overland Trail. They reinforced their advice with news of the discovery of gold, the first reports these emigrants received about the wealth that awaited in the rivers and streams of northern California. Offering more than just words, the Battalion Boys pulled out samples of gold dust and nuggets to display to the astonished emigrants, and their tales of easy riches lost nothing in the telling. "The glowing stories of the Mormons of the gold mines," one wagon-train member wrote in his journal, "nearly ran us all mad."[47] Vivid is the image of an elderly gentleman in the first party coming west across the plains, who, upon seeing the Mormons' gold and hearing about the diggings, pulled off his battered hat, flung it to the ground, jumped in the air, and exclaimed, "Glory Hallelujah! I'll die a rich man yet!"[48]

The new road by way of the Carson River and West Carson Canyon, the Mormon travelers told each group they met, was much easier and shorter than the old route that led back and forth across the Truckee River and over Donner Pass. Moreover, it had the advantage of leading directly to the American River drainage, where the first gold discoveries were concentrated. Stories of the Donner party disaster of 1846 had already circulated widely in the eastern states, making late-season emigrants dread the threatening weather that might overtake them in the mountains. The relative nearness of the Mormon-Carson Pass route was thus another reason for the 1848 emigrants and those who followed to prefer it to the older trail.[49]

The Mormon interest in this route continued strongly through 1849 and the next few travel seasons. Some of the battalion veterans who traveled eastward in 1848 returned to California the following year with LDS parties or hired out as guides for non-Mormon wagon trains passing through the Salt Lake region en route from the Mississippi Valley.[50] Moreover, in one instance they rudely ended the attempt of a money-hungry non-Mormon to charge a toll on the road they had built. One enterprising veteran, Ira Willis, prepared handwritten copies of his trail notes, which he and others sold in 1849 as a guide to westward-moving emigrant parties for one dollar per copy.[51] A more detailed *Mormon Way-Bill to the Gold Mines*, prepared by Joseph Cain and Ariah C. Brower, appeared as a guidebook in 1851 and remained a helpful reference for emigrant parties during the next few years.[52] A steady use of the route by LDS groups traveling both east and west can be documented through the early 1850s, but it was the non-Mormon immigrants—as many as forty thousand in 1850—who became the greatest benefactors of the trail-building Saints.[53]

In 1849 overland travelers coming westward across the Nevada desert found a first outpost (called Ragtown), near the site of modern Fallon, a camp that one emigrant described as "ten small tents, and one large one which was used as a trading post. . . . the rendezvous of the thieves and gamblers who came out from California to fleece the emigrants."[54] Here was the only place weary forty-niners might replenish their supplies until they reached the diggings at Weber Creek. In early June the following year a party from Salt Lake City founded a trading post in Carson Valley that became known as Mormon Station, located in a grove of pine timber close to the junction of the Carson and the West Carson Rivers. Selling foodstuffs and goods brought from the Sacramento Valley and locally grown produce, by the end of the 1850 season this post became a landmark and a welcome source of fresh supplies for emigrant parties. By 1851 Mormon Station was the focal point of a small settlement that overland travelers greeted as a true outpost of civilization and settled domesticity. Utah's territorial legislature created Carson County as part of western Utah early in 1854, and LDS church authorities in Salt Lake City dispatched additional parties of Mormon colonists to stake out the Carson Valley and secure it as part of an enlarging area of influence for the Saints.[55]

The beginning of gold mining in northern California and the opening of the Mormon-Carson Pass Emigrant Trail created a particularly delicate challenge to Brigham Young and the church leadership in the Salt Lake Valley. The popular allure of California was great, threatening the Mormon colony with the same sort of exodus, led by young men, that was disrupting society in Oregon, Hawaii, Chile, the eastern United States, and many parts of Europe and South China. The result could be a loss of able-bodied and skilled workers, abandoned farms and stores, abruptly rising prices for food and all sorts of goods, and a growing dependent class of women, children, and old people left behind: a potential social calamity for the newly transplanted Mormon community. As Young also came to realize sharply, many of those who tarried in California would be lost to the church, seduced away from their religion by the worldly temptations of California and its non-Mormon society.

Nearly as great a danger was posed by some who brought California ways back to the Salt Lake Valley. When the battalion veterans arrived from their mining and road building in September 1848, they included the young men who had adopted vaquero styles while herding the expedition's horses and cattle. Mounted on spirited horses, decked out in wide-brimmed hats with spurs on their boots and red sashes about their waists, clearly these were no longer the naive Midwestern farm boys who had marched away from Council Bluffs more than fifteen months earlier. They brought with them another Californio custom: On one or more occasions a few of the high-spirited young veterans came riding into the Old Fort at Salt Lake City with "a young Lady sitting in the sad[d]le before, & the man behind with his arms around the woman. One of the men was sawing on a violin. This they called Spanish manners or Politeness."[56] Some of the older church officials, particularly Amasa Lyman and Erastus Snow, took great offense at this provocative behavior. As a result, five of the miscreants were fined twenty-five dollars each, no small amount, and cut off from the church. But surely these were not the last California-improved Mormons whose manners and style would raise eyebrows and excite comment in the well-churched, narrow circles of Salt Lake's LDS society.

There was a danger that men, particularly the most able-bodied and enterprising, would run off and also a danger they would come back alarmingly changed. But for church officials California's gold fields presented too rich, too badly needed an economic opportunity to be ignored. From the time the Battalion Boys arrived in the fall of 1848, bringing several thousand dollars of gold into the valley, the flow of California gold into the church treasury—the result of tithing—became welcome income for the hard-pressed Mormon leaders. Gold dust became a common circulating medium, and by the close of 1848 church officers had set up a system for coining the dust into ten-dollar gold pieces. In January 1849, after the coinage equipment broke apart, the Salt Lake municipal council authorized Brigham Young, Heber Kimball, and Bishop Newel Whitney to issue handwritten bills, based on a reserve deposit of gold dust. The following September the arrival of new equipment made it possible for the church mint to resume operations, with gold pieces issued in denominations of $2.50, $5.00, $10.00, and $20.00. This coinage continued until early 1851, amounting to approximately $75,000 in total. The Mormon coins, designed with religious symbols and the initials "P. G." to stand for pure gold, circulated throughout the Salt Lake Valley and surrounding regions, with some returning to California.[57]

California's gold was responsible for an era of prosperity in the Salt Lake settlement that succeeded the earliest years of want. In another chapter of the story we can only briefly note here, church officials in the fall of 1849 instituted a little-known program, the Gold Mission, which sponsored two mining expeditions to California. The plan was to have older members of the Salt Lake community outfit younger men, including some, like Henry Bigler, who were experienced in the placers, to go to the gold country and dig out a fortune. The profits of these operations they proposed to divide in equal shares between the sponsor and the miner. Unfortunately, the profits were small, and this lack of success confirmed for Brigham Young his growing prejudices against California and California ways.[58]

Until 1857, when political events in Washington DC and Utah Territory constrained faithful Saints to retreat from California to Salt Lake City and environs, Mormon miners, merchants, and settlers took an active part in the economic and social life of this young state. Among other episodes, the establishment of a Mormon colony at San Bernardino, remote from the gold fields, was a short-lived pioneering effort that emphasized LDS interest in California's development.[59] During the crisis of 1857, moreover, while appealing to the California Saints to come to Utah and aid in the defense of the church, Brigham Young also sent a secret expedition to San Francisco to procure guns, powder, and lead for Mormon military forces.[60]

Because most faithful Saints did leave for Utah in 1857, they and their descendants were not on hand to remind California's pioneer historians of LDS contributions to the state's foundation. In Utah at the same time, a Zion-centric historical tradition obscured Mormon connections with California for at least three generations. Bigler, Brannan, and their companions clearly had major importance in beginning the California gold rush. Yet their activities represent only one small part of the Mormon role in the larger narrative of this world-changing event. Members of the LDS church, we can now recognize, were key to the entire process that opened California to Anglo-American occupation and made it a valuable, wealth-producing part of the American union. Without the Mormons, California might not have been conquered and pacified so quickly by U.S. military forces. Without the Mormons, not only would Marshall's gold discovery have been someone else's gold discovery at a different time and in a different place, but the beginning of intensive mining for placer gold might well have been delayed by months or perhaps even years. Moreover, Mormon trail makers took a prominent part in ending California's landlocked isolation: between 1846 and 1848 they opened three major wagon routes connecting California with the Southwest, the Great Basin, and the older regions of the United States. These routes included the trans-Sierra Carson Pass route that became most popular for overland immigrants during the early gold rush years.

Without the 1848 gold discovery and the rush that followed, we are also right to suppose, the Mormon Church and the community of LDS believers in the Great Basin would have taken a very different course of development, less economically prosperous and less likely to become reunited in time with the broader American society. When the Mormons evacuated Nauvoo, they hoped to find an isolated place in the West, away from U.S. authority and persecution by intolerant gentiles, where the community of the faithful could live apart. For a short while they found this isolated Zion in the Salt Lake Valley, but very soon the California gold rush brought the world by their doorstep. The parade of overland travelers offered opportunities to the church leaders that they could not ignore: opportunities to profit that would enable them to aid the poor, look after the weak, and sustain the ever-expanding mission of the church. "Get rich," President Young had written to the California Saints in 1847, "for the Lord designs that his should be the richest people on earth."[61] Following that principle in the Salt Lake Valley, Young and his associates seized the economic main chance brought to them by the gold rush, turned away from the alternative of isolation, engaged with the wider world, and directed the LDS church toward a far broader calling as the most successful Christian evangelical institution in American society.[62]

One final vignette can conclude the story of the Mormons and the California gold rush. In 1898, to commemorate the Golden Jubilee of the Coloma gold discovery, an organizing committee in San Francisco invited back to California four of the original Battalion Boys, all still living in Utah, who had been part of that event. Azariah Smith, Henry Bigler, William Johnson, and James S. Brown arrived in San Francisco on January 22. Two days later, January 24, 1898, the four men had a place of honor in the Jubilee Parade, a grand event with over fourteen hundred carriages or floats and thirty different bands. The four rode in a coach that proclaimed in large letters on each side "The Companions of Marshall." For a week they toured the city, posed for photographs, shook hands, gave autographs, and in general played the part of celebrities. Then they returned home, content to have seen again some of the places that were part of their adventures as younger men.[63] Just as in 1898, so again more than a hundred years later, we are right to keep in mind the companions of Marshall, the gold-rich Saints, and to give due respect to their sometimes forgotten contributions in helping create California's most famous moment in history.

Notes

1. For Marshall's career, see Gay, *James W. Marshall*. It is a commentary on changing historical tastes that Marshall has been virtually ignored during recent sesquicentennial commemorations of the California gold rush. The circumstances of gold discovery are thoroughly documented in Paul, *California Gold Discovery*.

2. Richard Dillon, *Fool's Gold*, provides the standard account of John Sutter's

American career. Owens, ed., *John Sutter and A Wider West,* reappraises Sutter's California career and his historical role in the American West.

3. For Mormon goals and the decision to move west, see Leonard J. Arrington and Davis Bitton, *The Mormon Experience: A History of the Latter-day Saints,* second ed.(Urbana: University of Illinois Press,1992), 95–96; Leonard J. Arrington, *Brigham Young: American Moses* (New York: Alfred A. Knopf, 1985), 123–29; and David L. Bigler, *Forgotten Kingdom: The Mormon Theocracy in the American West, 1847–1896* (Spokane WA: Arthur H. Clark Company, 1998), 24–36. Also informative is the discussion in Will Bagley, ed., *The Pioneer Camp of the Saints: The 1846 and 1847 Mormon Trail Journals of Thomas Bullock* (Spokane WA: Arthur H. Clark Company, 1997), 45–50.

4. Young to Brannan, September 15, 1845, Brigham Young Collection, MS 1235, LDS Archives, Salt Lake City, transcribed in Will Bagley, ed., *Scoundrel's Tale: The Samuel Brannan Papers* (Spokane WA: Arthur H. Clark Company, 1999), 91–92. Bagley's work reviews the evidence regarding Brannan's instructions from church authorities on pages 100–104. Bagley also provides extensive circumstantial detail on "The Plot to Conquer California," which involved Brannan with the machinations of various non-Mormon politicians and speculators.

5. Brannan to Young, January 26, 1846, Brigham Young Collection, LDS Archives, transcribed in Bagley, ed., *Scoundrel's Tale,* 122–24. Until the U.S. declaration of war against Mexico ended these plans, eastern LDS church leaders Jesse Little and William Appleby intended to charter another ship and follow Brannan to San Francisco Bay with a second colonizing expedition "to get beyond the reach of persecution as oppression," as Appleby wrote. Once the war began, Little received instructions from the Nauvoo authorities to have the emigrants instead "to go by land, as fast as they can." Bagley, ed., *Scoundrel's Tale,* 132, 134. Apostle Orson Hyde in the fall of 1846, after the *Brooklyn's* arrival at San Francisco Bay, indicated to Brannan his understanding that the main body of the Saints would be joining Brannan's colony on the Pacific Coast: Bagley, ed., *Scoundrel's Tale,* 154–55.

6. Samuel Brannan, "Fragmentary Remarks Re: His Expedition to California with the Mormons," Brannan Collection, HM 4089, Huntington Library, San Marino, California, transcribed in Bagley, ed., *Scoundrel's Tale,* 166–67. Brannan's Mormon party, as historian Will Bagley points out, was the first organized group of American emigrants to reach California by sea.

7. For this migration and the camps on the Missouri, see William W. Slaughter and Michael Landon, *Trail of Hope: The Story of the Mormon Trail* (Salt Lake City: Shadow Mountain, 1997), 40–48; Arrington, *Brigham Young,* 126–29; and Richard E. Bennett, *Mormons at the Missouri: "And should we die"* (Norman: University of Oklahoma Press, 1987).

8. The *Brooklyn's* voyage is thoroughly documented in Bagley, *Scoundrel's Tale,* 131–

68; and in Lorin Hansen, "Voyage of the *Brooklyn*," *Dialogue: A Journal of Mormon Thought* 21 (autumn 1988): 46–72.

9. Samuel Brannan, "Fragmentary Remarks," transcribed in Bagley, ed., *Scoundrel's Tale*, 142. See also Hubert Howe Bancroft, *History of California*, vol. 5, *1846–1848* (San Francisco: History Company, 1886), 550.

10. Neal Harlow, *California Conquered: War and Peace on the Pacific, 1846–1850* (Berkeley: University of California Press, 1982) is the fullest account. Harlow describes Commander Montgomery's ceremony of possession at Yerba Buena on pages 126–27.

11. Mary Holland Sparks to Maria and Holly Clark, November 15, 1846, MS 7519, LDS Archives, transcribed in Bagley, ed., *Scoundrel's Tale*, 158–62.

12. Bagley, ed., *Scoundrel's Tale*, 177–81, 183–86, 234. According to one of the men involved, the assets at New Hope—including the land, crops, oxen, a few houses, and tools—all went into Brannan's hands, "and the Company that did the work never got anything for their labor." William Glover, *The Mormons in California* (Los Angeles: Glen Dawson, 1954), 20–21.

13. Bagley, ed., *Scoundrel's Tale*, 204–5, prints Brannan's account of the journey across the Sierra, written from Fort Hall in mid-June, originally published in the *Latter-day Saints' Millennial Star*, October 15, 1847.

14. Bagley, ed., *Scoundrel's Tale*, 208–12. Bagley points out that Young's actions in sending Brannan "on a variety of odd errands" suggest that the church president was not very fond of Brannan's company, "but there is no direct evidence that relations between the two men were strained" (209).

15. Bagley, ed., *Scoundrel's Tale*, 213, quoting Howard Egan, *Pioneering the West, 1846 to 1848*, ed. William M. Egan (Redmond UT: n.p., 1917), 111.

16. Bagley, ed., *Scoundrel's Tale*, 213, quoting John Brown, "An Evidence of Inspiration," *Juvenile Instructor*, 16 (1881).

17. Bagley, ed., *Scoundrel's Tale*, 214, quoting Wilford Woodruff, *The Discourses of Wilford Woodruff* (Salt Lake City: Bookcraft, 1969), 322–23.

18. Brannan to Jesse Little, December 24, 1886, Brannan Papers, Lee Library, Brigham Young University, quoted in Bagley, ed., *Scoundrel's Tale*, 396–97.

19. Brigham Young to the Saints in California, August 7, 1847, Special Collections, Lee Library, quoted in Bagley, ed., *Scoundrel's Tale*, 219.

20. The history of the Mormon Battalion has received detailed treatment in Norma Baldwin Ricketts, *The Mormon Battalion: U.S. Army of the West, 1846–1848* (Logan: Utah State University Press, 1996). Among other valuable sources, David L. Bigler, ed., *Gold Discovery Journal,* contains a particularly candid account of the battalion's

march to California. These works have now been supplemented by an excellent documentary history, David L. Bigler and Will Bagley, eds., *Army of Israel: Mormon Battalion Narratives* (Spokane WA: Arthur H. Clark Company, 2000).

21. James Stephens Brown, *California Gold—An Authentic History of the First Find, with the Names of Those Interested in the Discovery* (1894; reprint, New York: William Abbatt, 1933), 9. The date of the contract between Sutter and Marshall, drawn up by Sutter's bookkeeper, John Bidwell, was August 27, 1847, the day after the veterans' committee opened negotiations with Sutter. The connection between the Mormons' arrival at Sutter's Fort and the sawmill partnership contract is clear in John A. Sutter et al., *New Helvetia Diary: A Record Kept by John A. Sutter and His Clerks at New Helvetia, California, from September 9, 1845, to May 25, 1848* (San Francisco: Grabhorn Press, 1939), entry for August 27, 1847.

22. Gudde, ed. *Bigler's Chronicle*, 78–79. See also David L. Bigler, ed., *Gold Discovery Journal*, entry for Wednesday, September 8, 1847, 102; Bagley, ed., *Scoundrel's Tale*, 221–23.

23. Brigham Young, October 18, 1857, *Journal of Discourses*, vol. 5 (London: Latter-day Saints' Book Depot, 1858), 341. I am indebted to Michael Landon, archivist of the LDS Church History Department, Salt Lake City, for calling this item to my attention.

24. David L. Bigler, ed., *Gold Discovery Journal*, 102.

25. Gudde, ed., *Bigler's Chronicle*, 99. Bigler's adventurous early life is well described in M. Guy Bishop, *Henry William Bigler: Soldier, Gold Miner, Missionary, Chronicler, 1815–1900* (Logan: Utah State University Press, 1998).

26. Gudde, ed., *Bigler's Chronicle*, 101. By this time Captain Sutter had visited the Coloma camp, confirming the gold discovery and urging the workers there to keep the whole thing quiet until he and Marshall could secure title to the land—an impossibility under the prevailing law, as the military governor, Colonel Richard Mason, soon pointed out to Sutter: Gudde, ed., *Bigler's Chronicle*, 92–94; David L. Bigler, ed., *Gold Discovery Journal*, 108–10; Colonel Richard B. Mason to John Sutter, March 5, 1848, printed in Paul, ed., *California Gold Discovery*, 81–82.

27. Gudde, ed., *Bigler's Chronicle*, 102–3. See also the reminiscences of James S. Brown, *Life of a Pioneer* (Salt Lake City: Geo. Q. Cannon & Sons, 1900), 96–102, for an account that differs in detail but agrees in substance with Bigler's narrative.

28. The most complete account of the gold discovery and early mining at Mormon Island is J. Kenneth Davies, *Mormon Gold: The Story of California's Mormon Argonauts* (Salt Lake City: Olympus Publishing Company, 1984), 31–49. Sources include S. George Ellsworth, ed., *The Journals of Addison Pratt* (Salt Lake City: University of Utah Press, 1990), 336–37; David L. Bigler, ed., *Gold Discovery*

Journal, 115–16; Brown, *Life of a Pioneer,* 102–5; and the unpublished diaries of John Borrowman in the LDS Archives.

29. Azariah Smith, who worked the diggings May 11–23, described his earnings: "I got there something near three hundred dollars . . . The most I made in a day was sixty five dollars after the toll was taken out, which was thirty dollars out of a hundred, which goes to Hudson and Willis, that discovered the mine, and Brannon [*sic*] who is securing it for them." Entry for May 26, David L. Bigler, ed., *Gold Discovery Journal,* 115.

30. David L. Bigler, ed., *Gold Discovery Journal,* 115.

31. Gudde, ed., *Bigler's Chronicle,* 107–8; Colonel Richard B. Mason's Report, August 17, 1848, reprinted in Paul, ed., *California Gold Discovery,* 91–92. Mason estimated two hundred miners were at the Mormon diggings in early July. His adjutant, William Tecumseh Sherman, later stated that three hundred miners were then at the site: *Memoirs of General William T. Sherman by Himself,* 2 vols. (New York: D. Appleton & Company, 1875), 1:52.

32. Writing his reminiscences a half century later, published as *Life of a Pioneer* in 1900, James S. Brown stated conclusions that merit a restatement: "Sutter's capital and enterprise and Marshall's shrewd sagacity have been given the credit of the great gold discovery in California. The facts are, that James W. Marshall discovered the first color; in less than an hour six Mormons found color as well, and within six weeks Mormons had discovered it in hundreds of places that Mr. Marshall had never seen, the most notable of which was Mormon Island, where the first rush was made, and from where the news was spread to the world. As to Sutter's enterprise and capital, he furnished the graham flour and mutton, wheat and peas, black coffee and brown sugar, teams and tools, while we, members of the Mormon Battalion, did the hard labor that discovered the metal. It is also true that we were in Sutter's employ at that date, and never received a farthing for it. I heard a number of other men say they never got their pay. It was our labor that developed the find, and not Marshall's and Sutter's, and we were never paid for it" (105).

33. Bagley, ed., *Scoundrel's Tale,* 265.

34. Bancroft, *History of California,* 6:56; Gudde, ed., *Bigler's Chronicle,* 110–11; Bagley, ed., *Scoundrel's Tale,* 264–67.

35. Sherman, *Memoirs,* 1:52–53. On the often misunderstood question of the fee charged by Brannan, see editor David Bigler's observations in *Gold Discovery Journal,* 115–16; Ricketts, *Mormon Battalion,* 200–201; Davies, *Mormon Gold,* 42; and Bagley, ed., *Scoundrel's Tale,* 263–64, 269–70. At Coloma, meanwhile, Marshall had begun supervising mining efforts by taking half of the gold that his workers gathered, a claim reduced to 30 or even 10 percent for those who came afterward.

36. Amasa Lyman and Charles C. Rich to Brigham Young, July 23, 1850, Young Collection, LDS Archives, printed in Bagley, ed. *Scoundrel's Tale*, 292–96.

37. Gudde, ed., *Bigler's Chronicle*, 106.

38. Brown, *Life of a Pioneer*, 107.

39. Rogers journal, cited in Will Bagley, ed., *A Road from El Dorado: The 1848 Trail Journal of Ephraim Green* (Salt Lake City: Prairie Dog Press, 1991), 51, n. 11; Ricketts, *Mormon Battalion*, 203; David L. Bigler, ed., *Gold Discovery Journal*, 113.

40. Ellsworth, ed., *Journals of Addison Pratt*, 337. Azariah Smith described the immediate results of this advance survey: "I scraped one day on the race [at Sutter's Brighton mill], when on the nineth [of May] the boys came back from the exploring expedition haveing went up to the back bones which was covered with Snow and they could not cross. They then concluded to go up to the [Mormon Island] Gold mine, so on Thursday the 11th we went up, and stayed there until Tuesday the 23d., when we came down." David L. Bigler, ed., *Gold Discovery Journal*, 115.

41. Gudde, ed., *Bigler's Chronicle*, 110.

42. Direct evidence of the returns from Mormon gold mining in 1848 is scattered and sparse. The indirect evidence of Brigham Young's Gold Account records, according to historian J. Kenneth Davies, indicates that at least $19,103.00 in gold dust and coins came into the Salt Lake Valley economy from California sources between October 1848 and June 1849, much of it representing the accumulated treasure of LDS church members who had been in the mines. Mormons known to have come from California in 1848 deposited into the Gold Account a total of about $6,561.00, for an average of $102.50 per depositor: Davies, *Mormon Gold*, 88. The Battalion Boys and others, of course, spent a substantial part of their mining profits in California, outfitting themselves and purchasing stock and equipment to take to the Salt Lake Valley before starting the trip eastward. Yet, as Henry Bigler subsequently wrote, in some places "where we got one dollar then, [other, more experienced miners] . . . could later get hundreds." Gudde, ed., *Bigler's Chronicle*, 109.

43. Kenneth N. Owens, "The Mormon-Carson Emigrant Trail in Western History," *Montana, the Magazine of Western History* 42 (winter 1992): 14–27. Greater detail can be found in Kenneth N. Owens, *Archaeological and Historical Investigation of the Mormon-Carson Emigrant Trail, Eldorado and Toiyabe National Forests*, vol. 2, *History* (Placerville CA: Eldorado National Forest, U.S. Forest Service, 1990). A day-by-day summary of the road-making expedition appears in Ricketts, *Mormon Battalion*, 205–21.

44. Most writers have adopted Henry Bigler's figures for the size of the expedition: "Forty-five men and one women (Sergeant Wm. Coray's wife) two small brass pieces bought of Sutter, seventeen wagons, one hundred fifty horses and about

the same of cattle, and I believe every man had a musket." Gudde, ed., *Bigler's Chronicle*, 114. Other sources give slightly different figures: Ellsworth, ed., *Journals of Addison Pratt*, 342; Richard Martin May, "A Sketch of a Migrating Family to California," Bancroft Library, University of California, Berkeley; Zadok Knapp Judd, Sr., "Reminiscences of Zadok Knapp Judd, Senior," typescript, Lee Library.

45. David L. Bigler, ed., *Gold Discovery Journal*, 134–35; Ellsworth, ed., *Journals of Addison Pratt*, 348; John Borrowman, "Journal from Dec. 23, 1846 to Mar. 1870, with Lapses of Several Years," LDS Archives, Salt Lake City; May, "Sketch of a Migrating Family." Ricketts, *Mormon Battalion*, 221–27, provides rosters of these various groups.

46. Zadok Judd describes this process in detail in his "Reminiscences."

47. May, "Sketch of a Migrating Family."

48. Daniel Tyler, *A Concise History of the Mormon Battalion in the Mexican War, 1846–1847* (Salt Lake City: Juvenile Instructor Press, 1939), 340.

49. Hazen Kimball to James Kimball, December 7, 1848, quoted in Charles L. Camp, ed., *James Clyman, Frontiersman: The Adventures of a Trapper and Covered-Wagon Emigrant as Told in His Own Reminiscences and Diaries* (Portland OR: Champoeg Press, 1960), 287; May, "Sketch of a Migrating Family"; Thomas Stock Bayley, "Five Chapters on Pioneer California," Bancroft Library.

50. William G. Johnston, *Experiences of a Forty-Niner* (Pittsburgh, 1892; reprint New York: Arno Press, 1973), 184, 192, 228, 237; James C. Sly, Journal, 1849 June–1850 March, photocopy of manuscript, LDS Archives, Salt Lake City; Will Bagley, ed., *Frontiersman: Abner Blackburn's Narrative* (Salt Lake City: University of Utah Press, 1992), 139–50.

51. Ira J. Willis, "Ira J. Willis Guide to the Gold Mines," Huntington Library. Cf. Irene D. Paden, ed. "The Ira J. Willis Guide to the Gold Fields," *California Historical Quarterly* 32 (September 1953): 193–207.

52. Joseph Cain and Ariah C. Brower, *Mormon Way-Bill to the Gold Mines from the Pacific Springs by the Northern and Southern Routes* (Salt Lake City: W. Richard, Publisher, 1851).

53. Owens, "Mormon-Carson Emigrant Trail," 16–19.

54. G. W. Thissell, *Crossing the Plains in Forty-nine* (Oakland: n.p, 1903).

55. Owens, "Mormon-Carson Emigrant Trail," 19–22. Mormon Station, located at the site of modern Genoa, Nevada, remained a center of LDS activities in what was then called western Utah until 1857, when the small settlement was abandoned in the general withdrawal of Mormon faithful to Salt Lake City to confront invading federal forces. See Russell R. Elliott, *History of Nevada* (Lincoln: University of

Nebraska Press, 1973), 50–57; Davies, *Mormon Gold*, 147–53; Arrington and Bitton, *The Mormon Experience*, 163–70.

56. John D. Lee, quoted in Bagley, *Frontiersman*, 177.

57. The story of gold coinage in Utah is admirably summarized in Leonard J. Arrington, *Great Basin Kingdom: An Economic History of the Latter-day Saints, 1830–1900* (Cambridge: Harvard University Press, 1958), 71–72.

58. Arrington, *Great Basin Kingdom*, 72–76, describes the gold mission project and its disappointing results. A more detailed treatment will be found in Davies, *Mormon Gold*, 109–30.

59. The history of the LDS San Bernardino colony is fully and expertly told in Edward Leo Lyman, *San Bernardino: The Rise and Fall of a California Community* (Salt Lake City: Signature Books, 1996). Leonard J. Arrington views this history from the perspective of one of the colony's founders and most earnest promoters in his biographical study, *Charles C. Rich, Mormon General and Western Frontiersman* (Provo UT: Brigham Young University Press, 1974), 152–213.

60. Peter Wilson Conover Reminiscences, LDS Church Archives, Salt Lake City; O. B. Huntington, "Incidents of Presentation by Inspiration in My Second Trip to Carson and Calafornia," Lee Library.

61. Brigham Young to the Saints in California, August 7, 1847, Special Collections, Lee Library, quoted in Bagley, ed., *Scoundrel's Tale*, 219.

62. Leonard Arrington's *Great Basin Kingdom* first examined the impact of the California gold rush on the Mormon enterprise in Utah. His assessment is reinforced in Eugene E. Campbell, *Establishing Zion: The Mormon Church in the American West, 1847–1869* (Salt Lake City: Signature Books, 1988). Among other relevant works, David L. Bigler, *Forgotten Kingdom*, emphasizes the separatist millennial tradition that remained strong in Utah until the 1890s. Thomas G. Alexander, *Mormonism in Transition: A History of the Latter-day Saints, 1890–1930* (Urbana: University of Illinois Press, 1986) describes the shift away from a closed community and the process of LDS accommodation to the wider non-Mormon society after Utah statehood.

63. The basis for this account is David Bigler's epilogue in his edition of Azariah Smith's journal, 147–51. See also Gudde, ed., *Bigler's Chronicle*, 134–35; Brown, *Life of a Pioneer*, 511–19.

2

"We Will Make Our Fortunes–No Doubt of It"

The Worldwide Rush to California

Malcolm J. Rohrbough

Like a stone dropped into a still pool, the news of James W. Marshall's discovery of gold in a millrace on the American River on the morning of January 24, 1848, spread outward in ever-widening circles. Eventually it would travel around the world and set thousands on the road to what they thought of as a better life. That this new Garden of Eden was in distant California, requiring for many a potentially dangerous journey of six months or longer, only added to its appeal. In addition to its immediate impact on families and communities world-wide, the gold rush was the beginning of the nation's and the world's fascination with California and things Californian as the embodiment of the American Dream.[1]

Those who rushed from other nations to take advantage of this astonishing opportunity to pick up gold nuggets from the sides of California's hills and along California's stream beds—for so it was foretold in the original accounts—included groups of diverse ethnic and cultural origins. The common denominator was that they came from all over the world. That they came—and most of them as rapidly as possible, with a single-minded intensity equaling that of their fellow Argonauts from the eastern half of the North American continent—was testimony to the power of this discovery and its spread. Most came greater distances than their American counterparts, hoping to find wealth in this alien country, despite its strange language and a peculiar culture that would, from the beginning, handicap them in a search for riches that became ever more competitive.

As news of the discovery of gold spread outward, it first reached those geographic areas closest to California: Mexico and the Hawaiian Islands, followed soon thereafter by Chile, Peru, and the other nations of South America. The story of the gold discoveries reached across the border into the Mexican state of Sonora in September 1848, where the response was immediate. Accounts of the arrival of Sonorans in the gold fields speak to the large-scale immigration. Jacques Antoine Moerenhout, the French consul at Monterey, wrote in these terms: "The emigration from all parts of the Americas to this place is still increasing day by day. Over ten thousand people from Sonora and lower California, men, women, and children, have passed within a few leagues of Monterey during the last two months, and more keep coming."[2] By December, according to one account, some three thousand Sonorans had taken the trails north into California's San Joaquin Valley. Many of those who came by sea disembarked at San Pedro and passed through Los Angeles on the way to the mines each spring. Another estimated four to five thousand gold seekers left Sonora between October 1848 and March 1849.[3] By the summer of 1849, at least six thousand Sonorans were in the southern mining region, with the largest concentration around the town known as Sonora. The long columns marched in a state of euphoria, convinced that the mines would make their fortunes and change their lives: "The whole state of Sonora is on the move, passing us in gangs daily. They say 'we will make our fortunes. No doubt of it'!"[4]

Sonorans sometimes took their families to the gold fields with them, returning home in the fall and making the trek to the gold fields again in the spring. Mining was, of course, seasonal, and for many from Sonora, the trip north could be made each spring, with a return the following autumn. As for the character of the Mexican immigration, the arrivals were almost exclusively miners and many of them skilled, at least by the standards of the day. The California gold rush, in its immigration and in its mining techniques, was initially the work of amateurs.

Because of their mining skills, the Mexicans were initially welcomed, but because of their gold claims, the growing pressure for space, and their clearly distinct culture, they soon found themselves discriminated against in the gold fields and the mining camps. The Sonoran influx peaked in 1850; subsequently this immigration seems to have decreased rapidly, and it largely ended by 1854. The beginning of the decline coincided with the passage by California's first state legislature in 1850 of the Foreign Miners Tax, a levy of twenty dollars per month on all miners not citizens of the United States. Whether the immigration decline was directly related to the tax is impossible to say, but certainly the proximity of the Sonorans to their homeland made it possible for them to return from California more easily than for many others.[5]

In accordance with the technology of the day, news of the gold discoveries (like all news) spread across long distances most readily by sea. This information first reached the seaports closest to California. A schooner sailed from San Francisco to Honolulu in late May 1848 with the startling news that California had gold, and it was available to anyone. The *Honolulu Polynesian* newspaper made the public announcement on June 24, 1848. The response was instantaneous. Over the summer prospective miners organized into groups and headed for the mainland, along with cargoes of goods. The *Polynesian* commented that summer: "[T]he little city of Honolulu has never before witnessed such an excitement as the gold fever has created. . . . The people of California now look upon their gold region as a bank upon which they have only to present a check, and withdraw what amount they wish. From this our planters and traders will doubtless reap a rich harvest."[6] In mid-July, Samuel Varney, a Honolulu-based merchant, wrote to his friend Thomas O. Larkin at Monterey: "The fever rages here and there is much preparation making for emigration. I hope they will realize all they anticipate."[7] Life in the islands was substantially disrupted, even among the missionaries. In one case, when a congregation was dissolved by emigration to California, the minister obtained a leave of absence and set out with his parishioners to the gold fields on the mainland.[8]

Native Hawaiian peoples went in numbers. In California, they were called Kanakas—the Polynesian word for "man"—and valued as cheap laborers. While their habits of diving for the precious metals in California streams entertained observers, they were isolated in the gold fields and seldom mixed with those outside their own groups.[9]

Unlike in Mexico, in Hawaii the response had a strong commercial element. The gold discoveries in the mountain streams of California would benefit individuals who departed for the mines; it also offered opportunities for profit on a larger scale to merchants, traders, and commercial men of many kinds. The gold fields were not only places where people sought wealth in the form of precious mineral; they were also places where people bought and sold. And as the numbers of miners increased—and in like proportion, the population of California—so the numbers of commercial transactions grew and expanded to touch the most remote streams of this golden land.

The Hawaiian Islands quickly became the source of large-scale agricultural exports to California, helping to satisfy the hearty appetites of gold rush immigrants. Hawaiian products included oranges, pineapples, bananas, turkeys, and chickens. Merchants shipped as well all the pickaxes and shovels that could be found in the islands, plus boots and clothing. Exports of domestic produce from Hawaii to California increased five times between 1848 and 1850, then declined in the face of competition from rising California farm production. Other notable exports were cattle and coffee. Hawaii's coffee production increased seven times between 1849 and 1850 to supply the enormous California market. Among the thriving new businesses was the laundering of clothes sent by ship from California.[10]

The impact of the gold rush on the Hawaiian Islands became a model for what would happen in other places that experienced the throes of the "gold fever." A severe labor shortage quickly developed, and the remaining workers demanded exorbitant wages. A sudden exodus of workers for California led to the abandonment of some sugar plantations and, on others, a decline in production. With the great export of foodstuffs, local food prices rose, inflated also by returning miners who had gold to spend. An indication of the commercial activity generated by the California gold discoveries was the rising number of merchant ship arrivals in the Hawaiian Islands, from 90 in 1848 to 469 in 1850, a peak figure not exceeded for the next half-century. Hawaii's gold rush commerce helped to bring about the introduction in 1853 of regular steam navigation between Honolulu and San Francisco.[11]

The commercial dimension of the gold discoveries was a powerful influence in both Chile and Peru. Perhaps these two nations were so greatly affected because they had trading ties well established with California prior to 1848. News of the gold discoveries first reached Valparaiso, the major trading and provisioning port on the west coast of South America, on August 19, 1848. Less than a month later another vessel dropped anchor with twenty-five hundred dollars in gold dust on board. Although newspapers generally ignored the reports, news of gold in California circulated by word of mouth, and soon people began to take passage on ships sailing northward. Finally, on November 4, 1848, an article appeared in the Valparaiso *El Mercurio* under the title "Las Minas de Oro de California" that brought the rumors into the open. Chileans learned that Upper California had been transformed by gold from a pastoral land controlled by a few wealthy landowners into a land of ordinary workers, where the poorest laborer was becoming rich. A miner needed only a knife to earn thirty to forty dollars a day.[12]

Who could resist such accounts? There was a frenzied search for berths on ships bound for California. By the opening of the year 1849, one thousand Chileans had already left for San Francisco, some two thousand by February, and the *Alta California* newspaper later estimated that more than five thousand Chileans had arrived in San Francisco during the first six months of 1849. When leaving Valparaiso, the departing Chileans were supposed to have passports, providing the government with some accounting of the exodus; but many of those boarding ships for California avoided or evaded the passport law, and soon it was abolished.[13]

From the beginning, the rush of Chileans to California had a strongly commercial character. The leading Chilean merchants quickly established commission houses in San Francisco. The most important export products were agricultural, especially wheat, flour, barley, maize, beans, and potatoes, as well as dried fruits and beef. But Chilean merchants also sent other gold-field staples such as mining equipment (shovels, picks, gold pans, and scales), several kinds of liquors, and even building materials—including prefabricated houses. In Valparaiso well-intentioned authorities also made plans to send to California "200 young, white, poor and virtuous girls to be . . . honorably married to the thousands of North Americans and other strangers who have made their fortunes at the mines."[14]

The Chileans did not blend easily into California's cultural landscape, and they were subjected to varieties of discrimination and violence—initially in the form of a riot in San Francisco in the summer of 1849. They were later among the leading targets of the Foreign Miners Tax of 1850.[15] Those outside San Francisco—a second wave of arrivals that was Spanish-speaking—congregated in the Southern Mines, where they worked and interacted with the Spanish-speaking Mexican peoples. Several Chileans brought their families to California, "an unusual procedure for immigrants in the early days of the gold rush."[16]

West across the Pacific, news of the gold discoveries reached Australia's Sydney harbor in December 1848. Soon the symptoms of gold fever could be seen throughout this British colonial capital; yet the first great rush from Australia came in goods, not as would-be miners. In part this difference reflected distance; in part it reflected the deliberate policy of Australia's editors and colonial leaders to minimize emigration, with its accompanying rise in local labor costs. But shipowners and commercial houses saw in the news from California a glowing opportunity to diminish their inventories, which had recently grown large and unprofitable because of a decline in the price of wool. The first vessel to sail from Australia to gold rush California was the ship *Plymouth*, which left Sydney, without passengers, on January 9, 1849. A dozen others soon followed. Most of these ships arrived at San Francisco in April 1849, making the Australian merchants among the first and most prominent to venture into a trans-Pacific gold rush trade. Despite the great distance between California and Australia, San Francisco was just as far away from America's East Coast ports (by way of Cape Horn) as from Sydney. When ships returned to Australia with reports that their cargoes had sold in California for unheard-of figures, making great fortunes for a few, the wildest hopes for quick profits seemed more than confirmed.[17]

By 1850 nearly every ship in Sydney harbor that could float was scheduled to sail for San Francisco. In addition to berths for miners, there were cargoes of nails, clothes, bottled beer, woolen blankets, and bricks. Among the important exports were dray horses, particularly valued for hauling goods to the gold fields. Australians even circulated reports of the opportunities for women in California. Sydney newspapers publicized the plan of Mrs. Eliza Farnham, a recent widow in New York City, to transport poor but marriageable girls from the East Coast to California, where they could find husbands while checking the evils that otherwise would prevail among a dominantly male population. This ill-fated proposal, which gained Mrs. Farnham only two recruits, roused talk of a similar scheme for Australian girls.[18]

The rush of men from Australia to California began in August 1849, when the first returning ships confirmed not only the opportunities for commercial ventures but also the high returns for individual miners in the diggings. Perhaps as many as two thousand men crowded aboard California-bound ships in the next six months.[19] Arriving in the wide-open, cosmopolitan town of San Francisco in the fall and winter of 1849, the Australians soon fanned out into the diggings. Although they were pleased by American informality and helpfulness, and amused by the American customs of constantly shaking hands and chewing tobacco on all occasions and in all settings, the Australians were made less happy by the American miners' habit of organizing themselves into a sovereign body and making whatever rules they liked. Perhaps they already instinctively sensed that these regulations might be used against all noncitizens, including Australians.[20]

News of California gold reached China in mid-1848. Despite the concern of merchants for expanded commercial opportunities, there was little immediate interest in emigration. This indifference changed in 1850 with the outbreak in southeastern China of the Taiping Rebellion, an internal upheaval that led to a widespread decline in trade and agricultural production and that encouraged overseas migration. Those who came to California during the gold rush years were predominantly male farm workers, members of the laboring class—although the term is an imprecise one. One historian has called them "free agricultural peasantry from the country districts and villages—young, thrifty and industrious." Not criminals and not paupers, they came for purely economic reasons, and few intended to stay longer than necessary to fulfill their labor contracts. They left their wives behind. Many came under arrangements for contracted labor over a specified period. Accordingly, the Chinese who came to California saved their wages and sent or carried them home. They spent little and became remarkable to other Californians for their penury.[21]

The Chinese were initially welcomed in California for their labor. In the gold fields they were regarded as a curiosity because of their unique appearance and language. Americans would visit Chinese camps on Sunday for entertainment and sightseeing. The immigration of Chinese into California reached a high point in 1852, with some twenty thousand arriving in that year. As competition for rich diggings grew more intense in the mining areas, the Chinese became victims of prejudice. Local authorities made them chiefly liable for paying the revised Foreign Miners Tax of 1852. The original legislation had been aimed at Mexicans and other Latin Americans, but its successor—with the tax reduced from twenty dollars to three dollars a month—fitted well into a growing popular reaction against the Chinese. While many miners and merchants from Mexico and Latin America left California in response to the antiforeign agitation, the Chinese continued to arrive in numbers through the 1850s, and they became the final targets for this discriminatory tax. After 1855 most of the revenue from the Foreign Miners Tax was collected from Chinese. By 1860, the Chinese, however unwelcome, had established themselves in several industries in California. The changing pattern of Chinese employment suggests that, like other immigrants, they had largely moved from the mining camps and gold-country towns to the cities, where they might find their best opportunities and perhaps their best chances to evade the hostility directed against them.[22]

In western Europe, news of the discovery of gold in California was the most celebrated event involving the United States since the American Revolution. It came at a time of great trouble and uneasiness. The Irish potato crop failure in 1846 had begun a series of years of blighted harvests and growing famine across Europe and the British Isles. There was also a widespread failure of the grain harvest throughout western Europe in 1846, with an accompanying rise in the price of bread. In responses to these catastrophes, massive internal immigrations began; in unheard of numbers, the population of the depressed countryside headed into the cities. Unfortunately, with the possible exception of England, there was not yet sufficient employment in urban industries to absorb these thousands of rural refugees. By 1848, there was much misery in France and Germany, with the countryside depressed and the cities full of unemployed.[23]

In England, the news of gold in California was greeted with astonishment mixed with a healthy skepticism. The London *Times* finally agreed that "[i]t is beyond all question that gold, in immense quantities, is being found daily." The appearance of President James K. Polk's address in print within a week, along with columns from the *New York Herald Tribune* and the *Washington Union,* offered further proof. Within a fortnight, if editors were not convinced, the public was. An observer in Liverpool wrote, "The gold excitement here and in London exceeds anything ever known or heard of. . . . Nothing is talked about but the new El Dorado. Companies are organizing in London in great numbers for the promised land. We hear it stated that no less than fourteen vessels have already been chartered and are nearly or quite filled with passengers and freight."[24]

Of the thousands of immigrants who came to California in the twenty years after the discovery of gold, the largest number came from the British Isles. These included tin and coal miners from Wales and Cornwall, who would comprise California's first truly experienced, professional miners. Ireland supplied the largest number of immigrants from the British Isles. This was an immigration of desperation, rooted in a collapse of the rural economy that had reached famine proportions. The Irish immigration to America had begun in 1847; the gold discoveries in California helped push annual immigration figures from 100,000 to well over 220,000 in 1851. The costs of traveling from Europe to California at midcentury were not cheap; hence, it was an option not available to the poorest families. But to those with means to do so, California was the subject of an Irish version of gold mania. As English speakers, the Irish were welcomed and prospered in San Francisco, in regional trade centers like Sacramento, Stockton, and Marysville, and in the mining camps.[25]

The several German states also sent substantial numbers to California. These immigrants responded in part to the upheavals associated with the revolutions of 1848 and, for some, the burden of imminent compulsory military service. There were also strong economic factors, especially in agriculture. Many of the German immigrant families had no thought of returning, and in California they did not intend to mine gold but rather to establish a farm or some kind of trade. Once they arrived, the Germans often learned English and assimilated very well, and they found themselves praised as disciplined and hard working. The census of 1850 already identified in California more than three thousand inhabitants from the German states, and this number had increased tenfold by 1860.[26]

Of all European peoples, the most unlikely in their enthusiasm for California gold were the French. France was not a nation of emigrants. The French preferred a life of hardship in France to a life of economic opportunity in a strange land. Even as they sojourned elsewhere for brief periods, their eyes were always fixed in the direction of France, the only place where a person of French nativity would want to live and, ultimately, to die. That the French noted the discovery of gold in California was to be expected; France was, after all, a cosmopolitan nation with interests around the world. That these discoveries would prompt widespread enthusiasm and a real movement of French people from western Europe to western America was quite extraordinary.

This unlikely ardor for California had much to do with France's internal conditions. The political upheavals associated with the winter and spring of 1848—sometimes called the Revolution of 1848, in which two factions fought over the right to be the legitimate heirs to French history— culminated on the barricades of Paris over four bloody days. In these so-called June Days, which resulted in the suppression of the revolutionary movement, some twelve thousand French men and women died on the barricades or in assaults on the barricades, twenty-five thousand were arrested, of whom eleven thousand were brought before the army's courts-martial, many executed and imprisoned, and five thousand deported. The bloody June Days and the subsequent retribution left deep divisions within French society. For those defeated and disgraced, the discovery of gold in California provided an opportunity to begin life anew under attractive physical and economic conditions. For the victors, it offered a place to send political prisoners and other undesirable elements within French society. And for those without strong political views but who wished to see a tranquil France with renewed economic opportunity, it offered the chance for investment in an enterprise that seemed to promise unlimited returns.[27]

News of the discovery of gold in California appeared in the French newspapers on November 13, 1848, where it was initially greeted, as elsewhere, with great suspicion. Then, in late December, the *Journal des Debats* suddenly offered its enthusiastic support for these claims. "The real facts are beyond the wildest dreams," its columns confirmed, "the auriferous fields" were eight hundred miles long and one hundred miles wide, with gold found everywhere in dust, nuggets, and ingots weighing up to twenty-four pounds. It continued, "The most remarkable development of our age in the field of material progress is beyond any contradiction the discovery and exploitation of the gold fields in California." The *Journal* announced that San Francisco was already a richer city than New York City (though not, of course, richer than Paris).[28] After almost two months of indifference, this burst of interest produced an unlikely outpouring of enthusiasm. On January 13, 1849, there appeared the first advertisement for a ship bound for San Francisco, the *La Meuse*, which would sail on February 15. It would make landfall in San Francisco in November, carrying fifty French forty-niners.[29]

There now appeared *la société*, the institution that would be the most popular way of involving the French public in the California gold rush. On February 1, 1849, we find mention of the first regularly constituted *société*: "L'Expédition Francaise Pour les Mines d'Or de Sacramento." This *société* and others that promptly advertised their organization were designed to offer to the French people a means of profiting from gold found almost halfway around the world. *La société* was what we would call a joint stock company. These companies, organized and registered under French law, offered shares of stock in their enterprises to the public. The roster of company officers, prominently listed on the prospectus, frequently included military officers, former ministers, retired mayors, holders of the Legion d'Honneur, judges, and other public figures whose titles inspired confidence. Of course, each of these directors received stock from *la société* in exchange for the value of his title and name.[30]

The formula pursued by the various *sociétés* was the same: the company would be capitalized at a figure between one million and five million francs—the numbers tended to rise over the history of the *société*; that is to say, the first were more modest in their capital ambitions, the later companies more shameless in their aspirations. Stock would be sold to the public in sums ranging from one hundred francs a share down to as little as five francs a share. The lower figure ensured that even the poorest farmer or worker could invest. The capital thus raised would be used to meet the immediate expenses of an expedition to California—most companies hoped their enterprise would be the "first" of several expeditions, and often referred to it as the first. The board of directors would charter a ship, advertise its passage, lay in goods to be traded in California, and make provision to carry workers to California and the gold fields. Those who bought several shares of stock in the company, generally equal to about one thousand francs, were entitled to free passage as *travailleurs associés* of the company. These "associate workers" would be transported to California free on the company's ship and fully supported while there—a support system that would include tools, food, medical care, and the services of a priest—with the arrangement that under the terms of their contracts, half the gold they mined would be remitted to the company in exchange for the company's support. But all *sociétés* intended to set up commercial enterprises, whether agriculture or trading, to make their large profits. These profits from commerce and the gold from their *travailleurs associés* would be used to pay dividends to the shareholders. That the number of *sociétés* reached eighty-five within a year testified to their popularity and their hold on the imagination and pocketbooks of French citizens.[31]

The *sociétés* were designed to sell stock in a risky commercial venture. The idea of promoting the emigration of French people, we can now judge, was a useful way of legitimizing the venture. If the company would take French people to California, support them there, and bring them home, then truly this must be a trustworthy venture, one in which French people could invest with confidence. It was really the investors, rather than the emigrants, who interested the company. To the extent that the company sought profits from the gold fields, they would come in the form of trade and commerce. It is important to remember that during the half-dozen years when the California gold rush was an important commercial dimension of French life, the French thought of California as what we would call a third-world country, ripe for the profitable trade of an advanced industrial nation like France. What made the exchange so attractive was that California, unlike other third-world countries, would not trade raw materials but gold, the most valued and universally accepted commodity in the world.[32]

The periodic departure of chartered ships, each carrying overseas a couple hundred eager French forty-niners, attracted much attention and generated much publicity. The advertising campaigns were elaborate by the standards of the day. Many *sociétés* had their own newspapers or broadside sheets for advertising their own achievements, generally measured in number of ships sent to California, the number of men, the varieties of goods for trade, and their value. The claims of the companies were extravagant, as each sought to make itself more attractive than its competitors. One company promised that each worker's share would increase in value fourteen times in the first year; another boasted that it had secured exclusive use of mining machinery invented by a university professor.[33]

These *sociétés* flourished. Companies with names like La Californienne, La Fortune, L'Eldorado, La Toison d'Or, and Compagnie Universelle des Mines d'Or sold millions of shares to the public. Cautious and thrifty petits bourgeois, who would have refused to lend money to family or friends, willingly invested in large companies headed by directors with well-known names and the Legion d'Honneur. The recent overthrow of the monarchy had also played havoc with government bonds and other safe investments, opening the way to wilder schemes. Into this new world of investment came these companies to promote immigration to and investment in California.[34]

About the character of the sojourners—for surely few intended to turn their backs on France permanently—evidence suggests that this opportunity prompted a temporary exodus of people of some standing and wealth, petit bourgeois if you like, men (for the most part) with skills (although some of these skills, such as those of lawyers, *petit fonctionnaires*, and clerks, would be of no use in the gold fields) and a degree of wealth. The cost of the trip to California by sailing ship—and many went independently of the *sociétés*—was on the order of one thousand francs. For those who went under the umbrella of a society, the cost was about the same, one thousand francs, depending on how many shares one had to buy to reach the status of an associate worker. Others went to pursue commercial ventures far removed from the mines. And some simply sought *la grande aventure*, the search for something new and startling in their ordinary lives, in the manner of many American Argonauts. A few went as observers, intent on writing up their experiences for newspapers and magazines.[35]

California and gold became the à la mode of a season. It is impossible to assess the influence or even the degree to which such information was disseminated widely; but among a certain reading public, it had a real if brief life in the popular press. Satirical cartoons on the French presence in California appeared in the pages of *L'Illustration*, a popular magazine. The fashion world designed special clothes suitable for California. And, finally, a restaurant, La Californie, opened in Paris. It offered the finest meal in town at a reasonable price—that is to say, it intended to reproduce the legend of the bounty of California in which everyone would receive much for little or no cost.[36]

The power of the news of gold in California—and its impact on the French people in a postrevolutionary period of national reconstruction—was summarized by an obscure commentator on social and economic conditions. Karl Marx wrote that in 1849 "the dreams of gold had replaced the dreams of socialism among the proletariat of Paris."[37]

The collapse of the French gold mania came in the last months of 1850, camouflaged by the rise of "The Lottery of the Golden Ingots." Officially sponsored and managed by the prefect of Paris police and the minister of the interior, this immensely popular scheme sold over 6.2 million tickets for one franc each, for a chance to win one of 244 gold bars, the *l'ingots d'or*, and hundreds of smaller prizes. With the proceeds, the government shipped 3,885 emigrants to California between 1851 and 1853. The French consul admitted that the emigrants included a number of "undesirables," although not as many as American officials suggested. These emigrants from France were put ashore in San Francisco with sufficient rations for two weeks, the mattress and blankets used during the crossing, a sailor's hat and coat, a pick, a shovel, an ax, a hammer, and a chisel. They were among the most remarkable of a diverse group of people who came from all over the world to make California of the 1850s a gathering place for people of every condition and every nation. By 1853, an estimated twenty-eight thousand Frenchmen were in California, making the Golden State the most populous of France's colonial outposts.[38]

In bringing the world to California, the lure of gold cut across cultural and class differences that spanned from agricultural peasants in China to professional miners in Wales, from small farmers in Sonora to lawyers in Paris. The gold rush offered wondrous testimony to the power of a dream of wealth, conjured up by a metal that lay within the reach of everyone. The influence of this dream was recognized so readily around the world that it submerged many differences in favor of a single objective. Within a few short years, James W. Marshall's discovery of January 24, 1848, made California into the most cosmopolitan place in the world.

Notes

1. Starr, *Americans and the California Dream*, observes: "After the Gold Rush, California would never lose a symbolic connection with an intensified pursuit of human happiness" (xiii). See also chapter 3.

2. Jacques Antoine Moerenhout, *The Inside Story of the Gold Rush* (San Francisco: California Historical Society, 1935), 57, quoted in Doris M. Wright, "The Making of Cosmopolitan California: An Analysis of Immigration, 1848–1870," part 1, *California Historical Society Quarterly* 19 (1940): 333.

3. Wright, "Making of Cosmopolitan California," part 1, "324–25.

4. Quoted in Cave Johnson Couts, *Hepah California!: The Journal of Cave Johnson Couts . . . During the Years 1848–1849*, ed. Henry F. Dobyns (Tucson: Arizona Pioneers' Historical Society, 1961), entries for December 1 and 17.

5. Ralph J. Roske, "The World Impact of the California Gold Rush, 1849–1857," *Arizona and the West* 5 (1953): 198–200. The Mexicans arrived in the southern mines at about the same time as the Oregonians in the northern mines. I have

not discussed the Oregonians because they were American. They were among the first to arrive in California and also the first to return home, thus inaugurating the state's firmly held conviction of 150 years duration that Oregonians would go to California to make money, but they would never stay a moment longer than necessary.

6. *Honolulu Polynesian,* July 15, 1848. Also note the reference to the commercial opportunities: "[A] vast population will be suddenly thrown into California; the demand for Hawaiian produce will be greatly increased." *Honolulu Friend,* August 1, 1848, quoted in Wright, "Making of Cosmopolitan California," part 1, 327.

7. Varney to Larkin, July 15, 1848, in George P. Hammond, ed., *The Larkin Papers: Personal, Business, and Official Correspondence of Thomas Oliver Larkin, Merchant and United States Consul in California,* 10 vols. (Berkeley: University of California Press, 1951–1964), 7:317.

8. Quoted in Wright, "Making of Cosmopolitan California," part 1, 327.

9. Wright, "Making of Cosmopolitan California," part 1, 328.

10. Roske, "World Impact of the California Gold Rush," 189–92.

11. Roske, "World Impact of the California Gold Rush," 192, 193.

12. Monaghan, *Chile, Peru, and the California Gold Rush,* chap. 2. In chapter 3, Monaghan analyzes the reluctance of newspapers to feature the news of gold discoveries.

13. Wright, "Making of Cosmopolitan California," part 1, 326–27.

14. Beilharz and López, *We Were Forty-Niners!* xiv–xx; quoted in Monaghan, *Chile, Peru, and the California Gold Rush,* 49. That the first wave of entrepreneurs was English-speaking explained the ease with which they established commercial houses in San Francisco.

15. On the anti-Chilean riots of 1849, see Monaghan, *Chile, Peru, and the California Gold Rush,* chap. 13.

16. Wright, "Making of Cosmopolitan California," part 1, 327. For an account of the Peruvians with special emphasis on the differences from the Chileans, see Monaghan, *Chile, Peru, and the California Gold Rush,* chaps. 7–9.

17. Monaghan, *Australians and the Gold Rush,* chap. 1, has an excellent analysis of the divisions within Australian society that made it particularly susceptible to the influences of the gold rush in California. Among the more remarkable inventions advertised was "California Gold Grease." If the purchaser covered himself with this grease and rolled down a California hill, loose gold would adhere to him (55).

18. Monaghan, *Australians and the Gold Rush,* 119. The astonishing feature of the

story of gold in Australia is that this continent "down under" soon had its own gold rush. The discovery of gold in 1851 rapidly concentrated a large population of gold seekers in Victoria in rich diggings that in 1852 would produce $60 million, equal to the California mines. Roske, "World Impact of the California Gold Rush," 196.

19. Monaghan, *Australians and the Gold Rush*, chap. 7 and p. 121. Interest in the California mines faded in direct proportion to the rising confirmation of Australia's own gold strikes.

20. Monaghan, *Australians and the Gold Rush*, chaps. 9 and 13.

21. Mary Roberts Coolidge, quoted in Wright, "Making of Cosmopolitan California," part 1, 329. On the observations of an American who contracted for Chinese labor, see Leslie Bryson to "Friend Stoddard," December 3, 1851, Henry E. Huntington Library, San Marino, California.

22. Rohrbough, *Days of Gold*, 228–29, discusses the changing reaction to Chinese gold seekers. See also Wright, "Making of Cosmopolitan California," part 1, 329–30.

23. See the analysis of the coming of the Revolution of 1848 in Alfred Cobban, *A History of Modern France,* vol. 2, *From the First Empire to the Second Empire, 1799–1871,* rev. ed. (Baltimore: Penguin Books, 1961), part 3.

24. *Times* (London), December 14, 22, 1848; *Liverpool Mail,* January 13, 1849, quoted in Doris Wright, "The Making of Cosmopolitan California: An Analysis of Immigration, 1848–1870," part 2, "Immigration from European Counties," *California Historical Society Quarterly* 20 (1941): 66.

25. Roske noted that prior to the news of the gold discoveries, the number of Irish women immigrants to California exceeded that of men. "The World Impact of the California Gold Rush," 216n.

26. Wright, "Making of Cosmopolitan California," part 2, 68–69.

27. Michel Le Bris, *Le Fievre de l'Or* (Paris: Gallimard, 1988), 22–23.

28. Gilbert Chinard, "When the French Came to California: An Introductory Essay," *California Historical Society Quarterly* 22 (1943): 289–314.

29. Chinard, "When the French Came to California," remains an excellent introduction in English. The most accessible account in French is Le Bris, *Le Fievre de l'Or,* which contains wonderful illustrative material.

30. Henry Blumenthal, "The California Societies in France, 1849–1855," *Pacific Historical Review* 21 (1956): 251–60, is a complete account.

31. Blumenthal, "California Societies in France, 1849–1855," lists many of the "societies" by name.

32. See, for example, the continuing accounts of French commercial life in California as reported by the Paris press in *Le Moniteur Universel*, June 28, 1849; February 15, May 12, 1850; July 17, 1851. One story (September 27, 1849) noted that several homes built in Bordeaux were to be shipped to California, where they would become a cafe-restaurant.

33. Abraham P. Nasatir, *The French in the California Gold Rush* (New York: American Society of the French Legion of Honor, 1934) is a standard account by the first American historian (in both nationality and discipline) to analyze the French and the gold rush.

34. Blumenthal, "California Societies in France, 1849–1854," offers a detailed analysis.

35. Among the journalists were Alexandre Achard, Martial Chevalier, Andre Cochut, Benjamin Delesset, and Octave Feuillet, who published their materials in the *Revue des Deux Mondes* between 1849 and 1854.

36. See, for example, an advertisement in *La Maison des Quartre Parties du Monde*, March 18, 1849, announcing that the house had received "a large quantity of wearing apparel intended for persons who wish to emigrate to California or any such distant country" (my translation). The suits were priced at six francs and up. The restaurant featured a menu that began at two sous (a large portion of vegetables), rose to four sous (a generous portion of meat), and then to six sous (add a half bottle of wine), and so forth. The acknowledged clientele of the restaurant: the unemployed and *des marginaux*.

37. My translation. His words were "les reves de l'or ont remplace les reves socialistes dans le proletariat parisien." Quoted in Le Bris, *La Fievre de L'Or*, 26.

38. On the Lottery of the Gold Ingots, see Abraham P. Nasatir, ed. and trans., "Alexandre Dumas fils and the Lottery of the Gold Ingots," *California Historical Society Quarterly* 33 (1954): 125–42; and Donna Evleth, "The Lottery of the Golden Ingots," *American History Illustrated* 23 (1988): 34–37.

3

"The Greatest and Most Perverted Paradise"

The Forty-Niners in Latin America

Brian Roberts

Theodore Johnson was the fastest of forty-niners. A would-be newspaper-man on the trail of a good story, he booked passage for California almost as soon as the first gold reports reached the eastern seaboard. He made every steamer connection on his way to the gold country; then, after a short stay to absorb the region's local color, he turned around and made every connection on his return to the East. Accordingly, he managed to write and publish an account of his adventures, *Sights in the Gold Region and Scenes by the Way*, before many of his fellow prospectors had even departed. As the title of his book suggests, Johnson was more interested in the adventure of travel than in finding gold. Early in his outward voyage, as they sailed into subtropical waters, Johnson and his fellow passengers keenly anticipated the novel sights and scenes of Hispanic America. Approaching the Caribbean, he reported, his shipmates filled "the lovely moonlight evenings with songs . . . till the ship almost danced in chorus." Then, when the dark outlines of San Domingo and Cuba loomed on a nighttime horizon, the sense of anticipation reached a climax. Johnson, like the rest, rushed to the rails, caught between feelings of revulsion and attraction, "having in sight at the same time," as he put it, "the two greatest and most perverted island paradises of the West Indies."[1]

Although they have rarely been included in the overall narrative of the event, forty-niner contacts with Latin Americans comprised a major part of the gold rush experience. Throughout 1849, thousands of gold seekers from the northeastern United States passed through Latin America. By January 1850, the harbormaster at San Francisco reported that some forty thousand persons had arrived aboard nearly fourteen thousand vessels, the largest number from the northeastern ports of New York, Boston, and New

Bedford. Two-thirds of these emigrants had sailed around Cape Horn; another third had steamed to the Colombian Isthmus of Panama, then crossed the isthmus to pick up a sail ship or steamer on the Pacific side.[2] Along these sea routes, gold seekers put in at Latin American ports and Yankee whaling stations: the suddenly burgeoning towns of Chagres and Panama on either side of the isthmus, Rio de Janeiro and the Brazilian island of Santa Catarina, and Valparaiso and Talcahuano along the coastline of Chile. In their visits to these ports, on the way to California and during their return, forty-niners would see much that offended their senses, many behaviors in stark opposition to Victorian sensibilities. Rather than resist these behaviors with the rhetoric of racism, many forty-niners shared the perspectives of Theodore Johnson and his fellow passengers. For these northeastern gold seekers, it seems, Latin America represented a free space where contradictions to Victorian standards of behavior might be revolting and attractive at the same time, where for a moment at least, these behaviors might even be embraced by respectable white males.

Most of these northeastern forty-niners, like Theodore Johnson, were men of a specific time and place. At the moment of their sailing and during the voyages, this time was not the "flush times" of the gold rush and the place was not California. Instead, these were men whose time was a period of class formation and market revolution, whose place was the industrializing northeast. Most came from growing towns and cities along the region's developing network of canals, railroads, and factories. These towns and cities, in turn, were the social, moral, and cultural opposites of gold rush era California. Beginning in 1827, Charles Finney, the father of the Second Great Awakening, had swept through the region, bringing with him the fires of religious revivalism, the guilty bench, and a renewed consciousness of the wages of sin. The result was a dramatic increase in the northeast's threshold of shame: certain behaviors, such as drinking, gambling, and swearing, were soon forbidden. In the following two decades, the region was flooded with etiquette guides and middle-class prescriptions. By 1849, specific standards of repression, refinement, and self-control pervaded the region; excess, from excessive sexual display to excessive laughter and even sneezing, had become examples of perversity.

The result of this great transformation in northeastern values was not what we might expect. For without the region's commitment to Victorian standards, without the spread of these standards throughout American culture, the California gold rush would have had very little meaning. The gold rush, as many forty-niners maintained—and as many later historians have confirmed—was a grand series of comic inversions. As a social experience, what made the rush particularly fascinating at the time—and ever since—was its exposition of forbidden behaviors, its dramatic challenge to Victorian standards through constantly repeated anecdotes of gambling and prostitution, and its sometimes violent, more often humorous examples of self-expression.[3] In composing these stories, forty-niners depended on one thing above all: that their readers, along with future generations of readers, would be middle-class enough to know the precise meaning of perversity. Gold rush era California, as one typical forty-niner had it, was characterized by "acts of deathless shame."[4] It was filled, added another, with the "darkest deeds ever recorded."[5]

These stories have given the rush its energy, its 150-years reign as America's most perverse and hence enjoyable historic event. But they have also accomplished something else. For elsewhere there is evidence that forty-niners meant this darkness literally, that is, that these deeds had originated with the dark people of the rush, with Mexican bandits, Chilean gamblers, and Latina prostitutes. An examination of forty-niner contacts with Latin America during their voyage to California reveals the social history of these "dark" deeds. It also reveals the extent to which the social reversals of the gold rush were also, perhaps primarily, racial reversals.

Theodore Johnson's thrill at his first sight of a Latin American environment, his conscious sense that these environments were somehow "perverted," was by no means unusual. Shortly after his arrival in Rio de Janeiro in March 1849, Bayard Taylor gazed in similar wonderment at the surroundings and streets of the city. "Strange it is," he wrote, "that the barbarians have the best corner of the earth." At Latin America's tropical ports, forty-niners discovered abundant landscapes, for each town appeared to be surrounded with hillsides "covered with orange trees plantain lemons limes coffee groves and hosts of other fruits." Amid such opulence, observed forty-niner John Callbreath, the natives could afford to be "careless of the future." "Nature does everything for them," Callbreath added, "they have abundance for life's wants." Throughout South America, nature and culture seemed intertwined: lush vines climbed the walls of giant cathedrals, Spanish castles slowly crumbled into the fertile soil. The strange blend transported and entranced many forty-niners. The natives were "barbarians," according to the travelers, but there was allure to their brutality; women and children might be nearly naked, but there was glamour in their lack of shame. In all, forty-niners found much that was wanting in Latin America society, but also much that they wanted.[6]

To be sure, many of these adventurers did what they could to maintain self-control in Latin America, and they found much that seemed revolting among these "savages" of the south. "Every thing is at least one hundred years behind the times," John Callbreath wrote to his sister in upstate New York soon after landing at Rio de Janeiro, "you cannot find a white man doing any kind of work and I do believe if it was not for the Yankees and English the race would run out." Boston Brahmin George Payson knew enough to recognize European stock among Brazilians but still noted what he perceived as a decline into primitivism. Unlike Anglo-Americans, these Europeans, he claimed, were degenerates of nature: "They have gained nothing of new life and vigour by being transplanted on to this virgin soil, but seem rather to have lost what little they possessed. This country has not proved to them the harsh stepmother that New England was to our Puritan ancestors; but like a foolish grandam, has spoilt them by her foolish indulgence. The result is that they can do nothing for themselves."[7]

Stuck in Panama City, Massachusetts-born Henry Peters echoed these sentiments: "The people are a miserable, degraded race with no trade, ambition or anything else desirable; a few of the proud old dons of pure Castillian blood are still left with some lovely specimens of Spanish beauty among the ladies, but these families are very rare." And truly, Peters seems to have seen little that was desirable among these people, noting for the most part only their offenses to his sensibilities and senses. Accordingly, it was "no wonder" that cholera was common on the Colombian isthmus, "for such a filthy set of people and such a compound of villainous smells as one's olfactories are regaled with from every shop, is enough to give the most sanguine unbeliever the infection."[8]

At times, these descriptions might reflect little more than racism and imperialist design, an idiom of complete resistance to cultural difference. As Callbreath added to his letter: "one thousand troops under Rough & Ready would take the place." As for the Panamanians, Peters felt they would soon disappear "before the march of improvement which is already beginning under the auspices of Americans who are about to establish a railroad across the isthmus." Similar dismissive assessments are sprinkled liberally throughout forty-niner journals of the voyage through Central America and points farther south. According to Charles Ross Parke, a physician from Illinois and Pennsylvania, Nicaragua was a "god forsaken country of niggers, monkeys, baboons, and lizards, to say nothing about the poisonous reptiles." Brazil, declared another observer, was hopelessly backward in its development: "[I]n agriculture, commerce, and invention, indeed in every branch of useful industry, they are, at least, fifty years behind the age."[9]

Still, even the most censorious of descriptions cannot disguise a creeping sense of attraction. Rio de Janeiro's nature and nudity revolted New York City lawyer John Stone. It was, he maintained, "a disgusting filthy city. . . . Very many of the negroes who make up the chief population live in a state of nature and nudity . . . their persons and their garments besmeared with grease and smut." While this description reeks of a self-conscious expulsion of the low and the excremental, something of a higher, more pleasing aspect was coming into his line of vision. "But the city has some redeeming features," he added, citing its ornate churches, fine older architecture, and its orange groves.[10] According to most forty-niners, it seems, what was most striking about Latin America was its strange contradiction of perceived backwardness and poverty amid exotic abundance.

Gold seekers might reject the apparent poverty of these scenes with seeming facility, but even then, the abundance of tropical environments remained charming. "The flowers are truly lovely," wrote steamer captain Cleveland Forbes of Rio's gardens. And with each exotically charged name on a list of delights, his wall of resistance seems to have slowly eroded. The camellias were plentiful, along with the moss roses; "Cape Jesmine, & every choice flower of the world grows finely here. The orange, the best in the world, the Banana, the Pine Apple, the coconut, the guava, the Tea, the coffee, Sugar Cane, Lime, Chocolate, or coco . . . and dozens of other fruit too many to name."[11] Discovering opulence amid what they first viewed as corruption, many forty-niners gaped in wonderment. According to Garrett Low, who joined the gold rush from the far northern reaches of New York state, the sheer size of Chile's apples, pears, peaches, and grapes must have made it "one of the most productive countries in the world." "It is said," he added in a typical bit of gold seeker fancy, "that five or six miles in the country one can travel for miles and step on nothing but strawberries, which are blooming and ripening all seasons of the year." As Benjamin Dore from the frosty coast of Maine had it, "every thing" would grow in the lush Brazilian soil: "pine apples oranges lemons . . . peaches figs bananers water melons onions sweet potatoes rice coffee corn cucumbers potatoes Ec." Within this "splendid surplus of vegetable life," according to Bayard Taylor, one's sense of self might be overwhelmed. In this natural paradise "as on the ocean," he noted, "you have a sense rather than a perception of beauty. . . . You gaze upon the scene before you with a never-sated delight, till your brain aches with the sensation, and you close your eyes, over-whelmed with the thought that all these wonders have been from the beginning—that year after year takes away no leaf of blossom that is not replaced, but the sublime mystery of growth and decay is renewed forever."[12]

For many forty-niners, Latin American abundance and patterns of behavior were evocative of brutality or, at the very least, vulgarity. And nearly always, as seen through the eyes of the forty-niners, they were perverse. Accordingly, their visions of the American South and African Americans were strikingly erotic, filled with passionate behaviors and excessive sexuality. These behaviors revolted many forty-niners. At the same time, they would find ways to give in to them. One way they could embrace these behaviors was through envisioning themselves as helpless captives to Latin American pleasures. John Beeckman, a well-born New York lawyer with political aspirations in California, found Rio's "free blending together" of races "disgusting and repugnant in the extreme." At the same time, he enjoyed his stay in the city, remaining there nearly a month while his ship put in for repairs. He portrayed this period as a captivity among the lowly, a typical dinner with one of Rio's leading citizens as a type of martyrdom. About a walk following the dinner, he wrote a fragmented description of his own descent into pleasure: "[R]omantic and beautiful scenery as the imagination could conceive—a Brazilian lady on my arm to whom I could not speak—that too was over and I hoped I might be permitted to escape—but no—there was music in the evening and dancing and I was a martyr for three hours longer. I will never again dine with a Brazilian."[13]

Giving in to these sorts of pleasures was one thing; indulgence in what many forty-niners saw as characteristic Latin American brutality was quite another. Yet here too they could envision themselves as captives, as having been "lured" by the natives into their own excesses. Sent by the Baptist Board of Missions as the first New England missionary to California, Francis Prevaux had been told that "the greatest cut throats in the world" roamed the Isthmus. To his surprise, he found these ruffians to be his fellow northeasterners. Indeed, abstention had given way to brutality: these Yankees, he wrote, "shockingly abuse, beat and mangle the poor natives for the most trivial offenses." In explaining this behavior, however, Prevaux placed the blame for these atrocities not on his "fallen brothers," but on the Latin American environment itself. "It is said," he wrote, "that 'man is a creature of circumstances,' that from the character of a man at home we cannot know what he will be in California. How fearfully has this been exemplified in our journey thus far! . . . Young men who at home were temperate, moral and of high promise, I see now with rapid strides in the high road to ruin."[14]

In a similar manner, the Reverend Joseph Augustine Benton noted that along the isthmus formerly respectable men had been "lured to indulgencies [*sic*] and excesses." According to the reverend, these men had been severed from their former ties, freed from all checks and restraints, surrounded by a "sense of lawlessness." As a result, he declared, they "care not what it is they do, provided it excites and gratifies them."[15] Certainly, Benton meant this as a moral critique of forty-niner self-indulgence. At the same time, harsh as his criticism was, it probably did little to halt this type of behavior. In a sense, Benton's criticism fit precisely with forty-niner desires: certain Latin American behaviors, in other words, might be revolting to respectable white men, but in specific contexts they were seductive and free for the taking. If seduction often led to corruption, it was not from personal moral failure but through extrinsic depravity, which they could not—or did not want to—resist.

In this respect, practically every forty-niner description of Latin American excess may be understood not only as examples of simple racism but also as attempts to increase their own pleasure. For by seeing Latin Americans as perverted, and then giving into perversity, gold seekers were able to intertwine revulsion with delight, hatred with love, making fun with having fun. "The Mexicans are a treacherous . . . cowardly set of ruffians, they hate the yankees, and would, if they dared, shoot every one that comes ashore," wrote New York's Henry Peters, and many other forty-niners undoubtedly shared his assessment.[16] At the same time, however, they delighted in mimicking the Spanish language, in learning exotic-sounding names for things: "jipijapa hats," "compadre", and "amigo." Balancing between engagement with and resistance to these cultural forms, Theodore Johnson wrote of his thrill at learning a few words of Spanish even while dismissing them as "jabber."[17] Elsewhere, rigid northeastern men could invoke the somewhat oxymoronic-sounding character of the "Yankee daredevil," joining the natives—or their "captors"—in a carnival of behaviors that back home would have been expressly forbidden. According to New Yorker John Linville Hall, the Americans on his ship arrived in Rio de Janeiro in an "unnatural state of excitement." There they reveled in a carnival atmosphere, leaving "a score of riot, excess and rowdyism . . . which ill beseems the American Character." Throughout the winter and spring of 1849, added Charles Coffin, Yankees took over the city. There they "did just as they pleased and the city authorities were powerless to restrain them; but . . . they can well put up with the Yankee dare-devil spirit for the sake of the Yankee gold."[18]

Elsewhere, as these forty-niners locked elbows to swagger through streets and bowl over passersby, the newly found spirit of Yankee daredeviltry found more disturbing expression. On the fifteenth of April 1849, Thomas Matteson of Oneida County, New York, docked at the island port of Santa Catarina off the Brazilian coast. Safely in port, the captain of the *George*

Washington, along with more than thirty passengers including Matteson, went into town to purchase supplies. There, claimed Matteson, a "row began between the Portuguese and the Americans. There was 2 Americans killed and 2 Portuguese, 1 American's leg broken, 10 wounded, 14 Portuguese were wounded."[19] Matteson was in the middle of the fray. A seminary student at home, he had crossed the southern frontier to find himself first a ruffian then a prisoner surrounded by three thousand angry Brazilians.

As much as it is an example of Yankee imperialism, the situation of those aboard the *George Washington* appears to have resulted from an excess of boisterous spirits. But if the scene reflected a playing-out of ambivalent longings for physical expression, its final act reveals connections between ambivalence and power. For three days Matteson and his mates remained under house arrest. Their ship languished at anchor, surrounded by island boats and unable to move while local authorities investigated complaints and prepared charges. Ultimately, the Yankees had the power to defend their excesses. On April 18, according to Matteson, the captain of the *George Washington* warned the locals that "he would resort to arms without they were released immediately." A day later, his ship was again on the high seas, its passengers freed at gunpoint to open lines of expression beyond both the confines of refinement and the port at Santa Catarina.[20]

Although typically on a smaller scale, similar slippages into brutality marked the passing of gold seekers throughout Latin America. For many, a touch of Latin American violence seems to have offered an exhilarating taste of the "real life." This type of contact may have been precisely the intention of Bayard Taylor, who, despite being repeatedly warned of robbers in the Mexican provinces, decided to take a lone pleasure jaunt into the countryside. As might be expected, it did not take long for Taylor to meet up with the adventure his soul craved. With a drawing of *pistolas* and a shout of "la boca a tierra," his yearned-for bandits made their appearance, trussing the travel writer while rifling his saddlebags. Taylor, if his account is to be believed, experienced the moment with a jaunty sense of brutality well met. "I never felt more alive than at this moment," he recalled. This kind of thing was a "genuine adventure": "I cannot say that I felt alarmed. . . . My feelings during this preceding were oddly heterogeneous—at one moment burning with rage and shame at having neglected the proper means of defense, and the next, ready to burst into a laugh at the decided novelty of my situation." In fact, immediately following the scene, Taylor recorded a rather curious feeling of refreshment: "It is astonishing how light one feels after being robbed."[21]

Indeed, added Taylor, there was something natural and quite enjoyable in this type of engagement with Latin American violence. For such adventures with the locals gave gold seekers a sense of freedom, offering them a rare chance, as he put it, to throw off the "little arts of dissimilation [practiced] in society."[22] Certainly, the fact that the "little arts" were there in the first place added to the excitement felt at breaking them in the name of instinct. Sin, in other words, would only remain a source of pleasure as long as it remained sinful. And if some northeastern missionaries missed this point, many forty-niners did not.

The passengers aboard the ship *Duxbury* recognized it; for they seemed always on the lookout for ways to increase pleasure. If inversions of proper behavior were the lifeblood of the gold rush, the *Duxbury* had to be the liveliest ship in the California-bound Yankee armada. A veritable floating fraternity house, the ship belonged to the Old Harvard Company out of Boston, a mining company composed entirely of Harvard students and alumni. Having sailed expressly for the adventure, its passengers sang, danced, and sought every opportunity to make contact with the passing examples of Latin American passion. On April 20, 1849, a group of the ship's passengers went ashore at Rio for a night on the town. The next day, the crew charged one member of the group, a certain John Burns, with the crime of soliciting a prostitute. Transcribed in the *Duxbury's* shipboard newspaper, the case of *Commonwealth v. Burns* began in seriousness. "Judge Frank," read the charge before an assemblage of passengers forming a "Police Court": "defendant did on the evening of the 20th day of April A.D. in the City of Rio de Janeiro, secretly, maliciously, unceremoniously, with evil intent and malice aforethought . . . seek to have private intercourse with one of the daughters of easy virtue . . . greatly to the injury of the good citizens of said city of Rio—his friends thereby encouraging vice, and greatly endangering his bodily health." One crew member testified that he had heard the defendant complaining of "a burning sensation," adding that "he had been strongly tempted, think he must have indulged a little." Another reported hearing Burns say that "a married man is excusable so far from home," and that "the prices were reasonable in Rio."[23]

John Burns pled not guilty to the charges. But the denouement of the proceedings may raise the question of why he was ever tried at all. For in the end, the "trial" was yet another example of the forty-niners' playful oscillation between Victorian standards of behavior and their tacit acceptance of perversity as manly adventure. According to the report, the next witness "declined answering any questions, as he might incriminate himself." At this point the ironic humor of the situation became obvious. "During the examination," claimed the reporter, "the court ruled several questions inadmissible, it appearing evident that thorough investigation would place his honor in a somewhat delicate position." As it turned out, both the prosecution and the defense were in a similar fix. Neither could raise questions without incriminating himself. Finally Judge Frank declared his verdict: Burns was guilty. As punishment he ordered the prisoner "to treat all hands."[24]

On the surface a clear case of the *Duxbury's* usual fun and games, on a deeper level the trial appears as a more serious exposure of the forty-niners' culture. Clearly the fact that these were married men made the passengers' intercourse with prostitutes something perverse. Interestingly, the men of the *Duxbury* seemed willing to admit their actions; far from glossing over their ethical transgressions, they exposed them in ritual, elevating them with the dramatics of a public spectacle. What the trial exposes is the circularity of forty-niner expression and action in Latin America. The abundance of Latin America, that is, its profusion and easy availability of temptation would give way to indulgence. Giving in to forbidden behaviors would be followed by an admission of guilt; punishment would then circle back to reembrace forbidden behaviors. In a sense, the ritual linked the secular pursuit of pleasure with the idiom of the Second Great Awakening. The admission of guilt, so central to the Christian revivalist movements of the mid-nineteenth century, seems here to have become a mode of pleasure enhancement. Back home, of course, ministers like Charles Finney would have fairly exploded in disgust at such a concept. Yet with its profusion of delights, both carnal and aesthetic, and with its distant and exotic apartness, Latin America rolled indulgence and redemption into a perfect circle of Yankee pleasures, even if—especially if—these Yankees had been respectable men back home. Here indeed, the men of the *Duxbury* professed, was a paradise where a self-consciousness of perversity only added to the carnival joy of free expression. As the *Duxbury* prepared to sail from Rio, one of the bards of the company newspaper summed up this perspective:

> O beautiful land
> By soft breezes fanned
> Where fruits in abundance are growing:
> Where cockroaches run
> Up our trousers in fun
> And where rivers of liquor are flowing
> Where each step in the street
> Dark damsels we meet,
> Tempting us their bananas to buy-o;

We cannot begin
To set forth our chagrin
At leaving thee; City o Rio.[25]

Such expressions would appear to indicate the free embrace of quintessential Latin American temptations and pleasures, its abundance of exotic fruits, liquor, crawling things, and even eroticized females. But as celebratory as they are of exotic differences between cultures, the engagements of forty-niners with these subjects rarely proceeded without an undercurrent of condescension and guilt. For nearly always, it seems, what made Latin American cultural expressions interesting to forty-niners was the fact that they came from below, they were forbidden, and they were consciously linked to vice. "Many of their dances," as one forty-niner noted, even as he appeared to enjoy watching them, "are got up for the purpose of carrying out their vices."[26]

Theodore Johnson shared this view. One night during his brief stay in Gorgona, he heard a distant rhythm. Always on the lookout for new and exotic experiences, he followed the drums to their source. What he found was a genuine South American "fandango." The dance, he wrote, "consists of a lazy, slow shuffle, until excited by aguardiente, and emboldened as night progresses, the women dance furiously up to their favorites among the men, who are then obligated to follow suit, all joining in a kind of nasal squeal or chant. There is nothing graceful in their mode of dancing, but, on the contrary, their motions are often indecent and disgusting." What for Richard Henry Dana had been a rather "lifeless affair" would for gold seekers like Johnson become "half barbaric orgies," erotic dances of "wooden drums" accompanied by "the na, na, na, of the women."[27] Clearly, the men who described such scenes were repulsed and attracted at the same time. Johnson was offended. Yet he stayed to watch the performance. From his choice of words to describe the dance—his reference to joined bodies, squeals, chants, and indecent, rhythmic motions—what he saw, and what seems to have disgusted and attracted him most, was the fandango's embodiment of women.

Even before the gold rush, the Latina's presumed lack of shame was a source of pleasure to male observers, her naked form one of the public legacies of the Mexican War. Stationed along the border at Matamoros, Zachary Taylor's men would watch as local women washed in the river. "Nearly all of them," wrote one of the gaping onlookers, "have well-developed, magnificent figures." These figures, in turn, could be uncovered with imagination: they dressed, the soldier added, "with as little clothing as

you can well fancy." "Their bosoms were not compressed in stays," wrote
another, "but heaved freely under the healthful influence of the genial
sun and balmy air of the sunny South." The gold seekers were similarly
attracted. In Chagres, according to Bayard Taylor, women wore only a
"single cotton garment" and children gamboled "in Nature's own clothing."
In Panama City, remarked forty-niner James Tyson, "many of the Women
[wear] nothing but a thin cotton cloth tied around their hips." Some of the
younger females, Asaph Sawyer confided to his diary in 1852, "were entirely
model artiste, at least as far as their clothing was concerned, but their forms
were rather indifferent."[28]

These obsessions with Latin American nudity reflected nothing new.
Early explorers in America had paid similar attention to the nakedness
of indigenous peoples. What is interesting about these passages, however,
may be their revelation that by the mid-nineteenth-century these images
reflected not so much the seen but a way of seeing. Here, the forty-niner
vision seemed capable of passing right through loose clothing to focus on
heaving breasts. As Latin Americanist Frederick Pike has noted, the North
American way of seeing the Latina was to link her with nature and with
"wanton physicality." She was completely sexualized, a source of admiration
and disdain filtered through the expectation of "available sex proffered
by inferior creatures who ostensibly welcome seduction and subjugation."
Yankee perception of Latin American women, claims Pike, was based on a
willful form of synecdoche: the prostitute stood for the whole.[29]

For Pike, the meaning of such perceptions is singular and clear, their goal
simply to reduce the Latin American other to inferior status and to open
the way for conquest along with sexual and later political or economic
exploitation. Yet this type of vision may have also been self-reflective
rather than wholly reductive. Perception notwithstanding, there were real
prostitutes in many forty-niner ports of call. The port of Talcahuano, Chile,
for example, contained a particularly large array of brothels and dives.
The reason for this thriving business had nothing to do with any natural
earthiness of Latin American women. Rather, it stemmed from the fact
that long before the Argonauts landed, Talcahuano was a favorite port of
the American whaling industry. What forty-niners were seeing in these
ports, in other words, was a sexual economy of their own creation: the local
prostitutes were manifestations of Yankee culture.[30]

Although prostitution was a flourishing industry in mid-nineteenth-
century seaport towns from Maine to Chile, we would not expect the
gold seekers to admit their patronage of these establishments. Despite

being steeled with resistance, however, they frequently found themselves, somehow, on the bad side of Talcahuano. "As we walked through the filthy narrow streets," wrote George Payson during his visit to the town, "the open doors on each side were full of women, who kept up an incessant cry of 'come in, Californe;' 'Californe, come in;' adding often other allurements of a yet more unmistakable character." Joseph Lamson may have tried to avoid these streets, but his straight path seems also to have been pleasured by furtive glances: "As I passed into the cross streets I saw a great many women seated or standing at their doors. . . . Many of them were very filthy, though some were neatly dressed, and were rather pretty. They had dark complexions, fresh, florid cheeks, bright, black eyes, and black glossy hair hanging down their backs. . . . They had a smile and a word for all strangers, but their smiles were those of the siren."[31]

For a man who was just passing by these exotic side streets, Lamson's vision is remarkably detailed. From this detail, it is easy to assume a certain repetitiousness in the placement of oneself in the path of temptation. What we have then is an image of straight-laced men walking stiff-necked past allurements and fleshly pleasures, eyes darting furiously, delightedly, right and left, passing on in self-congratulatory resistance, circling around the block and starting again. At the same time, however, there are indications that visits to Talcahuano might be marked by more than mere window-shopping. "In the city of Talcahuana," wrote one gold seeker to a friend, "there is nothing of special interest or remark but one, and that is its Prostitution. . . . I was informed by Mr. Frick, our consignee at that port, 'that there was not ten virtuous females among a multitude of three thousand' and what I saw while there confirmed his statement. This was just the port to suit the tastes and gratify the passions of many of our company among them I regret to say were those who had left confiding companions behind[.] Very soon after we put to sea, then certain kinds of medicines were in demand and freely administered."[32] Indeed, this account makes it clear that revulsion and attraction might be wed in indulgence. If the result of this mixture was conquest, to accept the sexualized elements of imperialism requires a recognition that the attraction was real.

Undoubtedly, some forty-niners expressed this attraction without a sense of ambivalence and without the additional thrill that came with a conscious sense of the Latina's position as an ethnic and erotic other. For Franklin Buck, the "ladies" of Lima were simply "the most beautiful women I have ever seen." More frequently, however, forty-niners seemed incapable of separating the Latina's allure from her supposedly intrinsic qualities of immodesty and "darkness." As his ship neared Brazil's main port of call, Samuel Upham reported that its passengers were busily engaged in bathing and shaving; all were desirous, as he put it, "of captivating the dark-eyed *senoritas* on their arrival in Rio." Similarly, Charles Parke noted desires for the "dusky senoritas" of Granada, Nicaragua. In such cases, dusk and dark, whether attached to eyes or bodies, conveyed the Latina's presumed internal passion and lack of shame: "[T]is only necessary to add," Parke made sure to mention, "*extreme* modesty is a scarce article in this country."[33]

Freed from shame and modesty, this vision of the Latina was a site for the projection of fantasy, a subject of perfect desire and limitless sexuality. Accordingly, forty-niner descriptions of her suggest much wide-eyed gaping. Theodore Johnson's eyes went toward a group of women pounding corn for tortillas: "One of these senoritas," he noted, "was quite pretty, and as she gracefully bent forward in her useful employment, displayed a bust which Saratoga [might] envy." Charles Parke directed his gaze on a part of the female anatomy that while now the subject of "fetishism," was a more central subject of erotic attraction and mainstream pornography through much of the nineteenth century. Like Johnson, Parke was transfixed by the sight of women pounding corn, with his eyes focused on their feet. "I saw the feet when they came out," Parke exclaimed in his journal, "and I know they were *clean*. Every time after when I ate tortillas, I imagined I could see those beautiful clean feet." Finally, gold seekers imagined that the Latina, like a host of ethnic and erotic beauties from Pocahontas to the Maid of Monterrey, would naturally return their desires. While dining with a Mexican family, James Tyson gave careful, friendly notice to the daughter. She, at least by his account, returned his interest: "being interrogated whether she preferred Americans or Mexicans, she quickly replied, '*Mexicano Malo, Americano bueno, grande!*"[34]

Rarely, however, could these yearnings proceed without a keen sense of guilt. As one of the poems printed aboard the *Duxbury* reveals, this type of fantasy could delve deeply into forbidden desires. These depths, in turn, might only increase the degree of shame, self-hatred, and ugly projection of destructive tendencies. "She stood there in her beauty," read the first line of the poem to "The Slave Girl at Rio," and through four verses its author expressed his attraction. His eye climbed from her "perfect woman's form" to "her bosom's swelling outlines" to her "dark and lustrous eye," and then came his penultimate admission: "I should I knew see naught on earth / So beautiful again." Yet the last lines of the poem reflect the ironic antithesis that so frequently characterized the forty-niner's inability to decide between attraction and revulsion:

But 'twas no use to figger
In setting up a wail;
For she's the blackest nigger
That I saw out of jail.[35]

John Cornelison's description of "Estafania," a vision encountered in Chile and a "specimen of South American beauty," reveals a similar inability to contemplate the attractions of the Latina without a consciousness of depravity. "Cheek bones somewhat high," began Cornelison's play with desire, "and complexion a shade darker than the brunette; vermilion color'd cheeks, and cherry lips, formed a sweet and expressive countenance at once attractive and romantic." But if Cornelison's desires are plain in this passage, so, as he continues, are his fears. Estafania's face, he claimed, was perfect "for embellishing a tale of love, murder and suicide. Pity it was that sensuality and depravity enveloped itself in such a lovely mould."[36]

These emotional qualities may be the constituent elements of the pornographic visions of Latin American womanhood and of a modern pornographic vision as a whole: love, suicide, and murder. If, that is, the Latina inspired forty-niner desires, these very desires also raised fears of complete self-dissolution, of a loss of respectability and whiteness. Perhaps the best and hence most disturbing example of this psychic tangle is Connecticut-born Charles Palmer's short story about his crossing of Brazil and Argentina. Palmer's story, which he seems to have penned after his arrival in San Francisco and which he planned to send East for publication, begins with reference to the gold seekers' self-conceptions as daredevil Yankees: "[W]e were all young," he wrote, "hearty, well armed and truly Yankee in our restless love of new scenes and adventures." Its central scene resonates with a pornographic way of seeing and experiencing the peoples and cultures of the Southern Hemisphere, with simultaneous longings to embrace and destroy specific elements within these cultures as the sources of forbidden pleasures.[37]

Palmer's "A Scene upon the Pampas" involves a meeting with a Spanish Don, Senor Munalta. The key figure, however, is his young daughter: "She is only sixteen," Palmer has one of his characters say, "and it is no wonder that her father is so careful of her, for she is beautiful as the virgin." Having established her virginity and ethnic exoticism, as well as his own position as Yankee adventurer, Palmer appears to be preparing the reader for a tale of seduction, manly rage, and the *duello*. Indeed, he begins in this manner. Senorita Munalta, as it turns out, has been taken captive by a group of Pampas "Indians." The heroes meet the marauding band and open fire.

They manage to kill five of the enemy, but one escapes with the girl. Palmer's main protagonist rides to the rescue; he grapples with the Indian, breaks his arm, and appears to save the virgin. At this point the stage seems set for passion. Even in imagination, however, Palmer cannot bring himself to embrace his subject. Instead of envisioning a romantic consummation, he pulls back to a disturbing resistance to miscegenation; his tale ends in a ritual of destruction that cannot conceal his pleasure. Senor Munalta rides up, and as he "gazed upon his daughter's upturned face," writes Palmer: "Ha! 'twas only to see the sharp spikes of a war-club crash into her tender brain, and to feel the hot gore of his child sprinkling his face with horrible profusion!"[38]

The fact that Palmer was a graduate of Yale College and a product of an emerging middle-class culture of respectability did not keep him from venturing far into the dark terrain of his fantasies. His narrative, however, appears to reflect a distressing maintenance of respectability and whiteness. Pleasure for men like him appears to have come at a price. The result here is a blend of anger, racism, and misogyny, an attack directed toward both the desire itself and the exotic subject that had called it into being.

Despite the forty-niners' celebrated penchant for social and cultural inversions, in their meetings with Latin Americans they generally left prescriptive hierarchies intact. In fact, much like the minstrel performers who dominated the nineteenth-century American stage, they may have strengthened them. If they pictured alternative behaviors and peoples as enticingly exotic, and if they desired to embrace—at least temporarily—these "low" elements, they still marked them with disgust and shame. Accordingly, Hispanics became lazy, intemperate, and sexually charged exemplars of raw passion, Latin America a site for the play of instinctual urges, for momentary but continuously repeated reversals of Victorian morality that seemed to place moral purity in the service of racism and pleasure enhancement. In imagining these subjects in this manner, forty-niners might do little but offend both themselves and others. Certainly, in perceiving the others they met as "primitives," as immoral exemplars of all the passions, violence, and raw eroticism lacking in respectable eastern manhood, and then in attempting to internalize or playfully mimic this excessive opposite, they left a trail of offenses through Latin America. It is easy to see such offenses as a natural result of Manifest Destiny. It may be more accurate, however, to view them as arising at least partly from a complex matrix of revulsion and desire. In effect, this type of contact would far outlast the wills of nineteenth-century filibusters and robber barons. Indeed, it appears to reflect a very modern tension: a blend of attraction and revulsion on one side pitted against resistance to being subjects of pleasure, revulsion, and disgusted embraces on the other.

Notes

1. Theodore T. Johnson, *Sights in the Gold Region and Scenes by the Way* (New York: Baker & Scribner, 1849), 6, 8.

2. James P. Delgado, *To California by Sea: A Maritime History of the Gold Rush* (Columbia: University of South Carolina Press, 1990), 7, 18–21; Frances Alida Hoxie, "Connecticut's Forty-Niners," *Western Historical Quarterly* 5, no. 1 (January 1974), 17–28, 20; John Haskell Kemble, "The Gold Rush by Panama, 1848–1851," *Pacific Historical Review* 18, no. 1 (February 1949), 45–56; Oscar Lewis, "South American Ports of Call," *Pacific Historical Review* 18, no. 1 (February 1949), 57–66.

3. On the role of social inversions in the history and historiography of the rush, see David Goodman, *Gold Seeking: Victoria and California in the 1850s* (Palo Alto: Stanford University Press, 1994), introduction.

4. John M. Callbreath to his parents, Dry Creek, California, October 1, 1850, Callbreath Collection, Bancroft Library, University of California, Berkeley.

5. Alonzo Hill to his sister, San Francisco, April 7, 1850, box 1, Hill Collection, Yale University Library.

6. Bayard Taylor, *Eldorado, or Adventures in the Path of Empire* (New York: George P. Putnam, 1850), 94; John Callbreath to his sister (Grace Callbreath in Sullivan County, New York), Rio de Janeiro, March 10, 1849, Callbreath Collection, Bancroft Library.

7. Callbreath to his sister, Rio de Janeiro, March 10, 1849, Callbreath Collection, Bancroft Library; George Payson, *Golden Dreams and Leaden Realities* (1852; reprint, Upper Saddle River NJ: Literature House/Gregg Press, 1970), 309.

8. Henry Hunter Peters, Journal, entries for March 5, 1850, March 8, 1850, TS, box 1, folder 9, Peters Collection, New York Public Library.

9. Callbreath to his sister, Rio de Janeiro, March 10, 1849, Bancroft Library; Peters Journal, entry for March 5, 1850, New York Public Library; Charles Ross Parke, M.D. *Dreams to Dust* (Lincoln: University of Nebraska Press), 1989, 134; description of Brazil's backwardness cited in Lewis, "South American Ports of Call," 58, 61.

10. John N. Stone, journal entry for April 14, 1849, in John E. Pomfret, ed., *California Gold Rush Voyages, 1848–1849: Three Original Narratives* (San Bruno CA: Huntington Library, 1954), 108.

11. Logbook of Captain Cleveland Forbes (on the Steamer *California*), entry for November 1, 1849, in Pomfret, ed., *California Gold Rush Voyages*, 195.

12. Garett W. Low, *Gold Rush by Sea* (Philadelphia: University of Pennsylvania Press, 1940), 130; Dore's fascination with Brazil's fruits cited in Lewis, "South American Ports of Call," 59; Taylor, *Eldorado*, 14–15.

13. John Beeckman to Margaret Gardiner Beeckman, Rio de Janeiro, March 17, 1849, box 27, Beeckman Collection, California State Library, Sacramento; Beeckman to Margaret Beeckman, Rio de Janeiro, March 27, 1849, box 27, Beeckman Collection, California State Library, Sacramento.

14. Francis Edward Prevaux, section of a letter—with the date missing—probably written in Panama and sent later from California to his parents in Amesbury, Massachusetts, Prevaux Collection, Bancroft Library.

15. Reverend Joseph Augustine Benton, *The California Pilgrim: A Series of Lectures* (Sacramento: Solomon Alter, 1853), 44–45.

16. Peters, Journal, entry for April 2, 1850, Peters Collection, NYPL.

17. Johnson, *Sights in the Gold Region*, 78.

18. The statements of Hall and Coffin are cited in Lewis, "South American Ports of Call," 60, 64.

19. Thomas Jefferson Matteson, Journal, entries for April 15–19, 1849, TS, Senter Family Papers, Bancroft Library.

20. Matteson, Journal, April 19, 1849, Bancroft Library.

21. Taylor, *Eldorado*, 121–22, 123, 178.

22. Taylor, *Eldorado*, 33.

23. "Police Court—Before Judge Frank," *Petrel*, undated issue, April–May 1849.

24. "Police Court—Before Judge Frank," *Petrel*, undated issue, April–May 1849.

25. "To Rio," *Petrel*, undated issue, April–May 1849; the fact that the poem appeared in the same issue as the report of the trial undoubtedly reflects another ironic touch. The irony here is romantic, however: the passengers of the *Duxbury* do not mind the victory of carnality over morality—as long, that is, as the victory is momentary and offers no sense of resolution or rationalization, and as long as sin and punishment remain in constant oscillation, both forming constituent and equally important elements of the individual.

26. Henry Hovey Hyde, "Journal of a Voyage from Boston to California via Cape Horn," TS, California State Library, Sacramento.

27. Johnson, *Sights in the Gold Region*, 38.

28. For the statements of Zachary Taylor's soldiers, see Robert Johannsen, *To the Halls of the Montezumas: The Mexican War in the American Imagination* (New York: Oxford University Press, 1985), 160. Argonaut comments are in Taylor, *Eldorado*, 11, 20; James Tyson, M.D., *Diary of a Physician in California* (Oakland CA: Biobooks, 1955), 17; Asaph Sawyer, diary, undated entry, Panama City, 1852, New York Public Library.

29. Frederick Pike, *The United States and Latin America: Myths and Stereotypes of Civilization and Nature* (Austin: University of Texas Press, 1992), 10–13.

30. See Eugene W. Ridings, "Foreign Predominance among Overseas Traders in Nineteenth Century Latin America," *Latin American Research Review* 20, no. 2 (1985): 3–27; Barbara Tenenbaum, "Merchants, Money, and Mischief: The British in Mexico, 1821–1862," *The Americas* 25, no. 3 (January 1979): 317–39; Margaret Creighton and Lisa Norling, eds., *Iron Men, Wooden Women: Gender and Seafaring in the Atlantic World, 1700–1920* (Baltimore: Johns Hopkins University Press, 1996); Margaret S. Creighton, *Rites and Passages: The Experience of American Whaling, 1830–1870* (Cambridge: Cambridge University Press, 1995); on nineteenth-century prostitution in American port cities, see Timothy J. Gilfoyle, *City of Eros: New York City, Prostitution, and the Commercialization of Sex, 1790–1920* (New York: W. W. Norton, 1992).

31. Payson, *Golden Dreams and Leaden Realities*, 55; Lamson's account cited in Lewis, "South American Ports of Call," 63.

32. Josiah Griswold to Benjamin Hill, "San Francisco," December 29, 1849, Benjamin Hill Collection, Bancroft Library.

33. Franklin A. Buck, *A Yankee Trader in the Gold Rush: The Letters of Franklin A. Buck* (Boston: Houghton Mifflin, 1930), 41–42; Samuel C. Upham, *Notes of a Voyage to California via Cape Horn* (Philadelphia: the author, 1878), 55; Parke, *Dreams to Dust*, 129–33.

34. Johnson, *Sights in the Gold Region*, 244; Tyson, *Diary of a Physician in California*, 111.

35. "The Slave Girl at Rio," *Petrel*, June 17, 1849, Bancroft Library; the poem appeared under the pen name of "Smike," one of the paper's most prolific writers.

36. John H. Cornelison, undated diary entry off the coast Chile, September 1849, Cornelison Collection, New York Public Library.

37. Charles Palmer (under the pseudonym Phil Brengle), "A Scene Upon the Pampas," unpublished manuscript sent from San Francisco, May 17, 1851, Bancroft Library.

38. Palmer, "Scene Upon the Pampas."

4

Clouded Legacy

California Indians and the Gold Rush

Albert L. Hurtado

In 1855 three California men succinctly characterized the gold rush: "Let none wonder that the time was the best ever made."[1] And so it seemed later in the century to the once-young men who grew old on a steady diet of green memories of their youth in that most extraordinary time. Their vision of the gold rush as the best of times influenced generations of Californians including California historians who described a rambunctious period that forever marked this place as the Golden State. Such memories materialized in the pipe smoke of middle-class, Anglo-American men who had good reasons to view the past with self-satisfaction and warm nostalgia. They reconstructed the gold rush past in their own image—their past was middle-class, Anglo-American, and successful. There was little room for people of color in their historical reconstruction. Indians were hardly to be seen at all.

Yet one of these successful businessmen, Hubert Howe Bancroft, took the trouble to consider California Indians in his multivolume history of the state. "The savages were in the way," he summarized. "The miners and settlers were arrogant and impatient; there were no missionaries or others present with even the poor pretense of soul-saving or civilizing. It was one of the last human hunts of civilization, and the basest and most brutal of them all."[2] The gold rush may have been the best of times for those white men who reminisced about it, but for Indians, as Bancroft recognized, it was something else again.

Early in 1848 no one—Indian or white—could have foretold the spectacular upheavals that were to come, or predicted the tragic history that awaited the California Indians. Indeed, at the close of the Mexican-American War, California Indians seemed to be in a relatively strong position. During the war most Indians simply stayed clear of the fighting, but some fought with the American forces and as allies of the victors could make a moral claim on the U.S. government. The Treaty of Guadalupe Hidalgo—the document that ended the war and settled outstanding disputes between Mexico and the United States—recognized Mexican citizenship rights. Under the laws of Mexico and the Constitution of 1824, Indians were citizens. According to Article VIII of the Treaty of Guadalupe Hidalgo, Mexican citizens could declare their intention either to retain their Mexican citizenship or to become U.S. citizens within one year of the treaty's ratification. Those who made no declaration automatically became U.S. citizens after one year.[3] Thus, optimistic observers might have predicted that the future for California's Native peoples (that is, the adult male part of the population) included immediate citizenship, a status that would not come to all Indians in the United States until 1924.[4] Only the most credulous student of the nineteenth century could believe that citizenship would fully protect Indians from the onslaught of miners who descended on California. At the least, however, citizenship status would have provided a basis for future claims against the government and Indian demands for equal protection under the law.[5]

The Treaty of Guadalupe Hidalgo also seemed to guarantee Indian property rights derived from Spanish and Mexican laws and traditions. Spanish law recognized Indians' rights to lands that they occupied, tilled, and hunted.[6] The crown established Catholic missions in order to Christianize and to Hispanicize Native peoples as a matter of colonial policy. In California the missions took up many thousands of acres and employed thousands of Indians. The crown intended missions to be temporary institutions that would eventually be secularized, that is, converted to parish churches. Then the government would distribute the old mission lands to the Indian inhabitants. In practice, Franciscan missionaries resisted secularization and maintained control of vast tracts of real estate throughout the Spanish era. When the Mexican government secularized the missions, most Indians either failed to gain land titles or soon lost their lands to California's Mexican rancheros through fraud and coercion. But some Indians at least had land rights that devolved from Spain to Mexico to Indians, land rights that the U.S. government should have recognized under the Treaty of Guadalupe Hidalgo.[7]

Many Indians in central and southern California had worked for Spanish and Mexican landholders; they were a vital part of the provincial workforce. Acting on behalf of the Spanish Crown, Franciscan missionaries converted tens of thousands of Indians to Christianity. Neophytes, as the new Christians were called, worked in the fields and shops of the missions. These Native farm workers, herders, and craftsmen literally built the twenty-one missions that stretched from San Diego to Sonoma. At first the Franciscans recruited most neophytes from the territory adjacent to the individual missions—Kumeyaay near San Diego, Gabrielino in the Los Angeles region, Chumash near Santa Barbara, the Costanoans and Miwoks surrounding Monterey and San Francisco Bays. In the early nineteenth century, missionaries turned to the central valley, where they induced Yokuts, Patwins, and interior Miwoks to relocate to the Franciscan's coastal establishments.[8] After Mexico established its independence from Spain in 1821, private landholders employed thousands of Indian laborers on the great cattle ranches that supplanted the missions. Whether as unpaid mission servants, waged labor, peons, or slaves, Indian workers built Hispanic and Mexican California. When Americans and other newcomers, such as John Sutter, immigrated to California during the Mexican era, they, too, rapidly came to depend on Indian labor.[9]

At the time the gold rush erupted in northern California, the U.S. federal government was working out a policy to replace the earlier policy of Indian removal that had served in the Midwest and the South. Congress meant the removal policy to resettle Indians from tribal territories east of the Mississippi to reservations established by treaties in the West. Acting under authority conferred by the Constitution, federal agents first negotiated removal treaties with individual tribes. Removal is best known in the popular imagination in the tragic case of the Cherokees, who recall their emigration from Georgia to present-day Oklahoma as the Trail of Tears.[10]

With the close of the Mexican-American War and the acquisition of former Mexican territory from the Rocky Mountains to the Pacific Ocean, a new Indian policy was needed. The United States was no longer willing to maintain a definite border from the Red River to Canada with Indians living on the west and non-Indians to the east. Federal officials now wished to open a path to California and Oregon and to reduce friction between Indians and whites as well as among tribes. Consequently, the United States began to develop a system of large reservations in the Great Plains region. As with removal, treaties were the foundation of this new policy. Typically, these documents provided that the tribes recognize federal authority, remain at peace with the United States and other tribal groups, and give up claims to some of their own home territory. In return, western tribes received substantial reservations in their home territory, along with gifts, annuity payments, livestock, teachers, farmers, agricultural implements, and other goods. Federally appointed teachers and farmers would instruct the tribespeople in agricultural and domestic skills so that the Indians could become self-sufficient farming their own land. These federal Indian treaties established nation-to-nation relations that had constitutional status as the supreme law of the land; they affirmed the unique legal status of Indians in the United States and provided homelands for them.[11]

Congress had strongly affirmed its obligations to Indians from the time of the American Revolution. In 1787 the Northwest Ordinance forthrightly stated that the "utmost good faith shall always be observed towards the Indians, their lands and their property shall never be taken from them without their consent; and in their property, rights and liberty, they shall never be invaded or disturbed, unless in just and lawful wars authorized by Congress; but laws founded in justice and humanity shall from time to time be made, for preventing wrongs being done to them, and for preserving peace and friendship with them."[12] Congress provided additional recognition and protection of tribal rights in Indian country in several laws culminating in the Indian Trade and Intercourse Act of 1834. This law defined Indian country as all U.S. territory west of the Mississippi River (except for the states of Missouri and Louisiana and the Arkansas Territory) and lands specifically set aside for Indians by treaty. The law prohibited non-Indian settlements, obligated the federal government to evict non-Indian trespassers in Indian country, and authorized the president to use military force if needed. Traders had to obtain a federal license to do business with Indians in Indian country. Non-Indians could not hunt, trap, or graze livestock in Indian country, and were subject to fines if they broke the law. Congress hoped this basic statute would eliminate some of the common causes of Indian and white frontier conflict by making Indian country safe for Indians under federal protection.[13]

So, knowing all this, a thoughtful person in 1848 might have predicted that the California Indians' encounter with Anglo-American society would be softened by the continuing need for Indian laborers, who would themselves have substantial claims to lands, citizenship, and political rights under Spanish, Mexican, and U.S. law. Our hypothetical observer might have surmised that independent Indian freeholders and reservation Indians alike would enjoy a relatively prosperous future. Many California Natives already knew how to raise crops and care for livestock and had done so for decades. It would not have been unreasonable to predict these people would swiftly take a leading role in caring for their own land, animals, and crops. Perhaps the future held economic self-sufficiency, independence, and citizenship for them. But that was not to be.

If I have proposed an overly optimistic counterfactual history for California Indians in the 1850s, allow me to say that no one in 1848 could have predicted the disasters that befell California Native peoples because of the unexpected, radical, revolutionary impact of the gold rush. When gold was discovered perhaps 150,000 Indians lived in California. Twelve years later only 30,000 were left. In 1848 Indians held most of the country north of San Francisco Bay, part of the Sacramento Valley and most of the San Joaquin Valley, the Sierra Nevada mountains and foothills, the Mohave and Colorado Deserts. In all, these territories amounted to perhaps 80 percent of the state's land area, although it must be admitted that much of this land was not suitable for European-style agriculture. Indians were in possession of virtually all the gold-bearing regions in the state, a sizeable proportion of the lands suitable for grazing and farming, and the richest timberlands in California, not to mention the headwaters of all the state's major rivers. In 1860 Indians retained legal rights to none of this land. Nor had the United States extended citizenship to California Indians. The Native survivors of the gold rush had been marginalized and, for the most part, grievously impoverished, with their well-being and their lives at the mercy of a dominant, mostly uncaring population of Euro-American invaders.

Why did things turn out so badly? Beginning in 1848 several revolutions struck California. First, the change from Mexican to U.S. sovereignty precipitated a political revolution that signified much more than a shift from one distant national capital to another. American republican government differed from Mexican in institutions, traditions, and practices. The United States incorporated frontier territories as states that were politically equal to the original thirteen. By 1848 new states carved from the old southwest and northwest territories comprised more than half of the Union. Representatives from these states had a great deal of influence on Indian policy, especially as it applied to their own states, as the Cherokees and other tribes learned by hard experience during the controversies over Indian removal. In most cases Congress required frontier communities to apply for territorial status before it granted them statehood. Territories had no voting privileges in Congress, and presidential appointees served as governors and other territorial officials. Territorial governors also served as superintendents of Indian affairs in their jurisdictions; thus they maintained (in theory) a degree of independence from local popular opinion on Indian affairs. In reality territorial government and politics were far from polite, tutelary institutions, and territorial governors did not always think first of the welfare of Indians when making decisions that concerned the Native peoples in their jurisdictions.[14]

Whatever the shortcomings of the territorial system, California's Native

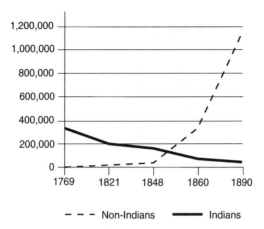

1. Indian and Non-Indian Populations, 1769–1890. Source: *Sherburne F. Cook,* The Population of California Indians, 1769–1970 *(Berkeley: University of California Press, 1976).*

people never had the chance to appeal to a territorial governor for protection. The rush for gold brought to California hordes of new settlers who clamored for immediate statehood. In 1850 Congress admitted California as the thirty-first state and gave white Californians a direct say in shaping federal Indian policy for their state.

There was a revolution in attitudes. The rising political philosophy of the time—ultimately expressed in the formation of the Republican Party—advocated free labor, free land, and free men.[15] According to this political program, the federal government was supposed to clear the land of Indians and give it to independent white farmers. Slavery, in this set of beliefs, should be abolished because it competed unfairly with free white men. The free labor of white men created personal and national wealth from the public domain. Indians were merely an impediment, an unproductive and potentially dangerous obstacle to white expansion and national prosperity.

There was a demographic revolution. The gold rush caused a massive change in the numbers, character, and location of California's non-Indian population. In 1848 California contained approximately 150,000 Indians and perhaps 14,000 non-Indians. Of the latter population, about half were Mexican citizens; the rest were Americans and foreigners.[16] In other words, Indian Californians outnumbered others by more than ten to one. In 1860 approximately 30,000 Indians remained in the state alongside about 360,000 non-Indians (see fig. 1). While the Indian population had declined

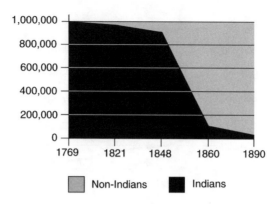

2. Indians as Percentage of California's Population, 1769–1970. Source: *Sherburne P. Cook,* The Population of California Indians, 1769–1970 *(Berkeley: University of California Press, 1976).*

by 80 percent, the Native peoples' proportion of the total population also became less than 8 percent (see fig. 2). Literally and figuratively, California's Native population was buried. Almost overnight Indians had become a demographically insignificant minority.

With this abrupt demographic change, the new population occupied new geographical turf. Formerly the non-Indian population had been limited to a narrow strip of territory west of the coast range and a few interior settlements (see map 1). Now miners flocked to the gold regions, the very places where Native populations had earlier maintained their autonomy and the substantial integrity of their populations.

The men who flooded the gold fields brought hardened attitudes toward Indians. Miners came to California from all over the world, but Americans with generations of hatred for Indians on older frontiers dominated the new population. As one of them succinctly put it, "[W]hen you are in a country where you know he is your enemy, and is not only waiting his chance but looking out for his opportunity, why not cut him down as he most surely will you?"[17] Some American immigrants believed fervently that preemptive murder was a sensible Indian policy. Thousands of men with such sentiments headed for the California gold fields in 1849. They had no experience with Indian laborers and precious little respect for Indian life.

The gold rush rapidly propelled California into the market economy. For Indians this revolution meant that money would replace barter as a mode of economic exchange and that free waged labor would replace coerced labor. The transformation to market-based capitalism was already well underway

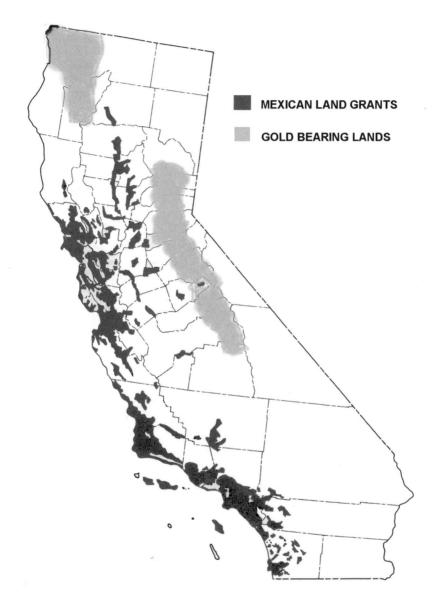

1. Mexican Land Grants and Gold Bearing Lands in 1848. Source: *Michael W. Donley, Stuart Allan, Patricia Caro, and Clyde P. Patton,* Atlas of California *(Culver City CA: Pacific Book Center, 1979), 14, and Warren A. Beck and Ynez D. Haase,* Historical Atlas of California *(University of Oklahoma Press, 1974), 23–24, map 24. © 1974 by the University of Oklahoma Press.*

in Mexican California, but the gold rush accelerated the process, and it squeezed Indians out of the labor force. With few opportunities to sustain themselves in the market economy, Indians were left behind, impoverished and marginalized in the new California.[18]

✗ Finally, the gold rush precipitated an environmental revolution that severely damaged or destroyed the Native domestic economy. Placer mining brought about the largest changes. Miners dug gravel from virtually every inch of the Sierra streambeds, loosening tons of silt that cascaded downstream. The silt choked off the salmon runs that formerly had fed Indian communities. Farmers and ranchers enclosed grasslands for their livestock and prevented Indians from gathering life-sustaining seeds and other plant products. Simultaneously, newcomers introduced exotic plants and animals that largely replaced the indigenous animal and plant regimes that California Natives had relied on. Domestic livestock were an especially important new element because they competed with Indians for wild grasses. Miners cut down oak trees and thus eliminated the acorns that were a Native staple. In the forty-niner scheme of things, lumber and firewood were important, Indian food resources were not. These changes rapidly transformed the California environment from a landscape producing wild plant and animal foods for Native peoples to one that sustained domestic animals and plants for sale in the new Euro-American market economy. Insofar as familiar landscapes remained intact, new owners claimed exclusive use of the land and kept Indians away—by force if necessary. The environmental revolution engendered a food crisis for Indians, who starved to death near prosperous farms and ranches that served the market economy.[19] Changes in the environment were not a "natural" transformation but the result of human choices. The dominant Euro-American population created a strange new world for California Indians in their own country, devaluing Native peoples and the resources that had traditionally sustained them.

Whether viewed from economic, political, social, or environmental perspectives, conditions in gold rush California were undergoing complicated changes that destroyed Indian rights, resources, and life. The Constitution, federal laws, national Indian policy, and human decency obligated the U.S. government to regulate Indian affairs and protect Indians in California. Because California was under military government until 1849, U.S. Army commanders, acting as military governors, appointed subagents to take care of Indian affairs. The subagents for northern California were John A. Sutter and Mariano Guadalupe Vallejo, two experienced and knowledgeable men who employed Indians on their Mexican land-grant ranchos.[20]

Governor Mason instructed Vallejo and Sutter to protect Indians from abuse by their employers. Since both men employed Indians, this directive was akin to ordering coyotes to guard a sheepfold. The discovery of gold immediately exposed Sutter's conflict of interests. James Marshall, Sutter's business partner, in the company of Indian and white workmen first found gold at Sutter's sawmill at Coloma in January 1848.[21] Without mentioning gold, Sutter drew up a lease with Yalisumni Indians that granted him exclusive rights to cut timber and erect "other necessary machinery" and sent it for approval to the military governor, Colonel Richard Mason.[22]

Sutter's lease was duplicitous in two respects. He failed to mention the discovery of gold, and he misled the governor about the Indians who had the strongest claim to the lands that he wished to lease. The Yalisumnis lived far downstream from the mill and had worked for Sutter for years. The Kolomas occupied the site of Sutter's mill, but he did not mention them in the lease.[23] Mason rejected the proposed lease, explaining to Sutter that such leases were contrary to federal law. "The United States do not recognize the right of Indians to sell or lease the lands on which they reside or to which the tribe may have a claim, to private individuals," the governor wrote. Mason expected the federal government to extinguish Indian land titles in the usual way—through treaty arrangements with tribes and the federal government. Only then would the land become part of the public domain and open to grant, lease, or purchase from the U.S. General Land Office by private individuals.[24]

Governor Mason was not the only federal official who believed the government would treat California like other western territories, although politicians and administrators disagreed about the applicability of current federal Indian law. In October 1848, Secretary of State James Buchanan predicted that Congress would soon establish a territorial government for California. "Our laws relating to trade and intercourse with the Indians will then be extended over them," he added, indicating that the laws did not apply to California without congressional action.[25]

Secretary Buchanan was a poor prophet, for Congress did not create a territorial government for California. While Congress debated the future of the Mexican cession, Californians elected delegates who wrote a state constitution, approved by voters in November 1849. With this show of popular support for statehood, California's self-designated political spokesmen demanded admission to the union, set up a state government, and awaited favorable congressional action.[26] In the summer of 1849, the secretary of war informed General Bennett Riley, the new military governor of California, that the Indian trade and intercourse acts were in effect despite Congress's failure to act on the matter. Crawford also believed that until Congress provided a territorial government or admitted California as a state, "the whole code of laws existing and of force in California at the period of the conquest" were operative, "with the limitation that they are not repugnant to the constitution and the laws of the United States."[27] As far as Crawford was concerned, these laws presumably included the military governors' edicts and the Mexican laws that applied to California before 1848. Five months later the commissioner of Indian affairs understood that the trade and intercourse laws were not in effect in California. Congress never did extend to California these laws' important safeguards for Indian life, rights, and property.[28]

While a state of confusion reigned in Washington, the gold discovery rapidly became a headlong rush for the precious metal. Sutter had hoped to keep the discovery a secret so that he could keep his workers on the job and gain an advantage, but his Mormon workers began to spread the news in the early spring of forty-eight.[29] Not surprisingly, in the first months of the gold rush, Mexican and Anglo ranchers took their Indian laborers to work in the mines. Given the extent of the gold deposits and the primitive placer mining technology then available, human labor was the chief factor that determined success in the mines. Men who controlled Indian labor had a significant advantage in the summer of 1848. As Mexican rancheros abandoned their cattle herds and headed for the mountains, Indian vaqueros transformed themselves into miners. After an inspection tour in July 1848, Governor Mason reckoned that there were about four thousand miners at work in the mining district and that "more than half were Indians."[30]

In that heady first season, large and small fortunes in gold came to white men through the hands of Indian laborers. John Sinclair, an associate of John Sutter and owner of the Rancho del Paso, well understood the economics of Indian labor. He employed about fifty Indian miners on the North Fork of the American River. They used closely woven willow baskets of Native manufacture to wash out sixteen thousand dollars worth of gold. Sutter, Sinclair, and other Californians customarily paid Indians in clothing, utensils, and other trade goods. It cost Sinclair and others about a dollar a day to employ an Indian worker, so profits could be enormous. He also benefited by using Indian baskets instead of expensive metal pans for washing gold. Sinclair was by no means the only Californian to make such gains from Indian laborers. After paying off their Native workers, seven men from Monterey netted 259 pounds of gold in seven weeks. At sixteen dollars per ounce, their profits came to more than sixty-six thousand dollars—a tidy sum for a summer's work in 1848.[31]

The value of Indian labor was so great that Sutter, John Bidwell, George

McKinstry, and other old California hands became labor contractors who supplied Indian workers to newcomers anxious to skim the golden grains from California mineral harvest.[32] These pioneers were happy to exploit Indian labor in the gold fields, but at least they paid their Native workers. Others were not so fastidious. Some unscrupulous entrepreneurs seized Indians and forced them to labor.[33] Needless to say, Indian agents Sutter and Vallejo did nothing to protect California Indians from this crude form of exploitation.

The success of experienced rancheros—especially Mexican Californians—confirmed notions about free labor held by most Anglo newcomers. Men who controlled Indian labor had an unfair advantage over individual white toilers, they believed. In the late summer of 1848, immigrants from Oregon began to arrive in the California mining districts. The Oregonians had fresh memories of the Cayuse Indian War in Oregon, and some took pride in killing any Indians they met. In the spring of 1849, one group of Oregonians had reached the Coloma vicinity, where they commenced mining. Evidently, some of these men raped local Nisenan Indian women. In retaliation, the Nisenans killed five Oregonians at a site later named Murderer's Bar, about ten miles northwest of Coloma. The enraged comrades of the murdered Oregon men decided to kill the Indian perpetrators, or at least to kill some Indians. In Coloma they singled out eight Indians, including some of James Marshall's Native workers, who almost certainly had nothing to do with the deaths at Murderer's Bar. Marshall tried to intervene, but the mob was drunk and out for Indian blood. The Oregonians paid no attention to Marshall's plea and held the prisoners overnight. When they took the captives out the next day, the frightened Indians ran and the Oregon men shot them down. Not all of the people of Coloma supported the bloody and misdirected revenge of the newcomers. As it became clear that the Oregon miners intended to kill Indians regardless of their innocence in the Murderer's Bar killings, someone (perhaps Marshall) sent for John Sutter, but the subagent was afraid that he would attract the wrath of the mob and declined to go to Coloma. Sutter's reluctance was probably well founded. Marshall's courageous but ineffective effort to protect his Indian laborers convinced some miners that Marshall was not to be trusted. Now fearful for his own life, the discoverer of gold fled from Coloma.[34]

The selective murder of Indian workers at Coloma marked a turning point in the use of Indian labor in the mines. From that time forward, with few exceptions free white labor dominated the mining districts. At some sites miners killed or drove away all Indians. In others, Indians lived on the margins of mining society, eking out a living as best they could.

Wherever possible, Indians worked as independent miners, trading their dust to merchants for the necessities of life. Prices were high for everyone, but Indians—with little knowledge of money, credit, and the value of gold—were at a great disadvantage. Some merchants employed a special "digger ounce," an overweighted slug with which to balance Indian gold dust in their scales. Other traders simplified exchange rates (and advanced their profits) by demanding the weight in gold for articles that they sold to Indians.[35] White miners staked claims to the best placers and allowed Indians to work only those locations that did not pay well enough to support a white miner. In some cases generous miners allowed Indians to wash tailings, which produced scanty piles of dust from the worked-over debris. Under such circumstances, Indians moved from one meager resource to another. Central California Indians had always moved from place to place in order to exploit plant and animal foods that were seasonally abundant. As miners drove away game and preempted Indian plant food collecting areas, small-scale gold mining and scavenging in white dumps were among the few replacement resources that Native people could turn to.[36]

In far away Washington DC neither Congress nor the executive branch had accurate knowledge of California and its Native peoples, so the federal government's first actions were tentative. The secretary of the interior reappointed John A. Sutter as Indian subagent for the territory drained by the Sacramento River and named Adam Johnston subagent for the San Joaquin region. The secretary issued no new instructions to the subagents, perhaps expecting them to carry on under the regulations established by the military regime.[37]

While the federal government moved slowly toward a policy for California, the new state government began to establish its own laws regarding Indians. The law "For the Government and Protection of the Indians" is perhaps the best known of the state's acts concerning the Native population. Passed by the first state legislature in 1850, the measure defined a class of Indian crimes (such as burning the prairies and livestock theft), prohibited Indians from testifying in court against whites, and provided for the indenture of Indian orphans and adults who were loitering—that is, who did not work for whites. Indentured orphans were to be released after they reached the age of majority: fifteen for women and eighteen for men, later extended to twenty-one for women and twenty-five for men. Courts could sentence loitering Indian adults to work for no more than four months for farmers who bid for their services and paid the county a fee.[38] The law also recognized certain minimal Native land rights, although the lawmakers left it up to white landholders to set aside Indian lands from their own holdings voluntarily.

The title of the law notwithstanding, this statute provided scant protection for Indian land or persons. It was designed primarily to give California farmers a legal claim to Indian labor. The law defined a class of "unfree" Indian persons, required them to work for whites, and punished them if they did not. While the law expressly outlawed kidnapping and other abuses, the exclusion of Indian testimony against whites (a provision also written into the state's constitution) made prosecution difficult. Few cases against whites came before the courts. Sometimes juries refused to convict; in other cases public sentiment cowed prosecutors, who simply released the accused.[39] These travesties occurred at a time when mobs lynched suspected criminals of all ethnic backgrounds on flimsy evidence and for comparatively trivial offenses against whites.[40] Under this dual standard of justice, kidnappers scoured the country for prospective Indian laborers. In the most outrageous cases, they killed Indian parents and took the orphans, who were then indentured according to law. This infamous law stood on the books until 1863.[41] There are few extant official records concerning the administration of this statute. Substantial archival evidence survives for the operation of the law in Los Angeles and Humboldt Counties—the geographic and cultural antipodes of the state—but there are only scattered documents elsewhere.[42] Consequently, we have no way of knowing how many Indians were subjected to this law and its abuses. Certainly the law compelled many hundreds, probably thousands of Indians to be unfree laborers in California's booming, labor-short gold rush economy.

As the 1850s dawned, Indian choices and opportunities were narrowing. Not surprisingly, some chose to steal from overland immigrants on the last leg of their journey in the Sierra Nevada mountains and from miners who had forced them out of work and overrun their lands. Sporadic fighting broke out throughout the mining districts. Few miners were willing to admit that their own presence was the root cause of these conflicts. Instead, they sought government help to secure their lives and property. In January 1851, Governor Peter Burnett bluntly assessed the situation in his annual message to the legislature. He explained that "the white man, to whom time is money, and who labors hard all day to create the comforts of life, cannot sit up all night to watch his property; . . . after being robbed a few times he becomes desperate, and resolves upon a war." The governor predicted that "[a] war of extermination will continue to be waged between the races until the Indian race becomes extinct."[43]

Following Governor Burnett's lead, the state legislature enacted laws that enabled the governor to call out the state militia and borrow money to fund Indian wars. State militia units campaigned against Indians from one end of California to the other. By 1854 the state's debt for these violent adventures totaled more than $900,000. State officials claimed that the federal government should pay this debt, arguing that it was the federal responsibility to protect its citizens from Indians. The federal government eventually paid most of the bill for these bloody forays.[44]

Federal inaction on California Indian affairs presented an opportunity to the new state that Governor Burnett and the legislature seized. The legislature passed laws governing Indians who were tried in state courts. While complaining that the federal government provided no military protection against Indians, the governor called out the state militia to make war on them. With these acts the state of California presented the federal government with a fait accompli, much as Georgia had done twenty years earlier when that state extended its laws over the Cherokees and demanded their removal. Congress was divided on the question of Cherokee removal, but President Andrew Jackson fully supported Georgia. Ultimately, Congress passed removal legislation, and the Cherokees moved under duress from their home country to treaty lands west of the Mississippi River. In the 1820s and 1830s, presidents, Congress, Georgia state officials, the U.S. Supreme Court, Indians, and their supporters (some of whom favored removal) debated the Cherokee removal issue. In the long run the state of Georgia won because it held a political ace in its hand: the U.S. government would not employ force against a sovereign state in order to uphold Indian rights.[45] In 1850 the state of California held the same card.

These conditions prevailed in California when the federal government finally acted to assert control over the state's Indian affairs. In late 1850, Congress authorized three agents to gather information about California Indians and to make peace. Although Congress did not specifically direct them to make treaties, the secretary of the interior instructed the agents to act as treaty commissioners and "make such treaties and compacts . . . as may seem just and proper."[46] Armed with these instructions, the three men began their mission in 1851. Working first in the Mariposa district, where a war was already underway, the commissioners negotiated eighteen treaties with scores of Native California communities from Mexico to Oregon. These agreements set aside approximately 8.5 million acres for reservations. The agreements resembled other treaties that federal authorities negotiated with tribal representatives elsewhere in the West during the 1850s. They set aside large tracts for reservations within traditional Native community districts. Some were several hundred square miles in extent (see map 2). The United States agreed to provide the Indians with teachers, farmers, livestock, tools, and other necessities. The Native leaders, if they understood the treaty language, recognized the United States as sovereign and agreed to remain at peace. In most cases the Native signatories took up residence on the lands that the treaties had reserved for them and which had been carved out of territory where they had long lived.[47]

Indians who negotiated in good faith could not have fully appreciated the treaty-making procedure. According to the Constitution, the U.S. Senate had to ratify all treaties, including Indian treaties, before they had legal force. Most Anglo-Californians, the state legislature, and California's congressional delegation in Washington opposed the treaties. These opponents argued that the reservations took up too much valuable mineral and agricultural land. Besides, they argued, California Indians did not need reservations because many of them already worked on white-owned farms and ranches. These people, some legislators asserted, "were already in the best school of civilization."[48] Treaty foes argued that neither Mexico nor Spain had recognized Indian land rights, so why should the United States? It did not help matters that many Californians accused the federally appointed commissioners of fraudulent dealings. The U.S. Senate heard the adamant opposition of the California legislature. In 1852, following standing rules concerning treaty ratification, the Senate retired to executive session, debated the treaties behind closed doors, and tabled them.[49] This action effectively killed the treaties and rendered nugatory the reservations that the treaties had seemingly established.

In rejecting the eighteen treaties, senators in effect told California Indians that the United States did not recognize any Indian land rights supposedly derived from Spain and Mexico, nor did they acknowledge in California the land rights that the federal government ordinarily recognized for tribes in the Midwest and elsewhere in the Far West. However, California's senators conceded that the nation had a humanitarian responsibility to provide for the Indians who were caught in the gold rush vise, and Congress provided money for that purpose.[50] After Congress rejected the treaties, federal officials devised a plan for temporary military reservations where Indians could gather. Edward F. Beale, the principal architect of this plan, explained that Indians would be "invited to assemble" at a farm between the Fresno and San Joaquin Rivers. There he would require the Indians to work under what he called a "system of Discipline and instruction." Laboring in the fields, Indian workers would feed not only themselves, but the soldiers who guarded them. When whites became numerous and clamored for the

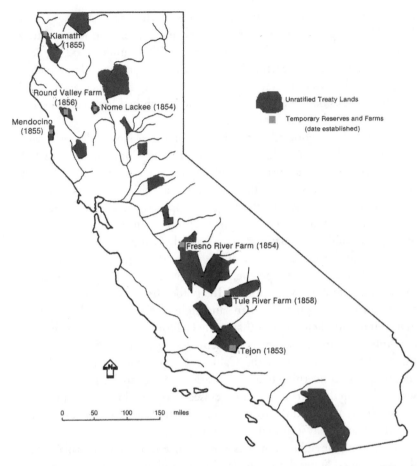

2. *Unratified Treaty Lands, Temporary Reserves and Farms, 1851–1860.* Source: *Warren A. Beck and Ynez D. Haase,* Historical Atlas of California *(University of Oklahoma Press, 1974), 57.* © *1974 by the University of Oklahoma Press.*

land, the federal government would simply move the Indians to another temporary military reserve.[51]

To administrators in Washington and to white Californians, the establishment of temporary reserves for Indians offered a plausible Indian policy for the state. Inexpensive because they were self-sustaining and inoffensive to local interests because they were temporary, these California reservations required no treaties. The federal government could pursue this scheme without recognizing formally any Indian legal rights or challenging white people's claims to mineral and agricultural land. Under such an arrangement, the gold rush and agricultural expansion could proceed unimpeded. Nor did national officials interfere with the state's Indian initiatives such as Indian indenture and state-sponsored Indian wars. Thus, federal authority in effect institutionalized gold rush chaos for California Indians while tacitly recognizing the legitimacy of the state government's actions in Indian affairs.

Bad as it was, this policy failed to work as its framers intended. Only a minority of the state's Indians voluntarily went to the temporary nontreaty reservations that Beale and his successors established. Most reservation residents were natives of the place or lived nearby. The majority of the state's Indians lived far from reservations, where whites often complained about them. The state responded to these complaints by sending volunteer militia units to round up Indian prisoners and herd them to the reservations. Militia members sometimes killed the old, young, and infirm who could not keep up. Prisoners who survived these forced marches often fled back to their homelands as soon as the state militia left the reservation. Most Native people preferred to take their chances with kidnappers, white farmers, state militia, and private Indian hunters.[52]

The reservations did not sustain themselves as planned. Instead they became a drain on the federal treasury. They were also riddled with mismanagement and graft that siphoned off federal funds intended for Indian welfare. Investigators from the Office of Indian Affairs deemed the reservations a failure in 1858.[53] "The Government provides a magnificent farm of 25,000 acres in one of the finest grain countries in the world, and stocks it at lavish expense," one puzzled investigator wrote concerning the Nome Lackee reservation. Even with "an unlimited supply of Indian labor," the farm could not feed all of the Indians in the vicinity.[54] Consequently, two thousand Nome Lackee Indians left the reservation to gather acorns, berries, grass seed, and other wild foods to stave off starvation. Similar scenes figured in reports from other temporary reservations.[55] Far from becoming self-sustaining, reservations depended on customary Indian food gathering outside the reservation boundaries. In other cases, nonreservation Indians merely stopped at reservations during the wheat harvest season, accepted food in return for their labor, then left for some different locality where food was available. Migrant California Indians merely incorporated reservations into their customary seasonal hunting and gathering cycle. By the mid-1860s, the federal government had abandoned most of these temporary establishments in favor of a few permanent reserves established by presidential executive orders (see map 3).

In effect, the federal government left most California Indians to shift for themselves during the gold rush, a neglectful policy that did nothing to halt the devastation of the Indian population. Federal and state actions made California's surviving Native peoples a landless and impoverished minority who eked out a living as migrant workers or as squatters on the public domain. In the worst cases, volunteer militia units under county or state authority (or on their own initiative) literally hunted and killed Indians without regard to age or gender. So it was that "in the best time ever made," Indians in the Golden State became objects of pity for all but the most hardened observers. On the streets of every gold rush boom town, on the sidewalks of Sacramento, Indians begged for food.

The gold rush left a clouded legacy for Indians and other Californians. Eventually state and federal officials, prompted by humanitarian pressure groups, recognized that a great injustice had been done to the state's Native population. As William P. Dole, Lincoln's commissioner of Indian affairs, put it, "the great error in our relation with the California Indians consists in our refusal to recognize their usufructuary right in the soil, and to treat with them for its relinquishment."[56] The recognition of this error did not lead to speedy and effective corrective measures. In the 1870s, prodded by public-spirited reformers, the federal government took tentative steps to address this problem by setting aside public lands for Indians in the southern part of the state. Over the next forty years, this practice evolved erratically to include land purchases for northern California Indians as well. These actions led to the establishment of scores of small reservations (customarily called rancherías) for Indians throughout the state but did not provide land for all Indians. Some rancherías were only a few acres in size—home sites perhaps, but not enough land to support the people who lived there. In the 1950s, a new federal policy called termination imperiled even these modest Native land holdings. Motivated by a desire to end the expense of administering Indian trust lands and a misguided desire to benefit Indians by forcing their total integration into white society, officials in Washington began to pressure Indians to terminate federal

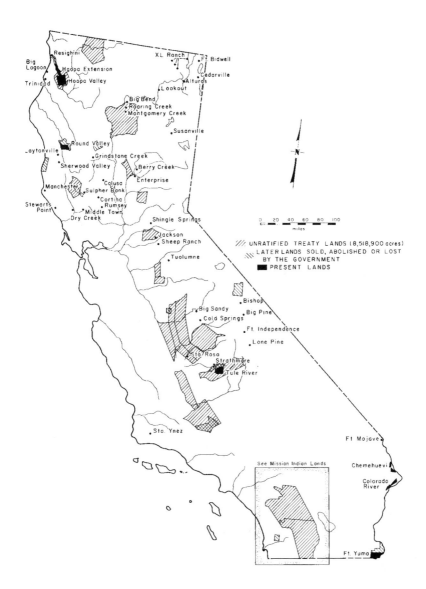

Map labels:

Resighini
Big Logoon
Hoopa Extension
Trinidad
Hoopa Valley
XL Ranch
Ft. Bidwell
Cedarville
Alturas
Lookout
Big Bend
Roaring Creek
Montgomery Creek
Susanville
Round Valley
Laytonville
Grindstone Creek
Sherwood Valley
Berry Creek
Enterprise
Colusa
Manchester
Sulpher Bank
Cortina
Stewarts Point
Rumsey
Middle Town
Dry Creek
Shingle Springs
Jackson
Sheep Ranch
Tuolumne
Bishop
Big Sandy
Cold Springs
Big Pine
Ft. Independence
Lone Pine
Sta. Rosa
Strathmore
Tule River
Sta. Ynez
Ft. Mojave
Chemehuevi
Colorado River
See Mission Indian Lands
Ft. Yuma

Scale: 0 20 40 60 80 100 miles

/// UNRATIFIED TREATY LANDS (8,518,900 acres)
\\\ LATER LANDS SOLD, ABOLISHED OR LOST BY THE GOVERNMENT
■ PRESENT LANDS

3. Indian Lands. Source: *Warren A. Beck and Ynez D. Haase,* Historical Atlas of California *(University of Oklahoma Press, 1974, 57. © 1974 by the University of Oklahoma Press.*

services and the Indians' trust relationship with the federal government. In return, California Indians were to receive title to their lands in fee simple—as well as responsibility for paying taxes. The residents of forty-one rancherías voted for termination in 1958. About thirteen hundred Indians received title to 7,601 acres of land (approximately 5.8 acres per Indian). Much of this land was marginal and could not produce income for the Indian owners. Many Native people eventually sold their land because they were unable to pay property taxes.[57] Despite federal attempts to eliminate California's reservations, many rancherías and small reservations still exist. Some rancherías are now equipped with casinos—one legacy of the attempts to correct gold rush wrongs.

In the twentieth century, many white Californians became concerned about the impoverished condition of the state's Native people. The state legislature decided that it had a responsibility to California Indians too. Instead of making amends for the Indian indenture law and the wars carried on under state authority, the legislators decided that the federal government should atone for its wrongs. Acting in accordance with the wishes of women's clubs and the Native Sons of the Golden West, the legislature took steps to sue the federal government on behalf of the Indians. The state attorney general argued that Indians should be paid for the lands that had been set aside for them in the unratified treaties. After obtaining necessary state and federal enabling legislation in 1928, the state attorney general initiated suit against the federal government. In 1942, a federal court decided the case in favor of the Indians, but the court subtracted the value of all goods and services that Indians had received from the federal government in the nineteenth century. After doing the math, the court awarded a little more than $5 million to the Indians. In 1950 each California Indian received $150, a payment that some derisively called the "TDP"—television down payment.[58]

The payment of these small awards did not put an end to California Indians' claims against the federal government. In 1946, Congress established the Indian Claims Commission to adjudicate all American Indian tribes' outstanding claims against the federal government. The California tribes submitted claims for 64.4 million acres, and eventually a compromise settlement was reached that awarded the Indians about $46 million. Each qualified Indian received a per capita payment of $668.51.[59]

Determining who was eligible for these two payments was not a straightforward matter. Each Native claimant had to prove descent from an Indian who was alive in 1852, a difficult task given the turmoil of the period and the inadequacy of vital statistics for Indians. The problem of proving identity also plagued California Natives who were not residents of a reservation and whom the federal government did not officially recognize as Indians. Even though the federal government provided land and services for some of these Indians, it did so without formally recognizing them as members of any tribal entities. Consequently, many nonreservation California Indians are still seeking federal recognition as tribes for their communities so they will qualify for federal Indian programs.[60] Nor should it be assumed that reservation Indians are in quiet, uncontested possession of their lands. Litigation frequently forces tribal councils to use scanty reservation funds to defend reservation interests.[61] The contemporary struggles of California's Native peoples provide additional examples of the clouded legacy of the gold rush.

The dismal historical facts of the gold rush and the technical details of Indian policy tend to obscure the horrifying conditions of Native life in the nineteenth century. The majority went to early graves because of starvation, murderous assaults, and lethal diseases. The surviving minority were so impoverished and debilitated that they were unable to begin recovering their former population levels until the twentieth century. Though small in numbers, the Native people who survived the gold rush were real heroes of that turbulent time. Struggling against every imaginable obstacle, they somehow persevered, held families together, and maintained a sense of community. Their contribution to the gold rush legacy is not clouded but clear as day: Indians will be an enduring part of the California future, just as they have been an abiding part of the California past.

Notes

1. Frank Soulé, John H. Gihon, and James Nisbet, *Annals of San Francisco* (New York: D. Appleton, 1854), 666.

2. Bancroft, *History of California*, 7:474.

3. The treaty is cited in full in appendix 2, "The Treaty of Guadalupe Hidalgo, as Ratified by the United States and Mexican Governments, 1848," in Griswold del Castillo, *Treaty of Guadalupe Hidalgo*, 183–99. See also Ferdinand F. Fernandez, "Except a California Indian: A Study in Legal Discrimination," *Southern California Quarterly* 50 (June 1968): 169; Robert F. Heizer and Alan J. Almquist, *The Other Californians: Prejudice and Discrimination under Spain, Mexico, and the United States to 1920* (Berkeley: University of California Press, 1971), 96; Donald C. Cutter, "Clio and the California Indian Claims," *Journal of the West* 14 (October 1975): 40; Van Hastings Garner, "The Treaty of Guadalupe Hidalgo and the California Indians," *Indian Historian* 9 (winter 1976): 10–13; Albert L. Hurtado, *Indian*

Survival on the California Frontier (New Haven: Yale University Press, 1988), 97–98; Griswold del Castillo, *Treaty of Guadalupe Hidalgo*, 69.

4. Francis Paul Prucha, *The Great Father: The United States Government and the American Indian,* 2 vols. (Lincoln: University of Nebraska Press, 1984), 2:681–86, 793–94.

5. In 1916 a California Indian sued Lake County for the right to vote on the basis that citizenship should have been conferred as a result of the treaty. The court found that the man was a citizen, but on different grounds. Albert L. Hurtado, "Herbert E. Bolton, Racism, and American History," *Pacific Historical Review* 62 (May 1993): 135–36.

6. W. W. Robinson, *Land in California: The Story of Mission Lands, Ranchos, Squatters, Mining Claims, Railroad Grants, Land Scrip, Homesteads* (Berkeley: University of California Press, 1948), 11–12; Samuel Trask Dana and Myron Krueger, *California Lands: Ownership, Use, and Management* (Washington DC: American Forestry Association, 1958), 35; Cutter, "Clio and the California Indian Claims," 38–41; Garner, "Treaty of Guadalupe Hidalgo," 10.

7. Chauncey Shafter Goodrich, "The Legal Status of the California Indian," *California Law Review* 14 (January 1926): 87; Robinson, *Land in California,* 13; Manuel Servín, "Secularization of the California Missions: A Reappraisal," *Southern California Quarterly* 47 (1965): 133–49; Daniel Garr, "Planning, Politics, and Plunder: The Missions and Indian Pueblos of Hispanic California," *Southern California Quarterly* 54 (1972): 291–312; Van Hastings Garner, "The Treaty of Guadalupe Hidalgo and the California Indians," *Indian Historian* 9 (winter 1976): 10–13.

8. Sherburne F. Cook and other scholars have argued that Franciscans used force to recruit neophytes. Franciscan historians and their supporters deny the charge. See Sherburne F. Cook, "Population Trends among the California Mission Indians," *Ibero-Americana* 17 (1940): 1–48; and "The Indian versus the Spanish Mission," *Ibero-Americana* 21 (1943): 1–194. These essays and others by Cook are reprinted in *The Conflict between the California Indians and White Civilization,* (Berkeley: University of California Press, 1976). See also Sherburne F. Cook and Woodrow Borah, *Essays in Population History,* 3 vols. (Berkeley: University of California Press, 1971–1979), 3:177–324; Robert F. Heizer, "Impact of Colonization on the Native California Societies," *Journal of San Diego History* 24 (winter 1978): 135, 136. The Franciscan critique of Cook's perspective is fully expressed in Francis F. Guest, O.F.M., "An Examination of the Thesis of S. F. Cook on the Forced Conversion of Indians in the California Missions," *Southern California Quarterly* 61 (spring 1979): 1–77; and Francis F. Guest, O.F.M., "Cultural Perspectives on California Mission Life," *Southern California Quarterly* 65 (spring 1983): 1–65.

9. Hurtado, *Indian Survival,* 24–54.

10. Prucha, *Great Father*, 1: 183–213.

11. Robert A. Trennert, *Alternative to Extinction: Federal Indian Policy and the Beginnings of the Reservation System, 1846–51* (Philadelphia: Temple University Press, 1975); Francis Paul Prucha, *American Indian Treaties: The History of a Political Anomaly* (Berkeley: University of California Press, 1994), 1–19.

12. Quoted in Prucha, *Great Father*, 1:47.

13. *U.S. Statutes at Large* 4 (1834): 729–38; Francis Paul Prucha, *American Indian Policy in the Formative Years: The Indian Trade and Intercourse Acts, 1790–1834* (Lincoln: University of Nebraska Press, 1970), 250–73.

14. John Porter Bloom "Territorial System," in Howard Lamar, ed., *The New Encyclopedia of the American West* (New Haven: Yale University Press, 1998), 1100–1102. For a discussion of political realities in the territorial system, see Kenneth N. Owens, "Pattern and Structure in Western Territorial Politics," in John Porter Bloom, ed., *The American Territorial System* (Athens: Ohio University Press, 1973), 161–79.

15. Eric Foner, *Free Soil, Free Labor, Free Men: The Ideology of the Republican Party before the Civil War* (New York: Oxford University Press, 1970).

16. For Mexican and foreigner population figures, see Bancroft, *History of California*, 5:643. On Native population, see Sherburne F. Cook, *The Population of the California Indians, 1769–1970* (Berkeley: University of California Press, 1976), 43, 44, 59, 65.

17. Charles D. Ferguson, *The Experiences of a Forty-Niner during Thirty-four Years Residence in California and Australia*, ed. Frederick T. Wallace (Cleveland OH: Williams Publishing, 1888), 105–6.

18. Hurtado, *Indian Survival*, 149–68.

19. Heizer, ed., *Destruction of the California Indians*, 11–39; Robert F. Heizer, ed., *They Were Only Diggers: A Collection of Articles from California Newspapers, 1851–1866, on Indian and White Relations* (Ramona CA: Ballena Press, 1974), 104–26.

20. Stephen Watts Kearny to John Sutter, April 7, 1847, and Kearny to Mariano Guadalupe Vallejo, April 14, 1847, letters sent by the governors and secretary of state of California, 1847–1848, National Archives Microfilm M182 (hereafter cited as M182).

21. James Rawls, "Gold Diggers: Indian Miners in the California Gold Rush," *California Historical Quarterly* 55 (spring 1976): 29–30; Bancroft, *History of California*, 6:33–35.

22. Sutter to George Mason, February 22, 1848, box 236, George McKinstry Collection, California State Library, Sacramento (hereafter cited as MKC).

23. The historic location of the Yalisumni community is in question. I follow Norman L. Wilson and Arlean H. Towne, "Nisenan," in Robert F. Heizer, ed., *Handbook of North American Indians*, vol. 8, *California* (Washington DC: Smithsonian Institution, 1978), 388, fig. 1. See also James A. Bennyhoff, *Ethnogeography of the Plains Miwok* (Davis CA: Center for Archaeological Research at Davis, 1977), 164, map 2; Alfred L. Kroeber, *Handbook of the Indians of California* (Berkeley: California Book Co., 1953), 394 and plate 37 (facing p. 446).

24. Mason to Sutter, March 5, 1848, M182.

25. James Buchanan to William V. Vorhies, October 7, 1848, 30th Cong., 2nd. sess., H. Doc. 1, serial 537, 48.

26. William Henry Ellison, *A Self-Governing Dominion: California, 1849–1860* (Berkeley: University of California Press, 1950), 22–77.

27. George W. Crawford to Bennett Riley, June 26, 1849, 31st Cong. 1st sess., H. Doc. 5, serial 569, 161.

28. Orlando Brown to Thomas Ewing, November 30, 1849, 31st Cong., 1st sess., H. Doc. 5, serial 570, 951–55. In 1852 Congress applied only those sections of the trade and intercourse acts to California that provided for the appointment of an Indian superintendent. See 32nd. Cong., 1st sess., *Congressional Globe*, vol. 24, pt. I, 447–48, 663–64.

29. John Walton Caughey, *Gold is the Cornerstone* (Berkeley: University of California Press, 1948), 6–16.

30. Mason to Brig. Gen. R. Jones, August 17, 1848, in *Message to the President. . . to the Two Houses of Congress . . .* , 30th Cong., 2nd sess., S. Doc. 1, serial 537, 60.

31. Mason to Jones, *Message to the President*, 56–64. See also Hurtado, *Indian Survival*, 103–4.

32. Johann August Sutter, "General Sutter's Diary," in Owens, ed., *John Sutter and a Wider West*, 21–22; agreement between William Dickey, John Bidwell, and George McKinstry, party of the first part, and Edward Kemble and T. H. Rolfe, party of the second part, August 7, 1848, MKC.

33. Lyman L. Palmer, *History of Napa and Lake Counties, California* (San Francisco: Slocum, Bowen, 1881), 49–62.

34. For Marshall's account, see Edward E. Dunbar, *The Romance of the Age; or the Discovery of Gold in California* (New York: D. Appleton & Co., 1867). See also George Frederick Parsons, *The Life and Adventures of James W. Marshall, the Discoverer of Gold in California*, ed. Ezra Dane (San Francisco: George Fields, 1935), 75–85; Gay, *James W. Marshall*, 255–62; Rawls, "Gold Diggers," 38–39.

35. Rawls, "Gold Diggers," 33–37; Hurtado, *Indian Survival*, 106–7.

36. For examples, see W. P. Crenshaw to Thomas J. Henley, December 16, 1854, Records of the Bureau of Indian Affairs, RG 75, Office of Indian Affairs, Letters Received, California Superintendency, 1849–1880, National Archives Microfilm Publication M234, reel 33 (hereafter cited as M234:reel number); Sutter to Thomas J. Henley, February 9, 1856, M234:35; Beilharz and López, *We Were Forty-Niners!* 52.

37. D. C. Goddard to A. S. Loughery, March 22, 1849, and T. Ewing to Orlando Brown, November 17, 1849, M234:32; George Crawford to Bennett Riley, August 24, 1849, *Annual Report of the Commissioner of Indian Affairs*, 1849, 31st Cong., 2nd sess., S. Doc. 5, serial 569, 166; and Bennett Riley to R. Jones, August 30, 1849, 31st Cong., 2nd sess., S. Doc. 5, serial 569, 170–71.

38. *Statutes of California*, chapter 133; *Statutes of California*, chapter 231.

39. Thomas J. Henley to J. W. Denver, November 30, 1857, M234:35.

40. For a sampling of accounts of California lynching, see Hubert Howe Bancroft, *Popular Tribunals*, 2 vols. (San Francisco: History Company, 1887). The best modern analysis of mob violence and vigilantism in California and the West is Richard Maxwell Brown, *Strain of Violence: Historical Studies of American Violence and Vigilantism* (New York: Oxford University Press, 1975).

41. For collections of documents concerning this issue, see Heizer, *Destruction of the California Indians*, 219–41; Heizer, ed., *They Were Only Diggers*, 1–3.

42. George Harwood Phillips, "Indians in Los Angeles, 1781–1875: Economic Integration, Social Disintegration," *Pacific Historical Review* 69 (1980): 427–51. Robert F. Heizer and Alan Almquist reviewed the Humboldt County indenture records in *The Other Californians*, 51–58.

43. "Message to the California State Legislature," January 7, 1851, *California State Senate Journal*, 1851, 15.

44. "Account Book," Indian War Papers, California State Archives, Sacramento; *Statutes of California*, 1851, chapter 125; Joseph Ellison, *California and the Nation, 1850–1869: A Case Study of the Relations of a Frontier Community with the Federal Government* (Berkeley: University of California Press, 1927), 97–102.

45. Prucha, *Great Father*, 1:183–213.

46. *U.S. Statutes at Large*, 9:519–58; A. H. H. Stuart to the Commissioner of Indian Affairs, October 9, 1850, M234:32; Harry Kelsey, "The California Indian Treaty Myth," *Southern California Quarterly* 55 (fall 1973): 225–38.

47. Prucha, *American Indian Treaties*, 243–46; Kelsey, "California Indian Treaty Myth," 230–31; Phillips, *Indians and Indian Agents*, 73–76, 92–94. The treaties are printed in Charles J. Kappler, comp., *Indian Affairs: Laws and Treaties*, 5 vols., (Washington DC: GPO, 1904–1941), 4:1081–128.

48. "Report of the Special Committee to Inquire into the Treaties Made by the United States Indian Commissioners in California," *California State Senate Journal,* 1852, 600–4; "Report of the Special Committee to Inquire into the Treaties Made by the United States Indian Commissioners in California," *California State Assembly Journal,* 1852, 202–5; "Report of the Special Committee on the Disposal of Public Lands in California," *California State Senate Journal,* 1852, 575–88.

49. Kelsey, "California Indian Treaty Myth," 231–32.

50. See, for example, the arguments of California Senator John B. Weller, 32nd. Cong., 1st sess., *Congressional Globe* 26, pt. III, 2172–81. Senator Weller was also concerned with preventing the suffering of contractors who had supplied beef to Indians on the short-lived reservations.

51. Beale to Luke Lea, September 16 and 30, 1852, M234:32; Beale to Lea, October 29, 1852, M234:32; Beale to Lea, December 14, 1852, M234:32. Beale is perhaps most famous in public imagination as the commander of the first U.S. Army camel corps that trekked across the Southwest. See Stephen Bonsal, *Edward Fitzgerald Beale: A Pioneer in the Path of Empire, 1822–1903* (New York: G. P. Putnam's Sons, 1912); and Gerald Thompson, *Edward F. Beale and the American West* (Albuquerque: University of New Mexico Press, 1983).

52. See Lynwood Carranco and Estle Beard, *Genocide and Vendetta: The Round Valley Wars of Northern California* (Norman: University of Oklahoma Press, 1981), 77–78, 84–97; William F. Strobridge, *Regulars in the Redwoods: The U.S. Army in Northern California, 1852–1861* (Spokane WA: Arthur H. Clark, 1994), 99–107, 139–60, 183–210, 247–48. For documentary accounts of reservation matters in this period, see Heizer, *Destruction of the California Indians,* 102–73.

53. J. Ross Browne, "Letter on the Condition of Indian Reservations in California," M234:35; G. Bailey to C. E. Mix, November 4, 1858, M234:36.

54. G. Bailey to C. E. Mix, November 4, 1858, M234:36.

55. Hurtado, *Indian Survival,* 150–53.

56. Dole quoted in Oscar H. Lipps, *The Case of the California Indians* (Chemawa OR: U.S. Indian School Print Shop, 1932), 5.

57. Edward D. Castillo, "The Impact of Euro-American Exploration and Settlement," in Heizer, *Handbook,* 8:122–23; George H. Phillips, *The Enduring Struggle: Indians in California History* (San Francisco: Boyd & Fraser, 1981), 67–69. I use Phillips's figures. Castillo states that "36 rancherias voted to terminate . . . which resulted in the loss of 5,000 acres of trust property" (123).

58. Kenneth M. Johnson, *K-344, or the Indians vs. the United States* (Los Angeles: Dawson's Book Shop, 1966), 58–59, 62–65; Omer Stewart, "Litigation and Its Effects," in Heizer, *Handbook,* 8:706–7.

59. Phillips, *Enduring Struggle*, 70; Omer Stewart, "Litigation and Its Effects," 8:707–8; Edward D. Castillo, "Twentieth-Century Secular Movements," in Heizer, ed., *Handbook,* 8:716–17. The belated attempts to write the debt to California Indians off of the ledger books did not come close to compensating for the disgraceful assaults on Indian life and property during the gold rush era. Certainly, no monetary payment could restore the Indian communities that the gold rush obliterated for all time.

60. Allogan Slagle, "Unfinished Justice: Completing the Restoration and Acknowledgment of California Indian Tribes," *American Indian Quarterly* 13 (fall 1989): 331.

61. Dan McGovern, *The Campo Indian Landfill War: The Fight for Gold in California's Garbage* (Norman: University of Oklahoma Press, 1995) shows how complicated reservation development can become.

5

"My Brother's Keeper"

Mexicans and the Hunt for Prosperity

in California, 1848–2000

Michael J. Gonzalez

Then the Lord said to Cain, "Where is your brother?"–Genesis 4:9

In California today, like long ago in the gold fields and mines of northern California, some Americans do not welcome the Mexican immigrants. Here, as in other parts of the nation, some citizens view the Mexican immigrant, not as a kindred spirit, but as a stranger or, for the most paranoid and xenophobic, as an invader bent on conquest. When Ernesto Zedillo, the president of Mexico, visited California in the spring of 1999, various people saw the trip as proof of Mexico's wish to reclaim lands lost in 1848. Glenn Spencer, president of a group named Voices of Citizens Together, told the Los Angeles Times, "This [visit] is a victory parade by the Mexican president through a conquered California."[1] Smile we may at the logic, but the fevered, nativist imagination draws on scenarios that may give pause to more sober minds.

The growing demographic importance of immigrants from Mexico and their descendants cannot be disputed. According to the United States Census Bureau, José is the most popular name given boys in California. By 2040, a time not too far away, demographers predict that 48 percent of California's populace will be Spanish surnamed, most of them Mexican nationals or Mexican Americans. Anglo-Americans, meanwhile, will shrink to 31 percent of the state's total population.[2] George Skelton, political columnist for the *Los Angeles Times*, notes that since 1994, Spanish-surnamed citizens have made up 85 percent of all new registered voters in

California.[3] The top two FM radio stations in Los Angeles in 1999 were stations broadcasting Mexican music. At the Universal Amphitheater, a venue for musical performances, also in Los Angeles, 40 percent of the shows featured Mexican singers or bands in 1998.[4] But one suspects that, even if current or future trends do not hold, individuals like Mr. Spencer will continue to feel alarm.

To help understand why Mexican newcomers raise such concerns, we should return to the gold rush and examine the first conflicts between Mexicans and Anglo-Americans. The controversies in the diggings may show why disputes and suspicions persist to modern times. Of course, a critic might ask whether we belabor the obvious. Disputes over language, concerns about culture, the particular way one group conducted itself as compared with the other, suspicions even about skin color could suffice as reasons for present-day animosity and division. Perhaps so, but we speculate that on some occasions similarities, not differences, historically separated many Americans from their Mexican compatriots.

The lessons presented by the gold rush require that miners from all backgrounds speak, but usually the only voice ringing forth from the diggings belongs to the Anglo Argonauts. In an outpouring of books, journals, and letters that in volume ranks behind only the literary efforts of the Civil War, the Anglo miners so vilified Spanish speakers that modern readers may think that the Mexicans and Latin Americans deserved contempt.[5] Of course, some individuals from south of the border gave good cause for alarm when, to satisfy a grudge or make a quick profit, they attacked and cheated American miners. As we will see, however, most Spanish speakers had honorable intentions, and they seemed no different from the Anglo Argonauts who prized hard work or respected the law. Unfortunately, we have little surviving evidence to describe the virtues cherished by the Mexicans and Latin Americans. It may be that the Spanish-speaking miners lacked the Argonaut resolve to compose detailed letters or memoirs about their California adventures. Or, if the Mexicans and Latin Americans did commit their thoughts to paper—and certainly no proof argues decisively either way—few of their accounts have survived to the present.

Those accounts that qualify as Mexican or Latin American testaments leave an incomplete record. One, Antonio Coronel's reminiscence, is a dictation transcribed by Thomas Savage in 1877. Composed by a prominent resident of Los Angeles, this piece only speaks briefly of the diggings and may suffer from the tricks that time plays on memory.[6] Another source, the official complaints Mexican diplomats fired off to their American counterparts about Anglo Argonaut outrages, comprises only a few letters and provides scant description of the miners who faced Yankee insults.[7] Newspapers could present Mexican and Latin American views, but any Spanish-language daily or weekly that might have flourished in the gold fields probably was short-lived and left no copies for study.[8]

As a consequence of this sparse Hispanic documentation, curiously enough, to retrieve the Spanish speakers' legacy we must rely on the writings of hostile observers. We can only guess that when the Anglo Argonauts persisted in seeing Hispanic troublemakers, they described those whom they thought they saw rather than those who actually walked before them. By picking through Yankee descriptions, we will determine what is true or, better, what is false, about each charge hurled against the Mexicans and Latin Americans. After the accusations undergo scrutiny, falsehood will fall away and reveal the Hispanic qualities that inspired Yankees to see scoundrels rather than industrious miners. California's modern ethnic hostilities stand ripe for fresh analysis, but first we go to the nineteenth century. On to the mines!

Mexican and Latin American Invaders

We can quickly dispense with the first canard that the Spanish speakers followed some sinister design. In the nineteenth century, many observers imagined that Mexicans and Latin Americans poured across the border to push their Anglo rivals out of the diggings. Early in the gold rush, Argonauts repeated tales that in Mexico "whole battalions" prepared for a march north, shouting "California's recovery or death."[9] Other observers may not have thought they had glimpsed advancing armies, but they conveyed the impression that Spanish speakers inundated California. During the debate on the state constitution in 1849, a delegate complained that among all the world's desperadoes who headed to California, the "refuse of the population from Chile, Peru, and Mexico" threatened the most trouble.[10] In the same year, an Anglo Argonaut counted "8000 Mexicans . . . [who] drive our people before them."[11] Meanwhile, the French consul at Monterey reflected the mood of the times by saying that Mexicans swarmed through the countryside. He observed that "ten thousand people from Sonora and Lower California passed within a few leagues of Monterey and more kept on coming."[12] Apparently, the huge number estimated by the diplomat was a popular figure. Thomas Butler King, in a report to the secretary of state in 1850, saw "ten thousand Mexicans" at the Sonora mining camp.[13] At the same time, a witness in Los Angeles counted, "ten thousand [Mexicans passing] through the city to the mines."[14]

The presence of an unfamiliar people excited speculation that war was imminent. If any Spanish speaker walked proudly or showed temper, anxious Yankees exaggerated the displays and expected that after defiance would come attack. For instance, J. D. B. Stillman, riding through camps apparently filled with Mexicans thrilled to mine, feared that the inhabitants wanted to make trouble. He worried in 1850 that "there are not enough Americans to hold the country which is in a state of anarchy."[15] During the confrontations sparked by the Foreign Miners Tax in 1850, a measure discussed later in this essay, agents who tried to collect the tax sometimes packed weapons or sought escorts when they heard stories that "uprisings" brewed in Mexican settlements. In the Sonora mining camp, a "collector of license" called for protection when he faced "hundreds of Mexicans and Chileans" who brandished guns or used threatening language to show their displeasure.[16] Later in 1851, other conflicts brought more reports of upheaval. After a lynch mob strung up Mexicans accused of stealing, rumors spread that the victims' friends would seek revenge by murdering all Americans in the Indian Gulch mining camp.[17]

Though rebellion did not convulse the diggings, in Los Angeles the threat of war turned real. In 1856, during the waning years of the gold rush, the Spanish-speaking populace rose up to protest the lenient sentences local judges gave to Anglos accused of killing Mexicans and Californios. During one case when the city sheriff awaited trial for gunning down yet one more victim, Mexican and Californio horsemen—"six hundred strong," remembered one observer—rode on the jail to seize the suspect and leave him swinging from the tallest tree.[18] The attack failed, but Anglo residents found safety on hilltops as riders tore through the city. During these tense times in Los Angeles, Judge Benjamin Hayes ordered the hanging of Mexican bandits to discourage any others who displayed "too many signs of hostility."[19]

Save for the upheaval in Los Angeles, which, as we will see, hardly resembled the Armageddon imagined by Yankee doomsayers, the outbursts attributed to Spanish-speaking insurrectionists did not culminate in full-blown, blood-dimmed attacks. One can sense how hearts raced when Hispanics (occasionally) robbed Yankees or cocked guns to answer a challenge. Yet when reason is applied, the portrait of angry rebels dissolves to the more sober description of a people who lacked the numbers to challenge massing Argonauts.[20]

Admittedly, the documentation that absolves the Spanish speakers sometimes lacks accuracy. The 1850 census, for instance, is a flawed instrument that failed to count the state's residents accurately. But, when used carefully, the census and other sources suggest that the Hispanic population did not in fact resemble the vast multitude that frightened the Yankees. The evidence reveals that nearly sixty-five hundred Mexicans inhabited the state in 1850.[21] Some may have lived in California prior to the American invasion, but others came north at the first mention of gold. Many came from the Mexican state of Sonora, which explains why most Anglo-Americans called the Mexican miners Sonorans. But historian J. M. Guinn added that large contingents also hailed from Baja, or Lower, California, Sinaloa, and Durango. Most Mexicans arrived in the spring, before the summer sun, and returned home in the fall to beat the cold.[22] Come next season, the migrants saddled up again for another trip north. Also in 1850, surveyors counted more than six thousand Californios, individuals born in the state when it was a Spanish or Mexican province. Next came nearly sixteen hundred Central and South Americans, with Chileans, followed by Peruvians, figuring as the largest contingent.[23]

When these migrants landed in San Francisco's harbor or made their way overland from Mexico, their growing presence could have multiplied menacingly in Yankee eyes. Yet, save for migrations to and from the mines, the Mexicans and Latin Americans probably looked less like a marauding force than a people who desired the permanence of home. A good number of Spanish speakers settled in San Francisco or Los Angeles, so much so that their population in each city supported newspapers and civic organizations.[24] When many more traveled to the diggings, they preferred the region south of the Mokelumne River and established camps like Hornitos or Sonora. In sum, the Spanish-speaking populace was large, but for Mexican and Californio miners, it was the Americans who resembled invaders. By 1850, sixty-four thousand Americans flocked to California, nearly four times the number of Spanish speakers. Two years later, a new and supposedly more accurate census showed little increase in the population of Mexicans and Latin Americans, while the Americans swelled to almost a quarter of a million.[25]

A state overrun with Yankees could dispirit the most ardent non-Anglo rebel—that is, potential rebel, if any existed. If additional convincing was needed, more heartfelt, intimate reasons gave Hispanics good cause to keep the peace. Since Spanish speakers brought their wives and children to California, it was unlikely that they would expose their families to violence. Admittedly, with no full study examining how the gold rush affected the Hispanic family, it requires creative thinking to reconstruct the personal ties of Mexican and Latin American miners. Enough material exists, however, to suggest reasonable presumptions. There seemed to be enough women to encourage a modest population of husbands and toddlers. The *Alta California*, an English-language newspaper published in San Francisco, estimated that between January and April 1849, 205 Hispanic women, including 70 from Chile and 57 from Mexico, came through the Golden Gate. Though dwarfed in number by the nearly 5600 men from the world over who landed during the same period, these ladies from south of the border outnumbered the 38 non-Hispanic women who likewise arrived by sea in San Francisco. A newspaper's estimate hardly proves that many women arrived at other times. But according to some observers, who admittedly used measures no more accurate than their own judgment, the southern diggings consistently held a high proportion of Hispanic women. William Perkins, a merchant who set up shop in the gold fields around 1850, noted that Mexican and Latin American women "probably" made the Sonora mining camp "the only place in California where the gentler sex could be found."[26]

This evidence prompts a few further suppositions. Some Spanish-speaking women headed to California without a spouse or a male partner. Apparently, a fair number—precisely how many we do not know—came to find their fortunes as saloon keepers, gamblers, or entertainers. One such woman, noted Perkins, was "Madame Abalos, ex-Prima Donna at the opera house in Mexico," who, accompanied by her adolescent daughter, delighted miners with her voice. The forty-year-old singer apparently bore a few more wrinkles and pounds than he liked, but Perkins confessed he still found her "an imposingly handsome woman."[27] Certainly, bold women found freedom and prosperity in the diggings. Yet, with many reared in the patriarchal, traditional ways of their native lands, most women probably lacked the daring of their independent sisters. For the sake of love or duty, they followed their Spanish-speaking companions and husbands to California.[28]

With women, came children, and as these intimates gathered in the diggings, mining's drudgeries would lift, if only briefly. Though families could have been a common sight in Hispanic camps, witnesses rarely commented on how relatives altered a gold hunter's life. The French consul at Monterey simply noted that children accompanied their Mexican parents to the mines.[29] In an aside, William Perkins observed that Mexican wives, some with infants, waited in camp while their husbands hiked into the Sierra to dig.[30] From such bare testimony, one can only imagine the tender feelings or emotions that bound miners to loved ones. Perhaps after the miner suffered through a long stretch of digging and shoveling, a child's smile could be a treasure. Wives no doubt cooked, cleaned, and warmed the miner's bed. If the husband's fortunes dimmed, the woman could try supplementing the family income. Antonio Coronel recalled, for instance, that the wife of one of his employees helped her spouse by selling tortillas.[31] The responsibility of supporting a wife and children could become a burden. When claims ran dry, money grew scarce, and tension ruined one's disposition, trouble might arise. William Perkins reported that once in a while a Mexican miner would ignore his family and drink to excess. He did not speculate about why the husband found comfort in a bottle, but in the risky, fickle world of digging, not even loved ones could always bring joy.[32]

These accounts imply that with women and children living in Spanish-speaking camps, fathers or husbands would fear for their loved ones if fighting broke out. Many reports show that even when Spanish-speaking miners possessed the numbers and firepower to fight off the Yankee foe, they displayed restraint. Witnesses in the diggings did not mention that wives and children cooled fiery spirits, but in a camp populated with family members, perhaps one can see why some Spanish speakers shunned all thoughts of violence. During a dispute on the Little Mariposa River in 1851, nine Mexican miners abandoned their claims to eight Americans.[33] The year before at the Sonora mining camp, when supposedly hundreds of Mexicans and Chileans challenged the collector of the Foreign Miners Tax, the angry populace chose to leave the area rather than fight the Anglo Americans.[34] After horsemen tried to hang the wayward sheriff in Los Angeles, they fired on the cell where sat their enemy, but did not carry the fight to Yankee families cowering on nearby hills. Though Anglo nerves certainly jangled at every rumor of insurrection, Spanish speakers showed little fervor for starting fights that could push wives or children into harm's way. It was easier to mine. For more than a few Argonauts, their insistence on magnifying isolated attacks by Mexicans or Latin Americans suggested that they feared the worst concerning their Spanish-speaking counterparts. If parents clutching children became confused with rebels, then little else could bring calm when Anglo Argonauts claimed other dangers lurked in Mexican and Latin American camps.

Black Mexicans and Latin Americans

The Mexican reputation, and to a degree that of the Latin American, declined further when each supposedly undermined the Anglo Argonaut's freedom. In the early nineteenth century, many American miners were reared in the tradition of the independent producer in which farmers or artisans largely depended on themselves to turn a profit.[35] Yet in the East and the Midwest, and apparently in the California diggings, changes in the American economy threatened traditional ways to reach success. The factory appeared with its retinue of wage laborers, bringing a potential to produce goods more cheaply than the artisan could. Meanwhile, on the farm, any cultivator who did not invest in reapers or effectively market his produce also faced hardship. In time, commentators, among them Abraham Lincoln, worried that craftsmen who failed to compete or farmers who went bust would toil for factory owners.[36] Like black chattel, a factory employee could face a lifetime of laboring for a taskmaster. Even more alarming for color-conscious Anglo-Americans, the work floor's chores suggested that neither skill, status, nor complexion could distinguish the white laboring man from his black counterpart in the South. In California, the Anglo Argonauts experienced psychic stress related to maintaining race and class distinctions when they beheld their Hispanic rivals employing workers to extract gold. Though a gold field swarming with work crews seemed far removed from a factory, an overseer exhorting laborers could be likened to the industrial regimens threatening to enslave American craftsmen or farmers. Apparently, in the opinion of some Argonauts, the men who worked for Mexican or Latin American entrepreneurs threatened to push the Anglo miner into servitude. At the same time, the struggling, gasping man sweating for pennies resembled the hated African American.[37]

Still, the Spanish-speaking practice of mustering cheap labor seemed far removed from the Southern habit of putting the lash to chattel. Work could certainly turn harsh, and a boss's threats could wreck the spirit, but the free Hispanic worker's most meager incentive exceeded many privileges granted to slaves. At the outset of the gold rush, Mexican and Chilean entrepreneurs hired their poor countrymen or Indians to work the mines.[38] The crews ranged from two to thirty men who labored for various rewards. Occasionally, the employees, called peons by Anglo-Americans—although Spanish speaker preferred the term sirvientes (servants)—received advances in money or supplies.[39] To repay the debt, all gold dust found by the workers went to the employer until they squared accounts. It is possible, however, that the debt could be so onerous that the laborers' length of service could remind onlookers of bondage. Yet, the workers rarely labored in perpetuity for a boss. When Mexican or Chilean patrones (bosses) returned home after making their fortunes or going bust, their employees were free to strike out on their own or seek a place with a new crew.[40] As an alternative working arrangement, some employers allowed workers to keep a portion of the gold they pulled from the mines. The amount usually varied—the boss enjoyed the biggest share—but such a share agreement could allow the miner to collect modest winnings.[41]

Initially, the reports of wage labor in the mines did not brighten American hopes. Commentators in the East predicted that men toiling for a pittance would supplant skilled workers, while similar warnings resounded in the diggings when Hispanic bosses called on peons to mine. During the debate over the state constitution, a convention delegate envisioned Yankee miners shoved into poverty because "Mexican peons, or any other class of that kind, degrades white labor."[42] Colonel James J. Ayers remembered how his Argonaut companions feared that Chileans "and their peones" would leave little work in the gold fields.[43] Another Anglo Argonaut, Hinton Helper, recalled that during his time in the mines, Americans feared they could not compete against the cheap labor of Mexican peons.[44] The association narrowed further over time until all distinctions vanished; although Chileans, Peruvians, and Indians labored for others, peons took on the look and habits of Mexicans, the largest mass of foreigners in the mines. Some Americans went one step further; for them, all Mexicans, rich and poor, the farmer, the merchant, the miner in the diggings, seemed little removed from peons.[45]

Unpleasant images intensified when the peons' dark skin, supposed ignorance, and servitude reminded observers of African American slaves. J. M. Guinn, writing years after the gold rush, related the descriptions that could prompt Argonauts to confuse blacks with Mexicans. "The Mexican peon," related Guinn, "wore a cotton shirt, white pantaloons, sandals, and a sombrero."[46] With the slightest alteration, such details provided the stuff for convenient connections. The sombrero shrinks to a straw hat; sandals transmogrify into bare feet or work shoes; and the complexion deepens in hue to reveal, not the peon, but the black slave.

These associations reached climax when Anglo Argonaut complaints about the peon's character hinted at Negrophobia. Throughout the nineteenth century, many Anglo-Americans dreaded the thought of blacks bedding down with whites. The fruit of such unions, according to popular racial doctrines, would inherit only the worst traits of each parent. When not consumed by desire, the blacks turned to other pleasures, and, as especially suspected by white southerners, they preferred drinking or throwing dice to work.[47] After the Argonauts trooped to California's diggings, antiblack sentiment flared up when Americans observed Mexicans. The mestizo (Spanish and Indian) heritage of the Mexicans only echoed the forbidden union between whites and blacks. When Mexicans organized fiestas or set up a game of cards, their public frivolity possibly reminded Argonauts of black people's supposed preference for good times. A distaste for Mexicans prompted so many reminders of black misconduct that condemnations against one group intertwined with critiques of the other. In a summation any Anglo-American could have uttered, William Perkins held forth against the objects of his revulsion. If one blocked out the name, there would be doubt about who excited his wrath. The Mexican, or just as well the African American, said Perkins, was "cruel, revengeful, sanguinary, and cowardly."[48]

This association of peon and slave, Mexican and African American, gave rise to more sensational images. If cheap labor triumphed in the mines, displaced Anglo-Americans requiring wages would need to work alongside Mexican social dregs. Though the portrait of a miner's decline rarely appeared in clear and vivid terms, there can be little doubt about why Argonauts disliked Mexicans. The spectacle of white man and peon languishing together dramatized the fear that once the Yankees sank in status, there would be nothing to stop them from becoming slaves. Of course, white Americans could never fall into permanent bondage. Nevertheless, the enthusiasm with which Americans linked Mexicans and blacks suggested that for many, the peons' resemblance to slaves foreshadowed the doom of the independent miner. Early in the gold rush, an Anglo veteran of the war with Mexico declared, "A Mexican is pretty near black. I hate all Mexicans."[49] Later Dame Shirley, one of the few women to chronicle the gold rush, complained "Of the Spaniards (i.e.: Mexicans) Oh! They are all half-crazed black men."[50] During the debate over the state constitution, a delegate observed that "Africans" looked like Mexicans.[51] In the twilight of the gold rush, President Buchanan picked up the refrain of his constituents and explained that Mexicans were descended from "blacks and Indians." (In an editorial, a Mexican journalist reassured his Los Angeles readers that their lineage was whiter than assumed by the chief executive.)[52]

Needless to say, the Anglo Argonauts used laborers whose responsibilities and work conditions compared with those of Mexican peons. Because Americans predominated in the diggings and usually possessed the sums to fund any endeavor beyond picking and panning, many work crews looked to Yankee supervisors. Indians, Spanish speakers, and Americans who contracted their services certainly received different treatment, but their deference to bosses and sometime their social and economic impotence accorded with Argonaut perceptions of peons or cheap labor. Though the growth of a servile class compromised the ideals of the independent miner, many Anglo Americans hired Hispanic work crews in the hunt for precious metal while condemning Mexicans or Chileans for similar practices. In time, the suspicions that hired work crews would drive Americans first into poverty, then into bondage, faded before the Argonaut urge to make money digging with just such a labor force.

Prior to 1850, the demand for workers swept up the abject and helpless. Historian Sherburne Cook relates that initially many Americans called on Indians to find gold. Following routines that paralleled Mexican custom, Anglo Argonauts advanced goods or money to the Native Californians or allowed them to keep shares of gold dust. One Indian crew handed over "275 pounds of gold," while another found "many thousands worth of dust" for Yankee employers.[53] After 1850, war and disease thinned Indian ranks, frustrating new Argonauts who desired the same kind of cheap labor that had benefited their predecessors. Alternative proposals soon circulated. Miners from the American South entertained thoughts of taking slaves to the diggings, but when the state constitution outlawed bondage, some speculated that Mexicans would do in the place of chattel. Thomas Jefferson Green, a state senator who had come from Texas, authored the Foreign Miners Tax to create the advantages of slavery for his constituents. He intended that foreigners would need to buy a license, or what he called a "pass permit," to work in the mines.[54] Many foreigners, who, in 1850, figured to be Mexicans, would supposedly lack the funds to pay the twenty dollar fee each month. Some could head home, but an equal number might seek loans from Yankee miners.[55] Green's plan no doubt followed a slaveholder's logic. The accumulating costs of the license, the advances for food or clothes, and perhaps a gratuity to play dice or cards, would so bind worker to boss that slavery would result, if not in law, then in practice. But the measure failed to meet Green's expectations. The law eventually evolved into a decree to force Mexicans and other foreigners from the mines.[56] In California, welcoming and later expelling foreign workers is old sport.

Green spoke for many Americans who ignored the dangers others saw in cheap labor. After 1850, when gold digging turned more expensive, enterprising Anglo Argonauts hired any set of hands to wash away hillsides with hydraulic power or to build dams that might uncover rich veins in downstream riverbeds.[57] Sometimes workers in these operations came from Mexico or other parts of Latin America. J. D. Borthwick, a traveler in the southern mines, remembered that around 1850 he saw Mexicans working for Argonauts.[58] Other laborers certainly included Americans down on their luck. The historian Rodman Paul explained that broke Argonauts sometimes sought work from their more successful compatriots.[59] With various populations willing to shovel and dig for pay, it is possible that Anglo-Americans and Mexicans worked together. The pairing, if true, unveiled a sight whose faintest trace had triggered outrage and dire prophecies in other quarters. In the mines, however, teams of workers spread out beneath the gaze of Yankee overseers.

Mexicans and Latin Americans as Abel

We come to the end of the gold rush era story, but questions linger why Mexicans and other Spanish speakers so often troubled Anglo-Americans. Reports of rebellion rang false, and the Hispanic enthusiasm for fielding work crews seemed no more excessive than the American ardor for pressing laborers into service. The point, however, is not to dismiss Yankee fears about their rivals. Rather, Argonaut worries suggest that while many claims about the Spanish speakers' treachery seem inflated, the concerns gave shape to, and as a consequence, masked what most perplexed the Americans. It is worth wondering whether Anglo Argonauts recoiled when the virtues they claimed for themselves also shined forth from Mexicans and Latin Americans.

Yankee hubris had offered more comforting scenarios. In the mid-nineteenth century, the triumphant spirit of Manifest Destiny convinced Anglo-Americans that Providence made them one of the most industrious and valiant races in creation. The recent war with Mexico provided proof of heaven's favor, and in the diggings the Americans once more expected to push aside the Mexicans and enjoy success.[60] Yet, when the Mexicans and other Spanish speakers startled observers with their vigor and pluck, it dawned on Americans that they had met their equals.

Already some Anglo Argonauts admitted that they and the Spanish speakers shared a taste for scandalous conduct. William Perkins claimed that although "Mexicans are . . . fond of butchering white men," the Argonauts who retaliated committed a "greater aggregate of crime and outrage."[61] If not locked in death struggles, less contentious pastimes brought each group closer to the other. J. D. Borthwick recalled that the town of Mokelumne Hill "was a mixture of equal portions of French, Mexicans, and Americans." When the populace attended a bullfight, all blurred into a colorful mosaic. The amphitheater in which the contest was staged seemed filled "with a mass of bright flowers. The most conspicuous objects were the shirts of miners, red, white, and blue . . . among which appeared bearded faces under hats of every hue."[62] Perkins, in a diatribe about Mexican gambling, could not deny that Americans like all others buckled before forbidden activities. One evening, Perkins, who prided himself on being a "staid and sedate man," watched two Mexican women play monte, a popular card game.

Perhaps tired, or attracted to the women—once before he had sighed "for the enjoyment of a genial smile from a pretty face"—or even amazed by the riffle of the cards, Perkins approached the gambling table, eyed the women, and confessed, "I sat down."[63]

Other ties appeared as Anglo Argonauts noticed, sometimes with approval, that the Spanish speakers matched the Americans' reputed devotion to work and business. The Argonauts in the field may not have known that the Mexicans had collected five million dollars worth of gold by 1849. But the bags of dust Sonorans plunked down during card games or the silver saddles and stirrups they flashed in camps presented evidence that miners from south of the border possessed admirable skills.[64] Indeed, for Americans new to the mines, as Rodman Paul observed, "more than one Anglo-Saxon acquired his first knowledge of gold mining by working alongside a Chilean or Sonoran in the Sierra gold fields."[65] One lesson absorbed by the Americans certainly involved the patience and skill needed to extract gold. Before the pan became popular, Mexicans used the batea, an Indian basket of tightly woven reeds, to separate sediment from ore. They filled the basket with gravel, then submerged it in water. After removing the batea and allowing the liquid to filter out sand and dirt, the miners hoped to find gold dust sitting at the bottom. In the southern mines, where water was scarce, Sonorans tossed soil in serapes, letting the wind blow off dust and leave pay dirt behind. When the Mexicans suspected that gold veins were trapped in granite ore, they employed better tools. Tethering mules to a long spoke, which in turn was attached to a millstone, they led the animals around in a circle to crush rock into ore.[66]

Industrious Spanish speakers who preferred not to mine, or who had amassed enough winnings and looked for new ventures, sought fortunes in trade and retail. Mexicans and Chileans peddled all sorts of delights. The *Alta California*, the newspaper from San Francisco, ever keen on advertising Hispanic depravity, noted in 1849 that Mexican merchants made Sonora rank ahead of Stockton in "gold, girls, music, and gambling."[67] Meanwhile, Thomas Butler King noticed that more benign diversions in Sonora, such as "hotels, restaurants, stores and shops," crowded the center of town.[68] In the spring, added King, various confectioners in Sonora collected snow from the Sierra and made "ice cream [which added] to the numerous luxuries."[69] The Anglo-Americans, of course, ran many businesses, but in a community where King claimed to see ten thousand Mexicans, one can suppose who owned most of the establishments and provided the comforts. Over time, Sonora, Hornitos, and other large Spanish-speaking camps apparently evolved into emporia where smaller traders and merchants collected goods to hawk in the mines. Livestock could be one thing enterprising Mexicans purchased in town to sell elsewhere. Sonorans peddled ten thousand mules between 1848 and 1851, the prices ranging from $150 to $500 a head.[70] Food found on a Sonora or Hornitos shelf would never want for buyers in the diggings. Laden with delicacies, at least by mining standards, Mexican traders trooped from camp to camp, selling potatoes and onions for the gold hunters' mess.[71]

The initiative shared by Spanish speakers and Americans only emphasized how other matters had entwined the two groups. From the early nineteenth century up through 1847, Yankees who wooed Californio women converted to Catholicism and pledged loyalty to Mexico. The nuptials persisted after the war, this time without pledges to Rome or Mexico City, but now the ceremonies occasionally featured Californio or Mexican men taking Yankee brides down the aisle.[72] The rate of intermarriage is unknown, but sometimes love, not hatred, tied the Spanish speaker to an Anglo-American spouse. When lonely Argonauts fantasized about their ideal mates, some disparaged the Yankee women in California and admired Mexican or foreign "lovelies." William Perkins noted that it was "too much . . . for a man to prefer the lean arm of a bonneted, ugly, board shaped . . . descendent of the Puritans to the full figured, sprightly and elegant Spaniard or Frenchwoman."[73] Spanish speakers attracted the Yankee eye in other ways. Prior to statehood, Americans in some regions followed Mexican laws to settle property disputes or punish wayward citizens.[74] In southern California, where Californio and Mexican influence remained strong, the city council of Los Angeles conducted business in Spanish until 1850. After then, the municipal body translated the minutes into Spanish for a decade until English emerged as the sole language for city affairs.[75]

For Anglo-Americans who believed that divinity had anointed the United States for some grand purpose, any entanglement with dark, Catholic mestizos compromised the national calling. To respect Mexican mining skills or other Latin American attributes implied an equality that was inconsistent with Anglo-American belief in Manifest Destiny. For white Americans convinced of their inherent racial and cultural superiority, occupying the same level as Spanish-speaking prospectors represented a loss of power or status. If the Anglo lacked strength, he became weak and vulnerable. Recall that most tales about Mexican belligerence or the recruitment of captive labor emphasized the slaughter, exploitation, and punishment of Americans.[76] Though claims about Mexican malevolence often approached fantasy, they expressed the Anglo Argonaut worry about looking helpless before their foes. To recover their standing, many white

Americans tried to deny any hint of equality with the Spanish-speaking populace and asserted that they, not Mexicans or Latin Americans, dominated life in the mines. To bolster their conviction of their own superiority, they degraded the Spanish speakers to banish all thought that any similarity, much less equality, existed between the two groups.

In some American commentaries, the Sonoran and Chilean mining expertise, which many Argonauts copied and perhaps envied, amounted to little more than luck. Hinton Helper, for instance, observed that "these delving countrymen of Santa Anna always had the peculiar knack for finding gold."[77] Other times, observers dismissed Hispanic talents as a simpleton's devotion to drudgery. The *Alta California* theorized that Americans sometimes suffered hard times in the mines because they proved "unwilling to give up the pleasures of civilized life." The Mexicans, who presumably had little taste for refinement, seemed the only ones suited "to develop the dry diggings of the county."[78] A bit later, the *Stockton Times* explained that life in the mines agreed with Mexicans, "who were milder in spirit, more contented to endure, more willing to suffer."[79]

At different times violence emerged as one more way for Anglo-Americans to humiliate Hispanic rivals. At this point we must step carefully; the topic of violence can trip up the most deliberate scholar. It is important to note that Mexicans, among other Spanish speakers, proved quite skilled with the rifle and pistol. Before 1846, Mexicans and their Californio compatriots treated Indians roughly. Once Michael White, an English émigré who lived in Los Angeles during the Mexican period, protested the indiscriminate killing of Indians. His Spanish-speaking companions defended their actions, saying, "No es pecado a matar indios" (It is not a sin to kill Indians).[80] But, for our purposes, we focus on the gold rush and consider who delivered the hardest blows. Of course, in the diggings some Spanish speakers attacked Anglo Americans. But remember that many Mexicans and Latin Americans probably had families in tow, and few would take up arms. If any of them turned violent, in most instances it was probably to seek revenge. The story of Joaquin Murieta, though largely a fable, relates what may have been the career path of many criminals who took to the hills to avenge Yankee atrocities.[81] His wife ravaged by forty-niners (other stories describe different atrocities), Joaquin spent the remainder of his life attacking Americans, whose pain and spilt blood never satisfied the bandit's rage. Though many details about Joaquin's life seem to be more legend than fact, the tale's account of Argonaut assaults on Spanish speakers may contain a bit of truth.

The frequency and severity of Yankee violence requires that we remain cautious. Consider, for instance, that the Yankees sometimes hacked each other to pieces. Many used guns or knives, while more ravenous souls bit and clawed their fellow Argonauts.[82] It may be that Yankees murdered each other more often then they did Mexicans and Latin Americans.[83] Think though: while Anglo American miners no doubt lit into each other, some may have turned on those who lacked the numbers to fight off attacks. If lynching episodes provide an accurate gauge, the Spanish speakers, among many peoples of color, risked the greater chance of suffering violence. Between 1849 and 1853, more than one-third of all cases involving popular justice featured a nonwhite victim. Because Spanish speakers, blacks, and Chinese were present in comparatively small numbers in relation to white Argonauts, they suffered a higher proportion of California's lynchings.[84]

Of course, we could fill pages with descriptions of more violent episodes. But more important, consider the intent of Yankee kicks and punches. Maybe, in some way, the Argonauts severely beat their Spanish-speaking compatriots to reduce any similarity between the two groups. By 1849, the Anglo-Americans, using words, had twisted the Mexicans and Latin Americans into inhuman shape. Thomas Jefferson Green, a recent arrival from Texas, apparently thought Mexicans lower than insects. He once boasted that he could "maintain a better stomach at the killing of a Mexican than at the killing of a louse." During a debate on the California assembly floor, a representative, while not mentioning Mexicans by name, nevertheless left little doubt about who aroused his ire when he said that immigrants had an "intellect but one degree above the beast of the field, and [was] not susceptible to elevation."[85] When Anglo Argonauts attacked the Spanish-speaking populace, it is not known if epithets like Green's or the good representative's dropped from the assailants' lips, but the logic that cast Mexicans and Latin Americans as beasts certainly directed the blows rained down by white Americans. By examining the wounds left by attackers, it seems clear that if a mangled Mexican or Latin American shared no physical characteristics with Anglo Argonauts, then there would be little else the two groups would have in common. Mexicans who crossed Anglo Americans could suffer bashed heads; a wrong word or indiscreet look by a Sonoran would be sufficient cause for lynching; Chileans who offended white Argonauts had their ears sliced off; and any Spanish speaker who seemed too proud might receive a knife in the back or a bullet in the stomach.[86]

Violence, though, could reach beyond dismemberment. White Argonauts wrought havoc on the few dignities and comforts Hispanic miners could enjoy. As with bodily punishment, lost privileges made Hispanics less like Anglo-Americans. One witness related an account in which Yankee Argonauts sailing around the Horn refused to bunk with Peruvians and forced them to sleep on deck.[87] The Mexican chargé d'affaires to Washington complained that a Yankee magistrate in California took from a "Mexican his legitimate wife and gave her up to an American with whom she was intimate."[88] Meanwhile, there persisted the Anglo Argonaut habit of jumping Mexican claims. Antonio Coronel blamed the offense on white miners "burning with gold fever."[89] Prospector Charles Kirkpatrick concurred. Tired of mining, he and his companions forced an old Mexican from his "pile of dirt."[90] When the aggrieved miner demanded his rights, Kirkpatrick remembered that "all he could get out of us was for him to vamoose."[91]

The hostility directed at Mexican and Latin American miners can recur over time.[92] At present, large numbers of Mexicans and Latin Americans stream into California. Some citizens, sounding quite like the Anglo Argonauts who once claimed that Mexican scoundrels or invaders darkened the mines, insist that among the newcomers come drug dealers, welfare cheats, and vagabonds. As in the past, current reports of Mexican wrongdoing may obscure what really menaces the white American populace. In a land that celebrates the self-made individual, Mexican newcomers and other immigrants follow the national mania to labor until they reach prosperity. Unlike their predecessors from a century and a half ago, they have few special skills to impart, but their diligence makes them no different from the many American citizens who likewise work long and hard.

Pause now, and go deeper. A century and a half ago, the close, almost intimate ties between Americans and Mexicans troubled those who wished to preserve their superiority. In the present, we should inquire whether the same worry circulates once more. The Mexican may seem far removed from the average citizens' life, but we say think again. The Mexican immigrant picks our food or prepares it; he or she may wash our dishes or make our beds; and perhaps, for some citizens, it is a Mexican nanny who puts a child down at night. Could it be that the American citizen refuses to find fellowship with a dark stranger who, like any citizen, burns with an equal desire to succeed? Or who, in some cases, is closer, physically and spiritually, than many Anglo Americans would care to admit? Already, no less a force than the Republican Party of California has recognized the virtues of Mexican immigrants and their descendants. (Nor must we forget those Californians who have origins in other parts of Latin America.) During the election for governor in 1998, the supporters for Dan Lungren, the Republican candidate, posted signs in Spanish-speaking neighborhoods that read, *Adelante con Dan Lungren* (Forward with Dan Lungren).[93] In a move to impress the Spanish-surnamed electorate, Republicans in the state assembly briefly named Rod Pacheco, a Mexican American, as their leader.

Recently, three California ballot initiatives sought to place restrictions on immigration, a person's qualifications for a job, and the opportunity to hear the mother tongue at school.[94] Good, honest people supported the initiatives, and none would think the measures resembled the violence in the gold fields. Others would say that the initiatives had nothing to do with the increasing Mexican presence in California. But see the measures anew; at their core, the initiatives limited movement, livelihood, and language. Did not, in some way, the Spanish-speaking miners face similar challenges? Their freedom to seek their fortune in a peaceful manner fell under assault. Despite the distance imposed by time, past and present controversies merge: to denigrate the newcomers is one way to deny all ties. When an American and a Mexican immigrant eye one another, each may glimpse his or her own reflection. The resemblance, however, does not necessarily invite embrace. Certainly, the desire to perceive an intimate as foe is an old story. We need only recall Yahweh's question to Cain, "Where is your brother?" The question persists, and answers go begging.

Notes

1. *Los Angeles Times*, May 20, 1999, A3.

2. *Los Angeles Times*, December 18, 1998.

3. *Los Angeles Times*, May 23, 1999, A3.

4. *Los Angeles Times*, "A Life's Passion," May 22, 1999, A1, 14–16.

5. For a good overview of Anglo American opinions on Mexicans and Latin Americans, see Raymund Paredes, "The Mexican Image in American Travel Literature," *New Mexico Historical Review* 52, no. 1.

6. For more on Californio and Mexican *recuerdos*, or memoirs, see Genaro Padilla, *My History Not Yours: The Formation of Mexican American Autobiography* (Madison: University of Wisconsin Press, 1993); and Rosaura Sánchez, *Telling Identities: Californio Testimonios* (Minneapolis: University of Minnesota Press, 1995). Meanwhile, Coronel's account may be the only reminiscence that scholars have noticed.

7. William Manning, ed., *Diplomatic Correspondence of the United States and Mexico, 1848 (mid-year)–1860,* vol. 9 (Washington: Carnegie Endowment for Peace, 1937).

8. This is not to say that Spanish-language newspapers did not exist during the

gold rush era. Newspapers served the Spanish-speaking populations of California's cities. *La Cronica* appeared in San Francisco, while in Los Angeles the bilingual newspaper *La Estrella* proved a popular choice. Each paper is on microfilm in the Bancroft Library at the University of California, Berkeley. The file for each, however, is incomplete. Surviving copies do not always mention life in the gold fields.

9. For a bold view of the gold rush, see David Courtwright, *Violent Land: Single Men and Social Disorder from the Frontier to the Inner City* (Cambridge: Harvard University Press, 1996), 73–75.

10. J. Ross Browne, *Report of the Debates in the Convention of California on the Formation of the State Constitution in September and October, 1849* (Washington DC: 1850), 150.

11. Doris Wright, "Making of Cosmopolitan California," part 1, 325–26.

12. Wright, "Making of Cosmopolitan California," part 1, 324.

13. An excerpt from King's account is in *Three Years in California: William Perkins' Journal of Life in Sonora, 1849–1852,* ed. Dale Morgan and James Scobie (Berkeley: University of California Press, 1965), 33. The introduction by Morgan and Scobie contains analysis and commentary on life in the mines. For the full text, see the "Report of Hon. T. Butler King" in Taylor, *El Dorado,* 332–75.

14. Wright, "Making of Cosmopolitan California," part 1, 325. The witness used the word "Sonorans." We will examine the term shortly.

15. Wright, "Making of Cosmopolitan California," part 1, 325.

16. Robert Wilson, "special correspondent" for the *Alta California*, May 22, 1850, in Perkins, *Three Years in California,"* 37–38.

17. Susan Johnson, "Bulls, Bears, and Dancing Boys: Race, Gender, and Leisure in the California Gold Rush," *Radical History Review* 60, no. 3 (1994): 29.

18. Benjamin Hayes scrapbook, Deposition of Judge William Dryden, vol. 43, 584, 588, manuscript in the Bancroft Library. Dryden's observation may be inflated. For another view of the same incident, see Pitt, *Decline of the Californios,* 164–66.

19. Pitt, *Decline of the Californios,* 160.

20. For a good overview of Mexican and California bandits, see Joseph Henry Jackson's, introduction to *The Life and Adventures of Joaquin Murieta by John Rollin Ridge* (Norman: University of Oklahoma, 1955); also see Jackson's *Bad Company: The Story of California's Legendary and Actual State-Robbers, Bandits, Highwaymen and Outlaws from the Fifties to the Eighties* (Lincoln: University of Nebraska Press, 1939).

21. Wright, "Making of Cosmopolitan California," part 1, 325.

22. J. M. Guinn, "The Sonoran Migration," *Historical Society of Southern California Quarterly*, 8 (1909–1911): 31–33.

23. Wright, "Making of Cosmopolitan California," part 1, 324–25.

24. For more on Mexican life after California became part of the United States, see Richard Griswold del Castillo, *The Los Angeles Barrio, 1850–1890* (Berkeley: University of California Press, 1985).

25. Pitt, *Decline of the Californios*, 52–53.

26. Perkins, *Three Years in California*, 103–4.

27. Perkins, *Three Years in California*, 304.

28. Introduction to Perkins, *Three Years in California*, 29–30.

29. Wright, "Making of Cosmopolitan California," part 1, 325. For another view of wives and children accompanying miners to California, see Guinn, "Sonoran Migration," 32–33.

30. Perkins, *Three Years in California*, 103–4.

31. Antonio Franco Coronel, "Cosas de California" (1877), Bancroft Library, translated and published as "Tales of California" in *Foreigners in Their Native Land: Historical Roots of the Mexican Americans*, ed. David J. Weber (Albuquerque: University of New Mexico Press, 1973).

32. Perkins, *Three Years in California*, 103–4.

33. George Cosgrove, "A Diplomatic Incident on the Little Mariposa," *California Historical Quarterly*, 21 (December 1942): 357–59; Manuel Larrainzar, Mexican Minister to the United States, to William Macy, Secretary of State, May 3, 1853, in Manning, *Diplomatic Correspondence*, 569–70.

34. Pitt, *Decline of the Californios*, 55–58.

35. Rohrbough, *Days of Gold*, 1–20; Christopher Lasch, *Revolt of the Elite* (New York: W. W. Norton & Company, 1995), 50–79; Foner, *Free Soil, Free Labor, Free Men*.

36. Lasch cites Lincoln's comparison of wage laborers and black slaves, *Revolt of the Elite*, 68–69.

37. For more on the link between slavery and wage labor, see Ronald T. Takaki, *Iron Cages: Race and Culture in Nineteenth-Century America* (New York: Alfred A. Knopf, 1979), 108–44, 229–239. For a good discussion on the problem of race in United States history, see Barbara Fields, "Ideology and Race in American History,"

in *Region, Race, and Reconstruction*, ed. J. Morgan Kousser and James McPherson, (New York: Oxford University Press, 1982).

38. J. M. Guinn, "Sonoran Migration," 32–33; Paul, *California Gold,* 26–27; Leonard Pitt, "The Beginnings of Nativism in California," *Pacific Historical Review,* 30 (February 1961): 24. American anxieties about Mexican and Californio laboring practices had some foundation. Prominent Mexicans and Californios certainly directed Indian captives to dig for gold or tend to a camp's domestic duties. Antonio Coronel, for instance, used Indian prisoners from New Mexico to dig for ore along the Stanislaus River. See Coronel, "Tales of Mexican California," 54. Any outcry against forced labor could also confess discomfort with Anglo-American habits. White southerners sometimes brought their slaves to the gold fields, while miners from north and south of the Mason-Dixon line exploited Native Californians. For more information, see Rohrbough, *Days of Gold,* 211–15.

39. Coronel, "Tales of Mexican California," 54.

40. Pitt, "Beginnings of Nativism," 24.

41. Paul, *California Gold,* 26.

42. Browne, *Report of the Debates,* 143.

43. Colonel James J. Ayers, *Gold and Sunshine: Reminiscences of Early California* (Boston: Gorham Press, 1922) 46–49.

44. Hugh Bailey, *Hinton Rowan Helper: Abolitionist-Racist* (Tuscaloosa: University of Alabama Press, 1965), 135–37, 149.

45. In "The Mexican Image in American Travel Literature," Raymund Paredes deftly explains why many Anglo-Americans considered the Mexicans nothing more than peons. For a comparative view of how Anglo-Americans viewed Mexicans in Texas, see David Montejano, *Anglos and Mexicans in the Making of Texas, 1836–1986* (Austin: University of Texas Press, 1987).

46. J. M. Guinn, "Sonoran Migration," 32–33.

47. For more on Negrophobia, see George Frederickson, *The Black Image in the White Mind* (New York: Harper Torchbooks, 1971).

48. Perkins, *Three Years in California,* 222–23. In fairness, William Perkins was born in Canada, but his attitudes differed little from those expressed by his American friends.

49. In Richard Peterson, "Anti-Mexican Nativism in California, 1848–1853," *Historical Society of Southern California Quarterly,* 62, no. 4 (1980): 313.

50. Peterson, *"Anti-Mexican Nativism,"* 313.

51. Browne, *Report of the Debates,* 143.

52. *El Clamor Publico*, October 16, 1856, Chicano Studies Library, University of California, Berkeley, microfilm.

53. Sherburne Cook, "The American Invasion, 1848–1870" in *Conflict between the California Indians and White Civilization*, 318–20; and Heizer and Almquist, *Other Californians*, 23–64.

54. Pitt, *Decline of the Californios*, 59–60.

55. Pitt, *Decline of the Californios*, 59–60. As a point of interest, the first Foreign Miners Tax collected $33,147.47 between April 1850, and March 1851. William Finkhauser, *A Financial History of California* (Berkeley: University of California Press, 1913), 137.

56. Pitt, *Decline of the Californios,* 59–60.

57. Paul, *California Gold*, 50–68, 124–46; Rohrbough, *Days of Gold,* 197–215.

58. J. D. Borthwick, *The Gold Hunters: A First-Hand Picture of Life in California Mining Camps in the Early Fifties*, ed. Horace Kephart (Oyster Bay NY: Nelson Doubleday, 1917), 307.

59. Paul, *California Gold*, 118–20.

60. For a review of American attitudes toward Mexicans, see Takaki, *Iron Cages,* 147–70. For a discussion on the fragility of American triumphalism, see Carroll Smith-Rosenberg, *Disorderly Conduct: Visions of Gender in Victorian America* (New York: Oxford University Press, 1985) 90–108.

61. Perkins, *Three Years in California,* 167–68, 175.

62. Borthwick, *Gold Hunters,* 275.

63. Perkins, *Three Years in California*: "staid and sedate," 219; gambling Mexican women, 103.

64. Five million dollars, in the "Report of Hon. T. Butler King," 367 (as a point of interest, Peterson says that the Mexicans collected two million dollars. See "Anti-Mexican Nativism," 314); bags of gold, Coronel, "Tales of Mexican California," 55–56; saddles, Perkins, *Three Years in California*, 101.

65. Paul, *California Gold,* 48

66. For a discussion of Mexican technology, see Pitt, *Decline of the Californios*, 53–55.

67. Cited in Paul, *California Gold*, 110–12.

68. King's report cited in Paul, *Three Years in California*, 33.

69. Paul, *Three Years in California*, 33.

70. Pitt, *Decline of the Californios,* 57.

71. Johnson, "Bulls, Bears, and Dancing Boys," 21.

72. For example, Platon Vallejo, son of the illustrious Mariano, married an Anglo woman. We could fill pages describing the people who intermarried, but at the moment, an exact count is difficult to tabulate. Nevertheless, a Spanish-speaking woman marrying an Anglo-American was not rare; however, a Spanish-speaking man marrying an Anglo-American, though infrequent, did occur.

73. Johnson, "Bulls, Bears, and Dancing Boys," 22. Johnson's interpretation of the material differs from my own.

74. When the Americans assumed control of Los Angeles, they continued to observe the laws that the *ayuntamiento* passed years earlier to regulate the people's consumption of alcohol. See *Los Angeles Ayuntamiento Archives,* vol. 5 (n.d.): 270, and July 3, 1848, 211, Bancroft Library.

75. Personal communication with Hynda Rudd, assistant city clerk for the city of Los Angeles.

76. For a good view on violence, masculinity, and dominance, see Courtwright, *Violent Land;* and Richard C. Trexler, *Sex and Conquest: Gendered Violence, Political Order, and the Conquest of the Americas* (Ithaca: Cornell University Press, 1995).

77. Bailey, *Hinton Rowan Helper,* 12, 42.

78. Cited in Paul, *California Gold,* 112–13.

79. Cited in Pitt, *Decline of the Californios,* 76.

80. Michael White (Miguel Blanco to the Mexicans and the Californios), *California All the Way Back to 1842* (Los Angeles: Dawson's Book Shop, 1960), 86.

81. See the story of Joaquin Murieta in Joseph Jackson, *Bad Company.*

82. Courtwright, *Violent Land,* 74–75.

83. One good study that focuses on violence in the gold fields does not concentrate on the 1850s but rather studies the decades after the gold rush period: Roger Mc-Grath, *Gunfighters, Highwaymen, and Vigilantes: Violence on the Frontier* (Berkeley: University of California Press, 1984).

84. David Johnson, "Vigilance and the Law: The Moral Authority of Popular Justice in the Far West," *American Quarterly,* 33 (1988).

85. The remarks by Green and the legislator are in Pitt, "Beginnings of Nativism in California," 28, 27.

86. Smashed heads, shootings, and stabbings, Coronel, "Tales of Mexican California," 55–57; sliced ears and other brutality, Ayers, *Gold and Sunshine,* 46–49.

87. *New York Herald Tribune,* March 9, 1849, in Victor Berthold, *The Pioneer Steamer, California* (New York: Houghton Mifflin & Company, 1932) 38.

88. José Ramirez, minister of foreign affairs of Mexico, to Robert Fletcher, United States minister to Mexico, November 19, 1851, in *Diplomatic Correspondence,* 432–33.

89. Coronel, "Tales of Mexican California," 61.

90. Charles Kirkpatrick excerpt in Paul, *Three Years in California,* 32.

91. Paul, *Three Years in California,* 32.

92. When the gold rush subsided and mining no longer pitted Hispanics against Yankees, Anglo Argonaut anxiety about resembling Spanish-speaking miners diminished and the violence between the two groups waned. Injustice, however, continued into the twentieth century. At times, Mexican-American children went to segregated schools when local authorities did not welcome children of other races sitting next to white students. In the 1930s, officials in Los Angeles deported thousands of Mexicans and Mexican Americans, a prelude to the zoot-suit riots that convulsed the city a decade later. These wrongs, though hurtful, were not exclusive California phenomena. One need only consult Jim Crow laws or xenophobic riots elsewhere in the nation to see that California was not alone in social conflict. For Mexicans and Mexican Americans in twentieth-century California, see Rudy Acuña, *Occupied America: A History of Chicanos,* 3rd. ed. (New York: Harper & Row, 1988), school segregation, 236; deportations, 200–201; zoot-suit riots, 253–59. For other views, see George T. Sánchez, *Becoming Mexican American: Ethnicity, Culture, and Identity in Chicano Los Angeles, 1910–1945* (New York: Oxford University Press, 1993); and Mauricio Mazón, *The Zoot Suit Riots: The Psychology of Symbolic Annihilation* (Austin: University of Texas Press, 1984).

93. Personal observation by the author in the San Gabriel Valley, an area east of Los Angeles populated predominantly by Mexicans and Mexican Americans.

94. Proposition 187 restricted benefits to immigrants; Proposition 209 overturned affirmative action in state agencies; Proposition 227 limited bilingual education.

6

Never Far from Home

Being Chinese in the California Gold Rush

Sylvia Sun Minnick

In the great competition for California's gold, men from different nations pitted themselves against one another to obtain a relatively small amount of gold. Beyond doubt, the California gold rush was the most momentous single episode in the development of the American West. The Sutter's mill discovery set off changes that the annals of history will continue to describe as perhaps the most extraordinary and strangest epoch of mankind: a voluntary mass migration from around the world that became the example and prototype for all later episodes of fortune-seeking. Scholars try to encapsulate the enthusiasm, the high spirits, the intense energy, and "can-do" mentality of the forty-niners, but they may find it difficult. For surely the California gold rush was a kaleidoscope phenomenon, unique in all its aspects. The coming together of people from multiple nations put into motion the meeting, the mutual confrontation, and in time the blending together of the myriad different languages, philosophies, religions, customs, and food and social habits that, 150 years later, the world identifies as a uniquely California lifestyle. The gold rush sesquicentennial also commemorated California's beginning as a launching pad for social and cultural innovation.[1]

In the gold rush competition, it may be unfair to compare the different competitors based on their background, their nationality, or their talents, as a means to measure individual successes. Some were luckier than others, some were better outfitted than others, and some—as in the case of the Chinese—started with far greater advantages than most. At first glance the Chinese stood out as a people so different in culture and society that they might be thought a disadvantaged group in gold rush California. But, as we should come to acknowledge, they were actually better equipped

Literal translation: "Within Four Seas the World Is My Home." This ancient saying, which has no association with any particular sea or ocean, indicates that within the compass directions of the universe a Chinese can make his home anywhere. A corollary verse is "Within the four seas all men are brothers," suggesting a universal brotherhood that precludes prejudice based on color or creed.

for success even than those who migrated from the eastern half of the North American continent. Their strong ethnic ties, sense of familial obligations, and the psychological drive to preserve "face" assured the Chinese miners of survival and prevented them from acting anything less than as Chinese, appearance and physical description notwithstanding. For California's Chinese Argonauts, to fail would mean they had done everything wrong—and then some.[2]

Even though the gold seekers in California—coming from Europe, North and South America, and East Asia—were endowed with different backgrounds and raised with parental and societal influences that were worlds apart, they created similar societal systems. Wisely, the easterner and the westerner had religious influences and personal convictions that instilled emotional and spiritual strength to meet mental challenges. In each case, their cultural store of adages and their folklore identified their ancestral beginnings. Their customs and culture dictated how each solved problems. The added difference for the Chinese, however, was the critical psychological attachment to "face," the absolute necessity of maintaining, at all costs, one's esteem, image, and family honor before the world.[3]

One of the earliest gold rush experiences for the Chinese occurred in 1848 when San Francisco merchant Chum Ming heard Sam Brannan's proclamation of the American River gold discovery as he stood in the doorway of his store. Chum Ming immediately wrote his cousin, Cheong Yim, in China, asking him to join in the bonanza experience and to bring help. As Chum Ming headed for the Sierra Nevada foothills, knowing that he served as his kinsmen's advance man, Cheong Yim quickly assembled his fellow villagers and boarded a ship bound for the Gold Mountain country, arriving in California some four months later.[4]

Coming from all corners of the world, driven by their energy and dreams

自求多福

In the Weaverville Joss House, Hanford Lee of San Francisco translated the tall wooden red signs with gold lettering that hang on opposite walls at each end of the altar table. Full translatin of the left sign reads: "I seek my victory (fortune) and now crossing ocean country to republic country." A less literal translation would be: I am crossing the ocean to reach the [free] country [America]. (Copies of translation provided by Diane Mercer).

of success, many adventurous Argonauts began their quest by sea. The men from the East Coast traveled by ship around Cape Horn. Their sojourn at sea, in time and conditions, matched the long and arduous voyage that the Chinese endured sailing the mighty Pacific from the Guangdong harbors. The men from China sailed the uncertain seas below decks in cramped quarters that reeked of sweat and vomit, and their conditions on deck were not much better. They not only heard but also contributed to the repetitive, monotonous dialogue about gold, adventure, and California opportunities with the same people, their shipmates, for weeks and months on end. Each bolstered the other's high hopes, at the same time feeling the need to reinforce their own thoughts. The voyage provided no space for solitude. For these village men, there was but the constant roll and pitch of the ship, a strange, perhaps frightening experience. Although the voyage felt like an eternity, the men knew their dreams lay just over the horizon.

As white and Chinese groups landed in San Francisco, the first staging area on the way to the gold country, they each confronted sights quite foreign to them and came in contact with exotic strangers. For each group, their first experience with the other could be dismissed as a temporary encounter; each had a more important mission at hand—to learn about the mines and to find a way to reach them. Eventually, a more finite assessment and permanent adjustment would take place. These men from east and west would test their mettle and test one another in the confines of California's rugged Mother Lode country. So opposite in background, they would eventually came to know one another's customs and something of the other's language and culture. Time and circumstances demonstrated that their opinions ranged from curiosity, admiration, and competition, to disdain, anger, and, eventually, respect for one another.[5]

One might suggest that the original passion for seizing the mineral from

自助者 天助者也

The Gods Help Those Who Help Themselves

the earth, "striking it rich," evolved into a realization that the actual gold would be dreams fulfilled by health, wealth, and opportunity. In town after Mother Lode town, residents in time paid tribute to pioneer leaders. Certainly, the individuals thus recognized were not praised for what they mined (mostly unsuccessfully), but for their keen sense of business, their ability to establish and shape local society and government, and their desire to build organizations for purposes of charity and fellowship so that their social group and brethren survived and thrived.[6]

The American miners' pursuit of civil society and government were evident as early as 1848. Those who came around Cape Horn brought with them compacts and agreements that were similar to business agreements. Those who came overland in wagon trains also had organizational systems in place. They typically began the overland journey by appointing wagonmasters or captains, designating hunting parties, and even agreeing on ordinances to regulate social behavior, settle grievances, and determine such matters as sentry watches. So it was not unusual that these same men quickly adopted regulations for establishing mining claims and punishing claim jumpers, and that these regulations were seriously enforced.[7]

By the fall of 1850, formation of counties and designation of county seats, elections of alcaldes or mayors and city councils, and the codification of mining and public safety laws, with a swift delivery of justice, guaranteed a type of government that would be ruled and controlled by the Americans. Many of the laws would, of course, favor the whites over the Native Americans, dark-skinned foreigners, and the Chinese. The Foreign Miners Tax, enacted in 1852, was among the many edicts that contributed to the disproportion of power between the gold seekers from the East, the West, and the South.[8]

The same drive to succeed existed in all those who entered the gold fields. Westerners were independent, individualistic in nature, taught to be self-reliant, and endowed with attributes that would serve them well in competition. A popular adage among those who spoke English in the mining communities was "To each his own, and the devil takes the hindmost." This attitude may not be associated with superiority, but it was enveloped in a psychic pride of being part of a new nation. After all, their fathers' generation had defeated the mighty English army, stalwarts of the British Empire. In addition, western gold seekers were also experiencing the early phases of a pervasive new era, self-confidently sharing a collective mindset that became identified as the spirit of Manifest Destiny.

Religious influence in California society began even before the gold rush with the Spanish missions becoming the focus of early coastal communities. Residents of Monterey and San Francisco welcomed visiting preachers other than the Catholic missionary priests. The Reverend Walter Colton, who landed in Monterey on July 30, 1846, became the first resident minister in American California. The following day, coincidentally, Sam Brannan of the Latter-day Saints sailed into San Francisco Bay with his shipload of Mormon colonists and purportedly gave the first Protestant sermon at Yerba Buena the following Sunday. Episcopal, Congregational, and Baptist ministers, among others, frequented Mother Lode camps and communities and preached in the streets or under temporary tents until their respective churches were built and their assignments became permanent.[9]

As cities grew and towns sprung up everywhere, temple buildings owned by the Freemasons and the halls of the Odd Fellows appeared in such towns as Columbia, Sonora, Sacramento, Stockton, Folsom, Jackson, and elsewhere. Sanborn maps from the 1880s, detailing California's urban geography, show evidence of ethnic organizations such as the German Turnverein halls, Jewish synagogues, and various other sectarian churches and schools, including those founded by early African American communities. So, too, one can find structures associated with Chinese societal influences.[10]

Visitors to the mining areas noted many Chinese camps throughout the Mother Lode. For example, J. D. Borthwick described the conditions at Mississippi Bar on the Yuba River: "There were about 150 Chinese living in a perfect village of small tents, all clustered together on the rock." Another sighting included two hundred Chinese at Mormon Bar and four hundred at Horseshoe Bar on the American River, while "a whole bevy" inhabited Weber Creek near Placerville. These and other descriptions provide us with images of numbers and the appearance of Chinese encampments. Actually, the number of Chinese in the mining camps fluctuated according to the gold's availability and the social and political conditions in each locality.[11]

By the mid-1850s, one of every five miners in California was Chinese. Towns such as Marysville, Oroville, Auburn, and Weaverville could show a higher percentage of Chinese among their residents than could be found in San Francisco. Even many small communities witnessed a growth in the number of Chinese stores and businesses.

Weaverville Joss house, translation of wooden sign on the right side of the altar table.
The literal translation is "I Came with Same Kind of People for My Happiness Year(s)."

As with other ethnic groups immigrating into new worlds, the Chinese quickly put in place all the services their community needed to make their Chinese camps and Chinatowns as "homelike" as possible. By doing so, these industrious gold seekers banished feelings of loneliness and their fear of strange surroundings. Sights, sounds, and the zest of living came through various forms of entertainment from gambling houses to traveling opera troupes to brothels.

Once they took up residence in a mining town, the Chinese quickly sought out and did business with stores and shops owned by fellow clansmen. Every service was reasonably accessible, from getting a haircut to securing a simple remedy for a stomachache or posting a letter. Even in the most remote mining areas, the Chinese had little difficulty obtaining food items in keeping with their traditional diet—items such as rice, dried fish, shrimp, fresh vegetables, and tea. Quickly the Chinese learned how to stash away their gold for safekeeping until it could be transported to San Francisco for processing. As yet another link in the service chain and as a form of security unmatched by the express companies of the American business economy, melting down and casting gold into the form of sooty pots, woks, and cooking utensils was done at jewelry stores owned by fellow clansmen. Once the precious metal was completely disguised, it was ready to be transported back to the Guangdong village to pay off debts and enhance living conditions for relatives at home.

The Chinese merchant was a vital link. Because of the fixed location of the shopkeeper, he served as the natural go-between and contact person for individuals and their clan associations. He had the ability to negotiate the transport of gold as well as to secure other services that fellow villagers needed, including services from members of white society. These shop owners and service providers helped maintain and reinforce the cultural practices of the homeland. They served as officials and were the decision makers in the family associations. Construction of today's historic Chinese buildings and temples was largely the result of their visions of permanency.[12]

In the spectrum of immigration history, each ethnic group brought to

Literal translation: "All who seek, necessarily finds." This motto was written on orange paper and pasted to the right wall of the main alter at the Daoist Tample in Hanford, California.

California a distinctive type of support system. Some were loose-knit points of contacts or had membership based on geographic origins, fraternal associations, or religious affiliations. Immigrants relied on these organizations for early help, contacts, or even to learn the rules of the land. Even though the early Chinese gold seekers intended their stay to be only a sojourn, it was natural to put support systems in place to provide protection and save time and energy for the betterment of the individual and the group. Records show that as early as the fifteenth century adventuresome South Seas Chinese created village associations in many Southeast Asian seaports. These organizations mirrored a number of immigrant European groups; but in California they were more noticeable because of their sheer numbers, their architecturally distinctive buildings, and their activities that prompted an ongoing curiosity on the part of other ethnic groups.[13]

The arriving Chinese miner knew he could access an immediate lifeline and could belong to one or more different associations once in California. These social support systems were of three types: clan, district, and regional dialect. Clan associations centered on surnames. Large groups of people sharing the same last name often had an association exclusively devoted to help those with that same surname, such as the Lees, Wongs, or Mahs. If immigrants with the same last name were few in number, leaders looked to established allegiances with other name groups that were already known in the homeland. For instance the Soo Yuen Association represents the Louies, the Kwongs, and the Fongs. Another similar amalgamation of surnames is the Loong Kong Association, which is dedicated to serving people whose last names are Low, Quong, Cheong, and Chew.[14]

District association members were natives of villages within the geographical border of a specific district. Because of the diverse terrain within the Guangdong province, natural barriers caused people within separate geographic confines to create distinctive regional dialects. Two examples are the Sam Yup Association, which encompassed people hailing from

Namhoi, Pun Yu, and Shuntak districts, and the Sze Yup Association, which represented people from Sunwui, Toishan, Hoiping, and Yanping districts.[15]

Historian Him Mark Lai has noted that the first Chinese organization in California began in 1849. Its function was to maintain internal order among Chinese immigrants and to deal with the larger white community. By 1851 the Sam Yup and Sze Yup Associations fully established themselves as leaders of the San Francisco Chinese community. Merchants, even in the smallest Mother Lode town, belonged to a local association that was affiliated with larger San Francisco organizations.

Commonly known as *huiguans* (associations), with their business offices known as *gongsi* (companies), these Chinese associations differed from tongs in their activities. As torchbearers of cultural continuity, the associations provided temporary shelter, guidance, and welfare services; administered burial needs; and operated cemeteries for their members. The tongs' interest, on the other hand, was in profiting through control of such social activities among the Chinese as gambling, prostitution, and drug operation.

The Chinese Argonaut's involvement in the various organizations seemed virtually limitless. If his family name was not among the numerous, he could gain support from his district or same-language group. He was, however, also expected to pay allegiance to as many of these associations as might provide him aid. Quite expectedly, it was a *huiguan* representative who would meet the arriving Chinese at the San Francisco docks and take him up the hill to Chinatown, where he was schooled on the available familial or clan contacts and given both temporary shelter and credit for food and supplies. The physical presence of a good many countrymen, along with opportunities to ask specific questions and enjoy the camaraderie of close bloodlines and relations, enhanced the familiar and lessened the fear factor for the new Californian.

The *huiguans'* purposes were to protect group interests and, therefore, the interests of the individual as well. *Huiguans* offered a place for respite. They also provided special services to handle funerals and return the bones of unfortunate individuals to the proper family burial ground in China when those occasions arose. This type of social insurance, with satellite offices in the far reaches of the Mother Lode, gave the Chinese the advantage of service and protection beyond that available to the other foreigners competing for California's gold.

The major association headquarters buildings in San Francisco, Sacramento, and Stockton served as a home away from home. These facilities were places to socialize, share news, celebrate holidays, and take part in all the traditions and customs that each immigrant enjoyed as a Chinese. All association main meeting rooms had some type of altar or worship table that contained an ancestor tablet, patron deities, or an illustrated image of the family's ancestor or ancestors. These altars served as the psychological and spiritual focus for reflection, reverence, and worship. Quite clearly, white journalists and other non-Chinese witnesses—as well as some present-day historians—mistakenly concluded that the secular societal systems of the associations included elements of religious significance. Understandably, interpretations of the altar's significance drew upon the witnesses' own background or experience. As an example, the Kwong Chow Temple was founded in 1854 when San Francisco's wealthy entrepreneur Yee Lo Tai of the Kwong Chow district bought a piece of land on Pine Street and built an association building for his fellow villagers. On the top floor he erected an ornate altar, which white observers described as extremely elaborate; thus they called the building a temple. Obviously, the building's intended use was restricted, meant for Chinese from the Kwong Chow district alone. Similarly, the Taoist Temple in Hanford served as the headquarters of the Sam Yup Association. Time and generational misinterpretations, mixed with the oversimplification of earlier explanations, have frequently clouded the historical character of these establishments.[16]

The *huiguans* had their own form of law and order. While they protected individuals, they capably meted out punishment in the form of ostracism from the association, which stripped the offending individual of benefits, banished him from *huiguan* activities, and—the most severe consequence—excluded him from being buried in the *huiguan* cemetery.[17]

The Chinese Argonaut's obligations included paying annual dues, tithing when asked, and extending a hand or advancing credit to other clans-men. And he needed to pay all debts before returning to China. When disagreements arose between *huiguans*, the Chinese stood by his own association, even when he disagreed with the issue or the position taken by the organization. When ill feelings arose or misdeeds occurred, everyone involved was affected. It was, after all, a matter of family honor and "face" that would be at stake. Loyalty, rather than independent thought, took precedence.

As part of their group-centered philosophy, Chinese pride themselves on conformity rather than on individuality. By definition, "face" is a perceived image, a visage one wants to project mostly of wealth, prestige, and integrity. Maintaining one's face is a primary responsibility learned in early childhood. A loss of face results in bringing dishonor to one's family. Causing someone to lose face is to create a doubt about that person's character. In the

Cantonese language, when one person accords another respect, he is "giving face." Hence, the concept of face encompasses many dimensions. For some, face formed the fundamental basis of one's purpose, decisions, and actions in life. At times, face guided motivation or, at other times, gave an excuse for vendetta and retaliation by instilling courageous feelings, loyalty, and purpose in the defense of honor.

One early example of defending a *huiguan*'s honor occurred in the Weaverville War of 1854, which pitted the Sze Yup against the Yeong Wo, the official name of the Heungshan association. This skirmish showed that long-standing feuds could easily be rekindled at a great distance from home. Participants in this particular confrontation prepared for the pitched battle an entire week and used a variety of weapons in the clash of arms, including tridents, shields, and swords. Caucasian witnesses vouched for the ferocity of the four-day pitched battle, which had begun earlier with the preparation of weapons forged at the local blacksmith shop. On July 4, 1854, the two Chinese groups assaulted each other in an open field. Accounts varied as to how many Chinese were involved, with estimates ranging from two hundred to six hundred participants. Eight died in the conflict, and an unknown number of individuals were wounded.

Other documented battles among the Chinese immigrants arose from time to time. Even tong wars that erupted in the early 1870s, again in the late 1880s, and clear into the 1920s originated to restore honor or face to the injured organization. Tong incidents oftentimes were caused by disputes centered on gambling debts, stealing or kidnapping women, or even a simple insult.[18]

In 1882 an umbrella organization officially titled the Chinese Benevolent Association of San Francisco came into being. Known in Chinese as Chung Wah (translated as the Great Center), it incorporated representatives of all Chinese district, regional, clan, and social associations, and it had the ultimate authority to adjudicate issues between feuding organizations. Other Chinese communities copied this same form of consolidation. As arguments spilled into various towns, leaders looked to the new organization to deal with sensitive issues. Their meetings allowed all parties to present their case. The elders of Chung Wah sought mediation and compromise, rather than punishment, to resolve problems. Most assumed that wisdom and not politics would prevail.[19]

The Chinese group mentality contrasted sharply with the Anglo-American sense of individualism and independence. Chinese organizational demands coupled with traditional Chinese ancestral worship, Buddhism, and

祐庇恩神

*Literal translation: "[May] the favors [grace] of the spirits [gods] protect you [everyone]."
This plaque, one of two written in black letters on gold background, is located on one
side of the wall next to the pillars parallel with the steps and railing in front of the main
altar of the Weaverville Joss House. (Interview with Diame Mercer, 1998.)*

Taoist strictures made the social obligations of the Chinese Californian even
greater than those of his western counterparts.

California's early Chinese houses of worship contained multiple deities.
Of the many popular mythical gods and goddesses, the early Chinese
miners preferred Kuan Kung (Kwan Di), god of war and wisdom; Tien
How, goddess of Heaven; Hua Tuo, god of medicine; Kuan Yin, goddess of
mercy; and Dai Tse, god of Earth. Rather than seek aid and spiritual comfort
from more than one god, which resulted in conflicts, miners turned to the
specific deity that could provide a solution to their temporary problems
and promote compatibility.[20]

In addition, the California's Chinese temples took on a Taoist nature.
A philosophical embodiment of regulations rather than a religious order,
Taoism instructs the believer in behavior that will create harmony and bring
order within that person's universe. The Taoist set of instructions instill day-
to-day moral conduct, social etiquette, and religious rituals that a follower
needs to maintain so he or she can find peace and happiness. Taoism is
frequently paired with the teachings of Confucius, the philosopher-teacher.
As Taoism provides personal behavior instructions, Confucius's teachings
focused on the obligations that the individual has to the higher order of
country, state, and family.[21]

It is understandable that some early Western observers tried to equate the
Chinese gods to the "saints" that are worshipped in the Roman Catholic
form of Christianity. Yet many of these same gods, and Kuan Kung in
particular, are also revered in some family/clan associations as well. So when
Western interpreters saw altars and urns maintained as sacrificial vessels in
family associations, they logically surmised that a headquarters building
was a temple when, in fact, the building was an association facility.[22]

Practical adages, precepts, homilies, and Christian sayings are a part of

众志成城

Literal translation: "The aspirations of multitudes makes a community [city]." On right wall of altar of the Daoist Temple in Hanford, California, this is one half of the couplet "All who seek."

the American fabric. A great many of these brief instructive admonitions remain familiar to us today:

Do unto others as you would have others do unto you.
Do good today, and every tomorrow will take care of itself.
To err is human; to forgive divine.
The Lord helps those who help themselves.
He who chops his own wood is twice warmed.

This sampling, suggestive of good behavior, could be readily found in homes, restaurants, and other social areas throughout mid-nineteenth-century middle America. Even reminders like "Home Sweet Home" are still popular today.[23]

Even though a great many of the early Chinese Argonauts were illiterate, their knowledge and culture was instilled during childhood in part by similar adages. They understood the importance of symbols such as the light and dark; Yin and Yang (the male and female elements of the cosmos); flowers that represented seasons (peony, spring; lotus, summer; chrysanthemum, autumn; and flowering plum, winter), or the lotus, a symbol of Buddhism and purity; and particular colors (red for luck and joy; white for mourning; yellow for imperial authority or royalty) or animals (dragon, goodness and virtue; bat, joy and longevity; or fish, wealth or abundance).[24]

Chinese characters and ideographs also evoked the same messages as the objects, particularly when used as parts of adages and precepts. California Chinese temples, family associations, and most buildings of importance were frequently decorated with artistic calligraphy, attractive frames encompassing elaborately embroidered symbols, bright posters, words carved in bamboo or on wooden planks, and simple sheets of bright red paper filled with homilies, slogans, and proverbs that spoke of inspirations, aspirations, and the Chinese sense of mission. Sayings similar to English adages decorated nooks and crannies. A strong repetitive theme of togetherness,

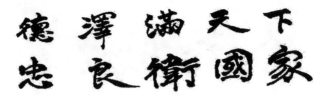

The red couplets at the doorway of the Weatherville Joss House translates to "The abundance of virtue fills the world / The loyal and good defend the country."

unity, work ethic, and responsibility to family and clan could be found over doorways, running downward on a pillar, above the thresholds of windows, along the top and sides of altars, and practically anywhere that space allowed.

Among the most notable of the few remaining religious temples bearing witness to the California Chinese experience are those in Marysville, Oroville, and Weaverville. According to Harry Chin, a retired scholar, the blue columns on either side of the main entrance to the Weaverville Joss House attest that the house of worship is dedicated to the Dragon in the Cloud and the Phoenix in the Forest. These columns represent the hopes and expectations of the believers. The dragon opens heaven so as to obtain utmost prosperity while the phoenix brings about great peace. Within the temple, in the attendant's quarters, and around the grounds are wall writings, placards, and plaques that speak of the reflections of those who sought solace in the temple and their aspirations. Among examples of couplets are:

> I came with my same kind of people for my happiness year(s)
> I seek my fortune and now crossing ocean country to republic country
> May the spirits (gods) protect everyone
> May virtue bring about success
> May you have luck at finding your fortune so you can return home early
> From this road together we put out our sincere hearts
> Let us walk into the temple together and gather good fruit (and be fulfilled)[25]

These sayings, while simple and direct, provided reassurance and instructive reminders of the purpose that brought the Chinese to California.[26]

It was common to have directional or missionizing names as official names for some clans and associations. While some clan names represent ideas and aspirations of the clan, others indicate the clan's origin. For instance, the Chan family organization's formal name is Gee How Oak Chin, which translates as "To Strive for Filial Piety and Extended to the Entire Clan." Bow On Tong, an enforcement arm of a district association, meant "For the Protection of Peace Among Ourselves." The Lee family's formal name, Lee On Dong, means "To Be at Peace With Our Neighbors."[27]

In *huiguan* buildings it was common to see phrases that reflected the members' thoughts and goals. Nonreligious couplets found in clan buildings often refer to prosperity and peace for their members. One such site is within the historic Chinatown in Hanford, California. The so-called Daoist Temple (a name coined because of early misinterpretations, but useful for attracting tourists into the area) actually is the meeting house of the Sam Yup Association of Hanford. The main room on the second floor houses two ornate altars and several other niches for various patron deities. On the wall to the right of the altar are these messages:

All who seek, necessarily (will) find.
The aspirations of multitudes make a community.
Of one mind and of one virtue.
All of [us] as one mind.[28]

Clearly, these and other visual signs, slogans, phrases, and adages served to bind, to reinforce a common purpose, and to add intrinsic strength to the psychological well-being of the early Chinese in California.

Together these adages, while centuries old, are still used as reinforcing thoughts by today's aging Chinese clan, district, and regional associations. By evoking the double issue of power and unity, the *huiguans* remind their members that survival and prosperity come not from independent action but from the good deeds of many. It also assures Chinese people that they can depend on support and aid from their own relations, which is part of their inherited legacy.

The California Chinese experience, on one hand, might be viewed as one of extreme sacrifice and limited success. History has not been able to assess how much gold the Chinese extracted from the Mother Lode, nor has there been sufficient documentation to suggest how much gold the miners sent back to China to relieve the economic crisis in their homeland. Yet, if a parallel can be drawn between the contributions of the Western forefathers and those of the Chinese association leaders, both made their mark in California's history. Both provided help to their brethren; both instilled

同 心 協 力
團 結 一 致

"Hearts Joined Creates Power / Muscles United Equals Strength." Dr. Sun Yat Sen, father of the Chinese Revolution, in his quest to overthrow the Manchu Government recognized the popularity and strength of this saying and adopted it as the slogan for the Free Chinese Movement. As he toured America raising funds among Chinatown leaders, he presented each of the funding towns' benevolent association office this slogan mounted in a black frame, a reminder to the overseas Chinese of the need to aid those still living in mainland China.

values; both promoted a civil society. With land purchased and buildings erected, both showed evidence of their influence, wealth, and legacy.

The uniqueness of the Chinese experience was created by many forces: strong ethnic ties, familial obligations, and a "collective individualism" mentality, meaning that whatever the individual does—good or bad—comes back to reflect on the family and clan. Susan Au Allen, a Washington DC, attorney, when asked by an *Asian Week* reporter her opinion on the high rate of Chinese success and their work ethic, commented: "I remembered that when I was growing up, you never shamed your family, you never shamed your village, you never shamed the community and that stopped us from doing bad things."[29]

It is this dominant thought of family, village, and community that drove a nation of Chinese to work and achieve. With a support system in place, one can conclude that no matter how strange the land, the language, and the dominant culture in the Gold Mountain, the Chinese survived and achieved because they were never really far from home.

Notes

A special debt is owed Dr. Chen F. Liem, who graciously provided artistic calligraphy for this paper, and to Harry Chin and Camille Wing for their energy in providing much needed translation of the couplets.

1. Carey McWilliams, *California: The Great Exception* (Santa Barbara: Peregrine Smith, 1976), 27. McWilliams suggests the uniqueness of the California gold rush was twofold: All resources of ocean transportation were available to those who cared to go to California. Also it was a great adventure for the common man, for it provided equality of opportunity (which was construed as equality of fortune).

2. Henry G. Schwarz, ed., *Chinese Medicine on the Gold Mountain: An Interpretive Guide* (Seattle: Wing Luke Memorial Museum, 1984), 16. This work, an interpretive guide to accompany the Washington Commission for the Humanities exhibit *Chinese Medicine in Washington and the Northwest: Past and Present*, reinforces the premise that "few Chinese were left alone without help from fellow Chinese. No Chinese emigrant lacked information on what to do, where to go or whom to see. They did this without ever having to move beyond the pale of the Chinese-speaking world. In this light, the advancing Chinese frontier in America assumes a much more structured and institutionalized form than heretofore thought to be the case. Especially after the late 1850s the Chinese immigrant world . . . had become a part of a complex network of organizations and groups that moved east on the heels of economic opportunity. It held together a global enterprise of men, money and power that functioned for nearly a century [and] while in America it helped to expand the Chinese frontier."

3. Dennis Bloodworth, *The Chinese Looking Glass* (New York: Farrar, Straus & Giroux, 1967), 264. While "face" is not only a matter of reputation and appearance, it creates a façade that demonstrates success even though the appearance may be far from reality. Additionally, the concept of "saving face" creates situations to allow for a "code of forbearance" to avoid humiliation or embarrassment for one's opponent.

4. Chinn, Lai, and Choy, eds., *History of the Chinese in California*, 9; Diane Mei Lin Mark and Ginger Chih, *A Place Called Chinese America* (Dubuque IA: Kendall Hunt Publishing, 1982), 6. Mark and Chih's work lists the first Chinese to the gold fields as Chang De Ming. Differences in dialect and pronunciation suggest that both names refer to the same individual. Chinn, however, provides a date of 1848, whereas Mark and Chih place his arrival year as 1849.

5. Paul Chace, "Dancing With the Dragon: A Study of Ritual and Inter-Ethnic Community Relations," *Origins and Destinations: Forty-One Essays on Chinese America* (Los Angeles: Chinese Historical Society of Southern California and UCLA Asian American Studies Center, 1994), 191. This study suggests that while the rituals of the Bok Kai Bomb Day Festival, with roots back to ancient China, was celebrated by the early Chinese pioneers, the event has evolved into "the annual re-creation of the festival tradition to promote and enhance inter-ethnic relations across the community." Bok Kai or Bok Ai, the God of Water or Flood Control, was known to ward off floods, and he was of particular importance to the Chinese working the various rivers in the Mother Lode.

6. Douglas McDonald and Gina McDonald, *History of the Weaverville Joss House and the Chinese of Trinity County, California* (Medford OR: McDonald Publishing, 1986), 23. Most of the deities on altars in California Chinese temples represent health, wealth, and mercy. The McDonalds observe that these are the three most sought after benefits by all people throughout history.

7. John Walton Caughey, *The California Gold Rush* (Berkeley: University of California Press, 1975), 225.

8. Carey McWilliams, *California: The Great Exception*, 28. Since no mining law existed in 1848, the early rules and regulations put in place by the miners' self-constituted mining districts emphasized a policy of one miner, one claim, and limited the size of the claim. This system purportedly ensured an equality of opportunity, although this equality did not extend to foreigners.

9. Caughey, *California Gold Rush*, 270; John W. Caughey, *California*, 2nd ed. (Englewood Cliffs NJ: Prentice-Hall, 1953), 330. By the mid-1850s San Francisco had thirty-two churches.

10. Frances Baltich, *Search for Safety: The Founding of Stockton's Black Community* (Stockton CA: F. Baltich, 1982), 58–61. The first African Methodist Episcopal Church in California was established in San Francisco in 1852, followed by another in Grass Valley in 1854 and in Stockton in 1855. Records show that that the small community of Stockton established a second African American church, the African Baptist Church, in 1855: Sylvia Sun Minnick, *SAMFOW: The San Joaquin Chinese Legacy* (Fresno CA: Panorama West Publishing, 1988), 38. Also in Stockton a German Turnverein Hall on Hunter Street abutted the Chinese joss temple, while the first Jewish synagogue (on Miner and Hunter Streets) was just one block north of both of these buildings.

11. Stephen Williams, *The Chinese in the California Mines, 1848–1860* (San Francisco: R & E Research Associates, 1971), 40.

12. McDonald and McDonald, *History of the Weaverville Joss House*, 4–5. Eleanor Briggs and Frances Leinginer, comps., *Chinese in Tehama Country* (n.p., n.d.), 16, describes Bo Do Hong, a business entity where the Chinese purchased herbs and groceries and did banking in the small Mother Lode community. Minnick, *SAMFOW*, 192–200, summarizes the career of Stockton merchant Lee Soon, who started his business in 1878 and provided lodging for fellow clansmen, sold herbs and sundries, and offered translation and interpreter services for county judicial officials and employers seeking workers.

13. Schwarz, *Chinese Medicine on the Gold Mountain*, 16; Him Mark Lai, "Historical Development of the Consolidated Chinese Benevolent Association/Huiguan System," in *Chinese American History and Perspectives, 1987* (San Francisco: Chinese Historical Society of America, 1987), 14. Lai suggests that the Chinese organization structure was equivalent to the German *Landsmannschaft*, an association of students from the same country or province.

14. Anonymous, *A Concise History of Lung Kong and the Genealogical Origin of the Four Families* (San Francisco: n.p, n.d.).

15. Lai, "Historical Development of the Consolidated Chinese Benevolent Association," 14–38.

16. Chinn, Lai, and Choy, *History of the Chinese in California*, 74.

17. Lai, "Historical Development of the Consolidated Chinese Benevolent Association," 23–24.

18. McDonald and McDonald, *History of the Weaverville Joss House*, 6–7. Chinese Camp in Tuolumne County saw a similar tong conflict in 1856, two years after the Weaverville War. Between 1902 and 1924 there were at least thirty-five tong-related incidents in Stockton. Frequently the victims were stabbed, shot, and even murdered. Many of these incidents involved the same organizations whose members acted simultaneously in other cities: Sylvia Sun Minnick, SAMFOW, 228–34.

19. Lai, "Historical Development of the Consolidated Chinese Benevolent Association," 23. Following the establishment of the Chinese Benevolent Association, it incorporated in 1900 and in that same year created the Tung Wah Dispensary, later named the Chinese Hospital. By 1905 this same organization founded the Chinese Language School. Disputes were settled by arbitration in a fashion similar to that of the Westerners. A panel announced their findings after allowing both parties to air their differences.

20. McDonald and McDonald, *History of Weaverville Joss House*, 18–23; Tom McDannold, "Chinese Place Names and their Significance," in *Origins and Destinations*, 183.

21. L. Eve Armentrout Ma, "Chinese Traditional Religion," in *Chinese American History and Perspectives, 1988* (San Francisco: Chinese Historical Society of America, 1988), 132–40. According to Ma, most of the temples were built between 1880 and 1890, while three in San Francisco date back to 1850.

22. Ma, "Chinese Traditional Religion." Family association members consider those with the same surnames as blood brothers. Frequently the altar in the association building houses one or more deities and gives the members a place to worship.

23. Marlon K. Hom, "Rhymes Cantonese Mother Sang," in *Chinese American History and Perspectives, 1999* (San Francisco: Chinese American Historical Society of America, 1999), 62. Hom indicates that nursery rhymes, lullabies, and children's ditties orally communicated from adult to child are instrumental in the growth of an individual. These oral narratives introduce knowledge and establish conformity in the young, thus molding the new generation to acceptable patterns of social behavior.

24. Hom, "Rhymes Cantonese Mother Sang," 68. Additional adages, rhymes,

and childhood ditties reinforce cultural knowledge such as seasonal festivals, folk science phenomena, and the natural order. Given the strong wish to recollect memories of the homeland, single males in the gold rush era clung to early childhood remembrances as structured educational tools to survive, particularly when they were without close familial influences. In Hom's research in Mainland China, he discovered songs and ditties that referred to Argonauts going to the Gold Mountain to earn gold and silver. He believes these early lessons have given way to immigration and Western influence.

25. Interview with Diane Mercer, 1998. In addition to the Taoist priest's quarters, there was a bachelors' quarter that provided temporary lodging for single men: McDonald and McDonald, *History of the Weaverville Joss House.*

26. Ma, "Chinese Traditional Religion." Ma indicates there were as many as thirty functioning temples in California, several in Nevada, one in Montana, one in Wyoming, three in Vancouver and Victoria, British Columbia, and at least three in the eastern United States.

27. Interview with Harry Chin, 1998.

28. Interview with Camille Wing, 1998.

29. *Asian Week*, November 20, 1997.

7

"Do You Think I'll Lug Trunks?"

African Americans in Gold Rush California

Shirley Ann Wilson Moore

From the early days of Spanish exploration and settlement, people of African ancestry were prominent among California's population. Indeed, of the forty-four *pobladores*, or settlers, of the pueblo of Nuestra Senora la Reina de Los Angeles de Porciuncula (Los Angeles) in 1781, people of African descent accounted for half of the city's founders. When gold fever gripped the nation in the mid-nineteenth century, California's population swelled as blacks, whites, and others from around the world poured into the gold fields, mining camps, and towns of California. In 1848 it was estimated that California's total population was ten thousand, but with the discovery of gold by the end of the year that number had doubled. The 1850 census showed one thousand black people living in California in a total population of nearly one hundred thousand. By 1852 California's population had climbed to over one hundred thousand, with black residents totaling two thousand. The 1860 census counted four thousand black Californians in a population of nearly four hundred thousand.[1]

African Americans entered California for a variety of reasons and came from all walks of life. Odell Thurman, writing of the black presence in this period, observed: "They came by land and they came by sea; they came in bondage and they came free; some came to escape the hazards of slavery; some came to search for the gold that was promised in the fabulous land of gold." Some slaves were brought by gold-hungry white slave owners to toil in the gold fields for their masters' benefit. As an extra inducement for faithful labor, slave masters sometimes promised to manumit their human chattel if they struck it rich. In some cases, slaves, with the consent of their owners, headed to the gold fields on their own, determined to extract enough gold to purchase their liberty and that of their wives and children, who were often left behind as hostages.[2]

Newspapers published accounts of large numbers of slaves and slave-holders swarming over the gold fields, working alongside white Argonauts, who feared unfair competition from slave labor. Slaves were used to work the gold sites, were hired out as laborers in non-mining-related work and were often employed as personal servants and assistants to whites in the gold regions. New Orleans slave George Washington Dennis sailed with his master to San Francisco and was used as collateral to pay for his master's shipboard gambling debts even before reaching California.[3]

In reality the panic over slave competition resulted from the presence of relatively few slaves in California's gold regions during the 1850s. Most of these men and women had accompanied their owners in groups of no more than three. Altogether between five hundred and six hundred slaves were involved in the gold rush. In 1849 delegates to the state constitutional convention drafted a provision that sought to bar slaves and free blacks from the state. The drafters opposed slave labor in the gold fields, but attempted to curtail the entry of free blacks as well. With the Compromise of 1850, California entered the union as a free state. However, the state constitution and other legislation placed such restrictions on the lives of people of color that freedom in the Golden State became a precarious proposition.[4]

California's Fugitive Slave Law of 1852 and litigation concerning runaway slave Archy Lee, California's last fugitive slave case, highlight the fragile nature of liberty for slaves who sought asylum on California's free soil. Archy Lee, an eighteen-year-old slave from Mississippi, had been brought to Sacramento in 1857 by Charles Stovall, the son of Archy Lee's master. Stovall settled in Sacramento to teach school and hired Lee out for a number of years. Claiming his freedom, Lee ran away but was arrested. The abolitionist community rallied around him, providing legal aid. After a series of intricate legal maneuvers, the state supreme court held the state Fugitive Slave Law valid if the slave owner was sojourning or only temporarily residing in the state. Despite Stovall's lengthy residency in California, the court ruled in his favor, citing the white man's youth and inexperience as legitimate defenses against forfeiture of his human property. As Stovall prepared to leave California with his slave, black abolitionists prevented his ship's departure from San Francisco. Lee was reprieved when his supporters went back to court to fight the extradition order. After weeks of legal wrangling, Archy Lee was declared free.[5]

So perilous was their status in California that in 1858 between seven hundred and eight hundred African Americans left the state for Victoria,

British Columbia, when gold was discovered on the Fraser River. This migration put them farther from reach of the Fugitive Slave Law. Archy Lee was among those who left for Canada.[6]

Slaves, however, were not the only blacks to enter California during the gold rush. Free black men and women made the journey as well. Some free black immigrants came as sojourners hoping to make their fortunes and return home; many came intending to settle permanently, and all aspired to economic and social advancement. Some blacks worked their way across country, hiring themselves out as cooks and "extra-hands" to California-bound immigrant groups or individuals. New England's maritime communities contributed their share to California's growing black population as African American sailors from New Bedford and other eastern maritime areas succumbed to the lure of the gold fields, jumped ship in San Francisco or other port cities, and set off to seek their fortunes. Booming economic opportunities also attracted dynamic black business entrepreneurs, who profited from the gold rush by supplying the Argonauts' unrelenting demands for food, clothing, shelter, and amusement.[7]

Black immigrants risked the hazards of arduous overland and sea journeys to reach California and attain their dreams. Traveling overland, black newcomers faced hardships on the Death Valley routes and treks that would carry them into parts of northern Mexico. Countless black men and women also traversed the treacherous Humboldt Sink region, the last overland barrier before travelers ascended into the heights of the Sierra Nevada. White forty-niner Amos Batchelder left a journal account of a "negro [*sic*] teamster" whom he met trudging across the arid expanse; his "perspiring face was completely whitewashed with white dust." In another account, Margaret Frink encountered a "Negro woman" as she crossed the Humboldt Sink in 1850, "tramping along through the heat and dust, carrying a cast iron bake stove on her head, with her provisions and a blanket piled on top—all she possessed in the world—bravely pushing on for California."[8]

While the Humboldt Sink presented a formidable challenge to thousands of immigrants, black and white, on at least one occasion an African American played a crucial role in assisting a caravan of white immigrants who had become stranded there. Sacramentan Ed Lewis, a "black man from Boston" who was an "expert with horses," rode to the aid of the imperiled group with a rescue party organized in Sacramento. On reaching the band and assessing their predicament, he rode back to Sacramento to muster additional help. Making the 250-mile round trip, Lewis returned with reinforcements and helped guide the newcomers to safety.[9]

Travelers who chose the ocean route to California also experienced their share of peril in sea voyages and isthmus treks that could last several months. Fierce storms, tropical diseases, and other natural disasters plagued white and black sea travelers alike, but racism imposed an extra burden on black gold rush immigrants.[10] Blacks taking the Panama route often endured racial insults and mistreatment from white shipboard passengers and crew members. Black immigrants recounted that ship captains often forced them to surrender their accommodations to whites, and they told of being compelled to wait for meals until all the white passengers had been served. Moreover, African Americans traveled under the constant menace of enslavement by slave hunters and bandits who flourished in the isthmus region. Central American kidnappers made a lucrative business of selling captives to the South American slave market, often targeting black travelers in Panama.[11]

Even before setting sail from their homes, however, black travelers were subjected to harassment by hostile whites. For example, freeborn Baltimorean Edward Booth, who had made a modest success in the gold fields in 1849, returned East for his family in 1851, planning for them all to sail for California together. The Booth family, which included four brothers and two sisters, were detained by Maryland authorities, who demanded proof of their free status before permitting them to leave. The family eventually sailed from New York to Panama, where they trekked across the isthmus. In Panama City the Booths waited three weeks for a steamer to San Francisco, but ticketing problems forced them to split up to continue their journey. Some of the group booked passage on a southbound "sailing ship" that was thrown off track when the captain "lost his route." Weeks later the exhausted travelers finally were reunited in San Francisco, where they immediately boarded a steamer bound for Sacramento.[12]

Despite these hardships, black newcomers continued to flow into California during the gold rush era. Although gold was the catalyst for voluntary and forced black migration to California, the black movement into the region is only partially explained by the prospects of material advancement. Noneconomic factors also persuaded black men and women to seek residency in California. Of course, those who were held in slavery had little choice in their owners' decisions to come west. Free blacks, however, swelled the ranks of California's African American population. Some sought economic freedom, but all pursued a liberty that could not be measured monetarily. For example, Miflin W. Gibbs, a black abolitionist from Philadelphia whose "entire life represented the achievement-oriented Negro," decided to migrate to California reasoning that "Fortune . . . may sometimes smile on the inert, but she seldom fails to surrender to pluck, tenacity and perseverance." Middle-class black intellectual organizations in the East, whose members had steadfastly opposed emigration to places like Canada, Africa, or Latin America, described migration to California as "healthy" and "enterprising."[13]

Ironically, African Americans invested their hopes in a territory where whites held them and other people of color in contempt. The census of 1850 showed 962 people of color residing in California. However, antiblack and other racist sentiments existed within a larger climate of xenophobia. In 1849 an estimated eighty-five thousand miners lived and worked in the gold fields. About twenty-three thousand of these were not citizens of the United States. Among this number were immigrants from non-European regions, including Australia, Asia, and Latin America.[14]

Native-born whites reserved their most virulent hatred for non-Europeans, although they demonstrated at times great hostility also toward the French Argonauts. Historian Hubert Howe Bancroft's description of the gold seekers resonates with the cultural and racial attitudes of the time:

> The flow from Europe alone equaled in variety that of the medieval crusades, with notable prominence to the leading types, the self-complacent Briton, the methodic and reflective German, and the versatile Gaul. The other continents contributed to swell the list. Africa was represented, besides the orthodox negro [*sic*], by swarthy Moors and straight featured Abyssinians. Asia and Australasia provided their quota in pig-tailed, blue-garbed Mongols, with their squat, bow-legged cousins of Nipon, lithe and diminutive Malays, dark-skinned Hindoos . . . , the well formed Maoris and Kanakas, the stately turbaned Ottermans, and the ubiquitous Hebrews, ever to be found in the wake of movements offering trade profits.[15]

The gold-hungry world rushed into California, but demographic diversity did not imply national, cultural, or racial egalitarianism. A correspondent to the *Panama Star*, a gold rush era newspaper, declared: "If foreigners come, let them till the soil, or do any other work that may suit them— the gold mines were preserved for Americans—we will share our interest in the mines with none but Americans." African American miners and their Spanish-speaking and Chinese counterparts were excluded from the gold-seeking fraternity envisioned by the writer.[16]

The California legislature codified xenophobic sentiment into law with the enactment of the Foreign Miners Tax in 1850. Ostensibly, the law levied a twenty-dollar monthly fee on all foreign miners, but it was published only in English and Spanish. The tax forced thousands of Mexican and Chilean miners to give up their claims and return home. It virtually barred Chinese and Indians from independent mining and compelled nearly one-half to three-fourths of Spanish-speaking and Chinese miners to quit the southern mining region, where they had their greatest presence.[17]

Ironically, African American gold seekers sometimes shared their white counterparts' condescending and exploitative attitudes toward nonwhites in gold rush California. For example, the relationship between Indians and blacks in the gold regions was complex, nuanced by issues of race, position, and situation. In general, California Indians "related to black men as [they] would to white men," seeing African Americans in terms of specific situations. Sometimes the situations called for mutual cooperation and other times they were fraught with mutual suspicion and hostility.[18]

Gold seekers' encroachment on Indian lands often provided the spark for violence, but sexual exploitation of Indian women was another situation in which racial tensions could erupt since Indian women were often a source of sexual gratification and competition for black and white men. This fact could have far-reaching and often violent consequences. For example, a quarrel between a Wintun (Nomlaki) Indian woman and her black common-law husband, identified only as Leroy, erupted into widespread violence that saw blacks and whites attack Indians in Northern California. The woman called on two men of her tribe to help her eject Leroy from the home. The black man, severely wounded in the ensuing struggle, killed the two Indian men and enlisted help from whites in the nearby community, who were more than willing to attack the Indians. This domestic squabble resulted in a general Indian-white war.[19]

In another situation, a black man identified only as Andy joined whites in an assault on an Indian woman. Andy was a cook for J. Goldsborough Bruff's group of gold seekers, who set out from Saint Louis in 1849 and arrived in California in 1850. In August 1850, Andy, along with two white men, raped an Indian woman. Bruff recorded the event in his journal: "Near sun set, Nicholas, Jas. Marshall and Andy, rode off, to visit the indian [*sic*] village above. As they purchase whiskey and drink along the route, it is probable that [they] will visit the indians drunk. They returned, at night intoxicated, and tell how that they reached the village and found the males all absent, and caught a Squaw, who offered them roots, willow baskets, &c if they would not molest her, but that they successively, *did molest* her [emphasis in original]."[20]

African Americans were often part of "pursuit and vengeance" posses that were organized by whites to hunt and kill Indians. Indeed, Andy gained a formidable reputation for his exploits as an Indian fighter in such a posse. In Northern California, where Indian-white wars raged, a newspaper described a posse that had returned from an Indian-killing expedition. The posse included "16 whites, two Indians and a negro . . . [who had the] muzzle of his gun decorated with the scalp taken from the enemy."[21]

Most African American–Indian relations in California were more tranquil, however. Blacks sometimes employed Indians as servants in the gold regions. There is one notable report of an Indian servant tenderly caring for his intoxicated black employer as the two left a "mining-town bar in Grass Valley." African Americans and Mexicans also interacted in the mining regions of California, mingling in dance halls, bullfights, and other activities. Similarly, blacks and Chinese routinely mixed in California's towns and mining sites, and African Americans often worked near Chinese mining camps in the northern and southern mines. Usually things went smoothly. However, in 1853 a battle between ten black men and one hundred Chinese over an "unreported issue" near Sonora stood as a glaring exception to the generally peaceful relations between these two groups.[22]

Despite the racially charged and often violent climate in California, free blacks, many from Eastern states where black people possessed comparatively more rights, were nonetheless eager to get to California.[23] As a land of opportunity, California had an abiding attraction for most African Americans. Optimistic black Argonauts and entrepreneurs in the East "brushed aside reports of prejudice, hardship, and death" and focused on more upbeat accounts of affluence, hope, and freedom. Word spread through newspaper reports, community meetings, and letters from miners to loved ones back home.

In 1850 the abolitionist newspaper the *Liberator* published a letter from a group of black miners who announced that they had formed a "mutual-aid society" to assist themselves and other black newcomers. The miners noted that their efforts in the gold fields were reaping between one hundred and three hundred dollars a month for each member. Similarly, an antislavery newspaper in Philadelphia reported in 1851 that two black men had returned to their homes in the East, thirty thousand dollars richer after only four months of toil in the gold fields. William H. Hall, a black forty-niner from New York, returned to marry his sweetheart in 1851 after striking it rich in California. His wedding was reported to be a "splendour . . . perhaps without a parallel in the history of coloured society in New York." Hall's good fortune, along with a public address he delivered in New York City titled "Hopes and Prospects of Colored People in California," is credited with inducing "more California-bound black migrants" from the state of New York than any other single event. Even those living far from the swirl of New York's black society were not immune to the lure of California. For example, Mrs. Alley Brown of Sainte Genevieve City, Missouri, became convinced of California's potential through corresponding with her husband, who worked the Cosumnes diggings in 1852: "This is the best place for black folks on the globe. All a man has to do is to work, and he will make money." Thus, California gold fever swept through black communities and touched off a flurry of activity and debate.[24]

African American abolitionist Frederick Douglass declared in his newspaper, the *North Star*: "So strong is the excitement that it has become a question of who ought to go and who ought not to go. . . . Discretion and reasonable consideration seemed to have been abandoned. Lovers hurried and married their sweethearts and left them. Young husbands left young wives. . . . Some have returned much better off and some much worse."[25]

So high were African American expectations of advancement in California that they were willing to risk their relative security to journey west. Indeed, their expectations and in some cases the realization of financial success led many African Americans to believe that old racial constraints that had confined them to America's social and economic margins would be swept away by gold fever. Residents of large black communities in New England and New York were lured by newspapers that ran stories proclaiming that "[t]he merest Negro could make more than our present governor," or asserting that in California "[t]here are no gentlemen here. Labor rules Capital. A darkey is just as good as a polished gentleman and can make more money."[26]

Reports by whites often gave credence to these claims. For example, in 1848 a freshly disembarked white newcomer to San Francisco recounted his futile attempt to hire a black porter for his luggage. A black man he approached indignantly rebuffed his offer of work, drawing a small sack of gold dust (estimated to be worth one hundred dollars) from his jacket and demanding: "Do you think I'll lug trunks when I can get that much in one day?"[27]

Mifflin Wistar Gibbs, a black forty-niner and publisher of California's first black newspaper, the *Mirror of the Times*, confidently advised black Californians to forgo menial work: "Let every Colored resident of the State . . . abandon such positions as bootblack, waiters, servants, and carriers, and other servile employment, and if they cannot engage in trading, mechanical pursuits or farming, let them pitch into mining from which they have not yet been debarred."[28]

African American material success in California was not uncommon. Black mining companies like the Sweet Vengeance Mine and the Rare,

Ripe Gold and Silver Mining Company proclaimed black achievement, but envious whites bestowed pejorative names on thriving black mining sites. In 1851 Nigger Bar (presently Negro Bar), on the American River where the town of Folsom is now located, boasted seven hundred residents, three hundred of whom were blacks who met with moderate success in their gold-panning efforts. Upstream on the American River's south fork, Nigger Hill (Negro Hill), located close to the Coloma site of James Marshall's original gold discovery, was founded in 1849 by blacks from Massachusetts. This site was consistently lucrative for the miners. There were "scores of hardy miners making good wages." Massachusetts Flat, founded by New England blacks and Portuguese immigrants in 1854, also turned a profit. Its success sparked another nearby black site, dubbed Little Negro (Nigger) Hill. The average daily earnings of most successful black miners, like those of their white counterparts, however, was estimated to be about five or six dollars a day.[29]

Despite black miners' skill and perseverance, white miners attributed black success to superstition and good luck. Gold-field lore among white miners held that blacks were "proverbially lucky at gold mining," and some of their "luck" might rub off on white miners who set up claims nearby. Folklore notwithstanding, black miners often fell victim to white claim jumpers.[30]

In addition to mining, black men and women were also able to achieve some success by providing services to the gold seekers. For example, George Washington Dennis worked with his white owner to establish the Eldorado Hotel in San Francisco with the promise that he would be able to purchase his freedom for $1,000. Dennis' monthly salary of $250 as a porter in the hotel enabled him to purchase his freedom and that of his mother, who joined him in San Francisco. He later bought a concession in the hotel, where his mother cooked meals for the hotel customers, gamblers, and forty-niners fresh from the gold fields. Dennis accumulated property in downtown San Francisco and became a prosperous businessman and champion of black civil rights.[31]

Mifflin Wistar Gibbs, one of the state's most successful African American entrepreneurs and civil rights advocates, arrived in San Francisco in 1850 and opened a shoeshine stand in front of the Union Hotel, where he also worked as a porter. An energetic businessman, Gibbs, in partnership with Peter Lester, opened the city's only retail and wholesale shoe and boot store and made a lucrative business supplying footwear to city folk and would-be prospectors headed for the gold fields. Putting his financial success and influence to work, Gibbs dedicated himself to the struggle for justice and fought vigorously for the right to testify in court and for the vote. His newspaper became the official voice of the California Colored Convention Movement that emerged in 1855.[32]

African American women also achieved a degree of success in gold rush California. Compared to their white counterparts, black women in the West were more likely to be married, were better educated, and had a lower childbearing rate. Whether they came as free women or as slaves, black women stood in the forefront of the battle for equality in California. Bridget "Biddy" Mason was born a slave in Georgia, and in 1848 came to California with her owners, the Smiths, a Mormon family from Mississippi who were trekking west in a wagon caravan. Mason, her sister, and her children thus became western pioneers, black slaves caught up in a white religious movement. Mason was one of the first English-speaking African American settlers in Los Angeles when the city had fewer than one thousand inhabitants.

The Smith party settled in San Bernardino in 1851. Not realizing that California was a free state, they planned to depart for Texas in 1854 with their slaves before anyone could stop them. On the way out, the band camped in Los Angeles. Biddy Mason, however, had made friends in the free black community in Los Angeles, including Robert Owens, who ran a flourishing stable business. Owens assembled a posse of vaqueros to rescue Mason and her kin and swooped down on their camp in the Santa Monica mountains in the middle of the night. Thirty-eight-year-old Mason was rescued, successfully sued for her freedom in court, and won in 1856. Ten years after her release, she had saved enough money working as a laundress, cook, and midwife to buy property on Spring Street in Los Angeles and build a house that would become the First African Methodist Church. Mason was a philanthropist, nurse, and community leader until her death in 1891.[33]

While Biddy Mason won freedom for herself and her family in California, not all African American women came to California as slaves. Mary Ellen Pleasant, a former Georgia slave, was sold from her Georgia plantation to a master who sent her to Boston to be educated. There she obtained her freedom and married Alexander Smith, a wealthy black Bostonian whose house was a hub of abolitionist activity. Upon her husband's death, Pleasant inherited more than fifty thousand dollars, which she vowed to use in the fight against slavery. In 1852 she migrated to San Francisco, where she opened a boarding house and immediately began to issue high-interest loans and speculate in real estate.

Pleasant became a successful businesswoman, networking with San

Francisco's leading political and financial figures. She was in the forefront of state and national antislavery crusades, contributing thirty thousand dollars to John Brown's ill-fated raid on Harper's Ferry in 1859, financing the California Colored Citizens Conventions, and participating in fugitive slave rescues in rural sections of the state. Pleasant successfully attacked racial discrimination in San Francisco public conveyances when she and two other black women were ejected from a city streetcar in 1866. Her lawsuit, *Pleasant v. the North Beach and Mission Railroad Company*, outlawed segregation in the city's public conveyances. Her efforts earned her the title "mother of the Civil Rights Movement" in California. Following a series of financial reversals, Mary Ellen Pleasant died in San Francisco in 1904.[34]

As Pleasant's life suggests, success in the gold fields and business made black Californians the wealthiest and most "culturally advanced" black community in the country in the first half of the nineteenth century. African Americans in California had more than two million dollars in assets, with half of it "located in San Francisco." Their financial and cultural position contributed to and sustained their drive for equality.[35] By 1860 the nearly five thousand black men and women who resided in the state had been fighting for equality and social justice for over a decade, yet they still suffered under a system that severely proscribed their most basic rights. Denied citizenship, they could not legally homestead public land; they were denied the rights to vote, hold public office, give court testimony against whites, serve on juries, send their children to public schools, or ride street cars unless fair skinned enough to "pass" for white.[36]

The black convention movement of the early 1850s was born out of this reality. Black Californians from ten counties established a statewide organization to address these ills. Meeting in Sacramento at the first Convention of Colored Citizens of the State of California, they took on issues of racial discrimination that barred them from full and equal participation in the life of the state. Sacramentan James Carter rallied support for the first Colored Convention declaring:

> Brethren:—Your state and condition in California is one of social and political degradation; one that is unbecoming a free and enlightened people. Since you have left your homes and peaceful friends in the Atlantic States, and migrated to the shores of the Pacific, with the hopes of bettering your condition, you have met with one continued series of outrages, injustices, and unmitigated wrongs unparalleled in the history of nations. . . . [W]e call upon you to lay aside your various avocations and assemble yourselves together . . . for the purpose of devising the most

judicious and effectual ways and means to obtain inalienable rights and privileges in California.[37]

One of the most pressing issues taken up by the convention was the state's antitestimony laws, which made it nearly impossible for black Californians to obtain legal redress. The laws, first enacted in 1852, provided that "no black or mulatto person, or indian [*sic*], shall be permitted to give evidence in any action to which a white person is a party, in any Court of this State."[38] Blacks mounted a series of impressive petition campaigns calling for the legislature to abolish such unjust laws. They managed to win a growing number of white supporters to their cause, but it was not until March 1863, two months after the Emancipation Proclamation went into effect, that the state legislature amended the testimony law. This proved to be a mixed victory since the amendment permitted black testimony but continued the prohibition against Indians and barred "Mongolians" and Chinese from testifying in court. The law was finally removed from the statutes in 1872.[39]

Black Californians held subsequent conventions in 1856, 1857, and 1858, tackling the issues of segregated public schools, Jim Crow public conveyances, and voting rights. While the Colored Convention movement galvanized African Americans across the state, black Californians found it virtually impossible to gain favorable consideration from a legislature that was controlled by antiblack Democrats.[40] Not until the advent of relatively "racially enlightened" state and federal administrations during Reconstruction did African Americans begin to feel more secure about their position in the Golden State as some of the old racial restrictions were loosened.

This new political climate was short lived, however. California returned to Democratic control in 1870 and joined the ranks of those states refusing to ratify the Fourteenth and Fifteenth Amendments. Thus, the last decades of the nineteenth century saw black Californians continuing their struggle for justice on a district-by-district, city-by-city basis. They achieved their most notable victory in 1894, when California's public schools were legally integrated. The fight for equal opportunity on all fronts would continue into the next century.[41]

California's gold rush was a catalyst for the activism and achievements of African Americans in the state. The spirit of adventure that compelled free black Argonauts to leave familiar faces and surroundings and the tenacity of those who were brought as slaves sustained all African Americans in their arduous trips across the deserts and oceans. The abiding hope that allowed them to dream of a society in which they could rise by their own merits forged a black community that would not settle for "lugging trunks" in the Golden State.

Moreover, African Americans sought more than material gain when they came to California. Many were immigrants in pursuit of other benefits as well. Black gold rush era settlers hoped to strike it rich, but their goals went far beyond materialism and can be discerned in the names they bestowed on their mines and claims, in the energy they brought to community building, and in their willingness to challenge racial and social barriers. These intangible expectations of life in California shine as brightly as any nugget extracted from the Mother Lode, as any gold dust panned from the American River. African Americans staked claims on the promise of California and demanded payment in full.

Notes

1. Census figures for 1850 and 1860 from United States Department of Commerce, Bureau of the Census, *Historical Statistics of the United States, Colonial Times to 1970, Bicentennial Edition*, part 1, series A, 195–209, Population of States, by Sex, Race, Urban-Rural Residence, and Age: 1790 to 1970, California (Washington DC, GPO, 1975), 25. For early black presence in California, see Rick Moss, "Not Quite Paradise: The Development of the African American Community in Los Angeles Through 1950," *California History, The Magazine of the California Historical Society* 74, no. 3 (fall 1996): 222–35; Kenneth G. Goode, *California's Black Pioneers: A Brief Historical Survey* (Santa Barbara: McNally & Loftin, 1974), 71; William Loren Katz, *The Black West: A Pictorial History*, 3rd ed. (Seattle: Open Hand Publishing, 1987), 119–20; Rudolph Lapp, *Afro-Americans in California* (San Francisco: Boyd & Fraser Publishing, 1979), 1–17.

2. Odell A. Thurman, *The Negro in California before 1890* (master's thesis, College of the Pacific, 1945; reprint, San Francisco: R & E Research Associates, 1973), 25; Lapp, *Blacks in Gold Rush California*, 21–22, 65.

3. Lapp, *Blacks in Gold Rush California*, 64–65, 75; for the story of George Washington Dennis, see Sue Bailey Thurman, *Pioneers of Negro Origin in California* (1949; reprint, San Francisco: R & E Research Associates, 1971), 5.

4. Goode, *California's Black Pioneers*, 44–54. For attempts to bar slaves from gold fields, see also O. Thurman, *Negro in California*, 29–32; Heizer and Almquist, *Other Californians*, 105–11; Larry George Murphy, "Equality Before the Law: The Struggle of Nineteenth-Century Black Californians for Social and Political Justice" (Ph.D. diss., Graduate Theological Union, Berkeley, 1973), 35–45; James Adolphus Fisher, "A History of the Political and Social Development of the Black Community in California, 1850–1950" (Ph.D. diss., State University of New York, Stony Brook, 1971), 14–19.

5. Lapp, *Blacks in Gold Rush California*, 147–52. For more on the Archy Lee case and earlier fugitive slave cases, see Heizer and Almquist, *Other Californians*, 121–28.

6. Heizer and Almquist, *Other Californians*, 239–54.

7. O. Thurman, *Negro in California*, 25; Lapp, *Blacks in Gold Rush California*, 18; Fisher, "History of the Political and Social Development," 12–14; Clarence Caesar, "The Historical Demographics of Sacramento's Black Community, 1848–1900," *California History* 74, no. 3 (fall 1996): 199–213.

8. Both accounts appear in Lapp, *Blacks in Gold Rush California*, 30–31.

9. Lapp, *Blacks in Gold Rush California*, 37–38.

10. For an account of the hazards of the sea route, see George D. Dornin, "Thirty Years Ago," and Bayard Taylor, "El Dorado," both excerpted in Kowalewski, ed., *Gold Rush: A Literary Exploration*, 59–65, 66–72.

11. Kowalewski, *Gold Rush: A Literary Exploration*, 40–43.

12. O. Thurman, *Negro in California*, 25–26; Lapp, *Blacks in Gold Rush California*, 39–40.

13. Lapp, *Blacks in Gold Rush California*, 16, 24.

14. Census of 1850 figures, see Lapp, *Blacks in Gold Rush California*, 49. Lapp notes that the 1850 census included Sandwich Islanders, or "Kanakas," in this figure as well as blacks from Latin America, chiefly Mexico and Chile. For population of gold fields, see Heizer and Almquist, *Other Californians*, 120–21, 144; Liza Ketchum, *The Gold Rush* (New York: Little, Brown & Company, 1996), 96.

15. Bancroft, *History of California*, vol. 6, 222.

16. The correspondent to the *Panama Star* is quoted in O. Thurman, *Negro in California*, 39.

17. For the Foreign Miners Tax, see, Heizer and Almquist, *Other Californians*, 121, 141–45; Ketchum, *Gold Rush*, 96.

18. Lapp, *Blacks in Gold Rush California*, 86.

19. For an account of the Wintun (Wintoon) War and other black-Indian encounters, see Lapp, *Blacks in Gold Rush California*, 86–88. See also Peter M. Knudtson, *The Wintun Indians of California and their Neighbors* (Happy Camp CA: Naturegraph Publishers, 1977), 15–17.

20. Quoted in O. Thurman, *Negro in California*, 24.

21. Lapp, *Blacks in Gold Rush California*, 87.

22. Lapp, *Blacks in Gold Rush California*, 88–89.

23. In 1849 five New England states had given black men the franchise, and Illinois extended the right of suffrage to its African American male residents. See Goode, *California's Black Pioneers*, 79.

24. Lapp, *Blacks in Gold Rush California*, 13; William Hall's wedding and address, 22; Alley Brown report, 22–23.

25. Lapp, *Blacks in Gold Rush California*, 23.

26. Lapp, *Blacks in Gold Rush California*, 13.

27. Lapp, *Blacks in Gold Rush California*, 12.

28. *Mirror of the Times* editorial of December 12, 1857, quoted in Katz, *Black West*, 135.

29. Mary L. Mainery, "The African American Experience: Gold Mining Along the American River," *Golden Notes* 42, nos. 1–3 (spring–fall 1996): 6–10; Lapp, *Blacks in Gold Rush California*, 52–53; "scores of hard miners," 55.

30. O. Thurman, *Negro in California*, 40; Lapp, *Blacks in the Gold Rush*, 55.

31. Lapp, *Blacks in Gold Rush California*, 5–10.

32. Goode, *California's Black Pioneers*, 72–73.

33. Judith Freeman, "Commemorating an L.A. Pioneer," *Angeles Magazine*, April 1990, 58–60; Goode, *California's Black Pioneers*, 90–91.

34. For material on Mary Ellen Pleasant, see Goode, *California's Black Pioneers*, 87–88; Katz, *Black West*, 139; Susheel Bibbs, "Chautauqua Enactment of the Life of Mary Ellen Pleasant," unpublished timeline and biographical sketch.

35. Katz, *Black West*, 132.

36. Goode, *California's Black Pioneers*, 75; O. Thurman, *Negro in California*, 44. For a discussion of the black fight for education in California, see Susan Bragg, "Knowledge is Power: Sacramento Blacks and the Public Schools, 1854–1860," *California History* 75, no. 3 (fall 1996): 215–21.

37. James Carter quoted in O. Thurman, *Negro in California*, 43–44.

38. The antitestimony act is quoted in David L. Snyder, *Negro Civil Rights in California: 1850* (Sacramento: Sacramento Book Collectors Club, 1969), 1. The antitestimony act defined a mulatto as anyone containing one-eighth or more "Negro blood." The law said nothing about Asians.

39. Lapp, *Blacks in Gold Rush California*, 203, 209.

40. Goode, *California's Black Pioneers*, 77.

41. Caesar, "Historical Demographics of Sacramento's Black Community," 209.

8

Disorder, Crime, and Punishment in the California Gold Rush

Martin Ridge

When James Marshall discovered gold at Sutter's sawmill, California was a Mexican province under occupation by the army of the United States. American military officers by and large permitted the existing local authorities—the alcaldes—to remain in office. Alcaldes exercised broad administrative and judicial powers. The military governors hesitated to limit their powers or to alter their rules of civil and criminal practice. There were exceptions. Colonel Richard Mason, military governor from May 1847 to February 1849, ordered a firing-squad execution for three army deserters who had murdered an Englishman and his family at San Miguel mission.[1] Mason also abolished all Mexican laws and customs relating to the private acquisition of land and mineral rights. Ignoring the Indian population, he turned California's undivided lands into part of the national public domain.[2] Mason acted on February 2, 1848, ten days before the signing of the Treaty of Guadalupe Hidalgo, which ended the Mexican-American War. That treaty guaranteed the property rights of all Mexican citizens, including Indians, living in the lands surrendered by Mexico to the United States.[3] Mason did not announce Mexico's surrender of California to the United States until August.

The treaty left California neither a territory nor a state, but with a legal system ill-designed to cope with a gold rush.[4] Moreover, the United States, never a center for precious-metal mining, lacked a strong gold-mining tradition.[5] The federal policy regarding mining became one of acquiescence. Under common law, however, a person disturbing a miner's claim on the public domain could be charged with trespass.[6] The army in California lacked both the power and the authority to prosecute or control gold hunters, even if it had been so ordered. So many soldiers began prospecting that the army granted furloughs to avoid wholesale desertions. Demobilized soldiers—Colonel Jonathan Stevenson's New York regiment consisted of men recruited to settle in California—Indians controlled, owned, or employed by whites; Mexican miners from Sonora; Chilean prospectors; and overland emigrants from the Middle West soon searched the foothills of the Sierra for signs of gold, pried huge chunks of it out of crevices along river banks, and panned the stream beds for nuggets.[7] The rewards were great, but they were dwarfed by exaggerated reports of easy money to be made in the mines. The result was an onslaught of California-bound fortune hunters. They traveled on foot, on horses, in wagons, and on aged and refitted vessels from ports in the United States, Europe, the Pacific Islands, and Asia.[8] Although some Argonauts, as the gold seekers were called, ventured alone, many formed companies with written constitutions. They planned to remain and work together. In many instances these companies—the Chinese and the French were major exceptions—broke up en route or quickly disbanded when the men reached the mines.

Most Argonauts came only in quest of gold they could take home. To them the California gold fields seemed a vast commons, like the sea to fishermen, open to anyone bold enough and lucky enough to exploit it.[9] Like fishermen, too, most understood the accepted rules of behavior and tried to abide by them. Conflict among them was rare as long as resources were abundant. Some, like many hard-working men elsewhere, found release in alcohol, cruel sports, gambling, and rough-and-tumble fighting. None left behind in the States the racial and ethnic prejudices characteristic of antebellum American society. No one in the mining camps expected the Argonauts to be concerned with chastity, piety, or sobriety, the benchmarks of middle-class society during the Victorian era, and they were not. Their behavior shocked foreign as well as easterner observers, who mistakenly saw the miner's world as chaotic and lawless. But an analysis of disorder, property rights, personal safety, crime, punishment, racism, xenophobia, and lynch law indicates that the miners from the United States, who dictated public behavior, ignored many practices of eastern society except when they affected person and property. They proved, by and large, to be lawful, even in fact replicating lawful behavior and legal procedures easily identified with existing customs.

Disorder

These first miners were not alienated, isolated, rebellious figures: they were socially acculturated men who sought wealth. They had small interest in anything else. Little wonder that when Colonel Mason toured the mines in late summer of 1848, he found them hard at work, untroubled by disturbances or social disorder. Weapons were rare. The army, concerned with pacifying the province, prohibited the sale of ammunition for fear of a Mexican uprising.[10] Many of the earliest weapons introduced into the early mining camps had probably been carried west by overlanders from the East who feared Indian attacks.

At first, the all-consuming quest for wealth and the abundance of surface gold meant that San Francisco was almost crime free. R. R. Taylor, on his way to the mines, wrote his wife Catherine: "Millions of dollars worth of goods of every description from Canton silks & toys to Yankee 'nick-nacks' lie stacked up in the streets or strewed about the vacant lots, for want of buildings to store them in. The place is quiet & orderly, nobody thinks of having anything stolen, & nothing is watched or locked up.'[11] But that condition did not last. The town soon confronted a wave of theft and disorder as newcomers drifted in. The "responsible" citizens resorted to a vigilance committee, scoured the town, arrested, fined, imprisoned, and overawed the rowdy and criminal element.[12]

While Congress wrangled over slavery and at length approved the Compromise of 1850, Californians had an election, held a convention, and organized a de facto government. As the basis for local legal administration, the state constitution replaced the office of alcalde with that of justice of the peace, an officer with limited authority. Most JPs behaved like alcaldes and exercised the same broad powers.[13] The effectiveness of the justices remained untested. At Governor Peter Burnett's urging, the 1851 state legislature passed an act making grand larceny—any theft over one hundred dollars—a crime subject to the death penalty. Petty larceny could bring a punishment of fifty lashes on the bare back. Moral behavior remained a private, not a public matter. Miners judged such action themselves. Therefore, crimes against property took precedence over social control.[14]

The gold rush lifted the lid off a Pandora's box of social disorder. The behavior of the forty-niners in the towns, especially San Francisco and Sacramento, earned the opprobrium not only of foreign journalists but also of many sober-minded Americans. "In the course of a month or a year [in San Francisco]," wrote the proper English travel author and amateur miner J. D. Borthwick, "there was more . . . money made and lost . . . more sudden changes of fortune, more eating and drinking, more smoking, swearing, gambling, tobacco chewing, more crime and profligacy . . . than could be shown in any equal space of time by any community of the same size on the face of the earth."[15] "The streets [of San Francisco] presented a scene of intense bustle and excitement . . . [but] here and there was a drunken man lying groveling in the mud, enjoying himself as uninterruptedly as if he were merely a hog."[16] Later, having spent more time among miners and picking up some of their spirit of laissez-faire individualism, Borthwick confessed that he had seen so much intoxication that, when he saw a drunken man arrested, he "was almost inclined to think it an infringement of the individual right of the subject . . . not to allow this hog of a fellow to sober up in the gutter, or to drink himself into a state of quiescence if he felt so inclined."[17]

But some Argonauts were less surprised by the social scene than by the honesty of the people. John Ingalls, on his way to the mines in August 1849, found San Francisco "very peacable [*sic*] much more than one would suppose where there are twenty-five different nations mixt [*sic*] up."[18] Israel Lord, writing in the evangelical Elgin, Illinois, *Western Christian*, found affairs in Sacramento similar: "I think there is less of what is ordinarily called stealing here," he noted, "than in any place I was ever in. . . . A vast amount of property, easily moveable, is daily and nightly exposed without a watch, or even a lock.—The security occurs, too, in a population composed of representatives of all parts of the Globe."[19] The historian Theodore H. Hittell believed that this honesty was less attributable "to the fact that every man went armed and to the knowledge of swift retribution that was almost sure to follow crimes of that nature, but it was probably much more due to the circumstances . . . [where everyone worked with his hands and money was easily earned] than to any consideration of prudence or fear."[20]

Protection of Property

Property rights were broadly but clearly defined. For example, a man's place in the post-office line was a possessory holding. This was no mean consideration: "Hours before the appointed time for opening the [post office] windows [in San Francisco], a dense crowd collected, almost blocking up two streets which gave access to the post office, and having the appearance at a distance of being a mob." Despite its length, "perfect order prevailed: there was no such thing as a man attempting to push himself ahead of those already waiting, nor was there the slightest respect of persons [regardless of wealth or status]. . . . The principle of 'first come first served' was strictly adhered to, and any attempt to infringe the established rule would have been put down by the omnipotent majority. A man's place in line was his individual property."[21] Isaac Barker waited in line unperturbed an hour and a half.[22] D. A. Shaw recounted that selling space to an anxious merchant—

called "selling out"—became a way an impecunious miner could make twenty dollars.[23]

"Rights of property are respected," a miner observed, "for the interests of all effects this; but for the tender sympathies . . . you must look in other land."[24] Frank Marryat, a British sportsman and popular author, agreed. Although life and property were safe in San Francisco, he wrote, the fact that so many men went armed meant that "cases of shootings were therefore very common, and dueling in particular became quite the rage."[25] Benjamin Baxter recorded that after a bullfight, which was a common form of amusement in San Francisco, "there was a street fight near the post office between some rowdies and some of the 'Buties' of the—[brothels]. The girls used their revolvers wounding several of the sterner sex. Next day they were hauled before police and fined for their bravery."[26] Little wonder that a crowd would gather to see a "difficulty between two gentlemen" referred "to arbitration [by the use] of knives or pistols," but if no one was killed the crowd would disperse just as quickly as it had collected.[27] Although dueling was illegal, a death in a duel was viewed by an alcalde or a JP as self-defense or justifiable homicide.

Both J. D. Borthwick and John Ingalls were struck by the greed, gambling, and lack of class consciousness in San Francisco and Sacramento. A "man might approach in appearance to the conventional idea of a gentleman," wrote Borthwick, but "the man standing next to him in the guise of laboring man, was perhaps his superior in wealth, character, and education." Even worse to this Victorian gentleman, a "man was judged by the amount of money in his purse."[28] Borthwick deplored the mad scramble for wealth. At the door of a saloon, he observed, "with one foot raised on the step, would be a well-dressed young man, playing thimblerig, on his leg with a gold pea, for the edification of a crowd of gasping greenhorns, some of whom would sure bite," while not "far off would be a precocious little blackguard of fourteen . . . standing behind a cask, and playing 'French monte.'"[29] John Ingalls, with some disdain, reported that Sacramento was "growing up like an *Irishman's family*," and was not much different. The environment, he believed, unleashed in their most naked and bold state the unrestrained inclinations and bad passions, the basest impulses of men. "Gambling is carried on here to an alarming extent," he wrote, and went on to add, it "is carried on here as openly as any mercantile business in New York. Sunday is usually their [the gamblers'] best day."[30]

Ingalls made no mention of Sacramento's squatters' riot, in which several men were killed. Israel Lord, editorializing in the *Western Christian*, sided with the squatters: "The people of the States who came in last, have taken, or are taking possession of the land where it was not actually occupied by improvements, and are building and improving in defiance of all SHOW or authority of law, except the natural or original *right*; and that in my opinion is not only best, but in reality, the only one worth a straw." In retrospect, the historian Hubert Howe Bancroft also felt that some of the squatters had a just case.[31] He could see little reason why those who had paid nothing for the land and made no improvements should profit from it.

Property, Person, and the Disorderly Element

Within three years of the Sutter's mill discovery, California had more than its share of unsavory and dangerous characters: "Sydney ducks," who were former deportees to the English penal colony in Australia; "Joaquin Murietas," since virtually every Mexican bandit—social, revolutionary, or otherwise—was given the name and denounced as well as romanticized; and an over-full quota of American ruffians, criminals, fugitives, ne'er-do-wells, and knaves. By and large, most miners were anonymous. "No one knew who anyone else was, wrote a popular writer, "and only the more ill-mannered and uneasy desired to be known."[32] A limerick ran:

O, what was your name in the States?
Was it Thompson or Johnson or Bates?
Did you murder your wife?
And fly for your life?
Say, what was your name in the States?[33]

There is some logic to the argument that the criminals, gamblers, and riffraff element that lived by its wits at first avoided the mines because of the rigors of camp life; but after confronting the increased pressures from law enforcement and vigilance committees in the larger towns, they moved to the gold fields.[34] Harsh times in the mines in 1850 forced many an impoverished miner back to San Francisco and may have made him a predator. Therefore, the mines for the most part remained peaceful.

Standing in the icy rivers and creeks that flowed from the snows of the Sierra or shoveling ore in a dry digging left men unfamiliar with physical labor bone weary. The less rugged fell fatal victim to disease and exhaustion. For the survivors in the isolated diggings in 1848 and early 1849, recreation before the coming of a saloon or a gambling hall was peaceable: reading, card playing, swapping yarns, and enjoying what music they could manage. Most miners sought companionship and worked with one partner or several. General Persifor F. Smith, who commanded the army's Pacific Division and wanted to exclude Mexican and Chilean miners, felt that any large city in the East would witness more disorder than all of California, and General Bennett Riley, who visited the mines in the summer of 1849, found that in the small camps the men had elected alcaldes and sheriffs who proved both diligent and loyal.[35]

Mining camps were anything but a stable society. Partnerships formed and dissolved quickly; claims were bought, sold, and traded; word of richer strikes drew off populations; and there were few mechanisms to control antisocial but not necessarily criminal behavior. Although the mines attracted many men who might look with disgust on the personal habits of their neighbors, they rarely did much about them. One group of miners did agree among themselves not to smoke, gamble, drink, swear—there was a four-bit (fifty-cents) fine for swearing—and to shave once a week, but they may have been a singular exception.[36] T. S. Eliot's chorus in "The Rock" asks: "Do you huddle so close together because you love each other?"[37] Miners, moiling in the river beds and tablelands below the Sierra, would have exclaimed, no!

Many camps appeared chaotic, and their very names are symbols of disorder: Whooping Boys Hollow, Hangtown—later Placerville—and Murderers Bar. Sherlock Bristol, a pioneer preacher, pointed out that the clergy were seldom welcome in the camps and that they were often harassed by "the boys."[38] Bullying tactics were not unusual. J. B. Borthwick tells of "two hulking [American] fellows who came swaggering in [a small Catholic church], and jostled their way through the crowd of Mexicans, making it evident from their demeanor, that their only object was to show contempt for the congregation and for the whole proceedings."[39] There was no authority to discipline them. A straight-laced German traveler, Friedrich Gerstaecker, was appalled by the pictures of seminude women displayed in gambling houses and saloons, noting "the farther you went into the interior, the more indecent these pictures became, becoming in the mines the most obscene points . . . every decent man would turn away in disgust from a shameless sight. These gambling houses are for California," Gerstaecker concluded with disgust, "what slavery is to the United States."[40]

Sarah Royce, a proper New England woman, recalled her unease when she and her physician husband moved into a tent: "Still, there was a lurking feeling of want of security from having only a cloth wall between us and out of doors. . . . But I soon learned that I had no reason to fear."[41] She had yet to discover that in most mining camps the tent was "held inviolate" and protected all that it enclosed. There "was a tacit disposition to make the canvas . . . as sacred as once were the portals of a church."[42]

Outside the sanctity of the tent, however, the absence of respectable women and the want of refined entertainment fostered dissipation in the saloon, the gambling den, and later the brothel. "All kinds of wickedness is done in these 'diggins,'" complained the religious writer Israel Lord, "drinking, swearing, swindling, litigation, quarreling and fighting."[43] He was specifically depicting life at Parks Bar, but he could have been describing almost any camp after 1850.

The camps succumbed to disorder, especially as predatory elements invaded the mines. Amador County was almost typical by 1851. There the dance hall, gambling den, and saloon prevailed.[44] "Take a sprinkling of sober-eyed, earnest, shrewd, energetic New-England business-men," wrote George F. Parsons of Marshall during its heyday, "mingle with them a number of rollicking sailors, a dark band of Australian convicts and cutthroats, a dash of Mexican and frontier desperadoes, a group of hardy backwoodsmen, some professional gamblers, whiskey dealers, general swindlers, or 'rural agriculturalists'... and having thrown in a promiscuous crowd of broken-down merchants, disappointed lovers, black sheep, unfledged dry-goods clerks, professional miners from all parts of the world, Adullamites generally, stir up the mixture, season strongly with gold-fever, bad liquor, faro, monte, rouge-et-noire, quarrels, oaths, pistols, knives, dancing, and digging, and you have something approximating... the early days."[45] David A. Shaw remembered a slightly more honest form of theft at Drytown: "The 'shingle,' of the man who neither used the 'hoe,' shovel, or rocker but reaped a rich harvest nevertheless. He was in evidence as elsewhere, bearing the 'legend,' 'Si compra oro aquí'—gold dust bought here."[46] Lucius Fairchild confessed that on the Cosumnes River, "it's dog eat dog & every man for himself in this country."[47] Fairchild probably exaggerated. Mrs. Royce, striving to establish a sense of community, felt that there were "about us selfish men, who would stop at nothing for the sake of gain; but I am glad to say... generous aid and ready sympathy were more common."[48] Although she would have conceded that a man might well be killed in a bar fight—fights were almost a spectator sport— and, unless he had friends, his death might simply be ignored as part of the general disorder. She did not mean that there was a lack of payback vengeance, but no one demanded that the camp take action against the culprit. At least one mining camp responded differently: after the shooting of a miner, Stringtown barred all gamblers.[49]

Alcohol contributed largely to the disorderly and violent behavior. Israel Lord noted with irony that many habitués of the saloons were temperance men at home. At Long's Bar, where he mined, Lord believed "that one sixth of the whole population will get drunk—dead—rolling down drunk."[50] Mrs. Royce wrote: "It was very common to hear people who had started on this downward moral grade, deprecating the very acts they were committing, or the practices they were countenancing; and concluding their weak lament by saying 'But here in California we *have to do such things.*'"[51] Lucius Fairchild thought Scott's Bar "decidedly the Roughest place and the miners the most Rowdy drunken set I ever seen in my life. Every night some party is on a spree whooping & yelling around town, fighting, swearing, and breaking the Rum holes up &c. One night it will be the Dutch (the most respectable portion of men) celibrating [*sic*] some annaversary [*sic*] of the 'Faterland.' The Irish will have a general drunk, when you may look for any quantity of fights, the French will take a turn, sometimes all together."[52] As long as drunkenness resulted only in disorder and not in serious property damage or homicide, it provoked little more than private censor.

Crime and Punishment

Crimes against persons were often handled in a summary way. What might start out as a verbal altercation between intoxicated men could lead to a fistfight and ultimately to a homicide.[53] As a result, even when an inquest was held, self-defense was broadly interpreted and accepted. Payback vengeance, too, seems rarely to have been punished. There was often a rush to judgment. The French physician Pierre Garnier, asked to serve as coroner, found that the inquest was held in the room with the cadaver. He was told to perform his work during the hearing, while witnesses testified. "Everything," he observed, "is very fast for Americans."[54]

There were very few women in the early camps and few recorded instances of crimes of passion, of domestic violence, or of acts of aggression directed against women. An attempted assault upon a woman provoked an immediate public response. A black man working on the Cosumnes River was charged with assaulting a white woman and promptly hanged.[55] In Stockton, as the journalist Bayard Taylor reported: "The night before my arrival, three negroes [*sic*], while on a drunken revel, entered the tent of [a] Chilian [*sic*], and attempted to violate a female within. Defeated . . . they fired their pistols at the tent and left. Complaint was made to the Alcalde, two of the negroes [*sic*] seized and identified, witnesses examined, a jury summoned, and verdict given, without delay." One man received fifty lashes, the other twenty, and both were ordered to leave town in forty-eight hours and not to return on pain of death. As "the negroes [*sic*] were stripped, tied to a tree standing in the middle of the principal street . . . bystanders jeered, laughed, and accompanied every blow with coarse and unfeeling remarks."[56] Some men objected to the cruelty of the decision, but with no prisons the alternative was a death sentence. Since the woman was associated with a Chilean, and there was intense ethnic hostility toward Chileans, neither the status of the woman nor her ethnicity seemed an issue; morality overcame prejudice.

Prejudice, however, was not absent. In 1851 a Mexican woman named Juanita killed an Australian miner in Downieville. He had burst into Juanita's cabin while quite drunk during the night of the local Fourth of July celebration. Later—as some sources assert—when the offending miner may have returned to offer an apology, she stabbed him. Juanita was taken before what amounted to a kangaroo court, convicted, and hanged before a jeering crowd of one thousand. (The woman's husband, present at the time of the miner's murder, was exonerated.) Men who protested against such brutality placed themselves at risk. The historian Hubert Howe Bancroft defended the actions of the miners. This episode was so unusual that it is reported in scores of miner's journals and memoirs. It is sometime seen as marking "a line drawn between the early and innocent . . . gold mining [era] . . . and the dawning of the second [more violent] phase of the California gold rush."[57]

Racism and Xenophobia

The racism and xenophobia characteristic of the United States in the 1850s produced both social disorder and interpersonal violence in the mining camps. The group that suffered most over time and that had the least hope of redress, other than vengeance, was California's Native people. For many miners the Indians did not warrant any consideration. Their lands were invaded, their property often taken, and their women abused.[58] "If he dares to strike a blow . . . even in defence [*sic*] of his wife and children," wrote Bancroft, "an outcry was raised, and mounted men with rifles would ride to the rancheria, and shoot down men, women, and children innocent and guilty promiscuously."[59]

Bancroft is often guilty of hyperbole but not in this case.[60] Murderers Bar earned its unenviable name because of an Indian raid. Seven Oregonians, prospecting on the American River, tried to take advantage of some Indian women. A fight broke out between the Indians and the miners that left three Indians dead. Later, when the miners made camp, the Indians took payback vengeance—a practice widely shared among Indians—by killing five of the whites. The remaining two fled to Coloma, about fifteen miles away, where, claiming their hands were clean, they incited the miners into attacking and killing a group of nearby peaceful Indians. White miners often acted against any Indians, usually the closest, even if they were peaceful.[61] This procedure was wholly outside the Anglo-American legal tradition, where only those persons are punished who are actually guilty.

In dealing with Indians, the white Argonauts did not treat all homicides the same way. When miners on the Feather River apprehended three Indians who had killed five white men, they were promptly hung.[62] A miner, William Tell Parker, recorded in his journal that after two whites had been killed, a group of men attacked an Indian village and slaughtered women and children as well as men. Parker, who thought in American legal terms, doubted that the guilty had been punished.[63] When a band of irate Indians in 1851 attacked and killed a group of white desperadoes who had been active near the mining camp, no one objected because the culprits had plagued the countryside.[64] Parker also reported the camp's dilemma when a white man shot a harmless, unarmed Indian: "The report is today that he is dead. Some of the citizens were in favor of delivering the offender up to the Indians for them to punish, & others were for arresting him by law, and others were in favor of letting him run at large. The latter council prevailed & the man has 'vamosed' [*sic*]."[65]

If whites had little enthusiasm for punishing a white man, not all whites had the stomach actually to whip an Indian for theft. Hungry Indian women often rummaged through miners' tents to take food, knowing that as women they were unlikely to be whipped.[66] Alfred T. Jackson reported that at Rock Creek, when an Indian was caught stealing gold, he was sentenced to fifty lashes on his bare back. But "[n]obody would volunteer to do the whipping," according to Jackson, "so we drew lots and Dick Stiles got the job . . . but the Indian after the first-half dozen strokes made such a howl that we let him go."[67]

African Americans in the camps were always potential victims of discrimination as well as interpersonal hostility. Southerners spurned social contact with blacks and refused to accept the fact that California was a free state and that blacks who lived in California before annexation were free under Mexican law.[68] Israel Lord pointed to the tensions in Marysville by noting a Dr. Jamison, who caused a row by refusing to drink with a man he called a "nigger." Lord, a northerner, put the word in quotation marks.[69] J. D. Borthwick found the race issue more complex than he had imagined. Some Americans were tolerant—"not that negroes [*sic*] were allowed to sit at a table with white men, but," he observed with irony, "the important fact that a 'nigger's dollars were as good as any others' . . . overcame their prejudice so far as negroes [*sic*] were permitted to lose their money in gambling houses; and . . . might be seen receiving drinks at the hands of white barkeepers."[70]

Racism could lead to cruelty. Jacob Henry Bachman, the so-called used-up miner, reporting cynically on a fellow from Bombay, demonstrated the underlying peculiar strain of racism in the miners' justice system. The fellow "says that he has been robbed of nineteen hundred dollars by some Indians near Douglas Flatt [*sic*] a party immediately start after them, kill one . . . and wound two others—burn their rancherie &c. . . . People in town talk of hanging the black fellow—say that his story about the robbery was false—get up a trial—jury cant [*sic*] agree. . . . The black fellow received twenty-five lashes in the presence of the Indians as a caution that he not be robbed again. The white men who shot the Indian go scot free—so all parties are satisfied."[71] What Bachman failed to realize was that for the Indians this was probably not an issue of individual culpability—who fired the shot—but of causation. Thus the whipping of the black man covered the eyes of the dead and whitened the path of peace between parties.

In the eastern states, xenophobia focused on Roman Catholic and Irish immigrants. In California it centered on Mexicans, Chileans, French, and later Chinese miners, all of whom tended to keep to themselves. There was much angry talk, threats, the enactment of a foreign miners' tax, and some criminal behavior.[72] The miners' tax, twenty dollars per month, was intended to drive out the Mexicans and the Chileans. Thousands of Mexicans and Chileans returned home or abandoned mining, much to the disappointment of local merchants. Others simply balked at paying the tax, and some in Sonora, where they were a majority, raised a ruckus. Alarmed, the Americans in the surrounding mining camps rallied for self-protection. There followed so drastic a reduction in the miners' tax that foreigners remained in the fields.[73]

Gerstaecker reported that when the American thugs found a lone foreign miner, they tried to drive him off by claiming that he had not paid the tax.[74] The Mexicans, fearful of these claim jumpers, when asked by a passerby, "Mucho oro acqui?" answered, "Si, poquito, Senor," which confused the American, who had exhausted his knowledge of Spanish.[75] Claim jumpers boasted that since California was part of the United States, they had a superior right to the mines. Sometimes they looted a placer mine before they were ousted. Their actions were, an American admitted, "an outrage on the Mexicans."[76] Little wonder that, even though the Mexicans tended to be accommodating, there were fights between them and Americans.

But bloodshed was uncommon unless banditry or gambling was involved. Violence and bloodshed were more frequent in the case of attacks on the Chileans, who were far from submissive. They were often driven from their claims, beaten, and even killed by toughs who escaped punishment.[77]

The French also faced hostility because they kept together and spoke and behaved differently. The same forty-niner who denounced the "outrage on the Mexicans" reported that, when some toughs jumped the claim of Frenchmen who owned one of the richest mines at Nigger Hill, there "was a big excitement and a miner's meeting called, which decided the Frenchmen's titles were as good as anybody else's and so the foreigners got the ground again." All this, he continued, shows "that we have more regard for other peoples than the Mariposa miners [who drove out foreigners]."[78] The response to the French miners often proved ambiguous. In a fracas at Mokelumne Hill concerning a claim, while "one of the Americans was attempting to drive the Frenchmen off, one man shot an American, mortally wounding him. The excitement was so great the Americans sent up [the Mokelumne River] . . . for men and arms." In recounting the event an American diarist wrote: "All they done with the French was to take away their arms as they could not find the Frenchman that shot the American, they let them all go."[79] The French were not always that lucky.

Of all the miners, none suffered more from discrimination and violence than the Chinese. Their dress, collaborative enterprises, food, eating habits, mining practices, use of opium, and especially their willingness to work mines considered unprofitable made them victims of the most vicious racism.[80] That other miners saw them as an economic threat is indisputable. "They are not looked upon as human beings," one wrote, "and have no rights that a white man is bound to respect." He added that after Mexican bandits raided the Chinese at Deer Creek, killed two Chinese miners, and reportedly got away with thirty thousand dollars, the Chinese appealed for protection, but local officials ignored their request.[81] A short time later at Deer Creek, some Chinese diverted water without permission, and "about fifty miners gathered together, ran the Chinamen out of the District, broke up their pumps, burned up their cabins, tore out their dams, destroyed their ditches, and warned them not to come back under penalty of being shot if they made a reappearance."[82]

J. D. Borthwick would have found the Chinese action unusual because they "did not venture to assert equal rights so far as to take up any claim which other miners would think worthwhile to work; but in such places as yield them a dollar or two a day they were allowed to scratch away unmolested. Had they happened to strike a rich lead, they would have been driven off their claim immediately."[83] Frank Marryat, who had lived in Amoy, knew the Chinese were not aggressive: "Chinamen are [a] long time coming to blows," he declared. "When a couple of Chinese dispute over the right to a claim," wrote Marryat, "the noise and gesticulations are frightful . . . but further than a dreadful uproar, no harm came from these rencontres."[84] The only time the Chinese fought, Marryat explained, was when someone "was driving poor 'John' into a corner."[85]

At Deer Creek, which was strongly anti-Chinese, the miners called a meeting and adopted a "law" that the Chinese should not be allowed to take up or hold ground unless it was purchased from a white owner. Some miners favored driving the Chinese out of the country altogether. "But," explained one observer, "the majority thought it was a good thing to sell them claims, as it was an easy way to make money."[86] Pringle Shaw, an Englishman, tells of miners defending the rights of Chinese against Arkansas claim jumpers, whom he called white trash, because the Chinese had bought their claim from a white.[87] But at Columbia, the miners decided that any person who sold "a claim to an Asiatic or South-Sea Islander shall not be allowed to hold another claim in this district for a space of six months."[88] For all practical purposes many mining camps tried to effect restrictive covenants, yet the desire to make money through the sale of mining claims conflicted with and often overcame racial and ethnic prejudices.

Gun Rule and Lynch Law

These examples of xenophobia, the prevalent gambling, and outbreaks of violence yield the impression, reinforced by the stories of Bret Harte and other authors, that early miners lived in a world with no law.[89] Even many miners believed that property and life were safe only because so many of them had guns.[90] "There was no law except the natural law of self preservation," wrote one. "Every man was armed and generally surrounded by armed friends." And, he added, "the delays of law and the tricks of lawyers could not avert the just doom of the criminal."[91] Frank Marryat summarized this point: "For the fear of the law, in the best regulated community, is not so strong as the fear of sudden death; and if quarrels and assassinations were rare, comparatively, in the mountains, it was owing to the fact that every man was able to protect himself. It is generally inferred, as a matter of course, that where all men carry arms, blood is shed on the first passion, and life is not safe. This is not so; it is where all carry arms that quarrels are rare."[92] A modern scholar agrees: "One reason the crime rate was so low," writes John Umbeck, "was because everyone carried a gun."[93] Moreover, Umbeck applies this belief to property rights: "In acquiring exclusive mining rights, the miners could have chosen [at least in theory] from a range of rationing methods which included the use of violence or the threat of violence. Because their ability to use violence was the basis of all property rights, every miner carried at least one gun."[94]

This idea that there was no law but individual force of arms defies historical evidence. Many miners no doubt owned guns. Hinton Helper thought that ninety-nine out of one hundred did, but that did not mean that they were always armed.[95] Quite the contrary; the work of mining would have made carrying a gun a burden. As the pioneer historian Theodore Hittell summarized, "Every man had to pick, shovel, remove boulders, carry earth, dip water, work the rocker or keep the sluice box—day in and day out, often standing in ice-cold water from the snow fields of the Sierra summits."[96] In gambling dens and saloons, no doubt disputes, slight misunderstandings or grave difficulties, or even a few misplaced words could result in an armed fracas. But there is almost no evidence of an individual on his own using a gun to settle either a civil or a criminal grievance. There is overwhelming evidence that such actions were taken by the group, especially in cases of claim jumping, theft, or homicide. Moreover, even if the group became an excited, wrathful mob, the participants argued that they were reclaiming and exercising legal authority because established institutions of law had failed or were yet lacking.

Contemporary observers were either appalled or impressed by what they called "lynch law"—instances when miners gathered to deal with crimes. Many critics misused the expression. Lynch law is the act of doing "justice" in an irregular or irresponsible manner by unauthorized, anonymous individuals, acting in opposition to the legally established and open courts. What took place prior to 1851 occurred most often where there were no courts, and where the alcaldes or JPs were either too far away or ineffective.[97] Action was taken by known persons in broad daylight. Critics of the miners' tribunals, contemporary writer Hinton Helper believed, "committed the very common error of judging the institutions of one set of people by the standard of another. They have applied to California the same rule which would guide them in their judgment of an Atlantic state. In reality there is no parallel between them."[98]

The American Argonaut carried more baggage in his head than in his hands—notions of God, rules of right and wrong, and the customs of lawful behavior. Like other pioneers, when he modified institutions—as in later mining law or water rights—he was conscious of how things should be done. At Eagle Gulch, for example, when Daniel Price was crushed to death, the miners held a mass meeting, selected a committee to take charge of his effects, posted a notice requesting that persons having claims against the dead man's estate come forward, liquidated the appropriate claims, and then sent Price's remaining assets east to his widow. The entire procedure— essentially a probate—was handled without a court.[99] The Price episode was not unusual.[100] Most miners kept their contracts and paid their debts.[101] They did not take loose property, even though mules and horses often ran free and housing seemed abandoned. They were concerned, not only that the rightful owners might come back to claim their property, but also that others might think the property, whether livestock or a residence, had been stolen—a conclusion to be avoided in the California gold fields. The miners in effect implemented the long-established common law principle that unexplained possession assured conviction, thus shifting the burden of proof onto the person who claimed the property without evidence of a clear title. One miner, A. J. McCall, believed that "men beyond the reach of the civil law or statute law are more sensitive to the [property] rights of others and so more disposed to regard them."[102] Tools were never taken or even moved because they indicated the location of a claim and the mining right of the owner. Evidence of occupation and use provided a possessory right. The miners had, in a sense, accepted the law as custom, sometimes even attempting to follow the legal forms with which they had been familiar in their home states.

The procedures and punishments pursued by miners' courts have been much criticized. Bancroft thought these courts were often no more than capricious mobs that inflicted punishment in an offhand manner. A trivial incident, he argued, could determine whether a culprit would be whipped or hanged. There were enough bizarre episodes after 1851 for Bancroft to picture the oak trees of the Sierra foothills as "tasselled with the carcasses of the wicked!" Mobs, he wrote, for good or evil, worked tyrannies on the populations of both cities and camps.[103] But there is no agreement on this issue. Alfred T. Jackson, an observant forty-niner, declared that although most miners were willing judges, only the riffraff would watch a sentence carried out: "There were few miners there," Jackson wrote of one episode, "and it would be hard to get together a worse lot of savages than those who stood around gloating over the wretches. The chances are that nine out of ten of the lookers-on, if they got their just desserts, deserved the same sort of punishment that was being dealt out to the culprits. The trouble is that most of the men are too ready to see themselves set up as judges, and swayed by their passions, inflict penalties, even the sentence of death, on insufficient evidence."[104] Most miners looked with disdain upon those who administered punishment and those who reveled in it. Charles D. Ferguson said that Butcher Bill, who accepted five hundred dollars to deliver thirty-five lashes to each of three convicted felons, "dropped to the lowest round of the social ladder, even to that of thieves themselves."[105]

J. D. Borthwick, in his own words, spent "two or three years cruising about in the mines and never saw a 'lynching.'"[106] Another miner, Charles D. Ferguson, said "never in my experience did I either know or hear of any excited crowd carry their design to execute until the culprit had a fair and impartial trial."[107] The journals and reminiscences of miners often noted cases where men were severely punished but recorded that such action was taken only after a trial where the truth was sought out: juries were selected, defenders and prosecutors named, and a judge elected. Witnesses were heard and often interrogated by any miner present. This was true in early civil cases—conflicts over mining claims—as well as in criminal cases. Punishment was determined often by consensus rather than by a judge. In Nevada City, Alfred Jackson reported, "the miners have elected an alcalde, but his decisions are not binding, only as they are accepted by the people."[108] After a verdict, another miner recorded, "Some were for hanging and some were for whipping & branding so there was a committee appointed to [decide] what the punishment should be. So the committee concluded that he be given fifty lashes and branded on the cheek with a letter & never to show himself in these parts or they would hang him."[109] Many contemporaries praised the rough-and-ready justice as a triumph of America's Anglo-Saxon heritage.[110] But a twentieth-century historian, looking to the philosopher Josiah Royce (himself a product of the mining town of Grass Valley), wrote: "A miners' court might conduct a splendid fair and 'earnest' trial. Then having convicted the accused, say of theft, the court would either hang him, which was immoral; or whip and banish him, which was equally immoral since it turned him loose, hurt and embittered to prey on other camps." Since miners would not build jails or send culprits to the towns for trial, this critic concluded, "Social irresponsibility led invariably to social immorality."[111] Others saw mining camp justice as the only practical solution to an intractable problem. "At all events," wrote Isaac Jones Wister, a veteran of the California gold rush, "the method was not without substantial advantage while it lasted, and it may be worth the while of philosophers to note that the novel judicial phenomenon need not necessarily be bad because worked out by practical men, not given much to speculation or remote consequences."[112] Wister may have been more insightful than many who have censured the miners' tribunals, for he recognized the moral patterns of behavior hidden in their apparent formlessness.

What critics and defenders of the miners' tribunals have commonly missed is that the men in the mining camps tried to follow the law and legal procedure as they understood it.[113] Yet California's miners distrusted judges and lawyers because they used rhetoric and narrow legal technicalities to shield the guilty or protect the patently dishonest.[114] Many Americans felt that the legal system in the hands of professionals generated random results. Israel Lord, defending the miners' tribunals, wrote: "The unsworn witnesses, no doubt, 'told the truth, the whole truth, and nothing but the truth,' which is more than I can say for them in any court of law I ever attended—and why? The lawyers will not let them. . . . In our case the jury was not sworn, and yet, I doubt not, did exact justice, which is more than the law, the judges, and the lawyers will allow them to do in the States."[115]

Lord's views were hardly unique, especially regarding alcaldes and JPs. Some untrained justices fared badly. Bancroft mentions one JP who was whipped by an unhappy plaintiff and another who was stabbed to death.[116] Stephen J. Field, later an associate justice of the Supreme Court of the United States, tangled repeatedly with an alcalde who was eventually forced from the bench. Field himself confessed that, when he was an alcalde, he knew little of Mexican law.[117] Some JPs, notorious for bad decisions, collecting high fees, and levying outrageous fines, were driven out of town.[118] Most, however, maintained their authority by relying on common sense. One example is the justice in the Columbia mining district. Facing an "American miner's complaint against a Mexican for stealing a pair of old leather leggings, that official, himself an American, remonstrated; but justice being demanded, he fined the Mexican three ounces (about fifty dollars) for the theft, and the miner one ounce for making a complaint over such a trifle."[119]

There is a tendency to depict the early California mining camps as being without law, as a Hobbesian universe where the gun prevailed, and where it was every man for himself.[120] Overlooked in this interpretation is the fact that the miners wrote rules establishing possessory rights and enforced them, following familiar legal principles and precedents. Even when they acted more like a lynch mob than a fair tribunal in punishing someone for homicide or theft, they were engaged in a group legal exercise, however coarse and crude. There is irony in the fact that after 1851, as county courts were established in California, with trained lawyers then arguing cases involving homicides, mining claims, water rights, and waste, true lynch law became a fact. Moreover, claim jumping and theft became increasingly prevalent. Miners hid their hoards and could no longer leave their tools to mark their claims. Bancroft points out that in 1855 there were 535 homicides, seven legal executions, but forty-nine extralegal, informal ones.[121] By the mid-1850s, as new gold mines became scarce and competition more keen, the social fabric, which had early been firm, though skewed by prejudice, had begun to unravel.[122] The first mention of a highwayman occurs in 1852, and the first stage robbery in California took place in 1856.[123] The opening of courts neither prevented crime nor ended mob violence, popular tribunals, and vigilance committees.

Both romantics and critics, relying on shocked Victorian observers, have overly dramatized the turmoil in the early California mining camps. Disorderly, brawling, intemperate, xenophobic, and racist, California's early miners surely were. But in cases of severe antisocial behavior, such as theft, homicides, or attempted rape, and in cases involving mining claims or possessory rights, they had a clear understanding of legal customs and tried to abide by them. Although the American miners were not members of a community in a technical sense, in their daily dealings with each other, most shared a moral code based on experience and logic that had little to do with the power of a sovereign. No one can deny that the record of abuses is sorry and disheartening, especially in dealings between American miners and the California Native peoples, Mexicans, Chileans, and Chinese. The California mines were not a peaceable kingdom. There was plenty of disorder, but the mines and the miners were never beyond the law.

Notes

1. See Bancroft, *History of California,* 8:450. For an extensive discussion of Mexican and American law in California, see Richard R. Powell, *Compromises of Conflicting Claims: A Century of California Law, 1760–1860* (Dobbs Ferry NY: Oceana Publications, 1977).

2. John R. Umbeck, *A Theory of Property Rights, with Application to the California Gold Rush* (Ames: Iowa State University Press, 1981), 69.

3. See Griswold del Castillo, *Treaty of Guadalupe Hidalgo,* 62–68.

4. Ray August, "Gringos v. Mineros: The Hispanic Origins of Western American Mining Laws," *Western Legal History* 9 (summer/fall 1996), 147–75. August argues that Mexican mining law, based on Spanish ordinances, was the true basis for American mining law. He further declares that historians who deny the significance of Mexican practice reflect an American or Anglo-Saxon xenophobia. Lacking evidence of specific genetic connections between Mexican and American mining codes, his case is unpersuasive.

5. August, "Gringos v. Mineros," 4.

6. Umbeck, *Theory of Property Rights*, 4.

7. Rawls, "Gold Diggers," 28–45. Rawls emphasizes the lack of hostility between Indians and whites in the early period and the large number of California natives who worked in the mines. See also Hurtado, *Indian Survival on the California Frontier.* Hurtado points out that in 1848 and 1849 some California settlers contracted to provide Indian labor to miners for a share of the proceeds (103).

8. J. S. Holliday, *The World Rushed In: The California Gold Rush Experience* (New York: Simon & Schuster, 1981).

9. For a discussion of the concept of the commons, see Arthur F. McEvoy, *The Fisherman's Problem: Ecology and Law in the California Fisheries, 1850–1980* (New York: Cambridge University Press, 1986); and Carol Rose, "The Comedy of the Commons: Custom, Commerce, and Inherently Public Property," *University of Chicago Law Review* 53 (summer 1986): 711–81.

10. John A. Swan, *A Trip to the Gold Mines of California in 1848*, ed. John A. Hussey (San Francisco: Book Club of California, 1960), 16–17. As late as early January 1850, guns cost more in Philadelphia than in San Francisco. If the need for weapons had been great, it would have been a seller's market.

11. John Walton Caughey, ed., *Seeing the Elephant: Letters of R. R. Taylor, Forty-niner* (Los Angeles: Ward Ritchie Press, 1951), 54.

12. For a discussion of the movement against the "Hounds," a group of thugs that terrorized Chileans and others in San Francisco, see Bancroft, *History of California,* 6:212. See also Roger W. Lotchin, *San Francisco, 1846–1856: From Hamlet to City* (New York: Oxford University Press, 1974), 188–96.

13. Theodore H. Hittell, *History of California,* 4 vols. (San Francisco: N. J. Stone & Company, 1898), 3:226.

14. Bancroft, *History of California,* 8:193. See also Jason Robert Beck, "California Gold Rush Violence, 1849–1854: A Psychological Interpretation" (Ph.D. diss., University of Southern California, 1978), 110; Gordon Morris Bakken, "Death for Grand Larceny," in John W. Johnson, ed., *Historic U.S. Court Cases, 1690–1990: An Encyclopedia* (New York: Garland Publishing, 1992), 34–36.

15. Borthwick, *Gold Hunters*, 58–59.

16. Borthwick, *Gold Hunters*, 59.

17. Borthwick, *Gold Hunters*, 313.

18. R. W. G. Vail, ed., *California Letters of the Gold Rush Period: The Correspondence of John Ingalls, 1849–1851* (Worcester MA: American Antiquarian Society, 1938), 13–14.

19. Israel Shipman Pelton Lord, "Journal of an Overland Trip to California by Way of the Oregon Trail, Life in the Mines, [and] Return Journey," December 26, 1849, manuscript collection, Huntington Library, San Marino, California.

20. Hittell, *History of California*, 3:175.

21. Borthwick, *Gold Hunters*, 89–90.

22. "Isaac Barker: Diary of a Voyage around Cape Horn from Boston to San Francisco . . . and Life in the Mines near Mormon Island, California," June 23, 1850, manuscript collection, Huntington Library.

23. David A. Shaw, *Eldorado: Or, California as Seen by A Pioneer, 1850–1900*, ed. Joseph Gaer (Los Angeles: Baumgardt & Co., 1900), 138. The sanctity of private property in the westering experience is strongly emphasized by John Philip Reid, *Law for the Elephant: Property and Social Behavior on the Overland Trail* (San Marino: Huntington Library, 1980).

24. John Cumming, ed., *The Gold Rush: Letters from the Wolverine Rangers to the Marshall Michigan Statesman, 1849–1851* (Mount Pleasant MI: Cumming Press, 1974), 74.

25. Frank Marryat, *Mountains and Molehills: Or Recollections of a Burnt Journal* (1855; reprint, Stanford: Stanford University Press, 1952), 315.

26. Benjamin Baxter diary, August 11, 1850, manuscript collection, Huntington Library.

27. Borthwick, *Gold Hunters*, 62.

28. Borthwick, *Gold Hunters*, 68.

29. Borthwick, *Gold Hunters*, 61.

30. Vail, *California Letters of the Gold Rush Period*, 50.

31. Lord, "Journal of an Overland Trip," December 25, 1849. Hubert Howe Bancroft provides an extended discussion of the squatters and their opponents. As in many such cases, the issues are complex: Bancroft, *History of California*, 6:332–35.

32. Roberta Evelyn Holmes, *The Southern Mines of California: Early Development of the Sonora Mining Region* (San Francisco: Grabhorn Press, 1930), 39.

33. Joseph Henry Jackson, *Anybody's Gold: The Story of California's Mining Towns* (New York: D. Appleton-Century, 1941), 100.

34. Caughey, *Gold is the Cornerstone*, 238. Caughey relies on Hubert Howe Bancroft, who believed that violence spread from the mines to the towns. But Bancroft refers to the conditions that resulted from the terrible state of the mines in the winter of 1850: Bancroft, *History of California*, 6:434,466. For the opposing view, see

Jackson, *Anybody's Gold*, 121. See also William Tell Parker, Journal, September 16, 1850, manuscript collection, Huntington Library.

35. Owen Cochran Coy, *Gold Days* (Los Angeles: Powell Publishing, 1929), 203–4.

36. Lord, "Journal of an Overland Trip," enclosing an article from the *Western Christian*, March 31, 1850.

37. *The Complete Poems and Plays of T. S. Eliot* (London: Faber, 1969), 155.

38. Sherlock Bristol, *The Pioneer Preacher: Incidents of Interest and Experiences in the Author's Life* (Chicago: Fleming H. Revell, 1887), 168–70.

39. Borthwick, *Gold Hunters*, 298–99.

40. Friedrich Gerstaecker, *California Gold Mines* (Oakland CA: Biobooks, 1946), 68.

41. S. Royce, *Frontier Lady*, 80.

42. Taylor, *Eldorado*, 1:93.

43. See Lord, "Journal of an Overland Trip," enclosing *American Baptist*, December 1850.

44. Shaw, *Eldorado*, 145.

45. Quoted in Charles Howard Shinn, *Mining Camps: A Study of American Frontier Government* (1885; reprint New York: Harper & Row, 1965), 158.

46. Shaw, *Eldorado*, 145.

47. Joseph Schafer, ed., *California Letters of Lucius Fairchild* (Madison: State Historical Society of Wisconsin, 1931), 59.

48. S. Royce, *Frontier Lady*, 96.

49. S. Weston, *Life in the Mountains: Or, Four Months in the Mines of California* (Providence RI: E. P. Weston, 1854), 26–27.

50. Lord, "Journal of an Overland Trip," April 4, 1850.

51. S. Royce, *Frontier Lady*, 107.

52. Schafer, *California Letters*, 185.

53. Beck, "California Gold Rush Violence," 43; Hittell, *History of California* 3:166.

54. Quoted in George W. Groh, *Gold Fever: Being a True Account, Both Horrifying and Hilarious, of the Art of Healing (so-called) during the California Gold Rush* (New York: William Morrow & Company, 1966), 255–56.

55. Beck, "California Gold Rush Violence," 113–14.

56. Taylor, *Eldorado*, 99.

57. Jackson, *Anybody's Gold*, 106. See also Bancroft, *Popular Tribunals*, 1:577–87; John R. McFarlan, "Journal of a Voyage to California via Cape Horn in 1850 . . . and Life in the Mines at Downieville, California," 156, manuscript collection, Huntington Library. McFarlan probably copied his account from a newspaper.

58. This point is clearly made in both Rawls, "Gold Diggers," 28–45, and Hurtado, *Indian Survival*, 101–24.

59. Hubert Howe Bancroft, *California Inter Pocula* (San Francisco: History Company, 1888), 235–36.

60. For numerous examples of Indians and whites shooting at each other, see Richard Brown Cowley, "Journal of a Voyage on the Barque 'Canton' from New York to San Francisco . . . [and] Life in the Mines on the Mokelumne," manuscript collection, Huntington Library. Borthwick remarks, "[A]s the country becomes more thickly settled there will no longer be room for them. . . . This may not be good morality, but it is the way of the world, and the aborigines of California are not likely to share a better fate than those of many another country." Borthwick, *Gold Hunters*, 275.

61. Hittell, *History of California*, 3:76–77. I am indebted to John Phillip Reid for the term "payback vengeance" and for setting out the different uses of vengeance among Indians and whites.

62. Parker, Journal, February 29, 1852.

63. Parker, Journal, October 15, 1850.

64. Reva Holdaway, "A Mormon Mission to California in 1851, from the Diary of Parley Parker Pratt," *California Historical Society Quarterly* 14 (March 1935): 69.

65. Parker, Journal, December 8, 1850.

66. Pringle Shaw, *Ramblings in California, Containing a Description of the Country-Life at the Mines, State of Society &c.* (Toronto: J. Bain, 1857), 76.

67. Chauncey L. Canfield, ed., *The Diary of a Forty-Niner* (San Francisco: Morgan Sheppard, 1906), 36.

68. For a brief discussion, see Bancroft, *History of California*, 6:313–14.

69. Lord, "Journal of an Overland Trip," August 5, 1850.

70. Borthwick, *Gold Hunters*, 163.

71. Jeanne Skinner Van Nostrand, ed., "The Diary of a 'Used Up' Miner, Jacob Henry Bachman," *California Historical Society Quarterly* 22 (March 1943): 72.

72. Bancroft, *California Inter Pocula*, 236.

73. Bancroft, *History of California*, 6:405.

74. Gerstaecker, *California Gold Mines*, 70.

75. Gerstaecker, *California Gold Mines*, 94–95.

76. Canfield, *Diary of a Forty-Niner*, 39–40.

77. Beilharz and López, *We Were Forty-Niners!* See also Monaghan, *Chile, Peru, and the California Gold Rush*.

78. Beilharz and López, *We Were Forty-Niners!* 40–41.

79. Cowley, "Journal of a Voyage, " April 27, 1851.

80. Regarding opium use, J. D. Borthwick wrote: "In the store I found the shopkeeper lying asleep on a mat. He was a sleek dirty-looking object, like a fat pig, with the hair scalded off, his head being close shaved excepting the pigtail. His opium pipe lay in his hand, and the lamp still burned beside him, so I suppose he was already in seventh heaven." Borthwick, *Gold Hunters*, 256. For a general discussion of anti-Chinese sentiment, see Alexander Saxton, *The Indispensable Enemy: Labor and the Anti-Chinese Movement in California* (Berkeley: University of California Press, 1971).

81. Canfield, *Diary of a Forty-Niner*, 202.

82. Canfield, *Diary of a Forty-Niner*, 211.

83. Borthwick, *Gold Hunters*, 144.

84. Marryat, *Mountains and Molehills*, 296.

85. Marryat, *Mountains and Molehills*, 297.

86. Canfield, *Diary of a Forty-Niner*, 202.

87. Shaw, *Ramblings in California*, 72–76.

88. Caughey, *Gold is the Cornerstone*, 230.

89. Bret Harte, "The Argonauts of '49, California's Golden Age" (pamphlet, n.p., n.d.).

90. The most popular gun in the gold fields was an Allen's pepper box, described as "a singularly ineffective gun, more dangerous to the possessor than anyone else . . . And was a most clumsy piece of mechanism, although thousands were sold in the East to the early gold seekers. A joke of the times was a standing reward for proof that anyone had been hurt or wounded by its discharge. In a trial of a miner for assault with a deadly weapon and intent to kill, held before a sapient justice of

the peace . . . the prisoner was discharged, the justice ruling that an Allen's pepper box could not be construed . . . as falling under the head of deadly or dangerous [weapon]." Canfield, *Diary of a Forty-Niner*, 26.

91. Julius H. Pratt, *Reminiscences Personal and Otherwise* (Privately printed, 1910), 76.

92. Marryat, *Mountains and Molehills*, 249.

93. Umbeck, *Theory of Property Rights*, 87.

94. Umbeck, *Theory of Property Rights*, 100

95. Hinton R. Helper, *Land of Gold: Reality versus Fiction* (Baltimore: H. Taylor, 1855), 157.

96. Hittell, *History of California*, 3:61.

97. Hittell, *History of California*, 3:241–42.

98. Helper, *Land of Gold*, 238. Actually Hinton Helper erred. Popular tribunals mirrored the legal system in using the whip, banishment, and the rope as penalties. See Gordon Morris Bakken, *Practicing Law in Frontier California* (Lincoln: University of Nebraska Press, 1991), 101–7.

99. *Reproduction of Fariss and Smith's History of Plumas, Lassen & Sierra Counties, California, 1882* (Berkeley: Howell-North Books, 1971), 213.

100. See Canfield, *Diary of a Forty-Niner*, 26.

101. Lord, "Journal of an Overland Trip," April 15, 1850.

102. A. J. McCall, *Pick and Pan: Trip to the Diggings in 1849, Reminiscences of California Life by an Argonaut* (Bath NY: Steuben Courier, 1883), 14.

103. Bancroft, *Popular Tribunals*, 1:152, 144.

104. Canfield, *Diary of a Forty-Niner*, 96.

105. Charles D. Ferguson, *The Experiences of a Forty-Niner during a Third of a Century in the Gold Fields* (Chico CA: H. M. Garson), 117–18.

106. Borthwick, *Gold Hunters*, 301.

107. Ferguson, *Experiences of a Forty-Niner*, 90.

108. Canfield, *Diary of a Forty-Niner*, 51.

109. Jane Bissell Grabhorn, ed., *A California Gold Rush Miscellany Comprising: The Original Journal of Alexander Barrington* (San Francisco: Grabhorn Press, 1934), 35–36.

110. Shaw, *Ramblings in California*, 69.

111. Saxton, *Indispensable Enemy*, 50.

112. Isaac Jones Wistar, *Autobiography of Isaac Jones Wistar, 1827–1905*, 2 vols. (Philadelphia: Wistar Institute of Anatomy and Biology, 1914) 1:123.

113. Stephen J. Field, later associate justice on the United States Supreme Court, wrote concerning his experience while practicing law during the gold rush: "The Americans in the country had a general notion of what was required for the preservation of order and the due administration of justice." Stephen J. Field, *Personal Reminiscences of Early Days in California* (1893; reprint, New York: Da Capo, 1968), 24.

114. Hittell, *History of California,* 3:291. Gordon Morris Bakken rightly points out that there were many lawyers in the early gold fields, and he demonstrates how they used their talents for personal advancement by deploying all their knowledge and skills: Bakken, *Practicing Law in Frontier California*, 101–7.

115. Lord, "Journal of an Overland Trip," April 24, 1850.

116. Bancroft, *History of California,* 7:210.

117. Field, *Personal Reminiscences*, 22–23.

118. Gerstaecker, *California Gold Mines*, 104.

119. Shinn, *Mining Camps*, 185–86. For other examples of the use of common-sense jurisprudence by justices of the peace, see Bakken, *Practicing Law in Frontier California*, 22–23.

120. Hittell, *History of California,* 3:162.

121. Bancroft, *Popular Tribunals,* 1:749. See also Beck, "California Gold Rush Violence," 105.

122. Rohrbough, *Days of Gold,* 216–17.

123. Canfield, *Diary of a Forty-Niner,* 189; Jackson, *Bad Company*, 44.

9

Where Have All the Young Men Gone?

The Social Legacy of the California Gold Rush

Elizabeth Jameson

When 1960s antiwar activists sang, "Where have all the young men gone?" they answered rhetorically, "Gone to soldiers, every one."[1] The same verse, in many parts of the mid-nineteenth-century world, might bring an equally automatic response: "Where have all the young men gone?" "Gone to miners, every one." James Marshall's discovery drew a demographically extraordinary influx, overwhelmingly young, overwhelmingly male, carrying ambitions born from the particular economic and political dislocations that pushed them to California.

Mark Twain indelibly etched the virile masculinity of these gold seekers. They were, he wrote,

> a driving, vigorous, restless population . . . a *curious* population . . . the *only* population of the kind that the world has ever seen gathered together, and it is not likely that the world will ever see its like again. For observe, it was an assemblage of two hundred thousand *young* men—not simpering, dainty, kid-gloved weaklings, but stalwart, muscular, daunt-less young knaves, brimful of push and energy, and royally endowed with every attribute that goes to make up a peerless and magnificent manhood—the very pick and choice of the world's glorious ones. No women, no children, no gray and stooping veterans—none but erect, bright-eyed, quick-moving, strong-handed young giants—the strangest population, the finest population, the most gallant host that ever trooped down the startled solitudes of an unpeopled land.

"And," Twain concluded wistfully, "where are they now?"[2]

Where indeed? What legacy remains from the thousands of men who interrupted their lives to flock to California's rocky streams and slopes?

How did an extraordinary experience impact hundreds of thousands of otherwise ordinary lives? How did they inscribe the gold rush in their social relationships and their social bequests?

The social outcome is less clear than the degree to which all those young men touched collective imaginations. Mark Twain's portrait of a mythic gold rush can still inspire nostalgic images of youthful adventure and reckless risk taking. The romantic world of these forty-niners evokes an adolescent fantasyland, free from parental constraint and familial responsibility—a place where young men worked hard, played hard, cursed, sweated, spit, whored, and gambled everything on an elusive bonanza and perhaps equally elusive good times.

Twain's gold rush, like most good fantasies, bore enough resemblance to reality to fuel generations of romantic histories. It *was* a curious population. And one of its most curious attributes was its ability to reproduce itself in collective memory out of all proportion to its capacity to reproduce itself biologically or socially.

These young men enter collective memory as leading actors in a history of an American West so unreal that historian Susan Armitage dubbed it "Hisland." In this imagined historical terrain "under perpetually cloudless western skies, a cast of heroic characters engages in dramatic conflict, sometimes with nature, sometimes with each other. Occupationally, these heroes are diverse; they are mountain men, cowboys, Indians, soldiers, farmers, miners, and desperadoes, but they share one distinguishing characteristic— they are all men. It seems that all rational demography has ended at the Mississippi River: all the land west of it is occupied only by men. This mythical land is America's most enduring contribution to folklore: the legendary Wild West. . . . The problem with Hisland," Armitage continued, "is that many people believe it is history, and some of those people are historians."[3]

In the context of gold rush California, Armitage's arguments with Hisland might sound like so much feminist equivocation. The gold rush was, after all, according to all available evidence, much as Twain painted it. It *was* a curious population. It *was* overwhelmingly male. In California, a year after the gold rush began, the U.S. census counted twelve men for each woman.[4] The odds were even more skewed in the mining districts. Men outnumbered women thirty-three to one in the Southern Mines, forty to one in the Northern Mines, twenty-one to one in the Klamath/Trinity diggings. All told, according to the 1850 census, the mining populations were 97 percent male. Two years later, the proportion of women had increased only slightly, to 6 percent in the mining districts. By 1860, approximately three Californians in ten were women, but in the mining areas there was still only one woman per twenty men. By 1870, as the placers dwindled and quartz mining stabilized, the ratios became somewhat more balanced—almost four Californians in ten were female. California, like the West as a whole, would remain disproportionately male for some decades. As late as 1920, the state still reported 112 men to every 100 women.[5] In the gendered settlement pattern, as with much of the trajectory of western placer and hard-rock mining, California set the model for mining communities throughout the West. The pattern would repeat ten years later in Colorado, where, a year after the Pike's Peak boom, there were 1,650 men per 100 women.[6] By 1900, when the industrial production of Cripple Creek gold mines peaked, there were still three men for every two women, the same proportion as in the industrial copper mining center of Butte, Montana.[7]

The early mining booms belonged to young men; the mines remained masculine terrain for decades. But the colorful antics of that first curious population cannot, in isolation, connect the gold rush to its social legacy. Over time, placer mining—sifting precious metals from gravel and streambeds—gave way to quartz mining, as capitalists followed the "leads" underground to mine complex ores that must be milled and refined. As the California placers developed into industrial lode mines, as a permanent class of mining wage labor replaced the exuberant forty-niners, as the impermanent placer camps gave way to settled mining communities and supply centers—as economic and social institutions became more stable— increasing numbers of women and children invaded Twain's masculine Eden. By 1870 women were outnumbered only two to one in Nevada City, while in nearby Grass Valley the ratio dropped to 180 men per 100 women.[8]

Like most adventurous young men, the forty-niners grew up, or went home, or settled down. They were seldom as footloose or unattached as the fantasy West would paint them. They did not, as Twain would have it, penetrate the virgin territories of their manifest destiny to startle "the solitudes of an unpeopled land." The land was, of course, quite "peopled" when they got there. To sift the mythic West from history, we must locate the Argonauts in their own contexts. Who and what did they leave, and why? Where did they settle? What relationships did they build, and with whom? For some youthful gold seekers, their sojourn in the diggings would represent, as it did for Twain, a brief adventure before they returned East to adult lives very like the ones they left behind. For others, however, the gold rush indeed was a step away from the familiar, toward something not yet formed.

Through multiple patterns of migration and settlement, Argonauts forged relationships of kinship and intimacy, of work and class, of identity and difference that, in numerous ways and to varying extents, both reproduced and transformed the social inheritances that pushed and pulled them to the gold fields. The "curious population" of gold rush California was part of the much larger international mass movements of people and capital engendered by the worldwide impacts of industrialization, colonial expansion, and the development of market economies.[9] These developments impelled an extraordinary but selective migration to California. The Argonauts came more often from the North than from the South or the frontiers; from Mexico and Chile, but not from Brazil; from China, but not from Afghanistan; from Ireland and Cornwall and Germany, but not often from Portugal or Greece. They left droughts, depressions, and workshops where their skills were being displaced by factory production, crowded farms and unhappy marriages, the chaos of revolutions. They hauled their social baggage with them to the gold fields. But to some degree the gold rush left its mark in a social legacy that altered previous ways that people related to one another as women and men, workers and owners, immigrants and native born, as they recharted the meanings of manhood, labor, and race.

It would require more than this single essay to chronicle all the social impacts of the California gold rush. My purpose here is to suggest the magnitude of this interpretive enterprise and some of the ways we might connect the impressive scholarship of a generation of historians who have, since the late 1960s, examined social relationships in the mining West. I focus on young men from the United States, Great Britain, and China to suggest some of the connected meanings of manhood and gender, work and class, race and ethnicity that developed in gold rush California.

In industrializing regions like the northeastern United States, wage labor and factories were replacing in the mid-nineteenth century the independence of the artisan's shop. Many young men whose hopes drew them to the gold fields came particularly from the northeastern and midwestern United States, places where industrialization and settlement limited the opportunities for native-born Euro-American men.[10] Craftsmen's skills and the price they could command were being eroded and with them the hopes of many Euro-American men of achieving what they called a "competency"—a secure financial future that guaranteed a respected social niche. Many of our most vivid gold rush records were penned by men who aspired to such stable middle-class status and who hoped that California opened a route to economic security that seemed increasingly tenuous in

New York, Maine, or Massachusetts. Susanna Townsend, who accompanied her husband, Emery, to his claim on Jackson Creek in Amador County, wrote her family in New York: "[I]f kind Providence smiles upon us Emery thinks he will be able to live the rest of his days without labor. A small capital in this country well invested brings in returns so much greater than in the older states that we could live handsomely on the interest of six thousand dollars while at home it would not be much."[11]

Men with more modest financial aspirations found that they could do better plying their craft skills in California than in the uncertain gamble of the diggings. New Englander Jotham Varney, who budgeted two years to improve his fortunes in California, became quickly "discouraged about gold digging" after a brief stint the summer of 1850. He soon found that it was much more profitable to work as a cooper, making kegs used to haul molasses and liquor to the mines. "A common hand," he wrote his wife, "can make from four to six of them in a day the ten gallons sell for five dollars, and the five gallons sell for a dollar apiece. If I had come out here a little more than a year ago and set up coopering I might have made something handsome them cags [*sic*] they say sold for sixteen dollars apiece."[12] New Yorker James Barnes calculated the value of mining against what he could earn plying his trade as a skilled carpenter, writing from Sacramento in March 1850, that "if work is good here this summer i shall not go to the mines if they get below 12$ a day i shall go to the mines it is thought by some that Carpenter work will be from 12 to 18$ a day all summer."[13]

Other men, pushed and pulled to California from all corners of the globe, soon joined Barnes and Varney and those like them who came seeking better opportunities than they left back East. William Ives Morgan of Bristol, Connecticut, wrote from Amador in 1850 that he "[w]orked all day near the road, and saw Yankee, English, Chinese, German, Scotch, Chileans, Mexicans, Californians, Manilla Men, Indians, Swedes, Norwegians, French men, Kanakas, and don't know how many other Nations pass us."[14] If Twain's curious population included "no women, no children, no gray and stooping veterans," it excluded such international diversity as well. The mythic Argonaut was a free white man from the eastern United States, a fitting agent of American national destiny. Many early migrants fit that bill. The 1850 census found that 95 percent of the male workers of Grass Valley and Nevada City were from the United States.[15] In the state as a whole, however, almost one person in four (23.5 percent) had been born in another country. By 1852, one resident of Calaveras County in three was foreign born, compared with 13 percent around the Northern Mines. In 1860 and 1870 some four Californians in ten were immigrants.[16] Ten years after the first influx of gold seekers, only 42 percent of male workers in Grass Valley were native born, 54 percent in Nevada City; by 1870 only one working man in four in Grass Valley was a native-born American, four in ten in Nevada City.[17] As these figures suggest, the international migrations that followed the gold rush were part of the process of class formation in the emerging social order, a process that determined who stayed around the mines, who worked them for wages, and who owned them; who grew food and who sold it; who supported families and who provided the domestic needs of a largely male and increasingly immigrant workforce.

Different dislocations pushed the men who rushed in from distant ports. Irish immigrants fled the potato famine and the constricted economic options of British rule. French Argonauts fled the failed Revolution of 1848, poor harvests, food shortages, and high prices.[18] French gold seekers and New England craftsman might both view the gold fields as a brief investment of time and labor, but for many migrants home was a much more uncertain point of return. Diminished possibilities at home set off distinct patterns of migration and settlement, patterns that are suggested in the particular social and economic niches occupied by the Cornish and the Chinese in post–gold rush California. By 1870, when four Californians in ten were immigrants, British and Chinese were disproportionately represented in that total. One migrant in four was Chinese, one in ten was English, one in four was Irish.[19] The designations "British," "English," and "Chinese" on a census form, however, did not show that migrants originated from particular areas where specific dislocations sent men toward the new gold regions.

The Chinese and the English who came to California were only a portion of larger migrations from their homelands and a tiny fragment of the international migration of labor caused by the global expansion of capitalism, which moved workers, capital, and technology to exploit resources and markets.[20] An estimated 2.5 million Chinese left their homeland between 1840 and 1900, after China lost the Opium Wars and was forced to open to European trade and political domination.[21] Almost all the Chinese who, by 1860, comprised 10 percent of the California population, came from the southern Chinese province of Guangdong, close to the ports of Hong Kong and Canton, a land approximately the size of Oregon but so poor and hilly that only 16 percent of the land was cultivated as late as 1955.[22] Much of the cultivated land in the nineteenth century grew commercial crops: sugarcane, fruit, indigo, and tobacco, rather than rice or other staple foodstuffs. Peasants in the Pearl River delta were particularly hard hit by increased taxes, loss of land, unemployment, and overpopulation. For common people, food was scarce and expensive, a situation aggravated by population growth. From 1787 to 1850 the population of Guangdong grew from sixteen million to twenty-eight million, stressing families that struggled to survive on extremely small plots of land. During the 1850s and 1860s, Guangdong was rocked by the Taiping Rebellion (1850–1864), the Red Turban uprisings (1854–1864), and Punti-Hakka interethnic warfare. Extreme political, social, and economic dislocations led to reports that "small families found it difficult to make a living and often drowned their girl babies because of the impossibility of looking after them."[23] Many of the sons emigrated, particularly from the most populous prefecture of Guangdong, Kwangchou, which contained the city of Canton and the colony of Macao; most sailed from the port of Hong Kong. While some could pay their own passage, many came as contract laborers, intending to work for wages to repay the cost of their passage. At least half were married, according to historian Shih-shan Henry Tsai, and intended not only to support themselves, but to support a family back home as well.[24]

The overwhelming majority of Chinese worked as laborers and miners. Of some forty thousand Chinese in California by 1868, a fourth labored on the Pacific railroad; a third were miners.[25] By contrast, in Grass Valley in 1870 only one U.S. native in four still mined; four in ten in Nevada City. Of the British 80 percent mined in Grass Valley, of the Chinese 80 percent in Nevada City.[26] Compared with native-born Americans, both the Chinese and the British were disproportionately working class.

The British miners came from Wales, from the Yorkshire coal fields, and especially from Cornwall, in southwestern England, where generations of Cornish had mined tin, copper, and clay used to manufacture china. The skills and techniques perfected in one of the world's oldest mining regions were passed from generation to generation in a system that allowed boys to begin working at age seven under the watchful tutelage of their fathers.[27] An estimated 11,639 men and 2,098 women worked in Cornish copper mining in 1827; 5,706 men and 130 women in tin. Combined with those who mined lead and iron, just over 20,000 Cornish worked at mining. Thirty-five years later, in 1862, some 340 mines employed 50,000 Cornish men and women, their lives marked by endless labor and marginal poverty, usually cut short by silicosis and other occupational ailments.[28]

Family survival required the labor of all family members. Children began working by age six or seven, often working ten hours a day for pennies, separating rubbish from the ore. Girls did not work underground but labored on the surface. Older women hammered rude ore with stone mallets and then passed it on to the "bal maidens," adolescent girls who "bucked" it with an iron hammer to the size of half-inch marbles. From ages twelve to fourteen, they earned twelve shillings a month; from fourteen to seventeen, fifteen shillings; and eighteen shillings thereafter. One observer noted that: "The use of hammers in dressing ores tends, perhaps, to the production of some fullness of breast, but the sedentary position necessary gives little or no exercise to the lower limbs."[29]

The poverty that forced all family members to endless labor was surely one impetus for Cornish migrations to other mining areas. By the time of the gold rush, even the meager living eked from the Cornish mines was threatened. An economic depression in the 1840s hastened emigration. From January to June, 1841, 795 people left Cornwall, most of them miners headed for the lead regions of southwest Wisconsin. By the 1850s high-grade copper was running out at depths of one thousand feet in Cornish mines. Competition from newly discovered copper deposits in Michigan and Chile led to mine closures and widespread unemployment. By the end of the century, Cornwall would lose, by most estimates, at least a third of its population. Some 230,000 left for Australia, Mexico, and Chile, for the Wisconsin lead-mining regions, the copper mines of northern Michigan, the gold mines of California, and the hard-rock camps that soon dotted western North America.[30]

Some sailed straight to California, like the Saint Agnes miner who wrote his wife back in Cornwall from Weber Creek September 25, 1850.[31] Others flocked to the diggings after intermediate stops, like Edward Skewis of Camborne, one of the first of the Wisconsin Cornish to arrive in California, in September 1849. His brother James joined him two years later, traveling from the Wisconsin mining center of Shullsburg to the diggings. Working a claim on Deer Creek, four miles from Nevada City, James Skewis reported that: "Most every day between three of us got six ounces of gold until the rainy season set in. Then we washed in smaller creeks between the hills, which also paid satisfactory. . . . Just then there was a strike at Grass Valley on a slide from a hill and we got a claim and sold it for 100 dollars. One day a man gave me ten dollars for one day's work on that hill to do some timbering work as he was not used to that kind of work." After three years of prospecting, the brothers heard of a gold strike in Australia and sailed on the first ship they could get. Disappointed in their hopes there, they returned to Cornwall, found that it was no longer home, and continued back to Shullsburg.[32]

The Cornish brought to the placers their knowledge of alluvial tin-streaming, introducing improved equipment such as long toms, cradles, and sluice boxes. John Roberts, who traveled from Wisconsin to Sonora, wrote that "the long tom is nothing but a washing strake such as we use in the lead mines of Wisconsin, with a sieve at the end of it, under which is fixed a box called the rifle [riffle] box, set in a diagonal position. . . . The place where I am working is on the side of a hill; we take away from one to two feet in depth of the surface of the ground (just like the farmers carry away a stope of Camborne town earth for dressing their land)." Roberts planned to dig into the quartz veins the next winter, which were "formed exactly like the copper lodes in Cornwall, only they lie very flat."[33]

Following placer deposits underground to develop quartz mines was a natural step for an experienced Cornish copper miner. Nevada City and Grass Valley became centers of Cornish settlement, where Cornish men became highly regarded miners, superintendents, managers, and foremen, working as skilled blasters and drillers and supervising specialized operations like timbering. Cornish shift bosses and foremen would hire newly arrived Cornishmen, in a world where Cornishness, regardless of actual prior mining experience, came to connote skilled miners.[34]

The Cornish brought to Nevada City and Grass Valley their brass bands and Methodist churches, and they fanned out from there to take their skills to the Comstock, to Leadville and Central City, and throughout the mining West. The Boise *Owyhee Avalanche* recorded a common estimate of these immigrants who soon became a common fixture of western hard-rock regions: "The Cornishman is probably the most skillful foreign miner that comes to our shores. For this he deserves no special credit, because it is a calling to what he has been accustomed since his childhood. . . . Generally speaking, he is satisfied to be working for others, but insists on being paid promptly for his services. . . . They are mostly stalwart, good-looking fellows, dress better than any other class of miners, and are very fond of women. They also appear more clannish than any other foreigner and a majority of them are very good singers."[35]

Although Twain did not, in all likelihood, picture the Cornish and Chinese among his "stalwart, muscular, dauntless young knaves," they lived in the company of other men in greater proportions and far longer than the "curious population" of native-born Americans he celebrated. The persistence of a male majority after the gold rush masked vast differences in the proportions of men and women among different ethnic migrants. During the gold rush itself, these proportions did not differ much. In 1852, both the foreign- and native-born white populations in the mining areas were 95–98 percent male.[36] By 1860, however, 30 percent of the white and free colored people were women, while Asian women were still outnumbered twenty to one.[37] The native-born population in 1870 was 43 percent female, while only three immigrants in ten were women, and only 8 percent of all Chinese.[38]

Cornishmen might be "very fond of women," but they often had to wait to marry them. The instabilities of mining and the excess of men in western mining camps meant that the Cornish, like many skilled working men, delayed marriage until they could support a family and often until they could send for Cornish sweethearts left behind. More Cornish men than women came to California. Coupled with the unbalanced sex ratios in all groups, this led to delayed marriages and some intermarriage. For many years Cornishmen shared bachelor cabins, most often with other Cornish miners, or boarded with the few Cornish and American women who provided domestic services for working men in the mining camps.

Ultimately, however, many Cornish miners married, settled, and raised families in western hard-rock communities. Generations of California miners traced their roots to the mines of Cornwall, or to the Yorkshire coal pits, or to Wisconsin lead or Australian copper mines. Those who came during and immediately after the gold rush often began a chain migration of family and friends who joined them where mining was stable and jobs could be had. Arthur Cecil Todd recorded some of these family stories as he researched *The Cornish Miner in America*. John and Fred Nettel recalled the story of their father, who began working the mines of Redruth at age twelve. He immigrated to Michigan in 1881 and then went to Prescott and Tuscarora before settling in Grass Valley, where his married sister lived. When he had saved enough and had been promoted to foreman at the Ledge mine, he followed the Cornish custom and wrote his sweetheart in Cornwall, asking her to marry him in Grass Valley. She agreed, and in time their sons followed their father into the mines.[39] Similarly, Stephen Thomas left Cornwall to prospect in Colorado, then traveled to Virginia City in 1873. Disappointed with Nevada, he visited his parents in Cornwall in 1875, then returned to Pennsylvania where his brother worked as a coal miner. He married an American and moved with her to Grass Valley near two more of his brothers. In 1889, he became foreman of the Sierra Buttes mine, twelve miles above Downieville.[40]

Class and race provide social lenses through which to examine wage work and domesticity. Chinese and Cornish men both labored on the mining frontier, but their ability to form families, father children, and establish permanent communities was sharply separated. Cornish miners and their wives reproduced generations of skilled workers, a variation on the pattern through which generations of Cornish sons followed their fathers underground. Their place in the process of class formation distinguished them from Chinese workers. Although Chinese labor was valued to work the placers and to build western railroads, neither capital nor labor welcomed Chinese women, who, it was feared, would bear a stable Chinese work force, who, owners feared, would demand higher wages and better working conditions, or who, labor feared, would drive wages down. The Chinese were restricted to the placers, allowed to mine underground only in the dangerous quicksilver mines, subjected to the Foreign Miners Tax, which provided more than half the tax revenues in California from 1852 until its repeal in 1870, and run out of mining camps throughout the West.[41]

Chinese women were restricted from joining Chinese men in American by patriarchal Chinese tradition, by poverty, and by racist anti-Chinese legislation. A series of laws restricted Chinese immigration and denied Chinese citizenship, with particular consequences for female emigration. The Page Law of 1875 sought to regulate the entry of Chinese prostitutes, while the 1882 Chinese Exclusion Act allowed only a privileged few women to emigrate, primarily the wives and daughters of merchants. Most of the Chinese women who were in the country when the doors closed in 1882 were prostitutes, most of them impoverished peasant women imported to serve as sexual companions for Chinese men. Since Chinese could not legally marry people of other races, these few women became virtually the only available marriage partners for single Chinese laborers who remained in America. The continued absence of women separated the Chinese from most other immigrant groups and ensured that only the small Chinese merchant class could legally establish families in California.[42]

Chinese workingmen generally attended to their own domestic needs, growing vegetables, cooking, and establishing a variety of businesses, from noodle houses to laundries, which served Euro-Americans as well as Chinese men. By 1880, almost 8 percent of the Chinese in the Northern Mines were cooks, 12 and 15 percent in the Sacramento and San Joaquin valleys, respectively.[43] Some became truck farmers, raising vegetables, hogs, and poultry.[44] Truck gardeners and laundrymen were, by 1860, among the few Chinese men with wives in California. As Sucheng Chan has noted, they practiced "sedentary occupations that benefited from unpaid family labor."[45] Farmers, domestic service workers, and the small merchant class represented the very few Chinese in America who could marry and physically reproduce their communities.

When we know that both Cornish and Chinese lived predominantly with other men, the *Owyhee Avalanche's* insistence that the Cornish were "very fond of women" takes on new meaning. It asserted the masculine and heterosexual identity of men who spent much of their time in all-male social worlds. Chinese men, by contrast, though legally prevented from cohabiting with women, came to be portrayed as feminized, as less than men. These images had little to do with which Chinese men, in fact, had wives and families in California but rather identified an "inferior" racial status with the lower status of Euro-American women. This association was then reinforced by images of men who did "women's work" such as cooking, gardening, laundry, and domestic service.

Masculinity was thus associated with class and race in social contexts that could be seen alternately as hyper-manly or as lacking women to perform "feminine" and feminizing domestic tasks. Who, after all, were the young men to depend on for food, clothing, sexual companionship, and sociability? If, indeed, we asked many of Twain's young compatriots about gold rush social life, they would have been mystified. "Society" implied women. The absence of women, by extension, defined what was missing in the tents, cabins, and settlements that mushroomed around the placers. James Barnes, who left New York for the gold fields in late 1849, wrote in December 1853 that he had "lived almost 4 years entirely excluded from society what makes society is females and a party of that kind i have not attended since i have been in the country." He soon elaborated: "[T]here is very little what we might call society here females are too scarce. [W]hat are here think themselves better than the Angels in heaven." That being the case, Barnes preferred "reading some books" to "a bar room where there is always card playing drinking smoking and swearing such is about all the society there is here but i am here and i intend to make the best of it."[46] Barnes's correspondence suggests how quickly the glamour of manly comradeship could pale, the adaptations that men made in the society of other men, and the extent to which the social conventions of home— wherever home was—would continue to shape Argonauts' perceptions of the social in their new and curious circumstances.

Though there were very few women around the mines, women were never entirely absent, psychically, emotionally, and in the social perceptions of men.[47] In the absence of women, men recharted a social universe, using as their compass the gender roles they had left behind. For most middle-class Euro-American men, this meant that things domestic—cooking, cleaning, sewing, doing laundry, making a space a "home"—had been done by women. Women nursed the sick, tended gardens, raised poultry and dairy cows, made butter and bread, championed moral behavior, and were essential for much civilized leisure. In the gold fields, then, men not only had to learn to care for their own domestic needs and amusements. They also had to decide what it meant that they did these things, what their new domestic and recreational arrangements meant for their personal and social identities.

They adapted in various ways, learning to provide for themselves and other men the domestic services that ideally belonged to women. As they did, they walked a fine line. In the social worlds they had left, men had greater status than women. Masculine status was a particularly precarious matter because a crisis in social status prompted many a gold seeker's journey. They thus hastened to assure the folks back home that they were prospering and living well, trying at the same time not to appear overly identified with the feminine domestic world. Much of their correspondence connected domestic needs with the pursuit of prosperity: they wrote of food and the cost of provisions and measured success in terms of health and income. Rodney Odall connected domesticity and finances as he described for his family back in Rochester the division of labor in his all-male household in Mariposa: "Harris makes our bread, Havens cooks in the morning, Fish at noon and I at night. . . . Everything looks to me that I shall make some money yet." Food and fortune appear in concert throughout his correspondence: "Wages are 60 dollars per month in this place, *eat yourself.* The mines are very healthy at present. Smoked salmon 25 cts, beans 38, rice 38, sugar 50, dried apples 50, everything sells by the pound." "The prospects for mining is rather dark compared with the past, but I can make double now and more too to what I can at home. *I ain't got the blues.* The money comes too easy for me to repine."[48] Six months later he reported from Brown's Bar: "I have been well and healthy; never in my life was I as tough as now. I weigh about 170 pounds." He was, he reported, making five dollars some days, some days a dollar.[49]

This connection of food with fortune, or more broadly of domesticity with prosperity, appeared repeatedly in Argonauts' correspondence. James Barnes wrote from San Francisco that it cost him and his group of friends eight dollars a week to live. "We live first rate we have one cook and baker we have good Oraing [Orange] County butter and potatoes and every thing els that is good."[50] Soon thereafter he wrote from Sacramento: "methinks i hear you say i wonder if he is not home sick far from it i did sometimes think of old daddy table when i was out to see feeding on salt beef some of it smelt strong enough to knock a Jack ass down our bread was mouldy and worms enough in it to cary it off, we have every thing that is good for breakfast something beter for dinner and tea and shortcake for supper that is beter than a seafaring life."[51] He left the mines both because they didn't pay as well as carpentry and because the food was bad. During his three months in the diggings he averaged about three dollars a day, and "lived on raw pork and sea bisket."[52]

With increasing time and distance, food began to evoke memories of home. Jotham Varney, after almost a year away from his family, wrote his wife: "I thought sometimes I should be glad to have a good drink of your buttermilk[.] Milk anywhere in the digging is 4 dollars a gallon and molasses is 5 dollars a gallon and hay is 75 cents a pound flour is 18 cents a pound beef 30 cents, potatoes 25 cents a pound, pork 35 cents so you must conclude that living in the mines costs something but in some places further off all kinds of provisions costs more than a dollar a pound. . . . So I concluded to leave and seek other employment."[53] As the glamour of the gold rush faded, Barnes wrote that he was well: "I now weigh 154 pounds and am gaining a little every day." But, he added, "[W]hat we live on here . . . is not buckwheat cakes for we do not get them more than once a week but the way we make them suffer even when we do get them is a caution." He paid, he reported, ten dollars a week for board "and get good board."[54]

Argonauts sought to assure home folks they were doing well, but for many home remained the measure of domestic comfort. The few women who joined the migration to the gold fields found that their domestic skills were in high demand. An unidentified woman wrote from San Francisco in 1850 that she was healthy and had no desire to return to Boston: "I am very fleshy. Weight 215 lbs." California was "the only country that I ever was in where a woman rec'd anything like a just compensation for work. I am perfectly contented and have no wish to return. I have been sewing ever since I came here but expect to change my business for some kind of housekeeping before long." She considered opening a boarding house for thirty to thirty-five boarders; she would pay a cook $150 a month. "People do not pretend to keep vary clean houses here," she wrote. "But if the houses and streets are dirty the money is clean."[55]

In a world so entirely masculine, women found a narrow, if remunerative, set of opportunities. Married or single, respectable or disreputable, rewarded in cash or indirectly through spousal support, they supplied the domestic needs, the heterosexual and heterosocial desires of the overwhelmingly male population. In the paid workforce or in their own households, they would cook, clean, sew, scrub, wait tables, and provide "society" for the male majority. They might be well paid, at least compared to what women could earn in the eastern states, but their options were limited to domestic arenas, in the marketplace or in the family household.

Their domestic concerns could, nonetheless, hold the key to family prosperity. Luzena Stanley Wilson would begin her road to gold rush prosperity when, much to her own amazement, she sold biscuits for ten dollars to a miner who missed bread baked by a woman. From that point on, she cooked for miners and operated hotels in Sacramento, Nevada City, and Vacaville. The day she opened her El Dorado Hotel in Nevada City, on a table she fashioned from two boards, she attracted twenty miners who paid her a dollar a meal and promised their continued patronage. "From the first day," she wrote, "it was well patronized, and I shortly after took my husband into partnership."[56]

Emery Townsend, who hoped "to live the rest of his days without labor," found that his wife's dreams pointed the route to their security. While Emery and two partners worked their claim, Susanna insisted on a garden.[57] Their future would be pegged as much to Susanna's grubbing after vegetables as to Emery's grubbing for gold in his much-worked diggings. "Our small garden has been so profitable this year," she wrote, "that they intend to enlarge it for the coming year and judging from this year they expect to make a thousand dollars each. . . . It is astonishing how the sale of a few vegetables mounts up. Our cabbages have been very fine solid heads and we have sold them at a gold shilling per pound and some of them weigh 8–10 and 12 pounds. A month or two back almost every day I would sell 2 or 3 or 4 heads and now and then Emery takes Jimmy and goes off with a load six and eight miles round. We have had all the tomatoes we wanted to eat, pickle and preserve and sold sixty dollars worth off quite a small bed. . . . People will use vegetables if they can get them no matter at what price."[58] The small garden financed turkeys, mules, hens, and a goat, "and all has grown out of that small garden which last year I coaxed and fretted into operation, not but that the trio were willing enough to have it but they knew it would hinder their mining operation."[59] From a half-acre garden, she "cleared twelve hundred dollars." "It has always been my hobby," she wrote, "since I came to California to get Emery to settle somehow on a small ranch. I have always felt sure we would do better at it than mining and not work half so hard." She got her way, and by fall of 1853 the Townsends moved to twenty-eight acres near Sutterville, where they intended to ranch. They pinned great hope on a cabbage crop "good for $2000 at least."[60] In April 1856, Susanna reported that they were growing grapes and had twenty-four hundred dollars worth of cabbages in the ground.[61] She further augmented their income teaching school.[62]

Class aspirations and assumptions distinguished their truck farm from those of their Chinese compatriots. Emery managed the operation, and Susanna had "a very nice American young woman who not only does all my housework very nicely but is company for me. Her husband does all the out of door work."[63] The company of an American woman would have been great comfort. Her one lack, Susanna reported in 1857, was female company. There were twelve women in town, but, she wrote, "I have not found one congenial acquaintance. They are all course, low, illiterate women."[64] In a world where most women labored at various domestic pursuits, many middle-class migrants went to great pains to reestablish clear lines of class and respectability. The reference point for acceptable society remained for Susanna Townsend, as for many middle-class Euro-Americans, the women she had left back East and whose correspondence provided her primary female companionship.

The most significant women in the Gold Rush were not the few exceptional ones like Susanna Townsend and Luzena Wilson who accompanied their husbands west or the even rarer souls who sought their independent fortunes in gold rush California. The men who constituted the "curious" population in California left behind equally "curious" communities, where "gold rush widows" managed farms and businesses in the absence of male guidance and authority. Women might have the help of their children or of other family members, but for most women the men's departure meant that they became responsible for family and business decisions they were not accustomed to handling on their own.[65]

The women and children left behind remained a constant presence in men's diaries and letters home. Jotham Varney wrote before he ever got to California that he "felt the loss of your company more than anything else which I have to regret."[66] He was particularly pleased with his wife's first letter. "I see in it feelings of love and affection which I could not expect from any other person and in this I hope you will receive as much satisfaction as I did in yours."[67] Ebenezer Sheppard wrote with concern about the married men in his company. "Sands says less but thinks to himself the more—I believe no one regrets the absence of his family more than he does."

> Charley Hifferd is bemoaning the imprudence of this wild goose chase and says with the experience he now has again $2000 would be no temptation to him for leaving his wife and child—If we ever get home I doubt not those married will love their wives better than heretofore as man does not usually duly appreciate his comforts while in the undisturbed enjoyment of them—I have been repeatedly assured that I could never appreciate the feelings of a newly married man under our present circumstances untill I were married and passed through the same fiery ordeal[.] But if such be the feelings of those who left in peace and

with mutual consent the joys of wedded love how poignant must be the reflection of him who ever violated his marriage vows and who by his vices cruelty and brutality has exchanged the bliss of pure wedded love for the anguish of contempt and abhorrence in the bosom of his desolated family.[68]

Separated couples expressed the gamut of emotions from affection to relief. Mining excitements might draw men who desired to improve their families' fortunes or those who wanted an excuse to leave. California's Argonauts pioneered a soon-common pattern of family separation. When John Bozeman set out in 1861 to search for gold in Colorado, both his wife and his mother knew that he followed his father, who had left home when John was twelve and died on the way to California.[69] Five years later, he wrote his mother that he did not intend to return to his wife, Catharine, and their three daughters. "I am a friend to Catharine and always will be, but the way we lived to gether my life was no pleasure to me. We never lived a week to gether without quarling and I do not think it right for us to live to gether that way." He had been gone long enough, he wrote, for Catharine to divorce him on grounds of desertion.[70]

Dearly missed or happily abandoned, the women left behind were often invisible partners in their husbands' adventures. Men who sought to escape debt and downward mobility left women with few resources to support themselves and their children. Accustomed to deferring to male management, women were forced to make decisions in their absence and to navigate legal and business matters in which, as married women, they had limited authority to act. They coped with the help of relatives and children, by expanding their own resources, and by relying on "respectable" sources of income like teaching, selling butter and eggs, and keeping boarders. Jotham Varney, like many absent husbands, tried to advise his wife on matters of farm management, such as what to do about the tenant who he feared was drinking too much and was not fulfilling his agreement to split the hay crop with Varney.[71] But he knew his family was essentially on its own. Sending advice for his children, he wrote, "Lincoln, I suppose is to work painting. I hope he will be a good boy and do the best he can. He will be the most of your dependence while I am absent. . . . As things look now," he added, "I shall not be able to send you any money at present."[72]

Women's efforts to sustain families, farms, and businesses in their husbands' absences remained largely invisible in a world that gauged economic value in the public marketplace. Yet their labor at home represented a very real contribution to the infrastructure of the gold rush, an uncalculated sum that supported the men's enterprises.[73] Economics and emotions subtly distinguished the separations of different gold rush widows. The "grass widows" left behind when Chinese men sought their fortunes in the land they called Gold Mountain might remain dear in memory, but they faced separations that could last ten years or a lifetime, depending on whether finances would enable a spouse to visit or return. An anonymous Chinese miner wrote his "Beloved Wife" from John Day, Oregon: "Because of our destitution I went out to try to make a living. Who could know that the Fate is always opposite to man's design. Because I can get no gold, I am detained in this secluded corner of a strange land. Furthermore, my beauty, you are implicated in an endless misfortune. I wish this paper would console you a little. This is all I can do for now."[74]

Chinese women left behind, like those left in New England, worked hard and were often sorely missed. But they had far less independence or leverage than did gold rush widows in the United States, remaining subordinate to men and dependent on relatives whom they labored to help support. A Cantonese folk rhyme captured their dilemma:

If you have a daughter don't marry her to a Gold Mountain man.
Out of ten years, he will not be in bed for one.
The spider will spin webs on top of the bedposts,
While dust fully covers one side of the bed.[75]

The length of separations and the contributions of Gold Rush wages to the family economy distinguished the situations of Chinese couples from their counterparts in the United States. While Chinese men struggled to support families in Guangdong, their wives performed their customary labor at home, and gold rush widows worked to underwrite men's enterprises in the gold fields by supporting families, farms, and businesses.

The effects of these extended separations are hard to calculate. It would be tempting to suggest that men who had done their own domestic chores valued women's work more highly when they returned, that women who had managed on their own became more independent and assertive in their husbands' absences. The men, however, seemed generally all too happy to relinquish domestic tasks to women when they were finally reunited. Some women, at least, appear to have been more reluctant to relinquish their newfound authority. Abiah Warren Hiller supported her two daughters and her mother in McDonough, New York, by teaching during her husband, William's, four-year absence in the gold fields. Abiah had to act decisively when her house burned down. She wrote William that she had spent three hundred dollars to build a new home and had finished a kitchen, bedroom, and schoolroom, but had left the rest for him to finish when he returned. "I hope what you have done to your house you have done well so it will be worth finishing when I get home," he replied. "I suppose the roof is too steep to suit you," she wrote in return, "but it suits me."[76]

The personal politics of separation could depend on many factors, including, of course, the previous relationship between husband and wife. Abiah Warren was already an independent woman when William Hiller courted her, and she remained an independent woman after he returned. Thirteen years his senior, she had supported herself teaching for years before they met when he became her student.

By contrast, Almira Fay Stearns remained less able to assert her own needs, though she bore and raised five sons during her husband, Daniel's, extended absences. He left her and their first-born in New Hampshire for almost four years, while he packed and sold supplies in the California and Oregon mines. Moving her and their growing brood west in 1854, he left her behind in various Oregon communities during his extended ventures as packer and merchant in the Oregon and Idaho mines for another eleven years. Finally reunited, she felt unable to oppose his plan to move from Roseburg to the isolated farm in Elkton, Oregon, that she detested. She had missed Daniel but had enjoyed the company of women friends and relatives in Roseburg. After years of coping alone, she found herself in almost unendurable isolation and suffered for years from poor health and depression.[77]

It is difficult to chart the long-term effect of gold rush separations on subsequent Euro-American gender relations. In individual couples, much seemed to hinge on the extent to which women recognized the value of their own contributions to family economies and the extent to which both partners shared and realized aspirations to middle-class respectability.

Although most gold rush men lived much of their lives in the society of other men, their ability to establish families depended in part on the ways that race and ethnicity operated in the emerging class system of California mining. While a majority of men in Nevada County were unmarried or separated from their families in 1870, more men born in the United States settled there with families than those from most other countries. In Grass Valley, 40 percent of the men born in the United States were married, compared with 27 percent of the British and 2 percent of the Chinese. In Nevada City, 36 percent of the Americans, 33 percent of the British, but virtually none of the Chinese lived with wives.[78]

These differences reflected how race and ethnicity connected with economic and social status. Merchants and professionals were more able to marry than were miners, and American men in disproportionate numbers moved out of the mines and into middle-class occupations. For the Cornish, marriages were postponed by distance, economic insecurity, and the paucity of available marriage partners. When they were finally able to marry, many skilled miners were older and often married considerably younger women. Their children often followed their parents' paths—the girls would marry miners, the sons would follow their fathers underground. Few Chinese men could marry in California, and after 1882, few could be reunited with their wives to raise families in America. The ability to reproduce was linked to class; skilled laborers and the middle classes were most able to establish families.

Social status also affected whose stories would be inscribed in the historical record. We have fewer published accounts of Cornish domestic life, either for the married men or for the many who shared cabins with their fellow miners, than we do for the Euro-American Argonauts. Even this brief examination suggests some of the silences yet to be filled with the voices of the Chinese and Cornish women left behind and of the men who lived together, not for a brief adventure in young manhood, but throughout most of their working lives.

We can, however, discern several patterns that illuminate the social significance of the California gold rush. For Cornish miners, Cornishness remained a positive identity in a world where Cornishmen were presumed to be skilled miners and where Cornish miners and superintendents would support a Cornish workforce. This is particularly notable because the Cornish remained, in the words of the *Owyhee Avalanche*, "clannish," though as Protestants and English speakers they were in a better position than most immigrants to assimilate. Ethnicity for them became a positive marketable identity, a commodity that assured the status and wages of highly skilled working-class men.[79]

Skilled miners could command wages sufficient to support families. Significantly, while Cornish sons might follow their fathers underground in California and throughout the mining West, Cornish wives and daughters did not become part of the mining workforce in the American West. It became a mark of achievement for western hard-rock miners, and ultimately for miners' unions, to ensure the wages that kept wives and daughters out of the paid workforce and their sons in school for an acceptable period.[80] While downwardly mobile American craftsmen sought access to middle-class respectability, immigrant miners from Cornwall, Yorkshire, and Ireland sought wages sufficient to support a family, or at least to keep married women out of the paid workforce and sons at school through the eighth grade.

One of the least-noticed social legacies of the California gold mines was the gendered assignment of labor it generated. Domestic work was marked as feminine, regardless of who did it, while mining itself was masculine. While this division was so commonly assumed it became somehow "natural," women were restricted from working underground in England only in 1842, when the Mines and Collieries Act forbade the employment of boys under ten and of all females in British mines, although they could work above ground, and women and girls, as we have seen, continued to perform hard labor for little pay in the surface workings.[81] The exclusion of women from the paid workforce rested on the unexamined assumption that women should not work in the mines, a social belief that might appear entirely "natural," although women did, in fact, perform mining labor in other times and places, and although Miwok women in California adapted gold mining to their seasonal round of activities, using tightly woven baskets to pan the California streambeds as they accommodated to the dislocations wrought by disease and dispossession.[82]

For the Euro-American men who succeeded in California, it became an equal mark of pride to establish middle-class homes, marked by wide separations between the public world of masculine commerce and the private domain of female domesticity. For the Cornish this ideal was a distinct achievement. The chance to keep women and children out of the mines represented a positive shift from the worlds of labor they left in Cornwall. Middle-class status for Chinese immigrants ensured that their homes became the sites of social reproduction for a Chinese American community, since only the tiny middle class *could* marry and raise children. As these brief examples illustrate, the social relations of class, race, and gender were international, linking people in California to others around the world. Their meanings were forged in the contexts of the particular "peculiar" migrations that configured the California population, the social aspirations and assumptions of diverse migrants, and the power relations that linked them after the gold rush.

Who did what work, how people of different races and ethnicities stood in relation to one another, which activities were considered manly and which womanly, these were some of the social legacies that remained after the gold rush. We cannot trace that social legacy from the partial perspectives of Twain's "erect, bright-eyed, quick-moving, strong-handed young giants." We can't tell the story of social relationships without all the actors.

It remains important to consider why Twain's fantasy remained for so long imprinted as history. The answer, I think, has to do with the ability of young, virile white American men to act in these stories as surrogates for the nation, to represent America's destiny to fill the continent with superior strength, pluck, and energy, to claim the imaginary "unpeopled land." The version of American history they serve endures in the legacy of Frederick Jackson Turner, who located the genesis of American character and American values on the frontier. Many historians have challenged this version of our national past, in part because it omits women and people of color, in part because it cannot connect the frontier with the present. If we stop the action where Twain's restless young giants startle the solitudes of an unpeopled land, then we can fit the gold rush into a nostalgic version of the American frontier. But if we widen the focus of our lens to include all the actors, and if we widen our historical perspective to see where they came from and what they did next, Twain's picture is revealed as an airy, socially shaped fantasy.

Fantasyland is a California cultural creation. It lies just next door to Frontierland. Frontierland fantasies do not explain adult lives, personal or social, not in 1849, and not now.

Where, then, to return to my rhetorical title, where have all these young men gone? With luck, they have forsaken the Wild West and left Hisland behind. That leaves historians to trace their complex routes to home and work. In these histories, the young men will represent, not the linear movement of the nation across the continent, but the complex and interdependent negotiations of family fortunes. With luck they will enter our collective memories, not as mythic heroes, but as our social ancestors who helped forge the worlds we inherit.

Where did all the *real* men go? Back to Massachusetts, Maine, and Guangdong; back to a place in Cornwall called Nevada Farm. To fetch their families or rejoin their wives. Underground, to timber the mineshafts. To cook dinner for their cabin mates. They grew up. Into history, every one.

Notes

1. "Where Have All the Flowers Gone?" words and music by Pete Seeger. David King Dunaway, *How Can I Keep from Singing: Pete Seeger* (New York: McGraw Hill, 1981), 186.

2. Mark Twain, *Roughing It*, (1872; reprint, New York: Signet Classic, 1980), 307

3. Susan Armitage, "Through Women's Eyes: A New View of the West," in *The*

Women's West, ed. Susan Armitage and Elizabeth Jameson (Norman: University of Oklahoma Press, 1987), 9.

4. Calculated from *Bicentennial Edition, Historical Statistics of the United States, Colonial Time to 1970* (Washington DC: U.S. Department of Commerce, 1970), series A, 195–209.

5. The following counties were included in each of the mining districts; the date in parenthesis is the first census year in which each appeared. Southern Mines: Amador (1860), Calaveras (1850), El Dorado (1850), Mariposa (1850), Tuolomne (1850); Northern Mines: Butte (1850), Nevada (1852), Placer (1852), Plumas (1860), Sierra (1852), Yuba (1850); Klamath/Shasta/Trinity: Del Norte (1860), Klamath (1852), Shasta (1850), Siskiyou (1852), Trinity (1850). Figures calculated from *Seventh Census of the United States, 1850: An Appendix Embracing Notes Upon the Tables of Each of the States, Etc.* (Washington DC: Robert Armstrong, Public Printer, 1853), 969 (hereinafter called "1850 Census"); "Population and Industry of California, By the State Census for the Year 1852," in 1850 Census, 984 (hereinafter called "1852 Census"); *Population of the United States in 1860; Compiled from the Original Returns of the Eighth Census* (Washington DC: GPO, 1864), 22–25 (hereinafter called "1860 Census"); *Ninth Census of the United States: The Tables of Race, Nationality, Sex, Selected Arts and Occupations* (Washington DC: GPO, 1872), 606–9 (hereinafter called "1870 Census").

6. Calculated from *Bicentennial Edition*, series A, 195–209.

7. The Cripple Creek District's population was 59 percent male and 41 percent female; calculated from Manuscript Census, Teller County, Colorado, 1900. Mary Murphy, "Women on the Line: Prostitution in Butte, Montana, 1878–1917," (master's thesis, University of North Carolina at Chapel Hill, 1983), 6.

8. Ralph Mann, *After the Gold Rush: Society in Grass Valley and Nevada City, California, 1849–1870* (Stanford: Stanford University Press, 1982), 208.

9. For European migrations, see for instance Timothy J. Hatton and Jeffrey G. Williamson, *The Age of Mass Migration: Causes and Economic Impact* (New York: Oxford University Press, 1998).

10. For regions of origin, see for instance Mann, *After the Gold Rush*, table 4, 225.

11. Susanna Townsend to Sister Mary, from Jackson Creek, November 23, 1852, Susanna Roberts Townsend Correspondence, 1838–1868, Bancroft Library, University of California, Berkeley (hereinafter called "Townsend Collection").

12. Jotham Varney to wife from Sacramento, September 8, 1850, October 27, 1850, Jotham Varney Collection, California Historical Society, San Francisco (hereinafter called "Varney Collection").

13. James S. Barnes, letter from Sacramento, March 21, 1850, in James S. Barnes Collection, Bancroft Library (hereinafter called "Barnes Collection").

14. William Ives Morgan, journal entry, William Ives Morgan Collection, Bancroft Library, 53.

15. Mann, *After the Gold Rush*, 229.

16. Calculated from 1850 Census, 972; 1852 Census, 984; 1860 Census, 33; 1870 Census, 36–37. In 1860, in the mining districts, almost half (48 percent) of the residents had come from other lands: 53 percent in the Southern Mines, and 45 percent in the Northern Mines and the Klamath/Trinity/Shasta district. Calculated from 1860 Census, 33.

17. Mann, *After the Gold Rush*, 229.

18. See Susan Lee Johnson, " 'The gold she gathered': Difference, Domination, and California's Southern Mines," (Ph.D. diss., Yale University, 1993), 113–15.

19. Overall, some 37 percent of California immigrants were British, 23 percent Chinese. 1870 Census, 336–37.

20. See Judy Yung, *Unbound Feet: A Social History of Chinese Women in San Francisco* (Berkeley: University of California Press, 1995), 16.

21. The Opium Wars occurred in 1839–1842 and 1856–1860.

22. The immigrants were particularly concentrated from selected districts. The largest proportions of Chinese emigrants to North America and Australia came from the district of T'oishan, to which an estimated 40–50 percent of the Chinese in America traced their origins. Sucheng Chan, *This Bittersweet Soil: The Chinese in California Agriculture, 1860–1910* (Berkeley: University of California Press, 1986), 17.

23. Shih-shan Henry Tsai, "Chinese Immigration, 1848–1882," in *People of Color in the American West*, ed. Sucheng Chan, Douglas Henry Daniels, Mario T. Garcia, and Terry P. Wilson (Lexington MA: D. C. Heath & Company, 1994), 110–16, 122; excerpt reprinted from Shih-shan H. Tsai, *China and the Overseas Chinese in the United States, 1868–1911* (Fayetteville: University of Arkansas Press, 1983).

24. Tsai, *China and the Overseas Chinese*, 114. Some seventy-five thousand Chinese lived in California in 1880, shortly before the Chinese Exclusion Act halted the entry of all but a trickle. Table 1, Chan, *This Bittersweet Soil*, 43.

25. Tsai, "Chinese Immigration," 116.

26. Mann, *After the Gold Rush*, 237.

27. Arthur Cecil Todd, *The Cornish Miner in America* (Truro, England: D. Bradford Barton; Glendale CA: Arthur H. Clark, 1967), 15.

28. Todd, *Cornish Miner*, 16–17.

29. Todd, *Cornish Miner*, 18.

30. Todd, *Cornish Miner*, 19, 21–22; A. L. Rowse, *The Cousin Jacks: The Cornish in America* (New York: Charles Scribner's Sons, 1969), 243.

31. Rowse, *Cousin Jacks*, 244.

32. Todd, *Cornish Miner*, 60.

33. Rowse, *Cousin Jacks*, 245.

34. Rowse, *Cousin Jacks*, 246. On the positive manipulation of Cornish identity in hard-rock mining, see Ronald M. James, "Defining the Group: Nineteenth-Century Cornish on the North American Mining Frontier," in Philip Payton, ed., *Cornish Studies Two* (Exeter, England: University of Exeter Press, 1994), 32–47.

35. Quoted in Todd, *Cornish Miner*, 68–69.

36. Calculated from 1852 Census, 984.

37. Calculated from 1860 Census, 22–27. The Asian population in the Southern Mines was 96 percent male, 97 percent in the Northern Mines and in the Klamath/Shasta/Trinity district. Among whites, the populations were 77 percent male in the Southern Mines, 90 percent in the Northern Mines, 81 percent in the Klamath/Shasta/Trinity District. The proportions among the "Free Colored" population were 78 percent male in the Southern Mines, 71 percent in the Northern Mines, 70 percent in the Klamath/Shasta/Trinity District. The small Indian population that was enumerated was 57 percent male in the Southern Mines, 73 percent in the Northern Mines, 51 percent around the Klamath/Shasta/Trinity District.

38. Calculated from 1870 Census, 606–9.

39. Todd, *Cornish Miner*, 55.

40. Todd, *Cornish Miner*, 77–78.

41. See Richard E. Lingenfelter, *The Hardrock Miners: A History of the Mining Labor Movement in the American West, 1863–1893* (Berkeley: University of California Press, 1974), 107–27; Sucheng Chan, ed., *Entry Denied: Exclusion and the Chinese Community in America, 1882–1943* (Philadelphia: Temple University Press, 1991); Alexander Saxton, *The Indispensable Enemy: Labor and the Anti-Chinese Movement in California* (Berkeley: University of California Press, 1971); Roger Daniels, ed., *Anti-Chinese Violence in North America* (New York: Arno Press, 1978); Duane A. Smith, *Rocky Mountain Mining Camps: The Urban Frontier* (Bloomington: Indiana University Press, 1967; paperback ed., Lincoln: University of Nebraska Press, 1974), 29–34.

42. The Chinese Exclusion Act was renewed in 1892 and then renewed indefinitely in 1904.

43. Chan, *Bittersweet Soil*, 73; for figures on occupations in 1860, 1870, 1880, and 1900, see tables 3–6, 54–55, 62–63, 68–69, 73–74.

44. Chan, *Bittersweet Soil*, 86.

45. Chan, *Bittersweet Soil*, 103.

46. James Barnes to Sister Mary from Sacramento City, December 31, 1853; from Sacramento July 30, 1854; from Sacramento May 26, 1854; Barnes Collection.

47. Andrew Rotter first explored Argonauts' preoccupations with home and family in "'Matilda for Gods Sake Write': Women and Families on the Argonaut Mind," *California Historical Quarterly* 58, no. 2 (summer 1979): 128–41. See also Rohrbough, *Days of Gold*.

48. Letter from Rodney P. Odall Jr., to his Parents, from Mariposa, November 25, 1850. Rodney P. Odall Jr., Collection, Bancroft Library (hereinafter called "Odall Collection").

49. Odall to Dear Parents, Brown's Bar, May 18, 1851, Odall Collection.

50. James S. Barnes, from San Francisco, February 28, 1850, Barnes Collection.

51. James S. Barnes, from Sacramento, March 21, 1850, Barnes Collection.

52. James S. Barnes, from Sacramento, October 13, 1850, Barnes Collection.

53. Jotham Varney to his wife, from Sacramento, September 8, 1850, Varney Collection.

54. James S. Barnes from Sacramento, January 28, 1851, Barnes Collection.

55. Unsigned letter to Catharine D. Oliver of Boston from a female friend in San Francisco, MS 1596, California Historical Society, San Francisco.

56. Jo Ann Levy, *They Saw the Elephant: Women in the California Gold Rush* (1990; reprint, Norman: University of Oklahoma Press, 1992), 91–92, 100–103, 107.

57. Susanna Townsend to Sister Fanny, from Jackson Creek, January 19, 1852, Townsend Collection.

58. Susanna Townsend to Sister Mary, from Jackson Creek, November 23, 1852, Townsend Collection.

59. Susanna Townsend to Skotty, from Secreta Ranch, February 20, 1853, Townsend Collection.

60. Susanna Townsend to Sister Mary, from Sutterville, October 25–November 13, 1853; Susanna Townsend to Skotty, from Sutterville, December 20, 1853; Susanna

Townsend to Skotty, from Scuppernong, October 3–9, 1854, Townsend Collection.

61. Susanna Townsend to Sister Mary, April 25, 1856, Townsend Collection.

62. Susanna Townsend to Skotty, January 23, 1857, Townsend Collection.

63. Susanna Townsend to Skotty, from Sutterville, December 20, 1853, Townsend Collection.

64. Susanna Townsend to Skotty, January 23, 1857, Townsend Collection.

65. See Linda Peavy and Ursula Smith, *Women in Waiting in the Westward Movement: Life on the Home Frontier* (Norman: University of Oklahoma Press, 1994); Linda Peavy and Ursula Smith, *The Gold Rush Widows of Little Falls* (St. Paul: Minnesota Historical Society Press, 1990).

66. Jotham Varney to wife, at sea, May 1850, Varney Collection.

67. Jotham Varney to wife, San Francisco, May 30, 1850, Varney Collection.

68. Ebenezer Sheppard, April 9, 1849, Ebenezer Sheppard Journal, California State Historical Society, San Francisco.

69. Peavy and Smith, *Women in Waiting*, 9.

70. Peavy and Smith, *Women in Waiting*, 17.

71. Jotham Varney, from Sacramento City, September 18, 1850, October 27, 1850, November 19, 1850, Varney Collection.

72. Jotham Varney, at sea, May 1850, Varney Collection.

73. See Peavy and Smith, *Women in Waiting*, 25.

74. Reproduced in Shannon Applegate and Terence O'Donnell, *Talking on Paper: An Anthology of Oregon Letters and Diaries* (Corvallis: Oregon State University Press, 1994), 215.

75. Quoted in Yung, *Unbound Feet*, 21.

76. Peavy and Smith, *Women in Waiting*, 43–88, esp. 43.

77. Peavey and Smith, *Women in Waiting*, 89–131.

78. Mann, *After the Gold Rush*, table 36, 255.

79. See James, "Defining the Group."

80. See Elizabeth Jameson, *All That Glitters: Class, Conflict, and Community in Cripple Creek* (Urbana: University of Illinois Press, 1998), esp. chapters 4 and 5.

81. See Angela V. John, *By the Sweat of Their Brow: Women Workers of Victorian Coal Mines* (London: Croom Helm, 1990).

82. The assumption that women should not mine underground has been breached in the United States since the 1970s against considerable resistance. In other times and places, it has not seemed so self-evident that mining was men's work. See for instance Patricia J. Hulden, "The Rhetoric and Iconography of Reform: Women Coal Miners in Belgium, 1848–1914," *The Historical Journal* 34, no. 2 (June 1991): 411–36; Zoila Hernandez, *El Coraje de las Mineras: Marginalidad Andino-Minera en Canaria* (Lima, Peru: La Asociacion, 1986); John, *By the Sweat of Their Brow*; Domitila Barrios de Chungara, *Let Me Speak: Testimony of Domitila, a Woman of the Bolivian Mines* (New York: Monthly Review Press, 1978); Lucy Murphy, "Economy, Race, and Gender Along the Fox-Wisconsin and Rock Riverways, 1737–1832" (Ph.D. diss., Northern Illinois University, 1995); Johnson, " 'The gold she gathered'," 379–80; Hurtado, *Indian Survival on the California Frontier*. In fact, for some British coal miners, the exclusion—or protection—of women from the mines was a distinct achievement they sought to extend to their children.

10

The Last Fandango

Women, Work, and the End of the California Gold Rush

Susan L. Johnson

In 1851 a California newspaperman published a tongue-in-cheek tribute to his town's most popular site of public amusement, titling it "The Fandango in Sonora." His was a romp of an article that compared Sonora's dance halls to the boulevards of Paris and the parks of New York City. Claiming that Sonora boasted five "fandango saloons," the writer described two, one French and the other Mexican. The French fandango was in "a stylish room, brilliantly lighted," where patrons danced a polka. In the tight embrace and unison gyration of couples, the writer detected "a Gallic fraternization"; indeed, only when the music stopped was it clear that "there were really two persons in the performance." The reader could not be sure whether the "two persons" were male and female, respectively or, as was common in the boom years of the Gold Rush, both male. Next the writer moved on to the Mexican fandango. In this saloon, it was dim and smoke filled the air. But the dancers were "going at it with a perfect looseness," urged on by a "brawny guitarist" whose music "lustily horrifie[d] the night." It was more likely here that men danced with women, since when the music ended, each "caballero" led a "fair dulcina" to the bar for refreshment. The caballeros, however, just as often as they were Mexicans, were "Sydney convicts" (that is, Australians), perfumed local officials, and youths who looked like mercantile clerks. It was the dancing women who made this fandango Mexican, women who, according to the writer, were "brown in complexion" and "blue" in moral character. At the night's end, each man left with one of the dancers, and the newspaperman drew the curtain, noting, "We only promised to daguerreotype the fandango, and would not outrage decency by introducing after scenes."[1]

Soon, Gold Rush journalists decided that describing the fandango itself—let alone the "after scenes"—was an outrage to decency. This decision was one marker of a transformation in social relations that occurred during the 1850s in the gold region known as the Southern Mines. The Southern Mines, like the Northern Mines, were located in the foothills of the Sierra Nevada in central California. But the diggings in the south were scattered throughout the drainage of the San Joaquin River, while the diggings in the north were found in the drainage of the Sacramento River. Residents of the Southern Mines turned to the valley town of Stockton as their supply center, while residents of the Northern Mines looked to Sacramento. These geographical distinctions matter because much of what we know about the California gold rush, both from scholarship and from popular culture, derives from the history of the Northern Mines, where Anglo Americans predominated and where the industrialization of mining followed a recognizable trajectory. In the Southern Mines, by contrast, non-Anglo-American gold seekers predominated in numbers, Native peoples persisted, and placer mining remained not the exception but the rule.[2]

During the boom years of the gold rush, certain forms of women's work flourished in the Southern Mines. A majority of the women who lived there just after the discovery of gold in 1848 were Native women, collectively known as Miwoks, but a growing number were newcomers from France, northern Mexico, and central Chile. The spaces in which these newcomers performed their work included everything from open-air kitchens to stream-side laundries to boisterous dance halls and gambling saloons. As the gold boom gave way to a bust, however, some spaces and forms of women's work came under attack. When Anglo-American women started to settle in the Southern Mines, for example, they joined with their menfolk in campaigns to banish popular amusements formerly frequented by lonely miners and often staffed by French- and Spanish-speaking women. Boarded fandango houses became signs of change in the Southern Mines, change by which an earlier social world of possibility and permeable boundaries gave way to more entrenched forms of dominance rooted in Anglo-American constructions of gender, race and ethnicity, and class position. In the very midst of this transformation, however, Chinese women began to arrive in ever-increasing numbers, most of them enslaved and indentured prostitutes. Chinese prostitutes did not enjoy the relative control over their labor and earnings that earlier women workers in commercialized leisure were able to exercise. But those Chinese women who endured (and those few who outwitted) the violent strictures placed on their everyday lives show how incomplete and unstable relations of domination remained, wherever a will to survival and dignity persisted among those with less access to power.[3]

Perhaps the most emblematic site of change in the Southern Mines was the ubiquitous fandango. Before the gold rush, "fandango" was a term that referred, not to a place for dance, but to a particular kind of dance event—one popular among poorer Spanish Mexicans in California. The "fandango house," often called simply a "fandango," was a gold rush innovation.[4] Fandango houses could be found throughout the California diggings as well as in San Francisco. But they flourished nowhere more spectacularly than in the Southern Mines and the supply town of Stockton. As the gold rush decade, from 1848 to 1858, progressed, fandangos came under attack. In the same issue of the Stockton newspaper that reprinted "The Fandango in Sonora" from the *Sonora Herald*, for example, there also appeared a frightful account of a murder that had taken place at Casa de los Amigos, a Stockton fandango. Apparently, two men, Caleb Ruggles and James McCabe, had quarreled over which of them would go home with a woman named Luz Parilla. A bowie knife, a pistol, drunken men, and Luz Parilla herself, shuttling back and forth between her angry would-be lovers, all figured in the account, which ended with Jim McCabe dead from a gunshot wound and the charges against Caleb Ruggles dismissed on grounds of self-defense.[5] After 1851 the Stockton paper would print many more articles of this type about dance halls—articles that directly or indirectly condemned fandangos as sites of vice and violence—and none at all of the celebratory type from the Sonora paper.[6] Even the very next piece on fandangos reprinted from the *Sonora Herald* sang a new tune: a year after Sonora's newspapermen winked at the town's most popular resorts, they ran an approving notice of a new city ordinance that prohibited fandangos, declaring, "the majority of the people are decidedly opposed to all such vile exhibitions."[7]

This was wishful thinking. Plenty of people in Sonora, as elsewhere in the Southern Mines, were decidedly attracted to such exhibitions, both as patrons and as workers. But the ordinance, along with a flood of newspaper reports about murder and mayhem in the dance halls, was evidence of a push that began in 1852 to curtail public amusements that had thrived in the early months and years of the gold rush, including not only fandangos but brothels and gambling saloons as well. This push was the consequence of two major transformations in the Southern Mines. The first involved a series of racial and ethnic conflicts, primarily among men, that had occurred between 1849 and 1851 and that had been resolved largely in the Anglo Americans' favor—events that came to be known rather extravagantly as the Chilean War, the French Revolution, and the Mariposa War.[8] The second involved an influx of Anglo-American women, particularly women with family ties to men who were helping to constitute a middle class in the more well-established towns of the Southern Mines. The resolution of the racial and ethnic clashes provided the engine for an assault on dance halls, gaming tables, and houses of prostitution. The arrival of white women from the eastern United States provided the fuel.

Census figures give an outline of the demographic change: In 1850 the non-Native population of the Southern Mines was less than 3 percent female—about eight hundred women in an enumerated immigrant population approaching thirty thousand. By 1860 an influx of women brought that figure up to nearly 19 percent—over nine thousand women in an enumerated immigrant population of almost fifty thousand.[9]

This was not a random increase. Although some women came to California on their own in the 1850s, many more came to join husbands or brothers or fathers already resident in the diggings. And those men in the best economic and social position to summon their wives or sisters or daughters to California were men who had weathered successfully the initial racial and ethnic strife of the gold rush—that is, Anglo Americans. Among Anglos, not all were equally able to send for their womenfolk; most merchants and professionals, for example, were more able than most miners. Another group of men who brought families from the East were those who established water companies, the entrepreneurial venture of choice in a region that had been known as the "dry diggings." Inadequate underground deposits meant that gold seekers in the Southern Mines persisted longer in placer, or surface, mining. Since placer miners needed water to wash gold-bearing dirt and water was scarcest in the south, entrepreneurs there sought their fortunes less by forming industrialized mining companies than by building systems of ditches and flumes and selling to placer miners the use of the water they tapped. Shopkeepers, lawyers, and water company managers were the progenitors of a homegrown middle class in the Southern Mines. But class making in the nineteenth century was a family affair, and this process was nowhere clearer than in the diggings. Only when women joined these men in California did a middle class begin to take root.[10]

One such woman was Mary Harrison Newell. Born a baker's daughter in Wilmington, Delaware, Mary Harrison had married a young man from Utica, New York, named William Newell. When William suffered a business failure in Utica, he decided to join a group of local men who headed to California in 1849. The Newells lived a continent apart for five long years, until 1854. Then Mary joined William in the gold rush town of Columbia. William first had tried his hand at mining, but then became secretary of the Tuolumne County Water Company (TCWC), perhaps the largest entrepreneurial venture in the Southern Mines. By the time Mary came, he had abandoned the TCWC, sold some of his stock, and entered into partnership with a man named Marcellus Brainard. The two white men kept a store that William described to Mary in one of the last letters they exchanged before she went west: "[I]t is the same as a Common Country Store at home Groceries Provisions Hardware Clothing Dry goods Mining Tools *Rum and Tobacco* fill a prominent place." Once Mary arrived, she entered easily into the world that William had described to her in letters: "Society is now growing a great deal better here a good many merchants and miners and others are sending for their Families."[11]

The wife of William's business partner, Clementine Brainard, was especially excited about Mary's arrival, noting in her diary on July 2, 1854, "Mrs. Newell arrived very unexpectedly this evening accompanied by her father: think I shall like her much." Although William Newell and Marcellus Brainard did not remain in partnership long, Mary and Clementine continued their round of visiting with one another and with women married to other up-and-coming white men in Columbia. Mary must have been a particular comfort to Clementine, as Mary's self-assurance in household and business matters was matched by young Clementine's awkwardness at domestic tasks and her astonishment at the pace and content of commerce in Columbia. Mary was an experienced baker, for example, while Clementine thought that learning to cook was "a bitter pill"—not surprising, since in one attempt at frying doughnuts she "came near setting the house on fire." Clementine also bemoaned her husband's frequent business trips to San Francisco and worried over the liquor he sold in his store—a worry Mary did not seem to share.[12] As much as the growing number of comfortably situated families, then, such female friendships helped to anchor the emerging white middle class of the Southern Mines.

The Newell family, however, was not long for this world. Just over a year after Mary arrived, William died. Now Mary turned her own sights to business, plotting with her sister, who was on her way west from Delaware with their father to open a store of their own. In the end, although Mary went into partnership with her father for a time selling paint, wallpaper, and glass, she found another road to economic security.

A year or so after William died, Mary Harrison Newell married Joseph Pownall, himself a long-time TCWC employee, now both a trustee and the secretary of the company. For his part, Pownall had worried over his bachelor state for years (he was nearly forty). He must have been pleased at long last to take his rightful place in the changing gold rush world he had described to a friend in 1854: "This country . . . is fast settling up with families of respectability wives daughters & other permanent fixtures of this class which assist so much in giving character & a healthy moral tone to the machinery regulating what is termed society."[13]

Unlike Clementine Brainard, Mary Pownall never seemed that concerned about Columbia's "moral tone." But the social transformation of places like Columbia did not require all the "respectable" wives and daughters of the white middle class to tinker with "the machinery regulating what is termed society." To a certain extent, it was enough that white women simply were present. Their presence, in turn, served as a reminder of middle-class cultural expectations whereby women acted as moral arbiters of society, thus encouraging men to exercise self-control.[14]

But Mary Pownall aside, some white women did bring with them a recognizable impulse for social reform. The impulse was recognizable, of course, because the social ills that white, middle-class women saw in the diggings—especially drinking, gambling, and sexual commerce—all existed in eastern places and had become targets of reform there.[15] So those who sought to do battle with public amusements in the Southern Mines came armed with an ideological arsenal—a discourse of reform, if you will.

Consider, for example, Elizabeth Gunn, who joined her husband in California in 1851. Gunn's mother was an antislavery woman, Elizabeth Le Breton Stickney, who after the death of her first husband was (unhappily) married to the abolitionist Henry Clarke Wright. So young Elizabeth grew up surrounded by antislavery Quakers and other antebellum reformers in Philadelphia, and then she married an abolitionist, Lewis Gunn, as well.[16] By 1850, however, Lewis was in California, working as editor of the *Sonora Herald*—the paper that first printed the tongue-in-cheek tribute to the fandango in July 1851. Elizabeth arrived in Sonora just weeks after the article appeared. If one can judge by the articles reprinted from her husband's paper in the Stockton press, the *Sonora Herald* soon assumed a disapproving tone on the subject of fandangos. It is not clear what role Elizabeth played in this change, but it is clear where she stood on such issues. In a letter to her mother and sisters, Elizabeth wrote that although there were "some good Anti-slavery and Temperance men" in Sonora, there were also many "of a different sort, lawyers and merchants who gamble and go to houses of ill fame and keep mistresses, mostly Mexican women." She went on to denounce a judge in town who had sold his house to prostitutes and who himself "kept" a Native woman.

It must have been evident to Elizabeth Gunn that women who worked in dance halls, gambling saloons, and brothels, as well as those who cohabited with men, had found viable livelihoods in Sonora. Up the hill from her own house, one of the finest and best situated in town, was another built by a young French woman—just seventeen years old—for herself, her mother, and her younger brother and sister. Elizabeth wrote that this woman earned her living "by going to the gaming houses and dealing out the cards to the players."[17] Reform-minded women had their work cut out for them.

Most white women who remonstrated against public amusements in the Southern Mines were not as well connected as Elizabeth Gunn. Some, like Clementine Brainard, had little or no prior experience in eastern reform circles but felt that social conditions in the diggings demanded their attention.[18] Another such woman was Lorena Hays. Her father had died in 1848, when she was twenty-two. In 1853 her widowed mother decided to leave Illinois and follow siblings west, taking along her four unmarried daughters. When they arrived in Amador County, the Hays women supported themselves by taking in boarders and by teaching. Immigrating as they did after the initial boom, their financial situations were always precarious. One by one, each of the women married, including Lorena's mother.[19] As for herself, Lorena mourned her lot. She longed to attend school in Sacramento but could not afford it. As consolation, she devoured every book and periodical she could find, from the *Water-Cure Journal* to *Hopes and Helps for the Young of Both Sexes*. Then she met an editor for *The Golden Era*, the first California publication to call itself "A Family Newspaper." He invited her to write a column, and she obliged, publishing seven letters in *The Golden Era* between 1854 and 1857. None of this altered Lorena's profound despair over her lack of schooling, which she had hoped would fit her to move in better social circles.

Like her mother and sisters, Lorena too married, though only after anguished indecision. Her suitor, John Clement Bowmer, was a man whom she "never really admired . . . as a lover," though she came to "love him for his goodness." Once married, she knew, "Friends, name, fame, all are given to husband—to one." She wondered if "in that one" she would find "an equivalent." She did not. In fact, after a brief period of bliss that probably coincided with her deepening sexual relationship with her husband, Lorena slipped back into despair over lost opportunities in her life. Her husband, it seems—though "*noble*" and "*good*" and capable of satisfying her in his "loving embrace"—shared none of her spiritual and intellectual passions. Lorena found an outlet for those passions by writing for publication.[20]

During the years that she wrote for *The Golden Era*, Lorena Hays gave voice to sentiments common among white women who were helping to constitute a middle class in the Southern Mines. In one column, for example, writing under the pen name "Lenita," she predicted that California would soon escape its status as a moral backwater. Rhetorically, she asked, "Towards what point are we to look for the light that is to break forth as sunlight to purify, cleanse, and irradiate our moral atmosphere?" "WOMAN," she answered, "is beginning to awaken to her true position." It was foolish, she went on, to think that men could enact reform alone, while women's hands were "folded in luxury, thus tacitly giving consent to the vice and immorality in which our land abounds." Privately, in her diary, Lorena wondered what caused vice and immorality in California: "Is it because of our peculiar situation—the mixed and incongruous mass of our population or the predominance of the male element in society?" But publicly and privately, she was sure that "WOMAN"—by which she meant white, middle-class women—would be instrumental in bringing about a cure.[21]

That Lorena Hays chose "Lenita" as her pen name for *The Golden Era*, borrowing Spanish-speakers' practice of creating diminutive, affectionate forms of female names, suggests a curious process of identification, projection, and reversal. It was only as "Lenita" that Lorena could express her deepest longings. Somehow, Lorena had come to identify her otherworldly passions with what she understood as the worldly passions of her Mexican and Chilean neighbors, in whom she took a great interest. Indeed, Lorena tried to learn Spanish as soon as she arrived in California, and she tutored a young Chilean who wanted to improve his English. Likewise, one of her longest journal entries denounced the reign of terror local vigilance committees had visited upon Mexicans and Chileans in Amador County after a small band of robbers assumed to be Mexican had killed several Anglos at a remote camp. As Lorena put it, "We fear a great deal more disturbance from these committees and white greasers than from the Mexicans who have been driven from their homes." Nonetheless, although she identified with Spanish-speaking people and projected upon them unfettered passions, the reforms she so wished for in California necessarily spelled a narrowing of opportunities for Mexicans and Chileans and especially for those women whose livelihoods depended on the worldly passions of a still disproportionately male social world.[22]

Other Anglo women were less concerned about what "Lenita" called California's "moral atmosphere" than they were about the ways in which social conditions in the Southern Mines intimately impinged on their everyday lives. In a divorce case in Amador County, for example, Chloe Cooper complained that when her husband, James, left their home in

New York State in 1849 and went to California, "he commenced to visit fandango houses . . . and kept company with divers women of ill fame of the Spanish race . . . and did commit adultery, and have carnal connection with them in said houses of ill fame." What was worse, when Chloe joined James in 1854, he continued his carousing. His behavior finally came to her attention, Chloe said, in 1857, and she left him.[23] Another case told a similar tale. Even though Mary Jane Anderson went west along with her husband, James, once in California this James, too, "spent his time among idle and dissolute persons, and frequenters of gambling saloons and brothels," and he slept with women Mary Jane called "spanish prostitutes" as well.[24] Likewise, Mary Ann Hayes called her husband, Nicholas, "a frequenter of houses of ill fame" in her divorce complaint, and Tuolumne County acquaintances backed her up. A teamster said he had seen Nicholas go off into private rooms with a "Spanish" prostitute in Sonora. And a neighbor claimed he had seen Nicholas at a brothel in Columbia asking a Mexican woman "what she charged." The neighbor recalled that the woman had said "three Dollars" and that the two had disappeared for a half-hour thereafter.[25] There is no evidence that women such as Chloe Cooper, Mary Jane Anderson, and Mary Ann Hayes participated in campaigns to shut down public amusements in the Southern Mines, but one can imagine that they did not stand in the way.

What did these campaigns look like? Interestingly enough, it is easier to find complaints about public amusements than to find evidence of action against them. Actual reform efforts on the part of Anglo-American women and their menfolk were limited. Despite their increasing cultural, economic, and political power, Anglos, according to the 1860 federal census, constituted less than half of the total population in the Southern Mines, ranging from a low of 37 percent in sparsely populated Mariposa County to a high of 49 percent in more populous Amador County. Since these figures do not include Native peoples, and since non-Anglo populations in general often were underenumerated by census takers, the actual percentages of white Americans in the southern diggings may well have been lower.[26] By definition, then, Anglos in the Southern Mines pursued reform from a precarious position. And by the mid-1850s, the white American population was fractured by growing class divisions. Furthermore, Anglo men were sharply divided over the need for reform, since many were enthusiastic participants in the leisure worlds reformers decried. Nonetheless, there were sporadic attempts to bring such worlds to an end, which took shape in temperance organizing, in campaigns for Sunday business closings and

Maine-style liquor laws, and in local initiatives against dance halls, gaming tables, and houses of prostitution.[27]

White women took an active role in these efforts. Women's diaries from the mid-1850s suggest that some merchants' wives worked behind the scenes, encouraging their husbands to give up selling liquor or to close their stores on the Christian Sabbath. Clementine Brainard, for instance, prayed in her diary that her husband, Marcellus, would "come to the determination soon that by the help of God he will deal in no intoxicating drinks whatever." She added, "may he feel that it is not good for his soul [even] if it is for his purse." Clementine may well have made Marcellus feel that it was not good for his marriage either.[28] Likewise, Lorena Hays Bowmer assumed a triumphant mood when her husband, John, "at last effected a settlement of his business" so that his store remained closed on Sunday, suggesting that she, too, had been an advocate for reform within her own home.[29]

But there were organized efforts among white women as well. In 1855, for example, the Stockton press noted that the "ladies" of Campo Seco, in Calaveras County, were the "prime movers" in advocating a Maine law. In 1856, a Tuolumne County newspaper observed that the "Ladies of Columbia" were petitioning merchants there to close their shops on Sunday. And in the same year, the *Weekly Ledger* in the Amador County town of Volcano poked fun at women's support of Sabbatarianism, suggesting that petitions to the state legislature in that town "were put in circulation by [marriageable] but not married ladies, in order to give the young 'lords of creation' one day in the week to devote at the shrine of bright eyes and bewitching ringlets."[30]

Even where white women were not distributing petitions, they were understood within their own social circles to be both inspiration for and prime beneficiaries of reform. The *Volcano Weekly Ledger* may have teased those with "bright eyes and bewitching ringlets" about their interest in a Sunday law, but the same newspaper routinely called on women readers to serve as moral beacons, whether by drawing men to church through their own regular attendance or by lending their aid in establishing schools for children and lyceums for adults. In the end, it was thought, this would all redound to the benefit of "ladies," as they would be able to walk peaceful streets that had once been "monopolized by rowdyism of every grade."[31]

The behavior of some Anglo women in the Southern Mines belied such middle-class cultural assumptions, which connected ladyhood, whiteness, and morality as interlocking links in a single chain. In addition to assaults on polyglot sites of public amusement, one of the means by which white women and their menfolk tried to redirect the leisure energies of gold rush participants was by creating alternatives to saloons, fandangos, and brothels. Among the alternatives were balls sponsored by community organizations and parties thrown by individual members of the emerging white middle class. These balls and parties often seem to have had the desired effect. But they could also become sites of contestation.

In March 1854, for example, Clementine and Marcellus Brainard received an invitation to what they thought would be such an event in Columbia. They intended to go to the party, but then Marcellus took sick. In the end, Clementine was relieved, noting in her diary, "I am very thankful something has happened to prevent our going . . . as I understand some are invited that are not fit for decent people to associate with." Her worst fears were realized when she learned that some had left the party in protest when a man named Cazneau arrived with a woman to whom he was not married. The next day, two separate duels threatened between Cazneau and the men who had departed when he arrived. (Neither fight actually materialized.) Clementine Brainard did not identify the woman who accompanied Cazneau to the party, but an 1852 court record provides a clue. In that year, an emigrant from Maine named Phoebe Quimby divorced her husband on grounds of cruelty; once, for instance, while she was pregnant, her husband had thrown her across a room. Phoebe's husband countered that Phoebe had been sleeping with Thomas Cazneau for almost a year and that she had moved in with Cazneau after filing for divorce. Despite these accusations, Phoebe won the divorce. In 1852, it seems, a white woman could leave a cruel husband and cohabit with another white man with relative impunity. But by 1854 a couple such as Phoebe Quimby and Thomas Cazneau could no longer go to a party attended by "decent people" without trouble erupting.[32] Times were changing.

Phoebe Quimby was not the only Anglo woman who failed to advance the cause of reform. Divorce records from the 1850s are replete with accusations against unruly white women. Such charges are hardly unique to the Southern Mines or to the gold rush era. Historian Robert Griswold has studied divorce in two nonmining counties of California between 1850 and 1890. He finds that although both women and men charged estranged spouses with adultery, husbands did so at twice the rate of wives. Accusations of adultery do not necessarily reflect how often women had sex outside their marriages. Instead, the charges represent a complex interaction among actual instances of extramarital sex, legal restrictions on admissible grounds for divorce, and cultural ideas about what constituted the most egregious affronts to marital vows for women.[33] None of this is unique to the diggings.

But charges of marital infidelity in the mines did reflect the particularities of changing social relations there. Some white women seem to have initiated extramarital romance, for instance, at the very balls and parties that other white women hoped would stem the tide of gold rush patterns of leisure.

Because there were still five times more men than women in the Southern Mines as late as 1860, even gatherings that middle-class people thought of as "respectable" could become arenas of contact between single men looking for women's attention and women looking for intimacy outside their marriages. The story of Mary Ann Chick is a case in point. When Mary Ann joined her husband, Alfred, in Calaveras County in 1855, their relationship quickly deteriorated. Mary Ann filed for divorce in 1859, charging Alfred with cruelty and violence. Alfred countered, however, that Mary Ann had taken up with a boarder in their household, Frank Averill, with whom she attended balls and parties and from whom she accepted "valuable presents."

That social events organized by middle-class people could become sites of moral ambiguity is also suggested by the divorce case of Emily and O. S. Davis. Emily charged her husband with extreme cruelty, and a neighbor backed her up, testifying that Mr. Davis called his wife a "damned stinking Shit ass" and a "damned wasteful bitch of Hell." Significantly, the same neighbor praised Emily by insisting that "she does not go out as other women do to balls and parties."[34] Those "other women," then—like Mary Ann Chick—must have used balls and parties to bask in the attentions of unmarried men.

While some white women dallied with men at "respectable" gatherings, others profited by gold rush gender divisions of labor, which took husbands away from family homes for much of every day and sometimes for longer stretches of time. When Sarah Philbrick of Amador County tried to divorce her husband, William, for cruelty and violence, for instance, William retorted that when he "was away from home at work on a Quartz lode," Sarah would visit an unmarried man named Bayerque. Furthermore, William charged, Sarah did this at night, often "dressed in men's apparel." William thought she wore men's clothing "so as to prevent being detected while on the streets." Whatever Sarah's reasons for cross-dressing when she visited her lover, according to William's friends she showed no remorse for her actions. After Sarah gave birth to a child, for example, William complained that the baby was not his but rather "a certain Frenchman's at Volcano." Sarah shot back that, in fact, the child did "[look] like the Frenchman." William's brother testified that this kind of wrangling was common between William and Sarah. The brother recalled that when William accused Sarah of "kissing a man," she rejoined that she "would do it again." So William slapped her. In the end, the judge disallowed the divorce, arguing, "Courts of equity cannot allow a woman who boldly avows her own turpitude to her husband to complain of her husband's anger when thus provoked."[35]

Likewise, in Tuolumne County, Joseph Hall complained that his wife, Celia, had "established a system of telegraphing or signalizing to inform her paramours" whenever Joseph was away from the house working. Joseph named three men with whom he was sure Celia had been intimate. One of these men, Charles Knight, testified that he indeed had slept with Celia and that he had seen one of the other men named in bed with her as well. Charles explained that the first time he and Celia had sex, he had gone to the Halls' house to dig a cellar while Joseph was off at work. When Charles went inside for a drink of water, he said, Celia "began to sing bawdy songs." Then she locked Charles in the house. He was able to escape, but when he went back inside later, Charles insisted, "she seized hold of me and forced me to have intercourse with her."[36]

There is no way of knowing whether the relationships between Celia Hall and Charles Knight or between Sarah Philbrick and the Frenchman Bayerque bore much resemblance to the descriptions deponents provided in divorce proceedings. But the descriptions in and of themselves, because they were designed to influence the court, had to tell stories that made sense to judges and juries. To those who heard them, stories about married white women cavorting with single men at balls and parties or when husbands were off working made all too much sense.

While plenty of white, middle-class women were advocating reform in the Southern Mines, the actions of others seemed to threaten those efforts. This would explain why narratives of unruly, aggressive white women who took advantage of gold rush social relations were so prevalent in the 1850s. At the very least, such stories suggest that keeping the chain linking ladyhood, whiteness, and morality in good repair required constant vigilance. The work of discursive repair must have sometimes frustrated the social practices of reform.

But there were other reasons why streets in the Southern Mines often remained stubbornly "monopolized by rowdyism." Put most simply, some Mexican, Chilean, and French women wanted it that way, for a rowdy street was a path to a living. During the early months and years of the gold rush, these women had helped to create both a domestic marketplace and a commercial sphere of public amusements in the Southern Mines. At the same time, exclusionary and extortionate practices on the part of white

American men were driving many Spanish- and French-speaking men away from the diggings altogether.[37]

Because these practices—the 1850 Foreign Miners Tax, for example—were aimed primarily at non-Anglo miners, those non-Anglos who toiled at different pursuits were less likely to leave. Women were overrepresented among those who worked in other parts of the boom economy and thus were overrepresented among those who stayed on in the gold regions. They carved out economic niches for themselves that exclusionists—whose goal was to reserve the placers for white American men—at first ignored. Such women's work did not threaten the "independence" of Anglo miners. In fact, some white men came to define their access to the services that French, Mexican, and Chilean women provided as part and parcel of their manly "independence." For those women who worked in the heterosocial leisure world of the diggings, the patronage of Anglo miners as well as that of those Latin Americans and Europeans who remained offered a measure of economic security. Recall, for example, Elizabeth Gunn's neighbor, a French teenager, who by dealing cards in Sonora had made enough money to build a house for her entire family.

French women such as Gunn's neighbor were omnipresent at gaming tables in the Southern Mines.[38] Documents from an 1856 grand jury investigation of gambling saloons in Tuolumne County make this clear. As a result of its investigation, the grand jury filed indictments against both women and men who worked at gaming tables. Just as grand jury members indicted a "John Doe" and a "Richard Roe" for gambling, so too did they indict a "French Mary," vaguely accusing such a woman of opening a "certain . . . game of chance called Monte" in a "certain house in Columbia."[39] They may have had a specific monte dealer in mind, but they made the indictment ambiguous enough that any one of a number of French women could have found herself in court.

Women from France did not content themselves with just working in saloons either. Many owned or managed such establishments. In the mid-1850s, for instance, court records show that several French women ran saloons in the town of Mariposa, including a Madame Clement, a Madame Follet, and a Madame Henry.[40] Emilie Henry seems to have been especially well situated. In 1856, San Francisco merchants Mills and Vantine sued Henry for failing to pay them for what they claimed was almost eight hundred dollars worth of supplies for her business. In the course of the suit, the court attached Henry's property, and the schedule of her belongings revealed an impressive collection of barroom furnishings in addition to large quantities of champagne, wine, brandy, port, and ale. For her part,

Henry sniffed that the goods she received from Mills and Vantine were "not of the quality contracted for" and "not of the value charged."[41] When middle-class Anglo women worried about the relative affluence of women who worked in saloons, then, these worries were not sheer flights of fancy.

And it was not only French women who owned and managed sites of public amusement in the Southern Mines. Mexican and Chilean women did so as well. A woman named Isabel Ortis is a notable case in point. It is not clear when Ortis arrived in the Southern Mines or even whether she came from Chile, from northern Mexico, or from elsewhere in Mexican California.[42] She was at least minimally literate, as she signed her own name in legal documents. Her business acumen must have been considerable. A variety of court records for a single year, 1858, show that she managed two separate fandangos in Amador and Calaveras Counties. An inquest into the death of a Portuguese-born man who had emigrated to California from Chile, for example, places Ortis as the proprietor of a dance hall at Camanche Camp in Calaveras County and as the owner of a house there. According to the inquest, the deceased had visited the dance hall one night and had later retired with a woman at Ortis's home, where he took sick and died. Ortis was among those called to testify before the jury of inquest. She was quick to point out that the man "did not eat or drink anything in the dance house."[43] (No charges were brought against her.) In addition, Amador County records reveal that Ortis leased a building on Main Street in the town of Jackson that she used as a saloon and dance house. The building belonged to a Mexican or Chilean woman, Natividad Shermenhoof, and her German-born husband, John. When Natividad divorced John in 1856, he retained control of their common property, including the dance house on Main Street. So in 1858, Natividad sued John for her share of their property, claiming that he had earned one thousand dollars in rent from Isabel Ortis since the lease began. Natividad won the case, and she got her share of Isabel's rent money.[44] For both Isabel Ortis and Natividad Shermenhoof, then, the gold rush commercialization of leisure spelled profit, though Isabel reaped the most direct rewards.

Indeed, so accomplished a businesswoman was Isabel Ortis that at least one Anglo American, a man named John McKay, tried to hide his failings behind her success. John may have been Isabel's lover; at least that is what one of his creditors maintained. In 1856 John McKay had joined with attorney Armsted Brown in building a livery stable on a lot that McKay already occupied on Main Street in Jackson, down the road from Ortis's fandango. Brown supplied the capital for the stable, and McKay mortgaged his half of the property to Brown in order to secure the loan. But McKay fell behind in his payments, and, in early 1858 he applied to the court as an insolvent debtor. In the meantime, however, he quietly had transferred his interest in the livery stable to Isabel Ortis. According to attorney Brown, McKay did this in order to shield the property from creditors. But Ortis, in turn, perhaps in order to defeat the mortgage, purchased title to the lot on which the stable stood from prominent Californio Andrés Pico.[45] Pico was among those landowning Spanish Mexicans who had led the resistance against Anglo Americans during the conquest of 1846–1848 (his brother, Pio Pico, was California's governor when the conquest began). After the signing of the Treaty of Guadalupe Hidalgo, however, Andrés Pico took his place in the new political order as a state legislator, while struggling to retain his landholdings.[46] His claim to the lot in Jackson where the livery stable stood rested in his Arroyo Seco land grant, which dated from the Mexican period and was as yet unconfirmed.[47]

In trying to nail down her interest in Amador County real estate by linking it to a Mexican land grant, Isabel Ortis entered a juridical maelstrom.[48] When Armsted Brown turned to foreclose the mortgage on the stable and to challenge John McKay's claim of insolvency, the attorney went after Ortis with a vengeance, making legal mincemeat of her appeal to the Arroyo Seco grant and dragging her character through the mud as well. As he prepared for McKay's insolvency hearing, Brown drew up questions for McKay designed to expose both McKay and Ortis as morally, not materially, bankrupt: "Were you at the time [you sold Ortis a half interest in the livery stable] living and cohabiting with her . . . ? Who is this Isabel Ortiz— where does she live and what does she follow for a living?" And among his notes about issues to bring before the court, Brown wrote, "McKay has for a long time and still does keep live with and maintain a Woman of Spanish [descent] known as Isabel Ortiz the Mistress of a Dance House and house of ill fame in Jackson." The attorney's notes continued, arguing that if McKay "has incurred any losses since commencing his business of stable keeping . . . they have been lavished upon his said Mistress and not in payment of [his] debts." Court documents suggest that Brown was disingenuous about who was keeping whom, since Ortis stayed afloat while McKay sank deeper into debt.[49] But the attorney's argument would have been an effective one among the Anglo-American men who heard it in court: A white man ought to remain master of his own resources, and not spend those resources recklessly on a "Mistress" of "Spanish" descent. What was the point of the military and economic conquest of California, whereby

Anglo-American men asserted dominance over Spanish Mexican men, if Latin American women could turn around and exact tribute from Anglo men with impunity?[50]

It is not clear from the historical record what happened to Isabel Ortis, but she may have met her match in Armsted Brown. According to Amador County historian Larry Cenotto, Brown was not only a prominent lawyer but also "an inveterate buyer of real estate." Indeed, when fire swept through Jackson in 1862, four years after Ortis and McKay tangled with him in court, Brown lost thirty separate properties in town. A native of Missouri but an emigrant from the lead-mining districts of Wisconsin, Brown had arrived in 1849 at the camp that would become the town of Jackson. Soon thereafter, he returned to Wisconsin for his wife, Philippa, a native of Cornwall, and their six offspring; they would have five more children as well. The Browns were one of the first white families in town. A Whig who turned Democrat when the Whig party collapsed, Armsted Brown held public office in the town, the county, and the state off and on throughout his life. Deep pockets, family ties, legal skills, political power: this was not a happy combination to find in an Anglo neighbor if one was a Mexican or Chilean fandango manager trying to hold on to one's livelihood in the Southern Mines. Indeed, the arrival of people like the Browns presaged the end of an era. Regardless of what happened to Isabel Ortis in the short term, then, the long-term outcome is clear enough. Left standing after the 1862 fire in Jackson was the Browns' impressive two-story brick home built atop the town's most prominent hill. One can still visit that home today; it is now the Amador County Museum, which preserves official collective memory of Jackson and its environs. Armsted and Philippa Brown are remembered there; Isabel Ortis and the hapless John McKay are not.[51]

For every Isabel Ortis in Jackson and every Emilie Henry in Mariposa, there must have been dozens of Mexican, Chilean, and French women in the Southern Mines who worked in fandangos, saloons, and brothels without owning or operating them. Dancing with men, dealing them cards, servicing their bodies—these were not easy ways to make a living, and each grew more difficult as the 1850s progressed. Consider, for instance, the problems Laura Echeverria faced in Sonora. She had married Juan Echeverria there in 1851. It is unclear from the historical record where Laura and Juan grew up, though evidence suggests that Juan came from Monterey County in California, where he worked a rancho near Mission San Juan Bautista. Laura and Juan did not stay together long. By 1852, Laura was on her own in Sonora. In 1857 she sued for divorce, claiming that Juan, though he was worth at least four thousand dollars, had failed to provide for her. Juan countered that since their separation he had given Laura some six thousand dollars, which she, in turn, had "squandered in dissipation."[52]

Those who testified on Laura's and Juan's behalf, respectively, fell in behind them. Several men backed Juan up, arguing that he had given Laura money out of the proceeds of livestock he had sold and that he had allowed her to collect rent on properties he owned in Sonora as well. When asked why Laura and Juan separated, a man named Pedro, who may have worked for Juan, answered bluntly, "I believe it was the woman's fault." Pedro acknowledged, however, that Laura had lost her livelihood when the reform bug bit the Southern Mines, explaining that "she dealt [cards at the Long Tom Saloon] until the gaming law was enforced." Another man named Bartolomé was scandalized when he saw Laura with a child that could not have been Juan's: "I told her at the time that she was in for it," he said. According to Bartolomé, Laura retorted "that she was young and could not live without a man."[53]

Some of the men and all of the women who testified took a more charitable view of Laura. They insisted that she had worked hard in the years she had been on her own, sometimes taking in washing and sewing, sometimes keeping a restaurant, sometimes working in a dance hall, sometimes selling "cold suppers" at the Long Tom Saloon, and sometimes dealing cards there. One of her coworkers at the fandango was a French woman named Anne Lyons. Anne told the court how Laura's work life had evolved since the Echeverrias' separation, which occurred while Laura was pregnant: "In 1851," Anne testified, Laura was "in a family way, and she was cooking at her sister's house." Anne continued, with markedly French syntax, "after [Laura's] confinement she was during two months sick. I lent her then two hundred dollars. She went over to the [L]ong [T]om and used to make up cold suppers; afterwards she was washing and sewing and afterwards she has worked with me for a long time."[54] As this testimony suggests, French, Mexican, and Chilean women struggled to earn a living, moving back and forth from work in the domestic marketplace to work in commercialized leisure to work in their own households. They also relied on one another—female relatives and fellow employees, women from their homelands and women from a half-world away. Indeed, when Laura Echeverria was "in a family way" and after she gave birth, not only her sister but also a French coworker stepped in to help.

The women who testified on Laura's behalf during the divorce bristled at the lawyers' questions. Rose Cartier, for example, had been Laura's employer. When asked "what kind of business" she ran, the French woman replied simply, "I keep an establishment in Sonora." Only when pressed would she say that the business was a "Dance house and bar room." When asked what kind of work Laura had done at the Long Tom Saloon, Anne Lyons answered that Laura prepared meals there. When asked if Laura also gambled, Anne retorted, "I do not know as I have never been inside a gambling house." When asked what kind of business went on at the Long Tom, among the most notorious gaming saloons in Sonora, Anne claimed not to know. Most obstreperous, however, was Laura's sister, Matilda, who was angry both with her brother-in-law, Juan, and with the attorneys attending the divorce case. Matilda insisted that her sister was often ill and that Juan "never contributed to her support at those times." Instead, Matilda said, she herself labored to support Laura and Laura's child, until Laura's health improved and the sisters were able to work together. When Laura asked Juan for money, Matilda fumed, Juan told his wife that "she might make tortillas to maintain herself." Disgusted, Matilda explained how diligently the sisters had worked to support themselves. When asked if Laura gambled, Matilda acknowledged that Laura had "had a bank" but claimed that Laura "never bet herself," adding, "that was the only mode she had of maintaining herself in Sonora." When asked if this was a monte bank, Matilda rejoined, "I don't know. I never paid any attention to it. I don't recollect." And when pressed to reveal her own occupation, she shot back, "That has nothing to do with my sister's affairs. It is nobody's business."[55]

The exasperation these women felt is palpable in their exchanges with the lawyers who handled the Echeverrias' divorce. The anger is not hard to understand. Here were well-heeled Anglo men putting non-Anglo women's work lives under a magnifying glass, arching an eyebrow at all they saw. Perhaps the attorneys themselves were patrons of Rose Cartier's dance hall and the Long Tom Saloon. Perhaps they were not. But it would have been easy for the women to see these men as representatives of a cultural category, the existence of which had once assured Spanish- and French-speaking women of a livelihood. Anglo men in and around Sonora had been among the best customers of local saloons and fandangos. Now some such men— no doubt backed by their womenfolk—threatened Mexican, Chilean, and French women with dispossession.

Indeed, it would only be a matter of time before women such as Laura Echeverria, Rose Cartier, Isabel Ortis, and Emilie Henry would drift away from the Southern Mines altogether. Gold rush social relations persisted into the 1860s, but they began to be overshadowed by a new social order as early as 1852, when the *Sonora Herald* wrote approvingly of the city ordinance that prohibited fandangos. The arrival of women such as Mary

Newell, Clementine Brainard, Elizabeth Gunn, and Lorena Hays presaged the changes. At the same time, the divorces of women such as Chloe Cooper, Mary Jane Anderson, and Mary Ann Hayes, who accused their husbands of keeping company with Mexican and Chilean women in the late 1850s, show just how protracted the struggle was between older and newer styles of heterosocial relations in this multiracial, multiethnic social world. It was protracted in part because white, middle-class women, perceived as those who both inspired and benefited from reform, were few in number; because white men were ambivalent about whether change should even occur; and because a handful of white women themselves rather liked the old order, which gave them intimate access to a wide range of lonely men. Just as important, however, was the will of Spanish- and French-speaking women to earn a living in the context of conquest.[56] The avenues that many of them chose—owning, managing, and working in dance halls, gambling saloons, and brothels—were wide open in the initial gold boom, and they narrowed only gradually over the course of the 1850s. It was not easy work and it would not last forever, but then neither would much of what constituted gold rush labor. Casa de los Amigos down in Stockton, Sonora's Long Tom Saloon, the fandango Isabel Ortis ran in Jackson, Madame Clement's saloon in Mariposa—for a time, these were places where California gold found its way out of the hands of men from around the world and into the hands of women from Mexico, Chile, and France. When these buildings closed their doors, just as surely as when the placers pinched out, the gold rush was over.

Sometimes you could even see it happening. One fall day in 1858, a stage-driver came to the office of a Stockton newspaper with word of a fire that had just ravaged the main street of Jamestown, near Sonora in Tuolumne County. It began, the driver said, "in an unoccupied building formerly used as a fandango house." The blaze spread quickly down both sides of the street, consuming all but the small number of fireproof structures. Many of the buildings that burned were hastily constructed wooden saloons. Next door to the boarded fandango house, however, was a dwelling that was still occupied. A woman lived there, the stage-driver said, and when the fire started, she rushed out into the street with a trunk containing three thousand dollars. In the fright and confusion that followed, the trunk was spirited away. According to the driver, many believed that whoever stole the trunk had anticipated all of this, that "the fire was started with the view of having the money thus exposed."[57] The historical record reveals nothing else about this woman. But it would not be far-fetched to imagine that she had worked in the fandango or maybe in one of the saloons that burned nearby. Her earnings neatly stored in a trunk, perhaps she was hoping to leave the diggings with assets for a new life. The fire would have destroyed those dreams. Most women did not end their careers in the Southern Mines in so dramatic a fashion, but a fandango in flames was surely a sign of the times.

In the end, however, Anglo-American, middle-class people did not succeed in ridding the diggings of commercialized forms of leisure in which men purchased proximity to women. Because at the same moment that French- and Spanish-speaking women were riding west in stagecoaches bound for Stockton or Sacramento en route to San Francisco, Cantonese-speaking women were riding east up into the foothills of the Sierra Nevada. By 1860 almost 450 Chinese women lived in the four counties that constituted the Southern Mines, roughly 4.5 percent of the Chinese population.[58] While a handful of these women may have been servants or merchants' wives, most worked as prostitutes. The lives of Chinese women engaged in sexual commerce, then, serve as a coda to stories of transformation in the Southern Mines during the 1850s.

Historians such as Lucie Cheng Hirata, Sucheng Chan, and Judy Yung have shown that Chinese women who sold sex for cash exercised far less control over their labor and earnings than did others employed in gold rush leisure establishments, including non-Chinese prostitutes. Many Cantonese-speaking women died on the job, stricken by sexually transmitted disease or cut down by violence at the hands of clients or employers. The women also came to California under different circumstances than did most of their menfolk. Chinese men often emigrated independently or under the credit-ticket system, whereby a man repaid the cost of travel out of the money he earned in the diggings. In contrast, most Chinese women arrived in San Francisco already indentured or enslaved. Secret societies, or tongs, which had roots in underground, antigovernment movements in south China, emerged in California as the major organizers of Chinese prostitution. It was a profitable business for procurers, importers, and brothel owners, if not for prostitutes. Hirata's work demonstrates that in any given year, a brothel owner could make much more money off an individual woman's labor than a male Chinese worker could hope to earn. It followed, then, that Chinese prostitutes lived under strict surveillance and control.[59]

Some Chinese prostitutes may have arrived earlier, but it is clear that by 1854 tongs had established brothels throughout the Southern Mines as well as in Stockton.[60] That year the region's newspapers began to report on a variety of largely unsuccessful attempts to close or at least regulate houses of prostitution. Fire companies in Stockton and Sonora, for example, did the job by turning fire hoses on Chinese brothels. The sexual and racial symbolism of such ejaculatory attacks could not have been lost on participants. Indeed, one such hosing in Stockton—itself an act of destruction and intimidation—provoked a wider anti-Chinese riot during which white men assaulted Chinese women. So violent was this event that newspapermen who earlier had winked at "the cold water remedy" now denounced fire hosing and upbraided those men who had perpetrated "indecent attacks upon frightened prostitutes." Soon, the Sonora town council tried a different tactic, passing a "stringent ordinance for the suppression of Chinese houses of ill-fame."[61] To the north in Jackson, town fathers took yet another approach. There, the marshal began collecting a licensing fee of twenty dollars a month from those who managed Chinese brothels. This practice did not last long. Within months an Amador County grand jury indicted Jackson's trustees for pretending that they "had the legal right to levy a Tax upon Chinese houses." In case anyone missed the point, grand jury members defined such establishments as "houses of ill fame kept for purposes of public prostitution and occupied by Chinese whores." One trustee indicted was Armsted Brown, the attorney and landlord who would soon set his sights on property claimed by dance hall manager Isabel Ortis and whose home would one day become the county's historical museum.[62] Again, white men's ambivalence about the commercialization of sex—a process in which they might find pleasure or profit or both—limited attempts at reform.

All in all, fire hoses, town ordinances, and license fees had little lasting impact on Chinese sexual commerce in the Southern Mines. No doubt such tactics increased the daily risks of prostitution but not to the extent of eliminating brothels as workplaces for Cantonese-speaking women. In 1856, for example, a Sonora grand jury indicted "Chinaman John" and "John Doe a Chinaman," two different men, for keeping houses where women sold sex for cash, though the local law prohibiting such establishments was already two years old. In 1858 a white woman in Amador County filed for divorce, accusing her husband of sleeping with a woman at a "Chinna Brothel" in Sacramento as well as with "various women of the chinese race" elsewhere in the diggings. And later that year, under the title "Americanizing," an Amador County editor reported that two Chinese prostitutes had "astonished and amused the people of Volcano by appearing on the streets in American colors—hoops and all!"[63] Chinese sexual commerce itself was no longer astonishing to white people, only the sight of Chinese prostitutes walking the streets in American-style clothing. For some—no doubt especially for white men—that sight was a source of amusement.

It was amusing for two reasons. First, it confounded racialized gender categories in ways reminiscent of the early years of the gold rush in the Southern Mines, when white men did their own domestic work, danced with each other, and developed new hierarchies of gender and race to accommodate the presence of Mexican, Chilean, French, and Miwok women. It must have reminded such men of the "world upside down" created in the Sierra Nevada foothills after 1848.[64] But now ten years had passed, and a new social order had taken hold in the diggings, brought about in part by an influx of Anglo-American women. So the sight of Chinese prostitutes promenading in "American" garments could amuse white men for another reason: it did not threaten that social order. There is no evidence that Chinese women who labored as prostitutes in the Southern Mines were able to achieve anything like the limited financial independence Mexican, Chilean, and French women gained by owning, managing, or even just working in leisure establishments. Historians have identified a tiny handful of Chinese women elsewhere who were able to profit from sexual commerce, such as Ah Toy and Suey Hin in San Francisco.[65] But no such women emerge from the historical record of the Southern Mines in the 1850s; there are no tongue-in-cheek newspaper accounts, no revealing court records, no white women's diaries filled with fears about the relative affluence of Chinese working women. For most white men, the world by 1858 was turning right-side-up, and Chinese women in hoop skirts were a curiosity, not a symbol of a world gone crazy.

For the promenading prostitutes, wearing hoop skirts must have meant something else altogether. The meanings these women attached to the act, however, are lost in a historical record generated by people who knew little and cared less about the inner lives of Chinese prostitutes. There is no way to know for sure, for example, who decided what these women would wear the summer day they appeared on the streets of Volcano. Higher-status prostitutes in San Francisco, who served a Chinese clientele, often wore elaborate and expensive clothing. But mining town prostitutes were generally of a lower status, and they served a multiracial clientele. Historian Lucie Cheng Hirata contends that prostitutes in the diggings endured especially harsh treatment. Indeed, banishment to a mining town brothel was a way to punish women who defied established controls in the city.[66] It seems likely, then, that a brothel owner, rather than the women themselves, decided on the hoop skirts and then sent his charges out walking, perhaps to drum up business. There was every reason in the summer of 1858 for a businessman to dream up new ways to attract customers: it was in the spring of that year that gold was discovered at the Fraser River in British Columbia, drawing thousands away from the California diggings and depressing the local economy. Just days after the women walked the streets in "American colors," the same newspaper complained about all those who had "left Amador county and gone to Frazer river."[67]

But even if a brothel owner hit on the idea of dressing Chinese women in "American" finery, it was not he but they who promenaded two abreast in skirts that took up a good deal of ideological as well as physical space. The flavor of that emotional experience is lost to the historical record, but one can imagine that appropriating symbols of ladyhood, whiteness, and morality provided an unexpected feast for women whom most other gold rush participants meant to starve. It was a rich joke in a poor world. It was a mockery of gentility, that great reservoir from which white, middle-class women drew so much of their social, cultural, and economic power. As Judy Yung has argued, Chinese women could take courage in knowing that their sale or indenture into prostitution helped their impoverished families back home in the Pearl River Delta.[68] Perhaps courage could come as well in a hoop-skirted march through the dusty streets of a town like Volcano.

Local newspaper reports on Chinese women, of course, reveal more about the discursive and social practices of Anglo-American, middle-class men than they do about the lives of Cantonese-speaking women. But in the absence of documents generated by the women themselves, such obdurate reports must be forced to yield every shred of evidence they contain about the ways in which Chinese women were able to maneuver in a tightly circumscribed social and discursive world. Along with the account of the promenading prostitutes, a handful of newspaper references to Chinese women in 1857 and 1858 suggest that some such women pushed at the boundaries of that world to good effect. The writer of one report, for example—tellingly titled "An Honest John Chinawoman"—was astonished to discover a married Chinese woman who had helped her husband build a house and who worked alongside him mining a nearby creek bed. There is no way of knowing if this woman accompanied her spouse to California or if she bought her way out of a brothel and married a suitor, though the latter is more likely. The writer's account of this house-building, gold-mining woman is drenched in his own arrogant understandings of race, gender, beauty, and morality. "The Celestial 'beauty,'" the editor gibed, "wields the pick and shovel with the air of a miniature Amazon."[69] Wring out this report, however, and there emerges an immigrant woman who with her own hands forged a different sort of life for herself in late gold rush California. Life with a pick and a shovel, a house and a husband improved on a servitude that might end in death.

Likewise, a second report reveals how a Chinese woman used a country-man's earnings and the local court system to gain her freedom. She had been brought to California by another Chinese woman—perhaps the famous Ah Toy herself—"as a slave for *any* purpose." The enslaved prostitute, in turn, borrowed four hundred dollars from a Chinese man in Amador County to purchase her freedom, "giving him a written mortgage of *herself* to secure the payment of the money." The Chinese man, the newspaper recounted, then "endeavored to enforce his lien," perhaps by insisting on free sexual services or by forcing the woman back into prostitution. Someone—it is not clear from the report whether it was the woman herself—then charged this man with abduction and took him to court. The man who had loaned the woman money failed in his attempt to enforce what he thought was his lien on her person. The judge in the case informed him that "persons could not be restrained of their liberty for evil purposes, even if they had originally agreed to it."[70] The account does not reveal what became of the woman who borrowed and bought her way out of bondage. But the act itself spoke volumes about her aspirations.

By the late 1850s, social relations in the Southern Mines had metamorphosed to accommodate the presence of new gold rush participants, the departure of others, and the continuing needs and desires of those who stayed on in the foothills. Anglo-American and Chinese women were among the latest arrivals. Mexican, Chilean, and French women were among those who were starting to leave. So were a wide variety of men frustrated by the declining placers and flushed with the promise of new bonanzas elsewhere in the West. Other men lingered, convinced that the Southern Mines yet would yield still greater treasures or that profits were possible in different pursuits. Miwok women and men stayed, too, dreaming that the decade-long invasion of their homeland might somehow end.

Anglo Americans, of course, had different dreams, as well as dispropor-tionate access to the power that could make those dreams come true. That power increased manyfold when white women from the eastern United States began to join their menfolk in the mines and set about supplanting with "respectable" gatherings popular recreations that had catered to men and provided work for polyglot women. As early as 1853, the *Sonora Herald* noted the increasing numbers of "the gentler sex dispersed among the hill-sides and ravines," as evidenced by the "female habilements in many directions hanging out to dry."[71] Like a flag flying, such recognizably white women's garments announced a consolidation of Anglo-American dominance in the diggings.

By 1856 the picture seemed even more promising. In that year, white men in Tuolumne County produced a booklet entitled the *Miners and Business Men's Directory*.[72] The directory included narratives detailing the history and prospects of camps and towns throughout the county. The entry for Columbia—home of reform-minded Clementine Brainard as well as monte-dealing "French Mary"—was particularly revealing of Anglo-American aspirations:

> This place is fast filling up with families—a surety of a permanent population and of improvement in society. The barberous [*sic*] amusements, introduced by Spanish customs, have long since ceased to disturb the peace of the community, while other Spanish customs that tend so much to the spread and continuance of immorality are fast dying, and in a short time will only be known as things that belonged to the past. The gambling saloon no longer, by its music, attracts the unsophisticated to squander their money on "dead things," and those who were connected with such houses have gone to other parts, or sought other occupations. . . . And as the Mexican population, and the class that are ever congregated around gambling houses are removed from our midst, the security of life and property may be soon considered equal to that afforded in most places in the older States.[73]

Things that belonged to the past, things that belonged to the future: the editors hoped that "Spanish customs," Mexican people, and gaming tables managed by the likes of "French Mary" were fading away and that (white) families and secure property were taking their place. Things that belonged to the past were "dead things." Things that belonged to the future were alive. Already, the editors noted, forward-looking residents were planting fruit trees and vines around homes and ranches. It would not be long, the writers predicted, "before most of our citizens will sit under their own vines and fig trees, with none to molest them or make them afraid."[74]

The *Miners and Business Men's Directory* was wrong about much: Neither "Spanish customs" nor Mexican people nor French card dealers disappeared so easily, and even where they did begin to depart, "Chinese customs" and Chinese people often stood in their stead. What is more, gambling saloons maintained a robust health throughout the rest of the decade, and women, on whom the increase of conventional families depended, still constituted less than one-fifth of the population as late as 1860. But white women and men together did begin to turn much of the Southern Mines into a place where few dared to "molest them or make them afraid." What they could not create was a world in which no Chinese woman would fly "American colors," straining the links between ladyhood, whiteness, and morality, and rattling the social, economic, and discursive chains that bound their own lives.

Notes

1. *San Joaquin Republican* (Stockton), July 30, 1851 (reprinted from the *Sonora Herald*).

2. See Susan Lee Johnson, *Roaring Camp: The Social World of the California Gold Rush* (New York: W. W. Norton, 2000). The Southern Mines comprised present-day Amador, Calaveras, Tuolumne, and Mariposa Counties, and included such towns as Jackson and Mokelumne Hill in the north, Columbia and Sonora in the midsection, and Coulterville and Mariposa in the south.

3. My argument is guided by the work of Elsa Barkley-Brown and Evelyn Nakano Glenn, particularly as it relates to the relational nature of differences among women. See esp. Barkley-Brown, "Polyrhythms and Improvization: Lessons for Women's History," *History Workshop Journal* 31, no. 32 (1991): 85–90; and Nakano Glenn, "From Servitude to Service Work: Historical Continuities in the Racial Division of Paid Reproductive Labor," *Signs* 18, no. 1 (autumn 1992): 1–43.

4. See Anthony Shay, "Fandangos and Bailes: Dancing and Dance Events in Early California," *Southern California Quarterly* 64, no. 2 (summer 1982): 99–113. A "fandango" was distinguished from the dance event among elite Spanish Mexicans called a "baile." For analysis of the meanings of gold rush fandangos for male patrons, see Johnson, *Roaring Camp*, chap. 3; and Johnson, "Bulls, Bears, and Dancing Boys," 4–37.

5. *San Joaquin Republican*, July 30, 1851 (from the *Sonora Herald*).

6. See, e.g., *San Joaquin Republican*, August 9 and October 25, 1853; March 11, April 11, November 22, and December 13, 1854; May 3, July 31, and November 20, 1855; August 24, 1856.

7. *San Joaquin Republican*, July 28, 1852 (from the *Sonora Herald*). Copies of most issues of the *Sonora Herald* are no longer extant, hence my reliance on articles reprinted in Stockton papers.

8. On these events, see Johnson, *Roaring Camp*, chap. 4. The Chilean War was a localized conflict that took place in 1849, when parties of both Chilean and Anglo miners decided to winter near the Calaveras River in a ravine called Chilean Gulch. Anglos created a mining district for themselves there and then ordered Chileans

out of the ravine. The Chileans resisted, and in the fight that followed at least two Anglos and perhaps one Chilean were killed. In the end, the Anglos organized an extralegal trial of the Chileans, in which Anglos sentenced three of the Chileans to death and several more to be whipped or to have their ears cut off. In this struggle, Anglo and Chilean men mutually constituted one another as adversaries, and Anglos invoked their rights as citizens on U.S. soil to enact vigilante justice. The second conflict was a broader one. It began in 1850, when California's governor signed into law an act that came to be known as the Foreign Miners Tax, which imposed a licensing tax of twenty dollars per month on all non-U.S. citizens at work in the diggings. Miners from Mexico, Chile, France, and elsewhere joined together across barriers of language and culture to voice their opposition to the law, parading through towns in the Southern Mines, flying flags and unfurling banners, and singing French revolutionary songs—hence the naming of this event as the French Revolution. Although the Foreign Miners Tax was eventually repealed, it, along with conflicts such as the Chilean War, drove many Spanish-speaking and French-speaking gold seekers away from the mines altogether. For those who remained, the tax sent a strong message about the Anglo-American will to dominate in the diggings and about the power of the state to give teeth to that will. The third struggle, the Mariposa War of 1850–1851, was an Indian-immigrant conflict in which a state-sponsored militia tried, with at best moderate success, to force Miwok and Yokuts Indians out of the foothills and onto reservations in the San Joaquin Valley.

9. See U.S. Bureau of the Census, *Seventh Census of the United States: 1850* (Washington DC, 1853), and *Population of the United States in 1860; Compiled from . . . the Eighth Census* (Washington DC, 1864) [hereafter cited as "1860 Census"].

10. On class-making generally, see, e.g., Mary Ryan, *Cradle of the Middle Class: The Family in Oneida County, New York, 1790–1865* (New York: Cambridge University Press, 1981); and Leonore Davidoff and Catherine Hall, *Family Fortunes: Men and Women of the English Middle Class, 1780–1850* (Chicago: University of Chicago Press, 1987). For a full discussion of class-making in the Southern Mines, see Johnson, *Roaring Camp*, chap. 5 and chap. 6.

11. For background on William and Mary Newell and on the TCWC, see Johnson, *Roaring Camp*, chap. 1 and chap. 5. The Newells' lives are documented in the Joseph Pownall Papers, Huntington Library, San Marino, California. For quotations, see William Newell to Mary Newell, April 24, 1853, PW 523; July 28, 1853, PW 524. And see Articles of Copartnership between B. M. Brainard and W. H. Newell, April 25, 1853, PW 76.

12. See, e.g., entries for October 20 and 24, December 17, 1853, and January 20, July 2, August 26, September 28, December 10, 1854, Clementine H. Brainard Journal, Bancroft Library, University of California, Berkeley.

13. Mary Newell to Benjamin and Lucy Harrison, December 18, 1855, PW 793; Mary Newell to Lucy Harrison, April 17, 1856, PW 769; Benjamin Harrison to Lucy Harrison, April 18, 1856, PW 356; "Receipt from Hotel International, San Francisco," March 17, 1857 (a receipt for Mary and Joseph Pownall's honeymoon suite), PW 146, Pownall Papers, Huntington Library. For Pownall's status in the TCWC, see Minutes of Board Meetings, May 1856 to November 1859, Tuolumne County Water Company Correspondence and Papers, 1853–1905, vol. 2, Bancroft Library. For Pownall's concerns about his marital status, see Pownall Journal and Letterbook, PW 553, passim, Pownall Papers; for the quotation, see letter labeled Joseph Pownall to "dear Friend," [1854].

14. The literature on this point is vast. See, e.g., Kathryn Kish Sklar, *Catharine Beecher: A Study in American Domesticity* (New York: W. W. Norton, 1976); Nancy F. Cott, *The Bonds of Womanhood: "Woman's Sphere" in New England, 1780–1835* (New Haven: Yale University Press, 1977); Ryan, *Cradle of the Middle Class*; Peggy Pascoe, *Relations of Rescue: The Search for Female Moral Authority in the American West, 1874–1939* (New York: Oxford University Press, 1990); Charles E. Rosenberg, "Sexuality, Class, and Role in Nineteenth-Century America," *American Quarterly* 35 (May 1973): 131–53; E. Anthony Rotundo, *American Manhood: Transformations in Masculinity from the Revolution to the Modern Era* (New York: Basic Books, 1993); Gail Bederman, *Manliness and Civilization: A Cultural History of Gender and Race in the United States, 1880–1917* (Chicago: University of Chicago Press, 1995).

15. For an overview of antebellum reform, see Ronald G. Walters, *American Reformers, 1815–1860* (New York: Hill & Wang, 1978). For an account of the urban worlds of leisure that so incensed reformers in the East, see Timothy J. Gilfoyle, *City of Eros: New York City, Prostitution, and the Commercialization of Sex, 1790–1920* (New York: W. W. Norton, 1992). An overview of reform efforts that impinged on sexual practices appears in John D'Emilio and Estelle B. Freedman, *Intimate Matters: A History of Sexuality in America* (1988; Chicago: University of Chicago Press, 1997), esp. 139–45.

16. See Lewis Perry, *Childhood, Marriage, and Reform: Henry Clarke Wright, 1791–1870* (Chicago: University of Chicago Press, 1980), esp. 172–82; and Anna Lee Marston, ed., *Records of a California Family: Journals and Letters of Lewis C. Gunn and Elizabeth Le Breton Gunn* (San Diego: A. L. Marston, 1928), esp. 3–15.

17. Marston, ed., *Records of a California Family*, 156–58, 170.

18. See, e.g., Brainard's support for temperance and Sabbatarianism expressed in entries for December 17 and 18, 1853, and July 4 and October 4, 1854, Brainard Journal.

19. Lorena L. Hays, *To the Land of Gold and Wickedness: The 1848–59 Diary of Lorena L. Hays*, ed. Jeanne Hamilton Watson (Saint Louis MO: Patrice Press, 1988), 1–14, 198–229.

20. Hays, *To the Land of Gold and Wickedness*, esp. 231–33, 235, 237–49, 252–57, 263–65, quotes on 238, 252, 255; *The Golden Era* (San Francisco), September 17, 1854.

21. Hays, *To the Land of Gold and Wickedness*, 261; *The Golden Era*, September 17, 1854.

22. Hays, *To the Land of Gold and Wickedness*, esp. 249, 251, 253, 259–61, quote on 261. On the murders and the subsequent siege of Spanish-speaking communities in Amador County, see Larry Cenotto, *Logan's Alley: Amador County Yesterdays in Picture and Prose*, 2 vols. (Jackson CA: Cenotto Publications, 1988), 1:159–73.

23. For his part, James accused Chloe of sleeping with a man named John Burridge and of leaving home only "for the purpose of having adulterous intercourse" with Burridge. See *James B. Cooper v. Chloe C. Cooper* (1857–58), District Court, Amador County, Jackson, California (hereafter cited as Amador County District Court Records).

24. *Mary Jane Anderson v. James W. Anderson* (1857), Amador County District Court Records.

25. *Mary Ann Hayes v. Nicholas Hayes* (1860), District Court, Tuolumne County, Sonora, California (hereafter cited as Tuolumne County District Court Records).

26. According to the 1860 Census, U.S. citizens constituted 45.55 percent of the population of the four counties that comprised the Southern Mines in 1860. White Americans constituted 44.75 percent of the enumerated population; blacks, including those designated as "mulattos," made up 1.8 percent of the U.S. population, and .9 percent of the total population.

27. Cf. Mann, *After the Gold Rush*, 56–59, which describes similar campaigns in two major towns of the Northern Mines.

28. Brainard Journal, December 17, 1853.

29. Hays, *To the Land of Gold and Wickedness*, 258–59; cf. Brainard Journal, December 18, 1853: "I do hope that merchants will decide soon to close their stores on the Sabbath and then we may hope for a reformation in Columbia."

30. *San Joaquin Republican*, February 6, 1855, and June 25, 1856 (the latter is reprinted from the *Weekly Columbian*); *Volcano Weekly Ledger*, January 26, 1856.

31. See *Volcano Weekly Ledger*, June 28 and December 13, 1856, and February 28 and July 18, 1857; *San Joaquin Republican*, October 16, 1857.

32. Brainard Journal, March 21–24, 1854; *[Phoebe] Quimby v. Z. M. Quimby* (1852), Tuolumne County District Court Records.

33. See Robert L. Griswold, *Family and Divorce in California, 1850–1890: Victorian*

Illusions and Everyday Realities (Albany: State University of New York Press, 1982), esp. 76.

34. *Mary Ann Chick v. Alfred Chick* (1859), District Court, Calaveras County, San Andreas, California (hereafter cited as Calaveras County District Court Records); *Emily Davis v. O. S. Davis* (1860), Tuolumne County District Court Records.

35. *Sarah E. Philbrick v. William H. Philbrick* (1860), Amador County District Court Records.

36. *Joseph L. Hall v. Celia E. Hall* (1860), Tuolumne County District Court Records.

37. See Johnson, *Roaring Camp*, chaps. 2–4.

38. Johnson, *Roaring Camp*, chap. 3; and Johnson, "Bulls, Bears, and Dancing Boys."

39. *The People v. French Mary* (1857), Court of Sessions, Tuolumne County, Sonora, California (hereafter cited as Tuolumne County Court of Sessions Records). Cf. *The People v. John Doe and Richard Roe* (1856), Tuolumne County Court of Sessions Records.

40. The saloons of Clement and Follet are mentioned in *Alfred Washburn v. Francis Williams* (1855), and *Alfred Washburn v. Sam Lord* (1856), District Court, Mariposa County, Mariposa, California (hereafter cited as Mariposa County District Court Records). Clement's saloon is also mentioned in the *San Joaquin Republican*, September 13, 1856 (reprinted from the *Mariposa Democrat*).

41. *S. R. Mills and James Vantine v. Madame Emilie Henry* (1856), Mariposa County District Court Records.

42. The 1852 state census lists a 40-year-old Chilean woman named "Elibe Ortiz" in Calaveras County, and this may be the Isabel Ortis (who also went by the names Elisa and Elizabeth) of the 1858 court records cited later in these notes. But, as we shall see, Ortis linked her property ownership in Amador County to the contested land grant of Californio Andrés Pico, suggesting some familiarity with the disposition of Mexican land claims in California. This familiarity might have been more likely for an ethnic Mexican than for a Chilean. Chilean names in the 1850 and 1860 federal census as well as the 1852 state census are usefully indexed in Carlos U. López, *Chilenos in California: A Study of the 1850, 1852 and 1860 Census* (San Francisco: R & E Research Associates, 1973), esp. 60.

43. Inquest, Francisco [Arayo] (1858), Inquest Records, Calaveras County, Calaveras County Museum and Archives, San Andreas, California.

44. *Natividad Shermenhoof v. John Shermenhoof* (1856), and *Natividad Shermenhoof v. John Shermenhoof, W. W. Cope, and James F. Hubbard* (1858), Amador County District Court Records. Another copy of the divorce record can be found in Amador

County Legal Records, box 1370, folder 6, California State Library, Sacramento (hereafter cited as Amador County Legal Records). Natividad accused John of violence and of trying to compel her to "open a house of prostitution." For his part, John accused Natividad of squandering his earnings in "riotous and dissipated living." He claimed she left him only to place herself "in a better condition to carry on an uninterrupted illicit intercourse with one Frederick Schober." Schober was a German butcher in Jackson, where a street still bears his name. See Cenotto, *Logan's Alley,* 2:223.

45. *A. C. Brown v. Isabel Ortis and John McKay* (1858), Amador County District Court Records; *John McKay v. His Creditors* (1858), County Court, Amador County, Jackson, California. Documents for both cases can also be found in Amador County Legal Records, boxes 1368 and 1369.

46. On Andrés Pico, see Pitt, *Decline of the Californios,* esp. 34–35, 139–40, 145.

47. The literature on California land claims is vast. See, e.g., Pitt, *Decline of the Californios*; and Camarillo, *Chicanos in a Changing Society*. For another perspective, see Paul W. Gates, *Land Law in California: Essays on Land Policies* (Ames: Iowa State University Press, 1991). On the meanings that Californios attached to dispossession, see Sánchez, *Telling Identities*.

48. I use "juridical" in both the ordinary and the academic senses of the word. In the first and most obvious sense, Ortis entered into the legal controversies over land tenure then underway in California. But the term "juridical" also has been used by Michel Foucault and scholars influenced by his work to refer to the ways in which systems of power (among them, legal systems) not only regulate or even prohibit certain kinds of people but actually produce and reproduce those kinds of people through the very practices that are assumed to constitute regulation and prohibition. In this sense, then, Ortis was not simply a Mexican or Chilean woman who managed fandangos and who thereby ran afoul of Anglo-American law. She was a person engaged in economic and cultural activity who became, through the imposition of the law, a representative of a cultural category: a "kept" woman of "Spanish" descent, the "Mistress" of a notorious fandango (for quotes, see references in the following notes). On juridical power, see, e.g., Michel Foucault, *Discipline and Punish: The Birth of the Prison,* trans. Alan Sheridan (1975; New York: Vintage Books, 1979); Judith Butler, *Gender Trouble: Feminism and the Subversion of Identity* (New York: Routledge, 1990).

49. *A. C. Brown v. Isabel Ortis and John McKay* (1858), Amador County District Court Records; *John McKay v. His Creditors* (1858), County Court, Amador County, Jackson, California. Documents for both cases can also be found in Amador County Legal Records, box 1368, folders 12 and 13, and box 1369, folder 8. The quoted material is from documents in this latter folder.

50. Cf. Deena J. González, "La Tules of Image and Reality: Euro-American

Attitudes and Legend Formation on a Spanish-Mexican Frontier," in *Building With Our Hands: New Directions in Chicana Studies*, ed. Adela de la Torre and Beatríz M. Pesquera (Berkeley: University of California Press, 1993), 75–90.

51. Cenotto, *Logan's Alley,* 2:182–85. As for Philippa Brown, she was actively engaged in efforts to supplant polyglot sites of heterosocial leisure with "respectable" gatherings. In early 1858, for example, she was among a group of women who planned a "Calico Party," the proceeds of which were to go toward building a schoolhouse in Jackson. After the ball, the managers met at Philippa Brown's home and decided how the funds would be appropriated. The women appointed Armsted Brown to "receive the funds and pay out the same" for the schoolhouse. See *San Joaquin Republican*, January 2 and 16, 1858.

52. *Laura Echeverria v. Juan Echeverria* (1857), Tuolumne County District Court Records.

53. *Laura Echeverria v. Juan Echeverria*, Tuolumne County District Court Records.

54. *Laura Echeverria v. Juan Echeverria*, Tuolumne County District Court Records.

55. *Laura Echeverria v. Juan Echeverria*, Tuolumne County District Court Records.

56. For historiographical context, see Camille Guerin-Gonzales, "Conversing Across Boundaries of Race, Ethnicity, Class, Gender, and Region: Latina and Latino Labor History," *Labor History* 35, no. 4 (fall 1994): 547–63.

57. *San Joaquin Republican*, October 8, 1858.

58. 1860 Census.

59. Lucie Cheng Hirata, "Free, Indentured, Enslaved: Chinese Prostitutes in Nineteenth-Century America," *Signs* 5, no. 1 (autumn 1979): 3–29, esp. 13–18; Sucheng Chan, "The Exclusion of Chinese Women, 1870–1943," in *Entry Denied,* 94–146; and Yung, *Unbound Feet,* esp. 26–37. My account of Chinese prostitution in the Southern Mines relies on the analysis in these groundbreaking works. See also Ronald Takaki, *Strangers From a Different Shore: A History of Asian Americans* (Boston: Beacon, 1989), 118–19.

60. According to Lucie Cheng Hirata, the secret societies gained control of Chinese prostitution in 1854, inaugurating a period of organized trade that peaked around 1870 but lasted into the early twentieth century. The Hip Yee Tong monopolized the trade in the years under consideration here. Hirata, "Free, Indentured, Enslaved," 8–13. On the relative importance of tongs and other social organizations among Chinese immigrants, see Eve Armentrout Ma, "Urban Chinese at the Sinitic Frontier: Social Organization in United States' Chinatowns, 1849–1898," *Modern Asian Studies* 17, no. 1 (1983): 107–35.

61. *San Joaquin Republican*, September 18 and 22, October 2 and 9, 1854.

62. Receipt Issued by the Jackson Town Marshal's Office, September 15, 1854; and *The People v. A. C. Brown, E. H. Williams, Hiram Allen, T. Hinckley, and Ellis Evans* (1854), Amador County Court of Sessions, Amador County Archives, Jackson, California. My thanks to Amador County historian Larry Cenotto for pointing out these materials to me. See also Cenotto, *Logan's Alley,* 1: 39, 53, 60.

63. *The People v. Chinaman John* (1856), and *The People v. John Doe a Chinaman* (1856), Tuolumne County Court of Sessions Records; *Mary Babbit v. Horace Babbit* (1858), Amador County District Court Records; *Amador Weekly Ledger,* June 26, 1858.

64. See Johnson, *Roaring Camp,* chaps. 2–3; and Johnson, "Bulls, Bears, and Dancing Boys."

65. See, e.g., Yung, *Unbound Feet,* 33–34.

66. Hirata, "Free, Indentured, Enslaved," esp. 13, 19.

67. *Amador Weekly Ledger,* July 3, 1858.

68. Yung, *Unbound Feet,* 31.

69. *Amador Weekly Ledger,* May 2, 1857. An account of a marriage ceremony for a Chinese woman and man appears in the same newspaper on May 8, 1858. Significantly, this couple chose to marry according to Anglo-American law, with a local judge presiding.

70. *Amador Weekly Ledger,,* July 18, 1857.

71. *San Joaquin Republican,* February 9, 1853 (from the *Sonora Herald*).

72. J. Heckendorn and W. A. Wilson, *Miners and Business Men's Directory for the Year Commencing January 1, 1856, Embracing a General History of the Citizens of Tuolumne . . . Together with the Mining Laws of Each District, a Description of the Different Camps, and Other Interesting Statistical Matter* (Columbia CA: Clipper Office, 1856).

73. Heckendorn and Wilson, *Miners and Business Men's Directory,* 8.

74. Heckendorn and Wilson, *Miners and Business Men's Directory,* 8.

11

After California

Later Gold Rushes of the Pacific Basin

Jeremy Mouat

The gold rushes were remarkable events. The excitement that they generated and the stories that surround them yet—stories of great endurance, bizarre coincidences, and, of course, sudden wealth—suggest their uniqueness. But a narrow focus on the particular can mask the fact that gold rushes were recurring phenomena. While the California gold rush was certainly a world event, it was one subsequently repeated around the Pacific basin. For fifty years—until the last dramatic rush to the Klondike in 1898—miners rushed from one newly discovered gold field to another, participants in a singular nineteenth-century experience. This essay looks at three major rushes that followed the first in California: the Australian gold rush of 1851, the New Zealand gold rushes, which began in 1857, and the rush to the Fraser River in 1858. The following pages describe the connections and similarities between these later rushes and the earlier rush to California, as well as the ways in which each rush was shaped by a distinct context and followed a specific trajectory. Before examining the three events in detail, however, it is helpful to consider gold rushes as a general phenomenon, to identify what they had in common as well as why they occurred when and where they did.

To many contemporary observers, the gold rushes seemed bizarre and inexplicable. With the passage of time it is possible to see them in a larger context and arrive at a clearer sense of their meaning. It was certainly no coincidence, for example, that the gold rushes were confined not only in time but also in space, occurring in roughly similar territories. By the mid-nineteenth century, Europeans had begun to move into the western region of the North American continent and to New Zealand and the Australian colonies. This process of colonization—a function of British and American

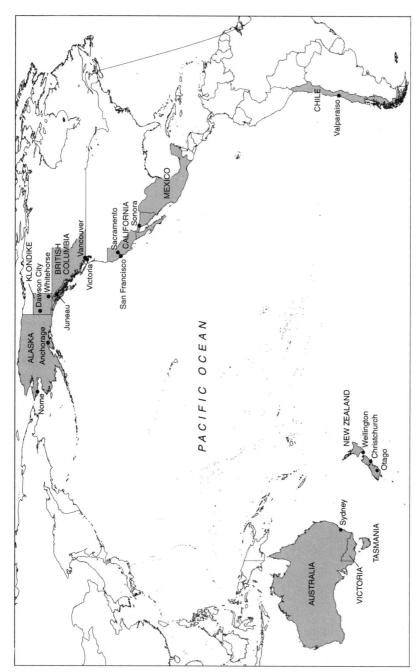

Pacific Rim Gold Mining Areas

expansion in the Pacific basin—meant that a growing number of Europeans lived in regions where large and hitherto unexploited gold deposits existed.

Europeans have valued gold for a very long time.[1] At the time of the rushes, gold-based coinage had been in circulation for thousands of years in the Mediterranean basin. Biblical references and Greek legend also suggest gold's considerable appeal to the people of that region.[2] Originally, this appeal likely reflected an aesthetic appreciation of the metal's properties as well as its relative scarcity. Unlike Europeans, most Native peoples of Australia, New Zealand, and western North America did not value gold, nor did they indicate its presence to early European visitors. Like other peoples, however, they did place a high value on decorative and relatively scarce materials. In New Zealand, for example, some Maori regularly made difficult journeys to an isolated region on the west coast of the South Island in order to obtain a highly prized type of greenstone.[3] Similarly, Native groups along the Pacific coast developed an intricate trading network to secure copper from Alaska.[4] And once aware of Europeans' desire for gold, Native peoples were quick to make the most of this new economic opportunity.[5]

The growing European presence in the Pacific was only one precondition of the gold rushes. Naturally enough, gold had to be found in sufficient quantity, but it also had to be gold of a particular type. The gold that was discovered in California and elsewhere in the mid-nineteenth century was placer gold—that is, water-borne gold—and these deposits were both rich and easily worked.

Placer gold was relatively pure, easily recognized, and represented instant wealth. It could be readily sold and its value was known to everyone; contemporary descriptions of miners' fortunes invariably listed their daily returns as a dollar value. In addition, the process of separating gold from the sand, gravel, or clay in which it occurred was straightforward. This reflected gold's unusually high specific gravity, one and a half times greater than lead.[6] Since it was by far the heaviest ingredient among the material with which it was found, gold was the least prone to wash away. As a result, the technology of placer mining could be crude but still be reasonably effective. The traditional tools used by gold rush miners—pan, rocker, and sluice—were inexpensive, portable, and required little skill to use. Few barriers stood in the way of aspiring miners; fitness, strength, and determination were certainly necessary, but little else. "Nothing, indeed," noted an observer of the first Australian gold rush, "can have a more levelling effect on society than the power of digging gold, for it can be done, for a time at least, without any capital but that of health and strength; and the man inured to toil, however ignorant, is on more than equal terms with the educated and refined in a pursuit involving so much personal hardship."[7]

Contemporaries almost always commented on the egalitarian nature of the gold rushes; the participation of people from every walk of life and from many countries was recorded with a regularity that suggests just how unprecedented this was. Few if any economic opportunities had previously offered such an equal chance of success.

In addition to the existence of gold, another obvious ingredient of a gold rush was the sheer number of participants. But if the gold rushes themselves offer proof that large numbers of people could travel across oceans and from one gold field to another by the middle of the nineteenth century, this was a relatively recent development and largely a function of the quickening pace of trade that accompanied the Industrial Revolution.[8] In addition to fostering a transportation system that extended around the globe, industrialization encouraged a burgeoning communications network: like people, information could now travel faster and with greater ease. And the news of the gold discoveries and the subsequent rushes—widely reported in newspapers—reached an increasingly literate population. Soon after news of the gold rushes appeared in magazines and newspapers, more extensive publications followed in a steady stream—self-help manuals, travel guides, and firsthand accounts of the gold fields—and were eagerly bought by a host of aspiring miners. Thus people who lived far from the Pacific basin grew confident that they could travel to the point where gold had been found and also believed that they would be able to mine the precious metal successfully upon their arrival.

Other changes also facilitated travel, particularly for people in Europe. In many countries, greater freedom of movement was now possible. Political upheavals such as the American and French Revolutions, as well as the lengthy Napoleonic Wars and the ongoing impact of industrialization, had had a cumulative impact, sweeping away the last vestiges of the feudal order throughout much of western Europe, while state bureaucracies had not yet formed to control the flow of migrants. The political turmoil in Europe during and after 1848 also encouraged people to seek adventure and economic advantage overseas.[9]

The factors underlying the gold rushes—European expansion in the Pacific, the presence in that region of rich placer gold deposits, a population able to travel and anxious to grasp economic opportunities wherever they existed—should not be overlooked when looking at particular discoveries and rushes. An examination of these specific episodes also reveals the connections that existed between them. Perhaps most important, many of the same individuals participated in two or more rushes. Gold discoveries in Australia, New Zealand, and British Columbia all owed a considerable debt to "Old Californians," a group that was quick to travel to new gold fields and often willing to instruct others in the basic techniques of prospecting and panning.[10]

The migration of people from one gold field to another suggests the role played by depletion. Once located, rich gold deposits never remained rich for long, one reason why gold fields rarely experienced a period of stability. Volatility was common, a consequence of the large labor force that was actively mining a resource prone to rapid exhaustion. Another problem was the number of people hoping to find their fortune. In California, for example, not all of the participants in the rush could secure a good paying claim; a substantial proportion of migrants were constantly on the move, looking for "payable ground." Rumors always circulated of richer rewards elsewhere, and dissatisfied miners moved randomly from one field to another. Gold rushes had a centrifugal dynamic, with the diminishing chances for success at one location making travel to more distant places an attractive alternative. Australia was the first to attract substantial numbers from California.

Three years after the first excitement in California, the second great gold rush began in the colony of New South Wales. (Australia was created on the first day of 1901. During the nineteenth century the island continent was British territory, comprised of a series of separate colonies. Australian Aboriginal people's rights to their traditional land remains a contentious issue.) The connection with the first gold rush was widely acknowledged. As one contemporary noted, "It was California, without doubt, that gave the direct impetus to seek, as well as the practical skill to find and to wash the golden alluvium of Australia."[11]

Various people had found gold in the Australian colonies prior to 1848.[12] Circumstances remarkably similar to the gold discovery in California occurred in New South Wales in 1846, although with very different results. Laborers constructing a mill uncovered what they rightly suspected was gold; the landowner dismissed the idea and claimed that they had found mica.[13] A handful of other discoveries took place as well. Perhaps the most notable came in the colony of Victoria in early 1849, when a shepherd sold nearly forty ounces of gold to a Melbourne jeweler. Local police had to be sent in to disperse the crowd that gathered in hopes of finding similar treasure.[14] Such events suggest the critical distinction between gold discovery and gold rush: gold discoveries could take place—and continue to do so—without a subsequent rush. For that matter, as over-optimistic miners sometimes discovered, gold rushes could occur without gold ever being found in quantity.

Despite the knowledge of gold's presence, common from the late 1840s, the Australian gold rush did not begin until 1851. The critical event that year was Edward Hargraves's discovery of gold in the region west of Sydney. Hargraves was one of the five thousand or more Australians who had earlier crossed the Pacific to California, eager for gold.[15] Although he did not make his fortune in California, Hargraves was struck by the similarity of the gold fields there to parts of Australia. He decided to return home, telling a number of people before he left California of his intention to discover an Australian gold field.[16] Whatever his shortcomings as a miner, Hargraves was to become a very successful publicist.

In January 1851, Hargraves returned to Sydney, where he persuaded a local merchant to underwrite his search for a gold field. In early February he set off over the Blue Mountains for an area rumored to be auriferous. Once there, it did not take him long to pan a few specks of gold at a promising spot on Lewis Ponds Creek. Delighted, Hargraves proudly announced to his puzzled companion the true significance of the few gleaming particles in his gold pan: " 'This,' I exclaimed to my guide, 'is a memorable day in the history of New South Wales. I shall be a baronet, you will be knighted, and my old horse will be stuffed, put into a glass-case, and sent to the British Museum!' "[17] On the rather slim evidence of four flakes of gold, Hargraves confidently concluded that he had found an extensive gold field. Fearing that others might get the credit and the reward for the gold discovery if he did not act swiftly, Hargraves gave instructions on how to build a Californian rocker and departed for Sydney to publicize his discovery.

Unlike most prospectors, Hargraves never attempted to disguise his find. Anxious to be recognized as the gold discoverer, he boasted of the new wealth to everyone he met, waving minute particles under the eyes of squinting sceptics.[18] Luck was on Hargraves's side: while he was busy advertising his modest find, his prospecting friends discovered gold in quantity with their rocker. Although Hargraves's claim to have discovered a payable gold field proved controversial, his proselytizing efforts did finally culminate in a gold rush.[19] And this first rush soon led to others.

Within a few months, people learned of the rich gold deposits of the adjacent colony of Victoria. In September 1851, two brothers returned from Ballarat with sixty pounds of gold, for example, helping to spark a rush to the gold field some fifty miles northwest of Melbourne. Other significant discoveries followed in the same region, bringing fame to such fields as Castlemaine and Bendigo. In October 1851, the governor reported to London that "[c]ottages are deserted, houses to let, business is at a stand-still, and even schools are closed. In some of the suburbs [of Melbourne] not a man is left." Although Victoria produced only slightly more gold than New South Wales in 1851, its production in the following years dwarfed that of its northern rival.[20]

When news of the gold discoveries in Australia reached California, many adventurous miners decided to travel "down under" and try their luck.[21] The presence in Australia of a large group of "Californians" was to help in the diffusion of mining technique, although they also became a source of anxiety. Some people in Australia did not welcome the gold rushes, since they appeared to threaten the fragile social equilibrium of the colonies, an apprehension fed by numerous reports of lawlessness in California. "There will doubtless be numerous robberies, perhaps murders, through the drunken quarrels of the miners," one woman wrote anxiously from the site of the first gold rush in 1851, "but I think we need not fear a repetition of the dreadful scenes of California, possessing as we do a Government who will guard against them."[22] The following year Lord Robert Cecil— later to become a prime minister of Britain—visited the Victoria gold field and noted that "[t]he most interesting point of view in which the diggings appeared was the marked contrast they presented to California. The rush of population was nearly if not quite as great; the temptations to come were as powerful; the country in which the gold lay was as wild and desolate; but the government was of the Queen, not of the mob; from above, not from below."[23] Such comments raise a common point of comparison between the California gold rush and the subsequent rushes that occurred in British territory.

Contemporary observers as well as later writers have emphasized the orderly and law-abiding behavior in the British-governed gold fields, con-trasting this with the more chaotic social scene in California. But a simple dichotomy is misleading; a closer examination suggests that the apparent differences were less dramatic than many claim and can be largely explained by the context in which individual rushes occurred. For example, the American government had considerable difficulty in exercising any real authority in California in 1848, and in any case it did not have a coherent policy that dealt with mining on federal land.[24] Consequently, regulations framed by miners on the spot became the basis of mining law, a state of affairs that the government could do little more than acknowledge after the fact. "The discovery of our precious metals," a mining expert recalled twenty years later,

> came in the midst of great excitement, right after the Mexican war; the mines were in a distant region, and before the government was able to acquire any definite knowledge of the extent of the deposits, hundreds of thousands were engaged in working them. . . . [T]he people, finding some law necessary, began to make regulations for themselves. Whenever a number of miners found themselves working together in a certain locality, they called a meeting, organized a mining district, established its bounds, defined the extent of ground each man might hold, and fixed the amount of work he should do per month, or per year, to retain it. . . . Very soon the courts, in the absence of other laws, and finding these codes well suited to the cases coming before them, adopted them as the rule of judicial decision.[25]

The situation was very different in New South Wales. The former penal colony had a relatively effective government, whose authority was not undermined by a widely held antipathy to state intervention, as was the case in the United States.[26] And the colonial government had every intention of exercising close control over events in the gold fields; the only issue was the most appropriate means for establishing this control.

The government at first greeted the news of the gold discovery with disbelief. The governor wrote to his superior in Britain, voicing his suspicion that Hargraves had actually brought the gold with him from California, intending to mislead people and create the false impression that an Australian gold field existed.[27] It soon became apparent that this was, in fact, Australian gold, and the government had no choice but to move quickly and devise a regulatory framework for mining. These regulations were a mixture of British law, current Australian practice, and the earlier Californian precedent.

The British concept of Royal Metals gave the government a means to control any mining of gold: the gold remained the property of the monarch, regardless of the ownership of the land on which it was found. Although Blackstone, the British legal authority, reiterated the point in his *Commentaries*, no one in the colonial government was aware of a British law that dealt explicitly with gold mining.[28] Since any regulations had to be enforceable, they needed the consent of the mining population, however reluctantly it might be given.[29] The existing regulations for managing the colony's extensive Crown lands were familiar to most people, and features of these—combined with others from California's gold fields—were adapted to gold mining.[30] For guidance on the Californian model, the colonial secretary got in touch with an American, A. E. Bush, who happened to be in Sydney. Bush later explained that: "I had with me a copy of the gold regulations in California, where I had been an Alcalde . . . something like a Police Magistrate here [in New South Wales]. I had these rules, which had been framed by the miners. I showed them to Mr. Thomson [the colonial secretary], and I had to explain to him why these rules and regulations were necessary, as he had never seen a gold field and knew nothing about it. . . . The regulations were framed almost exactly as I gave them to him, with very little variation indeed."[31]

The most striking feature of the New South Wales mining regulations, and one that subsequently became the basis of those in the other British jurisdictions, was the miner's license. Anyone determined to mine for gold had first to pay a substantial fee to a government official, the gold commissioner. On payment of 30 shillings ($7.50), a miner was licensed for a month. Police patrolled the gold fields and summarily fined any person found mining without a license. The cost of the license was deliberately high, to raise the necessary revenue to administer the gold fields and to discourage mining.[32] In practice the license acted more as an irritant than as a deterrent, provoking miners' anger and resistance. They saw the license as an arbitrary measure enacted by a government intent on restricting access to the wealth of nature, and the heavy-handed conduct of officials on the ground further antagonized them.[33] The license was a constant and visible symbol of the government's determination to regulate mining; only the relative richness of the gold fields deterred widespread opposition.

The gold rushes themselves were not greeted with unanimous approval. The proximity of the gold fields to Melbourne and Sydney meant that the metropolitan centers could scarcely ignore their impact. Some people worried that the labor supply for other industries would evaporate.[34] Others simply lamented the absence of servants and the lack of deference. "We find it literally impossible to get anything done, which requires labour," grumbled an English clergyman visiting Sydney in early 1853.

> None of the accounts which you have received exaggerate the complete dislocation of society which has been caused by the diggings. It is not so much the high wages . . . it is the restlessness & general demoralization which has come over the whole of the working class. No man will stay with one master for more than a few weeks. . . . Then they acquire of course a manner, not so much of independence, as of rudeness, quite

different from what I saw in the United States & in other colonies. The *sudden* transition from poverty to wealth, & from dependence to superiority, is too much for ordinary minds. . . . This inordinate wealth is gained at the price of all that makes wealth desirable—civilization, refinement, comfort, religion, morality. A nation of successful gamblers, & low-bred parvenus, from which all the best elements are continually drained off, & which is constantly recruited from the worst populations, the lowest classes, in the world, such appears to be the future of Victoria. Is not gold dear at such a price?[35]

Another contemporary remarked disapprovingly that "[t]he equality system here would stun even a Yankee."[36]

If the California rush evokes the image of the forty-niners streaming headlong across a continent, the Australian experience emphasizes the miners' bitter resistance to "that bloody license tax," opposition that culminated in Ballarat in early December 1854. In a final confrontation, opponents of the license—angered by other perceived miscarriages of justice—gathered at the Eureka stockade, a hastily erected fort. An armed government force soon arrived and attacked in the early hours of December 3. The government troops easily routed the miners, killing fourteen men outright and wounding many others. But if the miners lost the battle, they ultimately won the war. After an inquiry into the miners' grievances, the government abolished the licensing system and allowed the miners a far greater voice in the management of the mining districts.[37] Many saw the achievement of a measure of self-government as a vindication of their actions and a herald of democratic practice in Australia. The Eureka flag, which rallied the miners, retains its symbolic power to this day and is still flown at popular protests.[38]

Placer gold fields have only a limited life span, particularly for the independent miner with few tools and scant resources. By 1854 returns from southeastern Australia's richest and most accessible gold deposits were beginning to decline. The mining population shrank with the drop in gold production. Some diggers moved on to search for gold elsewhere; others returned to their homes. Many crossed the Tasman Sea, a decade after the first rushes, when men with Australian experience uncovered gold in various parts of New Zealand.

New Zealand's first gold rush took place in the northwest corner of the South Island in 1857.[39] As in Australia, surveyors and other early European explorers had reported the presence of gold in this area, but the information had little or no impact. In 1842, for example, a person "found several particles of what was believed to be gold, but the idea was universally ridiculed by the good folks of Nelson, who then never dreamed of the gold discoveries that were afterwards to take place in California, in Australia, and even in Massacre Bay [New Zealand]."[40] The following year a surveyor picked up a small gold nugget in the same vicinity, but again this find did not lead to further investigation.[41] In the mid-1850s, men with experience of the Californian and Australian gold rushes worked an area east of Collingwood after traces of gold were found there, and in 1856 there was a minor rush near Motueka, farther east again. These veteran prospectors recovered only a small amount of gold—"in such minute quantities as to render the occupation unremunerative"—but the incident once more raised the possibility of a local gold field.[42]

The significant discovery that triggered New Zealand's first gold rush occurred when two farmers found gold in a tributary of the Aorere River in late 1856. William Hough, a Nelson storekeeper, had been trying unsuccessfully to persuade a young veteran of the Australian gold fields, G. W. W. Lightband, to accompany him on a trip to the area for some time. Lightband, however, felt that limestone country such as western Nelson was not auriferous and so he was reluctant to make the journey. Evidently the farmers' discovery changed his mind, for Lightband finally agreed to go to Collingwood with Hough to examine the area. After looking over the discovery site, Lightband concluded that the location was not a promising one. Instead, he opted to work some two miles farther on, in what was to become known as Lightband's Gully. In early February 1857, Lightband sent five ounces of gold to Nelson, where it was sold by auction. Just as Sam Brannan's dancing down the streets of San Francisco with a bottle of gold helped to spark the California gold rush in May 1848, so Lightband's gold provided Nelson's skeptics with eloquent proof that, indeed, there was gold in the distant hills. The rush was on. Within a few months, two thousand people were hard at work in the Collingwood field.[43]

Julius Haast visited the field in the winter of 1859, toward the end of the rush, accompanying the geologist Ferdinand Hochstetter on his travels around the colony. Haast described the scene for a newspaper back in his native Germany. There were, he wrote, "men of all ages and conditions, sailors who had deserted, bankrupt merchants, doctors and lawyers without practise, farmers and traders, every trade is represented. But amongst them are many respectable people attracted by the love of gold, adventure or a free life. . . . Often, when I saw young people of good family in this picturesque 'Rinaldo Rinaldini' digger costume, I fancied that I was at a great masked ball, and all of us, they as well as ourselves, in fancy dress."[44]

The sense of incongruity that Haast felt in the gold field also comes across in the memoirs of a participant in the Collingwood rush, Edwin Hodder, who had recently arrived from England. Hodder was a good example of Haast's "young people of good family," and he later recorded his experiences in *Memories of New Zealand Life*:

I pictured every bit of romance which the [gold digging] mode of life seemed capable. I thought of its freedom from all conventional restraint, the novelty of living in the bush, with merry birds waking me up with their morning songs, and, above all, of turning up beautiful glistening nuggets of precious gold. I felt rather mortified when, after announcing my plans, several friends said, "My dear fellow, don't think of such a thing. Nature never cut you out for a gold digger." But I resolved to go. . . . I could not divest myself of a strange uncomfortable feeling, half of shame, half of pride, as I started off through town, with my tent, blankets and provisions on my back, and a spade, pick and shovel over my shoulder. . . . Nor did I feel any more at ease when the vulgar little boys said, "Go it, four eyes", in allusion to the spectacles I wore; or when old settlers murmured something about the sun spoiling certain folks' complexions, and other little innuendoes.[45]

But life in the gold field was hard, the weather was harsh, and the gold was never sufficiently abundant. Thomas Hewetson, the son of a Nelson farmer, was perhaps a more representative early digger. His letters home describe an environment where only the fit and the hardy could survive for long:

Slate River, September 13, 1857
    Dear Joseph
Here I am in the midst of mud and mire on the bank of this noted Slate River. On the 8th and 9th instant I stopped at Collingwood—thence started for Slate River—arrived and went out prospecting—unsuccessful.
    11th started for Red Boulder River—got lost—passed the most miserable night in the bush—rained very heavy. . . . If I cannot find a good claim soon, I shall seek employment of another kind. Tell all who are comfortable to remain at home.[46]

New Zealand's first gold rush was a rather modest affair, giving up few bonanzas to miners and passing its zenith within two years. But the flurry of activity did force the government to devise an administrative structure to regulate the gold fields, borrowed from the Australian example.[47] More importantly, the Collingwood rush provided clear proof that gold did exist in the country. Participants learned the basic techniques that they needed in order to explore other likely areas. The next rush came in 1861, after Gabriel Read located gold in central Otago, in the southern corner of the South Island.[48]

Like Hargraves, Read was an Australian with Californian experience, having sailed his own schooner from Tasmania across the Pacific to take part in the rush. He returned to Australia in the 1850s to work in the Victorian gold fields and then in 1860 heard rumors of gold discoveries in New Zealand. He went over to investigate in January 1861. After some un-profitable wanderings, he headed for the Tuapeka region of Otago, thought to be the site of an earlier gold discovery. In late May 1861, he panned significant amounts of gold—information that was soon published in local newspapers—and the rush was on.[49] Nearly fifty thousand people traveled from Australia to New Zealand over the next three years.[50] Just when the yields in the Otago district began to decline, the South Island's West Coast diggings came into their own, provoking another substantial rush.[51]

In California, southeastern Australia, and New Zealand, the most accessible gold deposits were soon exhausted. By the late 1850s, those still intent on mining in California were either turning to new methods of mining—which would require capital, more sophisticated technology, and larger claims—or searching for new gold fields. In early 1858, San Francisco was abuzz with news of a gold discovery on the banks of the Fraser River.[52] The next big gold rush outside the western states was soon underway.

The Fraser River lies just north of the forty-ninth parallel, which the Oregon Treaty of 1846 had established as the border between American and British territory in the Pacific Northwest. The only formal British possession along the coast was the colony of Vancouver Island, founded three years after the treaty. The Hudson's Bay Company [HBC] administered the colony; in addition, it had exclusive trading rights over a huge area—all of present-day western Canada, the Yukon and Northwest Territories, as well as much of northern Ontario and Quebec.

Gold fever first broke out along the north Pacific Coast in 1849, when news came of the gold discoveries in California. "In the Spring of 1849 a vessel appeared in the harbor," recalled Roderick Finlayson, an HBC official then in charge of Fort Victoria on Vancouver Island,

> the crew of which wore red flannel shirts, and when they landed we took them to be pirates. I ordered the men to the guns, manned the bastions

and made ready for defence. I then interviewed the men, from the gate,
who told me they were peaceable traders, come from San Francisco, with
gold, to trade for goods, as this was the only station on the northern
coast where they could get the goods they wanted. Having satisfied
myself that they were what they represented themselves to be, I let them
in, and they then told me that gold had been discovered in California in
large quantities the previous Fall, and that they had gold nuggets which
they would gladly exchange for goods. . . . After this our operations here
got considerably disarranged, by numbers of our men leaving for the
California diggings.[53]

As Finlayson indicates, the company soon had considerable difficulty
retaining workers. The next year, when a ship arrived at Fort Rupert
on the northern tip of Vancouver Island to pick up a cargo from the
Hudson's Bay Company coal mine there, the miners left with the coal.
"The presence of the *England*," grumbled James Douglas, head of the
Hudson's Bay Company's operations in the region, "and the tales of the
wealth to be acquired in Calefornia [*sic*] circulated by her highly paid
crew, is the chief cause of all the dissatisfaction that prevails among the
Company servants. . . . Their [*sic*] is little doubt about the intention of the
Miners their ardent wish is to get to Calefornia."[54] To add to the company's
anxiety, gold was also found within the region itself, on the Queen Charlotte
Islands.[55] The Haidas, the islands' Native people, had learned of the value
that Europeans placed on gold—likely through trading expeditions to
California—and brought some to a Hudson's Bay Company fort in the
summer of 1850.[56] This was not placer gold like that found elsewhere but
hard-rock gold, recovered from a rich quartz vein. Over the next two years,
[HBC officials and groups of American miners arrived to work the vein.
None of these forays was successful, largely because of Haida opposition
to mining. In addition, although the quartz deposit was rich, it was not
extensive and interest in the area soon faded.

The flurry of excitement over the presence of gold in the Queen Charlotte
Islands raised some troubling issues for the Hudson's Bay Company and
the British government. The first was simply their ability to maintain
authority and sovereignty in the face of an influx of miners. There was
also the uncertain political status of the area. The sudden interest in the
Queen Charlottes led the British government to extend the authority of the
governor of Vancouver Island to include those islands as well.[57] The British
government also wanted gold mining to be regulated in a manner consistent
with British law and precedent. "The property, both in land and mines,

in Queen Charlotte's Island being unquestionably the Crown's," explained
the colonial secretary to Douglas in 1852, "the Crown can delegate to you
the power of granting land and issuing licenses for procuring gold."[58] The
colonial secretary then indicated the best way to deal with the situation:
"I . . . send you copies of two papers which have been lately presented by
command of Her Majesty to Parliament, relating to the recent discovery
of gold in Australia, from which you will derive very valuable information
as to the course of procedure adopted by the respective Governors in that
country for granting licenses to persons to prosecute the search for gold. You
will . . . frame such regulations as you may deem practicable and advisable
for granting licenses for collecting gold upon the principle of those which
you will find, from the correspondence, have been granted to the Australian
Colonies."[59] Thus, despite the fact that no significant mining developed in
the Queen Charlottes, the interlude resulted in the extension of formal
British sovereignty and the establishment of mining regulations based on
the Australian model. But the most significant consequence was that other
Native people learned of the value that Europeans placed on gold. Following
the example of the Haidas, they started to bring gold to Hudson's Bay
Company mainland forts for trading purposes.[60] The company gradually
accumulated the precious metal while maintaining a discreet silence to the
world.

Farther south, the miners of California had begun to prospect well
beyond northern California's Mother Lode region. By 1855 some had
traveled nearly to the forty-ninth parallel, participating in a minor rush near
the HBC's Fort Colville on the Columbia River close to the international
boundary during that year.[61] As this northward movement continued
during the spring of 1856, Douglas advised the colonial secretary that gold
discoveries had been made "within the British territory."[62]

Douglas was anxious to maintain control over events on the mainland.
Although he was governor only of Vancouver Island, his second job was
chief factor and head of the Western Department for the Hudson's Bay
Company. Any disturbance on the mainland—an area over which the
company possessed exclusive trading rights with Native peoples—would
jeopardize its position. A gold rush would almost certainly bring chaos;
events in the Queen Charlottes, for example, demonstrated that conflicts
were likely between Native and white miners. South of the border, an Indian
war raged in Washington Territory during 1855 and 1856, something that
Douglas was anxious to prevent in British territory. He was also well aware
of the problems that the California gold rush had caused the company,
and no doubt expected that these difficulties would be far greater if the

rush was closer to home. In addition to the possibilities of Indian wars and mass desertions by company employees, he was also concerned that an influx of American miners would lead inevitably to a reprise of the events that culminated in the loss of the Oregon territory in 1846. By late December 1857, he determined on a course of action, issuing a proclamation "declaring the rights of the Crown in respect to gold found in its natural place of deposit, within the limits of Fraser's River and Thompson's River districts . . . and forbidding all persons to dig or disturb the soil in search of gold, until authorized on that behalf by Her Majesty's Government."[63]

Ironically, the rush of "adventurers from the American side" that Douglas dreaded was caused inadvertently by the Hudson's Bay Company itself several months after his proclamation. The gold that had slowly increased in the company forts through trade with the Native population—some eight hundred ounces—was shipped to the San Francisco mint in February 1858.[64] News of its arrival was all the encouragement needed to start the stampede from California northward; the first shipload of miners, over four hundred in number, arrived in Victoria in late April.[65]

The Fraser River gold rush of 1858 brought much publicity to British Columbia. In many ways the gold rush was an inevitable consequence of the earlier rush to California, ten years before. After all, by 1858 California's richest deposits were mostly depleted. "The miners," wrote historian John Hittell in 1869, "were spoiling for an excitement. Many of the rich placers were exhausted. . . . The country was full of men who could no longer earn the wages to which they had become accustomed. . . . They were ready to go anywhere if there was a reasonable hope of rich diggings, rather than submit to live without the high pay and excitement which they had enjoyed for years in the Sacramento placers. . . . These men welcomed the rumors that a new California had been found in the basin of the Fraser with joy and enthusiasm.[66] Between April and August 1858, some twenty-five to thirty thousand people rushed to the Fraser River, most coming via San Francisco."[67]

Despite Douglas's anxieties, the Fraser River rush was more or less an orderly affair.[68] Considerable tension arose between European and Native miners, culminating in a series of confrontations, assaults, and murders, but actual warfare was avoided.[69] Nonetheless, the situation caused Douglas a good deal of concern, and at the height of the tensions between the two groups—in August 1858—he traveled to the mining district to act as a mediator.[70] Overall, however, the rush was not particularly lucrative for the participants. They soon realized that the Fraser River was not another American River. Harsh conditions and meager returns left many with no desire to remain on the river bars, and soon the exodus began. The event, noted a California historian four decades later, "was the longest and most disastrous of all the mining excitements . . . a big mistake."[71]

Bonanza discoveries typical of other nineteenth-century gold excitements came only two years after the first stampede and the departure of many a disgruntled miner. This second gold rush was to the Cariboo district, some two hundred miles north of the Fraser River diggings. Preoccupied by the Civil War and perhaps overly cautious after the disappointments on the Fraser, few Americans took part. Substantial numbers arrived from the British North American colonies, however, and British Columbia boomed once more.[72]

This narrative of discovery and rush in the areas around the Pacific underscores the theme of continuity and sequence. One of the striking features connecting one gold rush to the next is the common personnel with feelings of shared experience. Another historian, after listing numerous individuals who participated in two or more rushes, speculated that "[p]erhaps I'm dealing not with Californian or Victorian or New Zealand colonists but with a variety of the *genus* Pacific Man whose habitat is no particular country but the goldfields."[73] The metaphor also applies to the rushes themselves; they are best seen as variations of the genus *Rush*.

While one may speculate why California, not Australia, was the site of the first rush, all of the gold rushes took place in areas of recent European settlement. The Australasian and western North American coastlines were among the last to be accurately charted and also among the last to be colonized by Europeans. Hence the near simultaneity of the rushes: a brief decade separated those examined here; barely fifty years passed from the first in California to the last in the Klondike. The rushes themselves were simply large groups of people, predominantly male, moving from one more-or-less rich placer gold field to the next. Their progress across the Pacific and up the North American cordillera was prompted by the diminution of the resource they sought. As returns declined in one region, the attraction of rumored wealth elsewhere became overwhelming. The goal was ever the same—alluvial gold in quantity—and it seemed to matter little whether one dug for it on the banks of the Fraser or the Sacramento or in Bendigo. Depletion, the unavoidable consequence of many an extractive industry, was the motor of sequence, the driving push that sent men from California to the Fraser, or from the colony of Victoria across the Tasman Sea to New Zealand's South Island.

As the value of gold production declined, the mining industry adapted to compensate for the diminishing returns, each field experiencing a shift to economies of scale. With this change came a more sophisticated technology and a more complex organization of the workplace. Hydraulic mining and river dredging took over from the pan and the ground sluice; companies replaced the loose partnerships of independent miners, reflecting the change from petty commodity production to full-fledged capitalism. The annual report of New Zealand's minister of mines in 1876 summed up the situation: "The character of mining . . . is very different to what it was in the early times of the gold fields: now a man without capital can hardly do else than work for wages."[74]

Lode or quartz mining facilitated industrial capitalism's control of the mining frontier, for such activity depended on advanced technology, absentee ownership, and a specialized labor force.[75] A lucrative business, the mining industry spurred investment and fueled growth. It remained a leading sector in the economies of each region well into the twentieth century. The frenetic communities created by the gold rushes had gone, replaced by company towns.

If the economic legacy of the rushes to Australia, New Zealand, and British Columbia was soon displaced by more sophisticated methods and industrial organization, their political legacy in the three former British colonies was more profound although more difficult to gauge precisely. Miners of the rush era challenged the status quo in each place, and numerous gold rush participants were active in the political arena. As an Australian historian argued in an article reasserting the significance of the gold rush's impact, "Quite suddenly there had appeared on the Australian continent a society of a kind not known before, on a larger economic scale, with larger ideas, larger demands, larger and more sophisticated connections with the great world, and with more diverse skills than any or all of the Australian societies of 1850. . . . There is a strong case for believing that the Victorian gold-society provided the power which set going the whole process of rapid economic growth in eastern Australia."[76]

The same argument could be made for New Zealand and British Columbia. In New Zealand, for example, the rush of miners fractured existing institutions on the South Island, and two of that country's more remarkable prime ministers emerged from their ranks. Julius Vogel left London as a teenager to participate in the Victoria gold rush, then crossed the Tasman Sea to join the Otago rush. As prime minister he launched an ambitious development program, financed by overseas loans, which had a considerable impact on New Zealand. Dick Seddon, a former miner and pub owner, became an immensely popular leader who oversaw the foundation of one of the world's first welfare states.[77] In British Columbia, the miners demanded full participation in the political life, forcing responsible government on a reluctant colony as the price to be paid for joining Canada as a province in 1871.[78] In each place, then, gold rush miners shaped a common political agenda that owed something to California, reinforcing the ways in which that first rush was a world event that reverberated around the Pacific Rim.

The significance of those who participated in the rushes can also be interpreted on a more analytical level. They became agents responsible for introducing new ideas and possibilities as they moved from one region to another. David Goodman, author of a fine comparative study of the Australian and Californian gold rushes, described those who took part in the rushes of the 1850s as "the true subjects of the new liberal ideologies. Self-seeking, self-regulating, morally and emotionally autonomous, transnational, the gold diggers were the citizens of nineteenth century liberal modernity." If anyone embodied the new doctrine that the individual pursuit of wealth was the fairest and most effective basis for a social order and that laissez faire was the ideal social policy, surely it was the gold seekers of the mid-nineteenth century. They were, as Goodman asserts, "boundary riders of modernity."[79]

Notes

1. For discussion of gold's history in Europe, see the opening chapters of Pierre Vilar, *A History of Gold and Money 1450–1920*, trans. Judith White (London: NLB, 1976).

2. There are numerous references to gold in Genesis and Exodus; perhaps the best-known classical allusions are to Midas and Jason and the Argonauts. Contemporaries often called gold rush participants "Argonauts" and most fields had either a mine or a community known as Ophir (the source of King Solomon's wealth in the Bible).

3. See Russell J. Beck, *New Zealand Jade* (Wellington: A. H. & A. W. Reed, 1984), esp. 73–115.

4. Mining in North America did not begin with the arrival of European peoples, of course; for an excellent portrayal of this point see "Prehistoric Trade," plate 14, in R. Cole Harris, ed., *Historical Atlas of Canada*, vol. 1, *From the Beginning to 1800* (Toronto: University of Toronto Press, 1987). This plate concentrates on the continent's northern region. See also Sandra Zacharias, "Historic Use of Metals by Native People on the Northwest Coast and in Alaska," *Datum* 6, no. 3 (spring 1981): 25–27. For a close study of Native mining in an area that is now part of the United States, see James B. Griffin, ed., *Lake Superior Copper and the Indians:*

Miscellaneous Studies of Great Lakes Prehistory, Anthropological Papers, No. 17 (Ann Arbor: University of Michigan, 1961).

5. In British Columbia, for example, the first gold discoveries were made by Native people. See especially the discussion in Patricia Vaughan's master's thesis, "Cooperation and Resistance: Indian-European Relations on the Mining Frontier in British Columbia, 1835–1858," University of British Columbia, 1978; note also the discussion of Maori participation in the New Zealand rushes in J. H. M. Salmon, *A History of Goldmining in New Zealand* (Wellington: R. E. Owen, Govt. Printer, 1963), 36–37.

6. A. H. A. Robinson, *Gold in Canada*, Mines Branch Monograph 734 (Ottawa: J. O. Patenaude, 1933), 5.

7. Godfrey Charles Mundy, *Our Antipodes; or, Residence and Rambles in the Australasian Colonies, with a Glimpse of the Gold Fields,* 2nd ed., rev. (London: Richard Bentley, 1852), 3:309. Some people regretted that hard work and muscle could lead to success. In London, for example, the *Times* observed that "[s]ociety is fairly turned upside down . . . the ignorant, the brutal and the criminal are raised by mere possession of bodily strength to the possession of that opulence which is hourly escaping from the grasp of their less fortunate superiors" (quoted in "Australia!" *The Morning News* [Saint John, NB], May 28, 1852, p. 2). James Wyld, the British cartographer, noted that "[w]hile the penniless look with hope on California and New Holland [Australia], the wealthy hear of them with dread. To the former they hold forth the chance of getting money, to the latter, fear that the value of their stores will be diminished. Among the many extraordinary incidents connected with the Californian discoveries, was the alarm communicated to many classes; which was not confined to individuals, but invaded governments." Wyld, *Notes on the Distribution of Gold throughout the World, Including Australia, California, and Russia . . .* (London: James Wyld, 1852), 20.

8. For a brief introduction, see L. Girard, "Transport," in *The Cambridge Economic History of Europe*, ed. H. J. Habakkuk and M. Postan, vol. 6, part 1, (Cambridge: Cambridge University Press, 1966), 212–73, especially the subsection "Railways and Packet Boats, 1830–69," 228–49; more generally, see the illuminating discussions of gold rushes in Eric Hobsbawm, *The Age of Capital, 1848–1875* (New York: Scribner, 1975), 78–82; and Goodman, *Gold Seeking*, 24–37. Delgado's *To California By Sea*, on the other hand, largely ignores the broader context, although it does contain a wealth of information on individual ships and people.

9. See, for example, Roske, "World Impact of the California Gold Rush, 1849–1857," esp. 217, 223; also, Seweryn Korzelinski, *Memories of Gold-Digging in Australia*, trans. and ed. Stanley Robe (Saint Lucia: University of Queensland Press, 1979), xi–xii. A Polish refugee in London, Korzelinski and a group of friends decided to quit Europe for the Australian diggings.

10. See especially Rodman Wilson Paul, " 'Old Californians' in British Gold Fields," *Huntington Library Quarterly* 17 (1954): 161–72.

11. Mundy, *Our Antipodes*, 394.

12. The most extensive treatment of prior gold discoveries is Lynette Ramsay Silver's *A Fool's Gold? William Tipple Smith's Challenge to the Hargraves Myth* (Milton, Queensland: Jacaranda Press, 1986), which presents compelling evidence that Hargraves simply went to the site of an earlier discovery. See also the comments in a letter published in the *Times*, September 8, 1851, p. 7 (published a week after the newspaper first carried news of the discovery of gold in Australia); Captain John Elphinstone Erskine, R.N., *A Short Account of the Late Discoveries of Gold in Australia with Notes of a Visit to the Gold District*, ed. George Mackaness (London, 1851; reprint, Sydney: D. S. Ford, Printers, 1957), 6–8; H. M. Suttor, "Early Gold Discoveries," Royal Australian Historical Society, *Journal and Proceedings* 8 (1922): 317–8; and Geoffrey Blainey, "Gold and Governors," *Historical Studies* 9, no. 36 (May 1961): 337–50. The same situation occurred in California: for references to gold discoveries there prior to January 1848, see Watson Parker, "The Causes of American Gold Rushes," *North Dakota History: Journal of the Northern Plains* 36 (fall 1969), 341; and Joseph Ellison, "The Mineral Land Question in California, 1848–1866," in *The Public Lands: Studies in the History of the Public Domain*, ed. Vernon Carstensen (Madison: University of Wisconsin Press, 1963), 88, n. 3.

13. See Geoffrey Blainey, *The Rush That Never Ended: A History of Australian Mining* (Melbourne: Melbourne University Press, 1963), 10; and Philip Ross May, "Gold Rushes of the Pacific Borderlands: A Comparative Survey," in *Provincial Perspectives: Essays in Honour of W. J. Gardner*, ed. Len Richardson and W. David McIntyre (Christchurch: University of Canterbury Press, 1980), esp. 102–3.

14. See Blainey, "Gold and Governors," 348; and B. C. Hodge, "Goldrush Australia," *Journal of the Royal Australian Historical Society* 69, no. 3 (December 1983): 161–62.

15. For discussions of the Australian and New Zealand rush to California, see Charles Bateson, *Gold Fleet for California: Forty-Niners from Australia and Zealand* (East Lansing: Michigan State University Press, 1964); and Monaghan, *Australians and the Gold Rush*. On Hargraves, see Bruce Mitchell, "Hargraves, Edward Hammond (1816–1891)," in *Australian Dictionary of Biography*, vol. 4, *1851–1890, D–J*, ed. Bede Nairn, Geoffrey Serle, and Russel Ward (Melbourne: Melbourne University Press, 1972), 346–47; Silver, *Fool's Gold?* 45–58; and Geoffrey Blainey, "The Gold Rushes: The Year of Decision," *Historical Studies* 10, no. 38 (May 1962): 129–40.

16. Monaghan, *Australians and the Gold Rush:*, 136–37. Hargraves also wrote at least one letter back to Australia, asserting that gold could be found there (125).

17. Edward Hammond Hargraves, *Australia and Its Gold Fields: A Historical Sketch*

of the Progress of the Australian Colonies, From the Earliest Times to the Present Day; with a Particular Account of the Recent Gold Discoveries. . . (London: H. Ingram & Co., 1855), 116. Hargraves admitted that this account may have seemed a little overstated but offered the following justification: "What I said on the instant—though, I must admit, not warranted as the language of calm reflection—has been since much laughed at. And though my readers may renew the laugh, I shall not hesitate to repeat it, because, as it was the natural and impulsive expression of my overwrought feelings at the moment, so is it the only account I can now give of what those feelings were."

18. See Blainey, *Rush That Never Ended*, 13.

19. In her book, *Fool's Gold?* Lynette Silver argues that Hargraves simply followed in another's footsteps, although her view is summarily rejected by Brian Hodge in "Gold and (Mrs.) Silver," *Journal of the Royal Australian Historical Society* 78 (June 1992): 30–47. Hargraves's role as the person who effectively provoked the gold rush seems indisputable.

20. The quotation is from Geoffrey Serle, *The Golden Age: A History of the Colony of Victoria, 1851–1861* (Melbourne: Melbourne University Press, 1963), 22. Serle's book provides an excellent account of the Victoria gold rushes, as well as including gold production figures and discussion in an appendix (390–91). See also Goodman's outstanding comparative study, *Gold Seeking*.

21. For a vivid description of how one group of miners decided to leave California, see Ferguson, *Experiences of a Forty-Niner*, 202–3. It is difficult to arrive at an accurate figure of how many Americans made the trip, but there were at least several thousand in the Australian gold fields in the early 1850s. One source cites 1,374 Americans in an 1854 census, although this figure includes only those who gave the United States as their birthplace, and not naturalized Americans; see E. Daniel and Annette Potts, "American Republicanism and the Disturbances on the Victorian Goldfields," *Historical Studies*, 13, no. 50 (April 1968): 156. Monaghan, in *Australians and the Gold Rush*, suggests a figure of "several thousand" (246), while Serle, in *Golden Age*, speculates that there may have been three thousand Americans before an ill-fated 1853 exodus to Peru (76). For reminiscences of Americans who took part in the Australian rush, see Amos S. Pittman, "The California and Australia Gold Rushes as Seen by Amos S. Pittman, with Introduction and Notes by Theressa Gay," *California Historical Society Quarterly*, 30 (1951): 15–37; John G. Williams, *The Adventures of a Seventeen-Year-Old Lad and the Fortunes He Might Have Won* (Boston: Collins Press, 1894); and Ferguson, *Experiences of a Forty-Niner*, esp. 325–28. These accounts make clear that many Americans were in the gold fields, a point that also comes across in George Francis Train, *A Yankee Merchant in Goldrush Australia: The Letters of George Francis Train, 1853–55* (Melbourne: William Heinemann Australia, 1970). Note also the reference to Americans in Korzelinski, *Memories of Gold-Digging in Australia*, 97.

22. From a letter dated May 15, 1851, reprinted in Henrietta Huxley, "The Gold Diggings at Bathurst in 1851," *The Nineteenth Century*, 45 (June 1899): 964. A newspaper in Halifax, Nova Scotia, reprinted a letter from Adelaide, dated April 14, 1852, which hinted darkly at impending chaos: "The gold seeking has turned almost all kinds of business, and trades of every description '*topsyturvy*.' . . . The 'Diggers' live in tents, and where there are thousands of all ages and both sexes thrown together, without order or law to protect them, you may conceive the state of society; however, hitherto things have been pretty orderly; and taking the population of Mount Alexander into consideration (45,000) crime has been light; but I do not think it can continue so for a much longer period." "Interesting from Australia," *The Nova Scotian*, September 27, 1852, 316 (the letter appeared originally in the *Cape Breton News*). Note also the comments in Goodman, *Gold Seeking*, 56–63, and Serle, *Golden Age*, 76n.

23. Lord Robert Cecil, *Lord Robert Cecil's Gold Fields Diary*, 2nd ed. (Melbourne: Melbourne University Press, 1945), 9.

24. In 1848, as Rodman Paul pointed out, "there were no well-developed American mining codes and no federal regulations other than the general policy that mineral lands not otherwise provided for were not subject to sale or preemption." Paul, *California Gold*, 211. For useful brief accounts of the framing of gold mining law in California, see Paul's chapter "The Law of the Mines," in *California Gold*, 210–39; and Ellison, "Mineral Land Question in California, 1848–1866."

25. E. F. Dunne to Rossiter Raymond, December 20, 1869, quoted in Rossiter W. Raymond, *Statistics of Mines and Mining in the States and Territories West of the Rocky Mountains* (Washington DC: GPO, 1870), 422. A similar view is expressed in the *Report of the Senate Committee on Mines and Mining*, May 28, 1866, 39th Congress, 1st sess., rpt. 105. A Californian periodical described the first comprehensive mining act passed by Congress—in the summer of 1866—as "nothing more or less than putting into the form of a congressional act those local laws, which a practical experience of sixteen years has induced the miners of the Pacific Slope to adopt as the 'Rules and Regulations' by which they have almost unanimously agreed upon among themselves to be governed, in the absence of all legislative enactments." *Mining and Scientific Press*, July 14, 1866, quoted in Paul, *California Gold*, 233.

26. For a useful discussion of the American context compared to British territories, see Paul, " 'Old Californians' in British Gold Fields," as well as "Mining Frontiers in the Americas and the British Commonwealth," in *Conference Proceedings: The Westward Movement and Historical Involvement of the Americas in the Pacific Basin* (San Jose: n.p., 1966), 17–28.

27. Governor FitzRoy to Earl Grey, May 22, 1851, quoted in Silver, *Fool's Gold?* 52–53. Similarly, when California traders first came to Vancouver Island in 1849, anxious to secure supplies from the Hudson's Bay Company fort, the company's

chief trader took a great deal of convincing that the gold was in fact genuine (Roderick Finlayson, *Biography [sic] of Roderick Finlayson* [Victoria BC: n.p., 1891], 21–22).

28. For a succinct account of the doctrine, see T. A. Rickard, *Historic Backgrounds of British Columbia* (Vancouver: Wrigley Printing, 1948), 297; also "Property in Mines Royal," in Robert Foster MacSwinney, *The Law of Mines, Quarries, and Minerals* (London: n.p., 1884), 40–41.

29. For example, the executive council recorded that "As . . . it is of the greatest importance that the license fee should not be so high as to afford any reasonable ground of resistance to its collection and that no opposition should be excited to the very small means of enforcing its authority which the Government will possess, the Council considers it desirable that the fee should not be higher than the persons engaged in the occupation would cheerfully and readily pay." Executive Council Minutes, May 23, 1851, no. 24, pp. 257–58, 4/1527, Archives Office of New South Wales, Sydney, New South Wales.

30. Here I am following the analysis in T. H. Irving and Carol Liston, "State Intervention and Equality: Administration in the New South Wales Goldfields 1851–1853," in *From Colony to Coloniser: Studies in Australian Administrative History*, ed. J. J. Eddy and J. R. Nethercote (Sydney: Hale & Iremonger, 1987), 103–19, esp. 107. See also the comments in Blainey, "Gold Rushes: The Year of Decision," 136–39; and Goodman, *Gold Seeking*, xvi–xvii.

31. Evidence of A. E. Bush, in the "Report from the Select Committee on Mr. A. E. Bush; Together with the Proceedings of the Committee and Minutes of Evidence," in New South Wales, *Votes and Proceedings of the Legislative Assembly During the Session of 1862*, vol. 2, (Sydney: Government Printer, 1862), answers 4–6. At this point, Bush was pressing the government for compensation for his services, which he claimed had been promised but never paid to him. While this may well have led him to exaggerate his role, the colonial secretary admitted before the same committee that Bush had provided the government with "very useful information, some of which information was acted upon in the establishment of our regulations." Evidence of Deas Thomson in "Report from the Select Committee."

32. When a group of miners petitioned the gold commissioner in June 1851, asking that the license fee be reduced from thirty shillings to seven shillings and sixpence, he rejected the suggestion outright, pointing out that "the Government had to consider the general interests of the Community and not those of the diggers alone and that those general interests would not be advanced by encouraging all the labouring hands of the Colony to be employed in Gold Digging" When the commissioner advised the executive council of the miners' request and his response, the group recorded "their entire approval of the answer given to the Deputation by the Commissioner." Executive Council Minutes, July 3, 1851, no. 32, p. 351, 4/1527,

Archives Office of New South Wales. For the adoption of the New South Wales precedent by the neighboring colony of Victoria, see Serle, *Golden Age*, 19–29. The idea of a high fee to discourage mining did not originate in Australia but in California, where the state government levied high fees on foreign miners. See Hittell, *History of California*, 3:262–65; and Ellison, "Mineral Land Question in California, 1848–1866," 77–79.

33. See the description in William E. Franklin, "Governors, Miners and Institutions: The Political Legacy of Mining Frontiers in California and Victoria, Australia," *California History*, 65, no. 1 (March 1986): esp. 52–57. The Australian artist S. T. Gill produced vivid contemporary sketches, reproduced in *The Victorian Gold Fields 1852–3: An Original Album by S. T. Gill*, ed. and intro. by Michael Cannon (Melbourne: State Library of Victoria, 1982): "Diggers licensing, Castlemaine camp," 22–23, and "The license inspected," 28–29. The various memoirs by visitors to Australia during the gold rush period always commented on the license: see, for example, Isabella Campbell, *Rough and Smooth, or, Ho! for an Australian Gold Field* (Quebec: Hunter, Rose & Co., 1865), 99–102; Korzelinski, *Memories of Gold-Digging in Australia*, 37; Ferguson, *Experiences of a Forty-Niner*, 242, 275–78; Antoine Fauchery, *Letters from a Miner in Australia* (Melbourne: Georgian House, 1965), 59–60. In Australia itself, as Blainey noted in 1962, "Millions of words have been written on the effects of the gold license." "Gold Rushes: The Year of Decision," 136.

34. For example, in the (Australian) spring of 1851 the governor of Victoria wrote anxiously to his superior in London that "your Lordship will easily conceive that, viewing the season at which these circumstances have occurred, and the agricultural and particularly the pastoral interests at stake, that this is the commencement of the shearing season, and that shortly the harvest will call for labour, great embarrassment and anxiety prevails." La Trobe to Grey, October 10, 1851, quoted in C. M. H. Clark, *Select Documents in Australian History* (Sydney: Angus & Robertson, 1955), 7.

35. Letter from J. R. Godley to J. E. Fitzgerald, February 22, 1853, copy in MS 2205 (typescript titled "Letters to J. E. Fitzgerald from E. G. Wakefield and J. R. Godley 1849–1861"), Alexander Turnbull Library, Wellington, New Zealand (emphasis in the original). Such comments were voiced frequently: see, for example, the revealing anecdotes in C. M. H. Clark, *A History of Australia*, vol. 4, *The Earth Abideth Forever, 1851–1888* (Melbourne: Melbourne University Press, 1978), 19; and Serle, *Golden Age*, 29–33; cf. the discussion in Goodman, *Gold Seeking*, 56–63.

36. John Capper, *The Emigrant's Guide to Australia, Containing the Fullest Particulars Relating to the Recently Discovered Gold Fields, the Government Regulations for Gold Seeking, &c.*, 2nd ed. (Liverpool: George Philip & Son, 1853), 235. Capper is quoting a recent letter sent from Australia. The writer went on to: "We have all grades and

classes, from the coalheaver to the 'Mantilini.' The outward garb forms no mark of distinction—all are mates."

37. For detail on the Eureka rebellion and its aftermath, see John N. Molony, *Eureka* (Ringwood, Victoria: Penguin, 1994); Bob O'Brien, *Massacre at Eureka: The Untold Story* (Kew, Victoria: Australian Scholarly Publishing, 1992), which reprints Samuel Douglas Smyth Huyghue's memoir, "The Ballarat Riots," arguably the best eyewitness account; and the special supplement to *Historical Studies* (December 1954), a centennial issue commemorating the event. For an overview of the event's legacy, see Weston Bate, *Victorian Gold Rushes* (Fitzroy, Victoria: McPhee Gribble/Penguin Books, 1988), 41–46, and the chapter titled "Battle Memories: Echoes of Eureka," in Chris Healy, *From the Ruins of Colonialism: History as Social Memory* (New York: Cambridge University Press, 1997), 133–58.

38. However, as the editors of a recent book on gold in Australia point out, "The use of a variant of the Eureka flag for a banner against the Chinese during the brutal riots at Lambing Flat in 1861 does a great deal to symbolise the limitations of goldfields democracy." Introduction to *Gold: Forgotten Histories and Lost Objects of Australia*, ed. Iain McCalman, Alexander Cook, and Andrew Reeves (Cambridge: Cambridge University Press, 2001), 7; cf. the account by Ann Curthoys in the same volume, "'Men of All Nations, except Chinamen': Europeans and Chinese on the Goldfields of New South Wales," 112–13.

39. The following section is based in part on Jeremy Mouat, "The Red Hill Swindle," unpublished master's essay, University of Canterbury, 1982, especially the first chapter, "Early Days on the Collingwood Gold Field: The Rush and After," 1–10.

40. J. L. Bailey, *The Nelson Directory and Companion to the Almanack for 1859* (Nelson, New Zealand: C. & J. Elliott, 1859), 9.

41. Ruth M Allan, *Nelson: A History of Early Settlement* (Wellington: A. H. & A. W. Reed, 1965), 228.

42. See Philip Ross May, *The West Coast Gold Rushes*, 2nd ed. (Christchurch, New Zealand: Pegasus, 1967), 63; Enga Washbourn, *Courage and Camp Ovens: Five Generations at Golden Bay* (Wellington: A. H. & A. W. Reed, 1970), 38; and Bailey, *Nelson Directory*, 16.

43. See the newspaper accounts of the early rush in the *Nelson Examiner*, February 18, March 18, and April 11, 1857.

44. From an article by Haast published in *Weiner Zeitung*, quoted in H. F. Haast, *The Life and Times of Sir Julius von Haast, K.C.M.G., Ph.D., D.Sc., F.R.S.: Explorer, Geologist, Museum Builder* (Wellington: the author, 1948), 34.

45. Edwin Hodder, *Memories of New Zealand Life* (London: Longman, Green, Longman & Roberts, 1862), 64–66.

46. Thomas Hewetson Letters, held in the Nelson Provincial Museum. Hewetson soon abandoned gold digging and took up storekeeping.

47. See Salmon, *History of Goldmining in New Zealand*, 38.

48. See Vincent Pyke, *History of the Early Gold Discoveries in Otago* (Dunedin, New Zealand: Otago Daily Times and Witness Newspapers Company, 1962), a reprint of the original 1887 edition; James Forrest, "Otago During the Goldrushes," in *Land and Society in New Zealand: Essays in Historical Geography*, ed. R. F. Watters (Wellington: A. H. & A. W. Reed, 1965), 80–100; and Murray McCaskill, "The South Island Goldfields in the 1860s: Some Geographical Aspects," in *Land and Livelihood: Geographical Essays in Honour of George Jobberns*, ed. Murray McCaskill (Christchurch: New Zealand Geographical Society, 1962), 143–69.

49. For detail on Read, see the entries in A. H. McLintock, ed., *An Encyclopaedia of New Zealand*, vol. 3 (Wellington: R. E. Owen, Gov't Printer, 1966), 55–56; G. H. Scholefield, ed., *A Dictionary of New Zealand Biography* (Wellington: Department of Internal Affairs, 1940): 2:204–7; and W. H. Oliver and Claudia Orange, eds., *Dictionary of New Zealand Biography*, vol. 1, *1769–1869* (Wellington: Allen & Unwin New Zealand/Dept. of Internal Affairs, 1990), 358–59. There is also a lengthy personal reminiscence by Read in Pyke's *History of the Early Gold Discoveries in Otago*, 121–32.

50. See table 1 in Forrest, "Otago During the Goldrushes," 86, and May, *West Coast Gold Rushes*, 503.

51. By far the best account of this rush is May's *West Coast Gold Rushes*.

52. In mid-July, the California correspondent of the *New York Times* described the impact of the Fraser River gold rush: "Throughout this State [California] the new gold fever has continued for nearly two months to rage with increasing violence, and no one believes the climax has yet been reached. Thousands of our citizens have been deploring for years past that the halcyon days of 1849 had gone for ever, when all of a sudden they are back again in full blast." *New York Times,* July 15, 1858, 2.

53. Finlayson, *Biography of Roderick Finlayson*, 21–22. Note also Helmcken's comments, in *The Reminiscences of Doctor John Sebastian Helmcken*, ed. Dorothy Blakey Smith (Vancouver: University of British Columbia Press, 1975), 293–94.

54. Douglas to Barclay, July 3, 1850, reprinted in *Fort Victoria Letters, 1846–1851*, ed. Hartwell Bowsfield (Winnipeg: Hudson's Bay Record Society, 1979), 102–3. The year before, Douglas had explained the impact of the California gold rush to a friend who lived east of the mountains: "The Company's servants are distracted at

the idea of losing so rich a prize and have deserted to the number of 30 from this establishment [Fort Vancouver on the Columbia River], the others so far steady, but we cannot depend upon them one hour." James Douglas to Donald Ross, March 8, 1849, in file 39, microfilm A-831, Donald Ross Collection, BC Archives, Victoria.

55. For detail on the Queen Charlotte gold discovery and subsequent events, see Margaret Ormsby's introduction to *Fort Victoria Letters, 1846–1851*, xci–xciv; Drew W. Crooks, "Shipwreck and Captivity: The Georgiana Expedition to the Queen Charlotte Islands," *Columbia* 8, no. 2 (summer 1994): 17–23; Bessie Doak Haynes, "Gold on Queen Charlotte's Island," *The Beaver* (winter 1966): 4–11; and Vaughan, "Cooperation and Resistance," 29–42. Much official documentary evidence may be found in two parliamentary papers: Great Britain, *Copies or Extracts of Correspondence Relative to the Discovery of Gold at Queen Charlotte's Island*, "Ordered by the House of Commons to be printed 19 July 1853" (London: Eyre & Spottiswoode, 1853); and Great Britain, *Copies or Extracts of Correspondence Relative to the Discovery of Gold at Queen Charlotte's Island*, "Ordered by the House of Commons to be printed 9 August 1853" (London: Eyre & Spottiswoode, 1853).

56. Vaughan, "Cooperation and Resistance," 29. She points out that "[t]here is evidence to suggest that the Haida were looking for new trade items."

57. See Sir John Pakington to James Douglas, September 27, 1852, reprinted in Great Britain, *Copies or Extracts of Correspondence Relative to the Discovery of Gold at Queen Charlotte's Island*, "Ordered by the House of Commons to be printed 19 July 1853" (London: Eyre & Spottiswoode, 1853), 12–14; also Barry M. Gough, " 'Turbulent Frontiers' and British Expansion: Governor James Douglas, The Royal Navy and the British Columbia Gold Rushes," *Pacific Historical Review* 41 (1972): 16–17.

58. Pakington to Douglas, September 27, 1852, *Copies or Extracts of Correspondence,* "19 July 1853," 13. Douglas had become governor of Vancouver Island in 1851, combining that appointment with his other position as chief factor of the Hudson's Bay Company in the West.

59. Pakington to Douglas, September 27, 1852, *Copies or Extracts of Correspondence,* "19 July 1853," 13. More than six months later, Douglas sent a copy of the regulations that he subsequently framed to London, pointing out in a covering letter "the conditions being nearly similar to those proscribed by the Governor-general of New South Wales on the discovery of gold in that colony." James Douglas to the Duke of Newcastle, April 11, 1853, reprinted in Great Britain, *Copies or Extracts of Correspondence Relative to the Discovery of Gold at Queen Charlotte's Island*, "Ordered by the House of Commons to be printed 9 August 1853" (London: Eyre & Spottiswoode, 1853), 3. For an analysis of Douglas's preparedness for the gold rush, see Clarence G. Karr, "James Douglas: The Gold Governor in the Context

of His Times," in *The Company of the Coast,* ed. E. Blanche Norcross (Nanaimo BC: Nanaimo Historical Society, 1983), 56–78.

60. F. W. Howay, *British Columbia: From the Earliest Times to the Present* (Vancouver: S. J. Clarke Publishing, 1914), 2:8–10; and Vaughan, "Cooperation and Resistance," 43–44.

61. William J. Trimble, *The Mining Advance into the Inland Empire: A Comparative Study of the Beginnings of the Mining Industry in Idaho and Montana, Eastern Washington and Oregon, and the Southern Interior of British Columbia; and of Institutions and Laws Based Upon that Industry* (1914; reprint, New York: Johnson Reprint Corporation, 1972), 15–23.

62. Douglas to Labouchere, April 16, 1856, in *Copies or Extracts of Correspondence Relative to the Discovery of Gold in the Fraser's River District, in British North America,* "Presented to both Houses of Parliament by Command of Her Majesty, July 2, 1858" (London: Eyre & Spottiswoode, 1858), 5.

63. Douglas to Labouchere, December 29, 1857, *Copies or Extracts of Correspondence,* "July 2, 1858," 8. Douglas candidly admitted to Labouchere that he had exceeded his authority in issuing the proclamation.

64. Howay, *British Columbia,* 14; "The Discovery of Hill's Bar in 1858," *British Columbia Historical Quarterly* 3, no. 3 (July 1939): esp. 217 (reminiscences of James Moore, one of the discoverers); "First Gold Excitement," in R. E. Gosnell, *The Year Book of British Columbia and Manual of Provincial Information* (Victoria BC: n.p., 1897), 88 (another account based on Moore's recollections); and Walter N. Sage, *Sir James Douglas and British Columbia* (Toronto: University of Toronto Press, 1930), 203.

65. See Douglas to Labouchere, May 8, 1858, *Copies or Extracts of Correspondence,* "July 2, 1858," 12–14; also *The Reminiscences of Doctor John Sebastian Helmcken,* 154–55.

66. John S Hittell, "The Mining Excitements of California," *Overland Monthly* 2 (May 1869): 415.

67. As a recent study points out, estimates vary from a low of ten thousand to a high of one hundred thousand: Daniel P. Marshall, "Rickard Revisited: Native 'Participation' in the Gold Discoveries of British Columbia," *Native Studies Review* 2, no. 1 (1997): 91–108. Marshall's thorough history of the Fraser River gold rush appeared after this chapter was completed: see Daniel Patrick Marshall, "Claiming the Land: Indians, Goldseekers, and the Rush to British Columbia," Ph.D. diss., University of British Columbia, 2000.

68. The best account of the rush is Morley Arthur Underwood, "Governor Douglas and the Miners, 1858–1859," B.A. essay, University of British Columbia, 1974.

69. For an opposing view arguing explicitly that there was a "Fraser River War," see Marshall, "Rickard Revisited: Native 'Participation' in the Gold Discoveries of British Columbia." My approach is largely drawn from Vaughan's "Cooperation and Resistance," esp. 43–55.

70. See Vaughan, "Cooperation and Resistance," 54; and Sage, *Sir James Douglas and British Columbia*, 225–28.

71. Hittell, *History of California*, 3:153–55; see also the comments of Jean-Nicolas Perlot, *Gold Seeker: Adventures of a Belgian Argonaut during the Gold Rush Years* (New Haven: Yale University Press, 1985), 359–62. The claim that the richness of the Fraser River gold deposits had been grossly exaggerated provoked several indignant responses: see, for example, Alfred Waddington, *The Fraser Mines Vindicated, or, The History of Four Months* (Victoria: P. de Garro, 1858); and R. C. Lundin Brown, *British Columbia, An Essay* (New Westminster BC: Royal Engineer Press, 1863). Note also the comments of James Bell, in a letter dated February 27, 1859, reprinted in "Gold-Rush Days in Victoria, 1858–1859," *British Columbia Historical Quarterly* 12, no. 3 (July 1948): 244. It is worth noting that some early commentators similarly described the California rush as a "miserable delusion, a magnificent humbug": see Jocelyn Maynard Ghent, "The Golden Dream and the Press: Illinois and the California Gold Rush of '49," *Journal of the West* 17, no. 2 (April 1978): 25.

72. The gold rushes in British Columbia have not attracted much scholarly attention. The best published studies are Trimble's *Mining Advance into the Inland Empire*; Gordon R. Elliott, *Barkerville, Quesnel and the Cariboo Gold Rush*, 2nd ed. (Vancouver: Douglas & McIntyre, 1978); and Sylvia Van Kirk, "A Vital Presence: Women in the Cariboo Gold Rush, 1862–1875," in *British Columbia Reconsidered: Essays on Women,* ed. Gillian Creese and Veronica Strong-Boag (Vancouver: Press Gang, 1992), 21–37. Netta Sterne assembled some excellent detail in her recent book, *Fraser Gold 1858! The Founding of British Columbia* (Pullman: Washington State University Press, 1998), although the critique by Dan Marshall is largely warranted: *BC Studies* 123 (autumn 1999): 95–97. A number of contemporary accounts of the Cariboo gold rush have been reissued; see, for example, *For Friends At Home: A Scottish Emigrant's Letters from Canada, California and the Cariboo, 1844–1864*, ed. Richard Arthur Preston (Montreal: McGill-Queen's University Press, 1974), esp. 259–313; W. Champness, *To Cariboo and Back in 1862* (Fairfield WA: Ye Galleon Press, 1972); Thomas McMicking, *Overland From Canada to British Columbia*, ed. Joanne Leduc (Vancouver: University of British Columbia Press, 1981). Richard Thomas Wright's popularly written *Overlanders* (Saskatoon, Sask.: Western Producer Prairie Books, 1985), describes the experiences of those who undertook the trek west across Canada to British Columbia. Little work has been done on the Fraser River gold rush since the early studies by Bancroft, Howay, and Sage. There are three excellent unpublished pieces: Underwood's "Governor Douglas and the Miners, 1858–1859"; Vaughan's "Cooperation and Resistance: Indian-European Relations on the Mining

Frontier in British Columbia, 1835–1858," 43–58; and, most recently, Dan Marshall's "Claiming the Land: Indians, Goldseekers, and the Rush to British Columbia."

73. May, "Gold Rushes," 100.

74. C. E. Houghton, in the General Report, New Zealand, *Appendices to the Journals of the House of Representatives*, 1876, H-3, p. 1. Thirty years later a government booklet on British Columbia's mines elaborated on this point: "[T]he placer is the "poor man's mine"; he needs little or no capital to work it; its product is cash, to all intents and purposes, and he is his own master—all attractions too great for the sturdy independence of the prospector to allow him to think of searching for lode mines, which, when found, require so much capital to work them as to leave but very small interest in the property with the original owner." *British Columbia, The Mineral Province of Canada, being a Short History of Mining in the Province, a Synopsis of the Mining Laws in Force, Statistics of Mineral Production to Date, and a Brief Summary of the Progress of Mining during 1906* (Victoria, 1907), 7.

75. For a detailed examination of this point, looking at the copper mining industry, see Logan Hovis and Jeremy Mouat, "Miners, Engineers, and the Transformation of Work in the Western Mining Industry, 1880–1930," *Technology and Culture* 37, no. 3 (July 1996): 429–56.

76. J. A. La Nauze, "The Gold Rushes and Australian Politics," *Australian Journal of Politics and History* 13, no. 1 (May 1967): 94. La Nauze was writing to counter the arguments of those who sought to discount the impact of the gold rushes on Australia.

77. See the entry on Vogel by Raewyn Dalziel in the *Dictionary of New Zealand Biography* (Wellington: Allen & Unwin/Dept. of Internal Affairs, 1990), 563–66; also, her book-length biography, *Julius Vogel: Business Politician* (Auckland: Auckland University Press, 1986). For Seddon, see R. M. Burdon, *King Dick: A Biography of Richard John Seddon* (Christchurch: Whitcombe & Tombs, 1955); and more generally David Hamer, *The New Zealand Liberals: The Years of Power, 1891–1912* (Auckland: Auckland University Press, 1988). The impact of the New Zealand gold rushes is discussed generally in Geoffrey W. Rice, ed., *The Oxford History of New Zealand*, 2nd ed. (Auckland: Oxford University Press, 1992); cf. the comments in James Belich, *Making Peoples: A History of New Zealanders From Polynesian Settlement to the End of the Nineteenth Century* (Auckland: Allen Lane/Penguin, 1996), 345–49, 369–71.

78. Curiously, British Columbia's political history during and after the gold rushes has attracted little attention, but see W. N. Sage, "From Colony to Province: The Introduction of Responsible Government in British Columbia," *British Columbia Historical Quarterly* 3, no. 1 (January 1939): 1–14; and W. George Shelton, ed., *British Columbia and Confederation* (Victoria BC: Morriss Printing, 1967), especially the essays by H. Robert Kendrick, "Amor de Cosmos and Confederation;" Olive

Fairholm, "John Robson and Confederation;" and Brian Smith, "The Confederation Delegation."

79. Goodman, *Gold Seeking*, 25. For a succinct argument about the impact of nineteenth-century liberalism, see Ian McKay, "The Liberal Order Framework: A Prospectus for a Reconnaissance of Canadian History," *Canadian Historical Review* 81, no. 4 (December 2000): 617–45.

12

From Gold Pans to California Dredges

The Search for Mass Production in Placer Mining

Clark C. Spence

Most forty-niners brought with them to California little in the way of technological baggage. At first, California placer mining was an individual kind of effort, requiring relatively little outlay of capital but substantial investment of labor. Gold found in the beds and along the banks and bars of watercourses could be recovered by simple methods using simple equipment—pans, rockers, long toms, or sluices, which seemed straight out of the pages of Agricola's *De re metallica*, published in 1556.[1] But the day of hand mining passed quickly. Reachable deposits soon became exhausted, usually in a year or two, and the pioneer miners were left frustrated, facing hard choices. If they didn't give up the pursuit of precious metal altogether or go to work as day laborers, they might search for the source of the free gold washed into the streambeds and hope to locate the quartz-embedded veins whence it came. But even if they found a quartz outcropping, it was arduous and expensive work to follow the veins underground. The work required more and more capital for tunneling, timbering, ventilating, blasting ore, transporting it underground, and hoisting it to the surface. Moreover, gold in hard-rock ores was often difficult to remove, "refractory" in the language of the mining engineers. At a minimum, quartz ores had to be crushed and amalgamated with quicksilver. In the worst cases, they might be locked in combination with other elements, in which case more intricate and costly processes would be needed. In short, lode mining was for corporate, not individual, effort except on a three-dollar-per-day wage basis.

Alternatives included devising new means of working the deeper placer deposits, located in ground beyond the reach of individual miners or, indeed, beyond the technological limits of the early gold seekers. One approach almost from the beginning was river mining, in which miners, usually groups of them working together, built wing dams and diverted the streams through bypass flumes long enough to work the beds by conventional sluicing methods. River mining was something of a "mass production" effort but was limited by seasonal flooding and cold weather, and it rarely reached the deeper gold.[2]

Another approach, hydraulic mining, added a more sophisticated modern twist to an ancient Roman technique described by Pliny the Elder in the first century. Devised by Connecticut Yankee Edward Matteson in 1853, hydraulic mining has been likened basically to directing a fire hose against a sand pile. By dropping a stream from a small reservoir above the mining site through a rawhide or canvas hose, miners could shoot a powerful head of water under strong pressure from a pivoting nozzle (a monitor) and literally wash away the sides of a gravel bank, with the gold-bearing dirt then run through a long sluice for recovery of its gold. Available water and hilly terrain were prerequisites, and the initial expense of setting up hydraulicking equipment did require a significant financial outlay. But operating expenses were low. Eventually, because of the destructive impact of river-borne mining debris, which was engulfing farmlands downstream, legal restrictions on hydraulicking in 1884 all but eliminated it as a serious mode of gold mining in the state.[3]

One remaining alternative was to contrive a new technology to handle the deeper gravels efficiently in large quantities, applying the economies of scale. Such equipment was usually lumped under the name "dredge," but for many this was a generic term that might mean any of a number of mechanical systems that involved digging auriferous gravel, separating the gold from it, and discarding the waste. Caisson mining, suction equipment, and steam shovels fell into that category. So did the dragline. If it had a single bucket suspended by a chain or cable from the end of a swing boom, it was a grab dredge. If the boom held a two-part bucket, it was a clamshell. Three- or four-piece scoops made it an orange-peel dredge.

The style of dredge that emerged preeminent was the bucket-line or connected-bucket dredge, which fitted the boom with an endless chain of heavy buckets to bring up the gold-bearing dirt from deeply buried deposits. Bucket-line dredges had first been used for cleaning canals in the Netherlands as early as 1623. Steam power had been applied in England in 1790, and by the mid-nineteenth century such equipment was commonly used to clear harbors and rivers in most parts of the world. But dredge technology still awaited adaptation to meet the difficult physical challenges in the California gold fields.

In California and in the American West generally, the search for new placer-mining technologies proceeded piecemeal and haphazardly. Individual inventors, both serious and crackpot, experimented with various pieces of "jackass machinery" that for nearly half a century failed to achieve success. Innovative tinkering brought its first rewards in the late 1890s, when designs of successful New Zealand dredges made their way to California, where they were wedded to features of an indigenous rig from Montana. The result of this hybrid design effort became the standard "California-type" dredge, a clever, sophisticated machine that combined efficient excavation of gravels, separation of gold from the gravel, and deposition of processed waste in its wake.

In the meantime, early Pacific Coast miners sought shortcuts—mass production techniques that would simplify and speed up gold mining and recovery at lower costs per unit of gold-producing ground. As would be true in later rushes, the California Argonauts all too willingly fell prey to sharp promoters, blood brothers of the snake-oil salesmen, who hawked "sure fire" contraptions that they guaranteed to reclaim precious metal with minimal effort. Onlookers described the "newfangled machines" shipped to the American River after the news of the northern California gold discovery reached the East. "They were of all imaginable shapes and sizes," wrote one observer, "some of them appearing most admirably adapted to the churning of butter." Others were not so small. Edward Buffum reported the spectacle presented by "hundreds of huge, bulky machines, which had been brought round Cape Horn, and which would require, each one of them, a large ox-team to convey them to the mining region, lying piled upon the beach of San Francisco, destined never to fulfill the object for which they were intended." Yet Buffum, something of a visionary, could foresee clearly the exhaustion of surface mining, when large-scale mining would continue. "Powerful steam machines," he predicted, "are to be set in operation for the purpose of tearing up the rocks, and separating the gold from them" and gold-bearing ground would be reworked and "re-washed in more scientifically constructed apparatus."[4]

On the South Fork of the American River in 1849–1850, the Englishman William Kelley saw some Kanakas (Hawaiians), "perhaps the most expert divers in the world . . . go down and bring up fine chunks, which suggested the construction of a dredging machine; but," Kelley explained, "it could not be got to work with effect, from the inequities of the bottom. Diving bells were also thought of," he added, "but I never saw any in use."[5]

Southerners sought to import techniques that they had heard of or were familiar with at home. At Rattlesnake Bar on the American River's North Fork, for example, a group of Georgians in 1852 had built a big scow, to be equipped with large digging shovels—"spoons long enough to sup with the devil," one onlooker noted.[6] More primitive versions of the so-called spoon dredge had been used in Georgia and would catch on in New Zealand during the 1860s. California experiments with the same type of technology, adapted best to areas free of boulders and lacking swift streamflows, would be sporadic and less lucrative.

Perhaps it was a miner from below the Mason-Dixon Line who had suggested the diving apparatus. In Georgia in the valley of the Chestatee, early in the 1830s, United States senator and former vice president John C. Calhoun had financed a steamboat with a diving bell attached, a rig that supposedly "proved successful" in gleaning gold from the river near Auraria. This experimental operation caught the romanticist's attention:

Wend you to the Mines and see,
The various things for your temptation,
Stand on the banks of the Chestatee,
Where the Diving bell's in operation.
Wend you to the pearly stream,
Where your eyes must be delighted,
Then of golden streets you'll dream,
If perchance you get benighted.[7]

Another early eyewitness to the California scene, James Delavan, thought "submarine armor and the diving bell" preferable to other approaches. "As experience has proven . . . ," he wrote, "these have been used to much advantage; but whether they can long be profitable instruments" in California mining "is very doubtful."[8] To what extent such underwater methods had been tried in the early placer era is uncertain; later years saw renewed but futile efforts.

At the same time, in 1850, while heading downstream from Sacramento, Delavan "met a steam dredging machine, urged upward by a screw propeller, to be used in mining operations." "In my opinion," he stated, "it is hardly possible for such a machine to be used to any advantage, as it can only operate in sandy or muddy soils, and not in the rocky beds of the rivers where most of the gold is found." Experience had taught him that "the only sure modes of obtaining adequate reward for labor will be by draining the bars, by diverting the river from its channels."[9]

Delavan no doubt was describing the *Linda*, one of the first two California dredges that actually materialized. (A third, a dredge "of most interesting design," was the work of a French group, La Torson d'Or, which published an illustration of the machine in 1850 but probably never shipped it to the gold fields.)[10] In 1849 the Linda Company of Boston fitted out a brig and carried on board a small, knocked-down, flat-bottomed steamer, with attending dredge gear. Its owners assembled the steam vessel—the *Linda*—at Sacramento and for several years ran it between this city and Marysville. Apparently the dredge, with its thirty-two-horsepower engine, remained untested until the spring of 1850, when several Californians became interested enough to raise twenty-five thousand dollars to take it over from the New Englanders. Once fitted out for dredging, the vessel headed for Ousley's Bar on the Yuba above Marysville. To help defray costs, she also carried a few passengers and a load of wheat. Unfortunately, a few miles north of Sacramento the *Linda* struck a snag, and her cargo shifted with disastrous results. All too soon investors learned, as one of them put it, "that damn dredge has gone to the bottom."[11]

To raise and refit "that damn dredge" cost about eight thousand dollars, but eventually the *Linda* reached Ousley's Bar, where it worked for several months without much profit, although one clean-up totaled about twelve hundred dollars. The machine was a variant of a spoon dredge, with a scoop at the end of a boom arm that lifted and dumped gravel into a series of sluices. Like much early equipment, the apparatus proved too light to handle the boulders or even the heavy clays in the California river bottoms, and this first operating dredge ended a discouraging failure. Investor Almarin Paul, a knowledgeable and experienced mining man, chalked it up to experience. "I entered about $7000 to profit and loss," he later recalled, "and wiped dredging from my mind."[12]

A second gold dredge also came aboard ship around the Horn in 1849, this one sent to California by a New York firm. The New York boat, its classical name misspelled *Phenix*, appears in illustrations to have been a sternwheeler. According to contemporaries, it was equipped with an endless chain of scoops to bring up gravel that was dumped into a rocker-washer arrangement, with screens to separate the material and a so-called Bogardus patent amalgamator to catch the gold with quicksilver. The story of the *Phenix* sounds much like that of the *Linda*, so much so that it is difficult to separate the short histories of the two. Some of the same investors were involved in both; both dredges were supposed to have been sunk and refitted; both were said to have worked the deposits at Ousley's Bar without success. As one historian wrote later, "It was soon found . . . that this machine dredged more money from the pockets of the owners than it did gold from the bed of the Yuba, and this kind of mining was soon abandoned." The proprietors of the *Phenix* spent twenty-eight thousand dollars on the enterprise and assessed shareholders even more, but the machine took out a mere one hundred dollars in gold, and trustees put the vessel up at auction. In February 1851, another group organized the Linda Steam Dredging Company, offering a hundred shares for sale, and ordered new machinery for the *Linda*, but the dismal showing of the *Phenix* put an end to the project.[13]

In the eyes of J. Ross Browne, early commissioner for collection of mineral statistics for the federal government, such episodes reflected the typical ignorance of eastern entrepreneurs. Such men "had never seen a placer mine," declared Browne, and they lacked any understanding of the nature of gold deposits in northern California's riverbeds and bars. Nonetheless, they sent untested equipment to dig the bottom of the Yuba, never questioning whether the stream was deep enough in the summer to float such a machine, or whether the tough clay and gravel in its bed could be dug up by a dredger, and entirely ignorant of the fact that the gold is mostly in the crevices of bedrock where the spoon and knife of the skillful and attentive miner would be necessary for cleaning out the richest pockets.[14]

From these inauspicious early beginnings, nearly half a century would elapse before truly successful dredge operations began in the California gold fields. For a time, while dredge technology remained still in its infancy, the profitability of large-scale river mining and hydraulic mining diverted capital and perhaps blunted the quest for a more efficient mechanical approach. Success in dredging depended on stronger, better-constructed machinery, cleverly designed to handle the peculiar problems of the western placer fields; greater knowledge of the gold deposits themselves; and improved gold recovery methods.[15]

Trial and error prevailed, on the part both of experienced technical people and of fly-by-night humbugs, and a good deal of capital vanished in the process. In 1872, when one group formed a company in San Francisco to work the rich gold sands off the California and Oregon coasts with a diving bell and a vacuum pump, the well-versed editor of the *Engineering and Mining Journal* suggested that the sands be raised by the steam-driven pump alone.[16] A few years later California newspapers were enthusiastic about a "New Mining Machine" costing ten thousand dollars that worked remarkably well in the river near Oroville. Probably this was the dredge designed by A. J. Severance, acquired for stock by a group of New Englanders and installed on the Feather River, only to be attached for debt after a short, futile run.[17]

Soon after this fiasco, in 1878 two new dredging companies—organized to use the latest state-of-the-art equipment—received a good deal of local publicity. One, the Camanche Gravel Mining Company, reportedly owned "vast deposits of auriferous gravel" near Camanche, twenty-five miles north-west of Stockton. These untapped riches, a credulous reporter declared, had been "discovered by means of Howland's Metallurgical Indicator," which not only determined "the precise location of the precious metals, but the particular kind, the extent and nearly the approximate value." The other firm, the Pacific Dredging and Mining Company, was nominally capitalized at $500,000 to work supposed rich deposits at Union Island in the Delta region of San Joaquin County. Both outfits were committed to use E. F. Dennison's patented "Ingurgitator Dredge," a steam-driven system of vacuum pumps floated on a barge to raise the gravel.[18] Neither operation showed any staying power.

Equally flamboyant was the so-called tube boat built for the American River Dredging and Mining Company in 1879. Apparently there were several of these "celebrated Daniel Moor's dredging machines," one working on the Feather River below Oroville, one designed for a location near Auburn, and a half-sized working model demonstrated in western Montana. Built on an eighty-by-thirty-foot hull, the Oroville rig resembled a floating sawmill in appearance. Its forty-horsepower steam engine warranted a tall smokestack and a large boiler. Sluices ran the full length of the deck, while over the bow hung an iron cylinder, forty-five feet long and three feet in diameter, fitted with a reversible valve-type door in the distant end. Hoisting gear lowered the tube to the riverbed, where it was filled with injected steam, which was then condensed with jets of cold water. The resulting drop in pressure created a vacuum, which forced sand and gravel into the tube through the reversible door. At this point the steam engine hoisted up the cylinder and swung it over the deck, where its contents would be dumped into the sluices. Seven men were required for the operation, which reportedly could handle about four hundred cubic yards of dirt per day. Even so, the rig recovered too little gold, and its backers soon discontinued the enterprise.[19]

At least the idea of using a large cylinder to be periodically brought to the top and emptied of its gravel could be thought feasible. About the same time, Rossiter W. Raymond, one of the country's foremost mining engineers, solidly endorsed adaptation to mining of a new East Coast harbor dredge that operated on this principle.[20]

During the 1880s, California dredge efforts multiplied. There were six in 1882 alone, although critics sniped away whenever a new enterprise was announced, whether it be on the Pacific Coast, in the Rockies, or in the Georgia Piedmont. Did not mining men ever learn from the mistakes of the early dredgers? As one faultfinder emphatically asserted, gold dredging "is always a most promising method to those who are ignorant of its history. There is only one difficulty connected with it—it has never been known to pay in the past; it does not pay now; and the chances are, that it never will pay."[21]

Some of the failed experiments were technically not dredges, although newspaper writers and other commentators used this label as a generic description. Early in 1886, J. J. Robinson, a civil engineer of some local renown, devised a pneumatic caisson plant at Oroville to tap gold deposits along the Feather River. Sinking heavy iron tubes into the river, he pumped in air at ten pounds per square inch and sent down miners—either quite brave or extremely desperate men—to work the gravel. The method may have been sound; but the necessary air pressure could not be maintained as the work went deeper, and so the operation had to be abandoned.[22]

Some, like the abortive suction dredge operation at Robinson's Ferry on the Stanislaus in 1887, were simply variations of earlier approaches, financed in this instance by Chicago capital. The Kise brothers' machine on the Trinity River, which began construction that same year, was apparently a bucket-line dredge. Sounding "like a four-horse gravel wagon on a rocky bar," according to one contemporary, it finally started up late in 1889 after many tribulations. But its owners and its San Francisco backer were denied a prosperous run when a raging storm and flood destroyed the rig early that winter.[23]

Still another type of apparatus achieved some success in the mid-1890s— the orange-peel dredge, so called because of its single bucket of four segments, operated by a dragline. At least one orange-peel dredge was at work in 1886 and two were active in the summer of 1887 at the Arroyo Seco mine, on the property of the A. D. Ranch near Amador, digging ground under a long-term lease from a railroad company. Their buckets carried a normal load of two cubic yards and were swung by booms 114 feet long. They dug to a depth of thirty feet, first removing and piling the overburden, then moving pay dirt to long sluices, through which pumps kept the water running. In the summer of 1887, with a crew that numbered from twenty-five to thirty whites and even more Chinese, all working in two shifts, this Amador County operation reportedly produced from eight thousand to twelve thousand dollars a month. With their machinery housed, each of these units could be shifted ahead on heavy sills, much as a house was normally moved along the street. This operation apparently was more than the usual experiment; it remained active for several years and produced profits for its investors.[24]

Also among the handful of dredge operators in the 1890s were the Distelhorst brothers, who started dredging the upper Sacramento River in 1894 "with very satisfactory results," and who continued profitably at least until the summer of 1898. Four of their rigs worked during the 1896 season on the Sacramento and another on the Klamath. Descriptions indicate that some of the Distelhorst rigs were outfitted with draglines to pull scrapers in and out of the stream, using an intricate cable system and two towers connected by an overhead cable—probably a variation of the Lidgerwood Radial Cableway manufactured in New York. One of the rigs in Siskiyou County had three hulls joined together to form a floating base thirty by sixty-five feet, with a twenty-horsepower steam engine. Its iron scrapers, each weighing half a ton, could handle one thousand cubic yards of gravel every twenty-four hours at a daily working cost of eighteen dollars. On the other hand, the Distelhorst machine on the Klamath River near Quigley's was a spoon dredge. The spoon was a large iron and steel scoop weighing about nineteen hundred pounds, which dropped into the river through an opening in the bottom of the hull, to then be hoisted by donkey engine and dump its gravel into a perforated grizzly located just over the sluice boxes on board the dredge. Construction of this dredge cost between seven thousand and eight thousand dollars. It ran day and night, operated by a crew of five men, in 1896 raising six hundred cubic yards a day that yielded on average about ten cents a yard. One of the bedrock scrapers cleaned up about twenty thousand dollars in 1896. During the 1898 season, the same dredge was taking out five hundred dollars a day.[25]

The success of the Distelhorst brothers inspired other dredge enterprises, among them the Gold Sand Placer Mining Company, organized in 1895 by four Oaklanders to operate along the American and Feather Rivers. Under the supervision of General George B. Tolman, a veteran forty-eighter, the group converted a stern-wheel steamer and outfitted her with an endless chain of buckets. Each bucket held one gallon of dirt that dumped into a screen hopper, with the gravel then being washed into one of A. C. Rumble's Gold King amalgamators to separate the gold. But the bucket-line approach apparently did not work for Tolman and his associates, who abandoned it in favor of a clamshell bucket.[26] The New Era Mining Company put a bucket dredge on the Yuba River near Brown's Valley. The Tortillata Gold Mining Company received a charter to dredge above Keswick on the Sacramento River. The Shasta Dredging Company also incorporated to dredge somewhere in California; and Samuel Theller bought the rights to Alphonzo Bower's suction dredge, proposing trials for the machine as soon as possible.[27]

The 1890s were years of cautious optimism for placer mining in northern California. Supporters of the various unsuccessful California dredging ventures failed to build on previous efforts, but they were not operating in total ignorance. They must have known something of the technological progress that had been made in New Zealand and to a lesser extent in the Transbaikal region of Siberia, although experts were surprised that the transition of ideas from "down under" was not felt in California until the end of the nineties—especially since miners with California experience had played an important role in New Zealand placer mining and early dredging there.[28]

Like their counterparts on the Pacific Coast, New Zealand mine operators had experimented with a variety of dredge machinery—including Welman's suction dredge, Parke's combination dredge, Priestman's grab-and-cataract pump, the Ball dredger, Taylor's "dry-land" dredge, and even Villaine's novel "gold-fishing" submarine, the "Platypus," none of which proved any more effective than their counterparts in California.[29]

At the same time, New Zealanders were pursuing more promising ideas, with a clear continuity in their development. As early as the 1860s, they were profitably using small spoon dredges in rich spots on the Clutha (or Molyneux) River. The first were very similar to the contraptions used by the ancient Chinese and Assyrians and later by western Europeans for clearing canals. They began with primitive iron rings to which was riveted a rawhide bag, the whole being attached to the end of a long pole aboard a sturdy boat and dragged along the river bottom by means of a rope. The New Zealanders added a hand-powered windlass to lift and dump the contents of the dredge bags or early buckets into rockers or sluice boxes. Next they attached pontoons to the dredge for stability and added an auxiliary scow to hold the washing apparatus. Some of these outfits were powered by wheels driven by the current of the swift-moving river, but by about 1870 a crude steam-driven spoon dredge had proved successful on the richer bars.[30] One of the next stages was to lift gravel from the river bed by an endless chain of buckets, which were also energized by current wheels. By 1877 at least six of these rigs were at work along the Clutha, paying their way "handsomely."[31] The next, inevitable advance came in 1881: the substitution of steam power for current-wheel power, first in Scott's rig at Muttontown Gully, then Charles McQueen's iron leviathan with dual bucket lines (later reduced to one), which managed to take out fifteen thousand ounces of gold over a sixteen-year period. The apparent profitability of Scott and McQueen's ventures touched off a flurry of dredge building. By March 1889, forty-nine gold dredges were at work in New Zealand, almost all of them on South Island. Otago had thirteen at that time, of which only two were current wheelers.[32] The New Zealand dredging boom from 1889 to 1892, declared one authority, was "a shaft of light on the clouded economic scene," the so-called long depression that characterized the three decades after 1865.[33] The number of dredges rose steadily: 36 in 1893; 84 in 1895, the year the first successful American gold dredge was launched; and 236 by 1900. The vast majority of these dredges were steam-powered, and 80 percent of them operated in Otago. A few were on the western coastal sands, some were along the Waikaia River, and a few others could be found on the Shotover, where Chinese entrepreneur Sew Hoy had remarkable success on ground that others had already worked over three times. But most of these machines were digging into the gold-bearing gravels along the Clutha River itself, where observers counted fifty-seven dredges at work on one seventy-mile stretch in 1896.[34]

Along with the increase in sheer numbers came an improvement of dredge equipment. Revolving sizing-screens separated the fines—the finely granulated auriferous soil—from larger material. W. H. Cutten's tailings elevator disposed of waste, stronger bucket ladders extended digging depth, and larger buckets increased capacity. More sophisticated mooring winches and gold-saving sluices or shaking tables became standard. Soon electricity began to replace steam power, with the advantage of variable-speed motors for different aspects of dredge operation.[35] Over the years, one improvement built upon another, in a way that did not happen in California, although it remained true in New Zealand that advances in gold-saving equipment always lagged behind improvements in the digging mechanisms.

American mining periodicals carried detailed information on dredges down under, noting profits and reflecting optimism for the future. As the editor of *The Engineering and Mining Journal* noted in 1889, past successes were leading to more powerful and perfect dredges. "We may expect," he predicted, "to learn from New Zealand a great deal with respect to this comparatively little-known branch of the gold industry."[36] Within less than a decade this prediction would be amply fulfilled.

Enter onto the Pacific Coast mining scene Robert H. Postlethwaite, a Dunedin, New Zealand, electrical and mechanical engineer who brought to California considerable experience with dredges. Thomas J. Barbour of the Risdon Iron Works in San Francisco later recalled that a few California mining men, including Thomas Couch of Butte and Wendell P. Hammon, an Oroville orchardman with a vision of mechanizing placer mining, had sought information on gold dredging and on builders and designers to put such a machine on ground in Butte County. According to Barbour, Risdon was aware of New Zealand's leadership in the field. He sent a representative there to examine dredge equipment and concluded that Postlethwaite's dredge designs seemed the most satisfactory of those inspected.[37] In 1896 Risdon enticed Postlethwaite to join his firm, where the newcomer laid out plans and built the *Archimedes*, a single-lift, steam-powered dredge with three-cubic-foot buckets designed to dig to a depth of twenty-five feet. Set to work in the Yuba River near Smartsville in 1897, the rig showed great promise until it was wrecked during flood season and never reclaimed.[38]

Postlethwaite's presence was important. He was a leader, a booster of dredging, and he came fortified with ideas and technical know-how based on years of experience. When Hammon and Couch decided to go ahead with a dredge on the Feather River, it was Postlethwaite who designed it and Risdon who built it and supervised its first operations in 1898. Some modern writers, unfortunately, have ignored the New Zealander's role completely, erroneously crediting Hammon with taking the design concept from Bucyrus-built machines in Chicago. One jingoistic Oroville editor noted only that prior to Hammon "an attempt at dredging had been made in a crude manner in New Zealand."[39]

In any event, Postlethwaite's second dredge—the Hammon-Couch boat—launched a large-scale dredging boom that totally revolutionized the California placer industry at the turn of the century. With backing from the Lewisohn Brothers, Hammon and Couch's Feather River Exploration Company added additional dredgers and prospered. Hammon became the undisputed king of California dredging, not only with countless machines in the field, but also because of his expertise in their manufacture. Close behind came dozens of other entrepreneurs. A flourishing new industry had been born and would rapidly expand along the Yuba, the Feather, the American, the Trinity, and other northern California rivers, and into the rich ancient beds of gold-bearing dry gravels found in half a dozen California counties.[40]

While Californians like to claim the first successful gold dredge in the United States, that honor goes to Montana. In Bannack, where the Montana gold rush had its start in 1863, the Bucyrus-built *Fielding L. Graves* was christened with a bottle of champagne and slid gently into the waters of Grasshopper Creek in the spring of 1895. Thus opened the "Dawn of a New Era of Placer Mining Methods," according to a local editor.[41] Electrically operated from its own power plant on shore, the *Graves* was a double-lift bucket-ladder rig; the gravel was raised by the buckets and dumped into a rotary grizzly, whence the finer dirt was carried by a second bucket ladder to a higher level and, with water coming from a centrifugal pump, washed into long sluice boxes suspended by cables on land. After a mediocre initial season, its operators rebuilt the *Graves* with larger buckets, improved pumps, and pontoon-held sluices. Its good showing in 1896 then established it as "the basic model for many dredges built thereafter."[42]

How much the design of the *Graves* drew upon the New Zealand experience is not clear. Samuel Harper, the man who interested Chicago backers in the dredge, "no doubt received some information from New Zealand," according to the company's first president. Tradition has it that Harper got the idea after watching the machines building Chicago's drainage canal. The story has one problem: experts agree that a variety of digging equipment helped construct the waterway, but contend that "the endless chain bucket or ladder dredges, so much used on the [eastern] seaboard, were not employed here at all."[43]

It is clear that Thomas Couch and others associated with Wendell Hammon at Oroville knew of the *Fielding L. Graves*, and they had also consulted harbor dredge specialists from New York. It is equally clear that the first few Risdon bucket dredges bore the New Zealand stamp. By 1900, Risdon's firm had produced at least seventeen rigs for California operators; by 1909, two years before it was absorbed by Union Iron Works, the company had turned out fifty-four California dredges to meet growing demands from all parts of the world. Bucyrus of Milwaukee had built an even dozen machines by the turn of the century, half of them for Montana, and constructed an additional sixty-one by 1910.[44] Soon, other dredge builders—among them Marion Steam Shovel Company of Ohio, Link-Belt Company of Chicago, Vulcan Iron Works of Toledo, New York Engineering Company, and Wendell Hammon's Yuba Construction Company—were busy turning out hundreds of placer dredges for the global market. With the great gold dredging boom underway, California was its center, and its experts took the lead in fashioning a unique "California-type dredge" that became the standard around the world.

The new hybrid emerged gradually, representing a blending and enrichment of the technology developed on the Clutha and the Shotover Rivers in New Zealand with what had been initiated on Grasshopper Creek in Montana. The cumbersome double-lift arrangement of the Bannack boats gave way to the single-lift system of Postlethwaite's early design, in which the bucket line carried the gravel to its highest point, thereby eliminating the need for a second elevation. Close-connected buckets of special steel replaced the open-connected type championed by Postlethwaite, with the advantage that, linked one to another, they caught material loosened and dropped by previous buckets. The four-sided upper tumblers, large sprockets to power the bucket line, now became pentagonal, hexagonal, or even round. Eventually they were cast in one piece, body and shaft together, in units weighing as much as twenty tons. The smaller lower tumblers that kept the line in place at the bottom of the digging ladder evolved with a new type of steel alloy flanges and bearings for sustained underwater use and conditions of high abrasion. First high-carbon, then chrome, vanadium, and especially manganese and nickel steel combinations came into use to lengthen the life of bucket-line parts subject to heavy wear. If the digging mechanism evolved more rapidly than the gold-recovery equipment, time brought improved scrubbing and screening devices, huge revolving screens or trommels washed by jets of water; but the banks of gold-saving tables, which had replaced the New Zealand shaking screen, remained the most primitive part of the apparatus.[45]

Because of the heavy river boulders and rough terrain in which they dug, California-type dredges needed to be heavier and stronger. Their designers abandoned the down-under system of headlines to keep the boat in position and relied instead on steel-pointed spuds—massive posts dropped into the soil that provided a pivot around which the dredge could swing while its buckets removed a cut of gravel. To discharge the tailings, the belt stacker became standard except in parts of Alaska and Montana, where flumes were used, and on the early Risdon dredges, which handled debris with bucket conveyors. In time, metal hulls and pontoon construction replaced the beautifully crafted wooden bottoms that had been skillfully fashioned by shipbuilders.[46] Low cost and the versatility of variable speed motors made electricity the preferred source of power for the new-style dredges, although isolation from hydroelectric dams often forced the use of steam or internal combustion engines.[47]

The new tough, efficient, crossbreed machines meant that mining men could now work the deeper gravels, heretofore unreachable. Eventually dredges would dig 150-feet deep to reach pay dirt. Moreover, low-grade gravels with no higher gold value than eight to ten cents per cubic yard now became profitable to work under the right circumstances, while ground earlier worked by hand, first by white miners and again by Chinese, could return fresh dividends. Following specific advice from Robert Postlethwaite, dredge operators learned also to abandon the rivers themselves and float their dredges in pits "inland," away from the river bars, bringing in water by ditches and pumps as required. In addition, the dredge brought a measure of predictability to placer operations. As Postlethwaite pointed out in 1899, the use of the Keystone drill to dig test holes before sinking substantial capital into machinery or property gave the dredge operator an excellent projection of his eventual outtake of precious metal, estimates that in many instances were remarkably accurate.[48]

By the turn of the century, it was clear that placer mining was about to be transformed. In 1900, 16 gold dredges were at work in California, 6 in Idaho, and 5 in Montana, producing a total of more than $520,000 in gold. In 1914, there were 120 dredges in operation—60 in California, 42 in Alaska, 5 in Colorado, 5 in Montana, 4 in Idaho, and 4 elsewhere in the West. Of the $12,512,783 worth of gold dredged that year, according to federal statistics, California accounted for more than half, $7,783,394. In 1911 dredges produced 38.84 percent of all gold mined and 85.32 percent of all placer gold in California. Nine years later, the California dredge fleet was responsible for 51 percent of all gold recovered and 98 percent of all the placer gold mined in the state.[49]

Gold dredging became a global industry, although American manufacturers predominated. Heavy equipment companies, spread across the country from San Francisco to New York, produced dredges for markets near and far. Wherever built or wherever used, the California-type dredge (sometimes called the Yuba-type) came to be accepted as the standard of excellence. Of the world's 225 operating dredges at the end of 1915, 166 were in the United States and only 11 were not American-made. By 1940, over 200 bucket-line dredges had been manufactured in California alone, half of them for use within the state. "The California-type dredge, known all over the world," wrote one observer in 1938, "is so efficient that it is being used on every continent where large quantities of low-grade metals are found."[50]

If California was one of the leading producers of gold dredges, it was also a global pool of experienced dredge personnel and regularly provided engineers and dredge men to install and operate California-type dredges the world over. All the while, California continued to be the leading gold-dredging and gold-producing state in the Union.

Already by World War I, gold dredging was big business within the state. Although dredge opportunities ranged from Siskiyou County in the north to Merced County in the south, the great dredging fields lay along the belt where the Sierra slope merges into the valley plain, along three of the largest rivers draining the principal mining region of the state—along the Feather River near Oroville, on the American River near Folsom, and along the Yuba River between Marysville and Smartsville.

Although a number of small operators produced considerable gold, much of these rich fields came to be controlled by three large concerns: Oroville Dredging, Ltd., which was British financed; Natomas Consolidated, which drew its capital from San Francisco; and Yuba Consolidated Gold Fields, a Boston firm.[51] The big three ran multiple dredges, which increased in size, cost, and efficiency with the passage of time. Eventually, dredges came to cost three-quarters of a million dollars or more. Natomas's flagship, No. 1 weighed 2,200 tons and was as large as many ocean freighters. Each of its sixty-five buckets weighted two tons and held sixteen cubic feet. In 1934 the largest of the three companies, Yuba Consolidated Gold Fields, had four huge dredges with eighteen-foot buckets capable of digging to depths of one hundred feet or more, and the firm was building two others. Over its life of sixty-five years, Yuba Consolidated used twenty-two dredges on its property near Marysville, dredging a total of more than a billion cubic yards with a gross return of nearly $138 million. The last of the big dredges, Yuba No. 21, closed down in October 1968, bringing an end to California's dredge era so far as regular operation was concerned. But half a dozen years later it was brought out of mothballs to dig tailings along the Yuba, in an effort to get operating cost figures that might attract capital for a deeper operation.[52]

The California-type dredge brought a revolution in the mining of placer gold everywhere, with a special boost to the economy of California, in the production both of dredges and of precious metal. To be sure, California never again came close to matching its peak gold rush output of 1852: 3,932,631 ounces worth $81,294,700. Production had gradually diminished to about 10 percent of that by World War I, but dredge yield stabilized the level of output and sometimes even boosted it substantially, as in 1940, when it reached nearly 1.5 million ounces.[53]

The California-type bucket dredge applied the spirit of Henry Ford's America to the placer gold fields, and it paralleled another new mass-production technology applied to low-grade porphyry copper by means of steam shovels, huge open pits, and massive concentration plants. In both cases, mining engineers applied the economies of scale to ground that previously could not be worked profitably. In like fashion, ever-changing methods would bring forth in the 1980s new ways of handling low-grade gold ores not amenable to dredging or other existing approaches. The new process of heap leaching was applied first in the desert areas of California and Nevada and soon spread. Heap leaching involved sprinkling or dripping a dilute sodium cyanide solution over immense piles of crushed ore to dissolve the gold and drain the resulting "pregnant" gold-bearing solution into a large plastic-lined pond, whence it was pumped through tanks and chemically treated to remove the gold. Despite environmentalists' concern over the use of deadly cyanide, grand-scale heap leaching enterprises helped the United States produce far more gold in 1993 than in 1852, the previous record year.[54] By the use of technology and scientific methods drawn from a century and a half of experience around the world, the search for mass-production in mining placer gold had reached a new level of success— though not in ways that might be recognized by any of the Argonauts of '49.

Notes

1. For early California placer-mining techniques, see Otis E. Young, Jr., *Western Mining: An Informal Account of Precious-Metals Prospecting, Placering, Lode Mining, and Milling on the American Frontier from Spanish Times to 1893* (Norman: University of Oklahoma Press, 1970), 108–24.

2. Young, *Western Mining*, 114–15. For a good description of river mining as practiced by the Chinese in California, see Randall Rohe, "Chinese River Mining in the West," *Montana, the Magazine of Western History* 46 (autumn 1996): 14–29.

3. Paul, *California Gold*, 152–70. The standard work on the subject is Robert L. Kelley, *Gold vs. Grain: The Hydraulic Mining Controversy in California's Sacramento Valley* (Glendale GA: Arthur H. Clark, 1959).

4. Buffum, *Six Months in the Gold Mines*, 99–100, 107–8, 135–36.

5. William Kelly, *An Excursion to California over the Prairie, Rocky Mountains, and Great Sierra Nevada* (London: Chapman & Hall, 1851), 2:32–33.

6. *Sacramento Daily Union*, June 23, 1852.

7. Fletcher M. Green, "Georgia's Forgotten Industry: Gold Mining," part 2, in *Georgia Historical Quarterly* 29 (September 1935): 217; E. Merton Coulter, *Auraria: The Story of a Georgia Gold-Mining Town* (Athens: University of Georgia Press, 1956), 11. See also David Williams, *The Georgia Gold Rush: Twenty-Niners, Cherokees, and Gold Fever* (Columbia: University of South Carolina Press, 1993).

8. James Delavan, *Notes of California and the Placers: How to Get There and What to do Afterwards* (1850; reprint, Oakland: Biobooks, 1993), 126.

9. Delavan, *Notes of California*, 126

10. Chinard, "When the French Came to California," 309.

11. Almarin B. Paul, in *San Francisco Chronicle*, August 4, 1907; Charles S. Aiken, "Farming for Gold," *Sunset* 23 (December 1909): 652–53; *Mining and Scientific Press* 81 (October 6, 1900): 403.

12. Almarin B. Paul, in *San Francisco Chronicle*, August 4, 1907.

13. Almarin B. Paul, in *San Francisco Chronicle*, August 4, 1907.

14. J. Ross Browne and James W. Taylor, *Reports upon the Mineral Resources of the United States* (Washington DC: GPO, 1867), 20.

15. W. P. Hammon, "Dredge Mining in Butte County," *A Rich Region, Illustrative and Descriptive of the Natural Resources and Development of Butte County* (Oroville CA: Oroville Register Office, 1899), 52. Copy in Charles Romanowitz Papers, Elmer E. Rasmusen Library, University of Alaska, Fairbanks.

16. *Engineering and Mining Journal* 14 (August 27, 1872): 138.

17. *Sacramento Record-Union*, June 20, 1877; R. G. Dun California Book 19, p. 243, Harvard School of Business Library, Boston.

18. *The Engineer of the Pacific* (San Francisco) 1 (June 1878): 2–3; 2 (June 30, 1879): 8.

19. *San Francisco Bulletin*, November 11, 1878; *The Engineer of the Pacific* 2 (June 30, 1879): 8; *Helena Daily Herald*, March 1, 1879; Anna Morrison Reid, "The Gold Dredging Era," *Overland Monthly* 39 (June 1902): 990.

20. Rossiter W. Raymond, "A New Method of Dredging, Applicable to Some Kinds of Mining Operations," *Transactions of the American Institute of Mining Engineers* 8 (1879–1880): 254, 257–58.

21. Anna Morrison Reid, "The Gold Dredging Era," *Overland Monthly* 39 (June 1902): 990; *Mining and Scientific Press* 41 (October 23, 1880): 264; "A. W." to editor, *Engineering and Mining Journal* 35 (June 23, 1883): 360.

22. *Mining and Scientific Press* 74 (June 12, 1897): 496–97; Reid, "The Gold Dredging Era," 991.

23. *Hailey, Idaho Wood River Times*, April 6, 1887; Commodore C. Kise, "Dredges Along the Trinity," *Trinity* (Weaverville CA: Yearbook of the Trinity County Historical Society, n. d.), 18–20.

24. *Mining and Scientific Press* 90 (April 22, 1905): 247.

25. *Mining and Scientific Press* 72 (February 8, June 13, June 17, 1896): 103, 479, 523; 73 (August 29, 1896): 171; 74 (June 19, 1897): 523; 77 (July 2, 1898): 15; *Engineering and Mining Journal* 66 (July 3, 1898): 15.

26. *Sacramento Record Union*, January 23, 1896; *Mining and Scientific Press* 71 (November 9, 1895): 299; 72 (February 15, 1896): 123.

27. *Mining and Scientific Press* 71 (August 10, September 28, 1895): 87, 199; 73 (July 25, November 28, 1896): 67, 489; 74 (May 1, 1897): 363.

28. Charles M. Romanowitz, "California's Gold Dredges," California Division of Mines and Geology, *Mineral Information Service* 33 (August 1, 1970): 158; *Engineering and Mining Journal* 64 (July 10, 1897): 31.

29. Robert McIntosh, *Three Prize Essays on the Present Condition and Future Prospects of the Mineral Resources of New Zealand, and the Best Means of Fostering their Development* (Wellington: John McKay, Government Printer, 1907), 85–86; *The Evening Star* (Dunedin, N.Z.), August 4, December 13, 1873; January 31, February 2, 1874.

30. Charles Janin, *Gold Dredging in the United States*, U. S. Bureau of Mines Bulletin 127 (Washington DC: GPO, 1918), 12; Hennen Jennings, *The History and Development of Gold Dredging in Montana*, U. S. Bureau of Mines Bulletin 121 (Washington DC: GPO, 1916), 3; Lewis E. Aubury, *Gold Dredging in California*, California State Mining Bureau Bulletin 57 (Sacramento: California State Printing Office, 1910), 2; *Engineering and Mining Journal* 46 (November 26, 1898): 637; 70 (August 4, 1900): 126; Province of Otago, *Votes and Proceedings of the Provincial Council*, Session 21, 1865–1866 (Dunedin, N.Z.: Daniel Campbell, 1866), 42A; *Dunstan Times* (N.Z.), April 30, 1869; James Forrest, "The Otago Goldfields, 1860–1870: Some Geological Aspects—A Study in Historical Geography" (master's thesis, University of Canterbury, N.Z., 1960), 53, 78, 117.

31. Romanowitz, "California's Gold Dredges," 158; *Engineering and Mining Journal* 66 (November 26, 1898): 637; Thomas A. Rickard, "Alluvial Mining in Otago," *Transactions of the American Institute of Mining Engineers* 21 (1892–1893): 464; "Appendix to Report on the Gold Fields of New Zealand," *Appendix to the Journals of the House of Representatives of New Zealand* 2 (Wellington, 1876): 8.

32. Janin, *Gold Dredging in the United States*, 5–6; *Engineering and Mining Journal* 70 (August 4, 1900): 129; *A Plea for Protection: Together with an Account of the Industries of the South Island* (Dunedin, N.Z.: Fergusson & Mitchell, 1888), 102–5; *Dunstan Times* (N.Z.), June 3, July 22, September 23, 1881; June 30, July 21, September 1, 1882; E. J. Von Dadelszen, comp., *The New Zealand Official Year-Book, 1899* (Wellington: John McKay, Government Printer, 1899), 509; "The Goldfields of New Zealand," *Appendix to the Journals of the House of Representatives* 1, C-3 (Wellington, 1899): 141.

33. Vivian Maureen Cartmell, "Pactolian Sands of Otago: An Historical Geography of Gold Dredging in the Otago Mining District" (master's thesis, University of Otago, N.Z., 1969), 4–5.

34. McIntosh, *Three Prize Essays*, 92; *Mining and Scientific Press* 72 (June 20, 1896): 504. An estimated 270 had been built by the end of 1902. *Engineering and Mining Journal* 78 (August 4, 1904): 170.

35. McIntosh, *Three Prize Essays*, 90–91; "Report on Goldfields," *Appendix to the Journals of the House of Representatives of New Zealand* 1, C-3 (Wellington, 1890):

168; "Report on Goldfields, Warden's Reports," *Appendix to the Journals of the House of Representatives of New Zealand* 2, C-3 (Wellington, 1895): 41; Rickard, "Alluvial Mining in Otago," 464; *Mining and Scientific Press* 74 (March 13, 1897): 212.

36. *Engineering and Mining Journal* 48 (November 16, 1889): 426.

37. Thomas J. Barbour to Edward H. Benjamin, San Francisco, November 14, 1902, in *Proceedings of the Eleventh Annual Convention of the California Miners' Association held at Golden Gate Hall, San Francisco November 17, 18, 19, 1902* (San Francisco: Hicks-Judd Press, n.d.), 144.

38. Frank W. Griffin, "Reminiscences," *Western Mining News* (San Francisco) 3 (June 1935): 13; handwritten list of Risdon dredges in notebook, George P. Hurst MSS, box 4, Stanford University Libraries, Palo Alto; Jack R. Wagner, *Gold Mines of California: An Illustrated History of the Most Productive Mines* (Berkeley CA: Howell-North Books, 1970), 41.

39. "W. P. Hammond, A Man of Mighty Achievements in the Development of Northern California," *Oroville (Calif.) Daily Mercury*, undated clipping, Natomas 2:98–99, California Room, California State Library, Sacramento.

40. Hammon, "Dredge Mining in Butte County," 51–52; *Mining and Scientific Press* 75 (September 4, 1897): 216–17; Wagner, *Gold Mines of California*, 41, 43; *Proceedings of the Eleventh Annual Convention of the California Miners' Association*, 144; "W. P. Hammon, A Man of Mighty Achievements in the Development of Northern California"; James Lenhoff, "The Dredging Era," Butte County Historical Society *Diggin's* 2 (winter 1959): 4; Peter J. Delay, *History of Yuba and Sutter Counties California, with Biographical Sketches* (Los Angeles: Historic Record Co., 1924), 1195.

41. Charles J. Lyden, *The Gold Placers of Montana*, Montana State Bureau of Mines and Geology Memoir 26 (Butte: Montana School of Mines, 1948), plate 1 (caption), no page; *The Dillon (Montana) Examiner*, April 10, May 22, 1895.

42. Lyden, *Gold Placers of Montana*, 6, quoting Samuel Helper; Janin, *Gold Dredging in the United States*, 8–9; Jennings, *History and Development of Gold Dredging in Montana*, 5, on ladder dredges; *Mining and Scientific Press* 71 (November 30, 1895): 353, 357; *Engineering and Mining Journal* 64 (November 20, 1897): 607.

43. H. J. Reiling to Charles H. Janin, Denver, September 13, 1915, Charles H. Janin MSS, Huntington Library, San Marino, California; *The Dillon (Montana) Examiner*, October 2, 1901; *Mining and Scientific Press* 71 (November 30, 1895): 353; Norman Cleaveland, "Bucket Line Dredge Methods," *Mining Congress Journal* 27 (November, 1941): 19; Charles Shattuck Hill, *The Chicago Main Drainage Channel* (New York: Engineering News Publishing, 1896), 44–49, 63–65, 110.

44. Handwritten list of Risdon dredges in notebook, George P. Hurst MSS, box

4; copy, handwritten list of Bucyrus dredges, courtesy of David M. Lang, Bucyrus International, Inc., South Milwaukee, Wisconsin.

45. Romanowitz, "California's Gold Dredges," 165; Aubury, *Gold Dredging in California,* 38, 40, 41; Griffin, "Reminiscences," 14; *Mining World* 24 (May 19, 1906): 607–8; *Mining and Metallurgy* 25 (May, 1903): 461; Norman Cleaveland, "Some Comments on Dredging as a Mining Method," *1967 Proceedings of Wodcon, World Dredging Conference* (n. p.: World Dredging Conference, 1967), 13; William M. Rosewater to Charles H. Janin, Milwaukee, June 7, 1915, copy, box 2, Janin MSS, Huntington Library.

46. H. H. Dunn, "Eight-Cent Gold-Digger Earns Millions," *Popular Mechanics* 49 (January 1928): 77; *Engineering and Mining Journal* 90 (July 30, 1910): 202; 91 (March 4, 1911): 483; Aubury, *Gold Dredging in California,* 54, 55–56, 57; Charles Romanowitz, "The Uses of Floating Dredges for Mining" (paper presented before the National Western Mining Conference of the Colorado Mining Association, Denver, February 4, 1966), Romanowitz Papers.

47. D'Arcy Weatherbe, *Dredging for Gold in California* (San Francisco: Mining and Scientific Press, 1907), 74; George Walsh, "Economy in Mining with the Modern Gold Dredge," *Mining World* 24 (May 19, 1906): 608; Charles Janin, "Gold Dredging in Alaska and the Yukon," *Mining Magazine* 6 (January 1912): 45.

48. *Mining and Scientific Press* 78 (March 4, 1899): 227; Wagner, *Gold Mines of California,* 41, 43.

49. Janin, *Gold Dredging in the United States,* 11; *Mining and Scientific Press* 112 (March 4, 1916): 346; *Mineral Resources of the United States, 1911* (Washington DC: GPO, 1912), pt. I, p. 462; *Mineral Resources of the United States in 1920* (Washington DC: GPO, 1921), pt. I, p. 163.

50. *Mining and Engineering World* 44 (January 1, 1916): 41–44; "Flagships of the Gold Fleet," *Popular Mechanics* 64 (May 1938): 730–31; Norman Cleaveland, "Bucket Line Dredge Methods," 20.

51. Wagner, *Gold Mines of California,* 49.

52. Wagner, *Gold Mines of California,* 51; Romanowitz, "California's Gold Dredges, 166; *Los Angeles Times,* August 12, 1975; George W. Rathjens to D. D. Muir, Jr. (No place, November 29, 1934), copy, United States Smelting, Refining and Mining Company MSS, Sharon Steel Company, Midvale, Utah.

53. Romanowitz, "California Gold Dredges," 155; *Mineral Resources of the United States, 1915* (Washington DC: GPO, 1916), pt. I, p. 213.

54. For the pros and cons of heap leaching, see Jessica Speart, "A Lust for Gold," *Mother Jones* 20 (January/February 1995): 58–60; Perri Knize, "The Price of Gold," *Sports Illustrated* 85 (October 14, 1996): 86.

13

The Last Great Gold Rush

From California to the Klondike in the Nineteenth Century

Charlene Porsild

At the end of a half-century of gold rushes, the Klondike episode (1897–1901) was touted as the "Last Great Gold Rush" by its participants and promoters.[1] Like California had been fifty years earlier, the Yukon was a fabled, faraway place in the late 1890s. Following the series of rushes in the North American West that began with the 1849 stampede to California and included the 1858 rush to British Columbia, the 1860s and 1880s rushes to Colorado, the Klondike drew its largest crowds in 1898 and 1899.

The Klondike excitement started when the steamship *Excelsior* arrived in San Francisco in July 1897, with dozens of newly wealthy miners on board, fresh from the gold fields of the Yukon. As news spread of "tons of gold" lying around the creek beds of the Klondike, men and women from all walks of life and the four corners of the globe began hasty preparations for the biggest adventure of their lives. Altogether, over one hundred thousand people left homes in more than forty countries to travel to the farthest northwest corner of Canada, and nearly half that number reached their goal. Artists abandoned their studios in London, merchants packed up their shops in Colorado, husbands left wives in San Francisco, and homesteaders abandoned homesteads in Kansas to join the mad rush that was the Klondike stampede of 1898.

And what a stampede it was! The average Klondiker traveled a minimum of twenty-five hundred miles and spent one thousand dollars on transportation and supplies. While the majority of these gold seekers came from more settled areas of Canada and the United States, many traveled great distances, leaving homes in Egypt, France, Belgium, Great Britain, and New Zealand to try their luck in the Klondike.[2]

Once stampeders had reached the West Coast, they chose from four major routes of travel. By far the fastest, easiest, and most expensive was the "all water route." This journey brought Klondikers north from San Francisco along the coast to Seattle, Vancouver BC, and then St. Michael, Alaska, at the mouth of the Yukon River. From St. Michael it was a mere six-hundred-miles trek upstream to Dawson City.

Those stampeders on a budget selected among the other major routes. The largest number journeyed by ocean steamer to the southern Alaska coast and disembarked at Skagway or Dyea. Here they packed or hired others to pack their mandatory one thousand pounds of supplies over the coastal mountains via either the Chilkoot or the White Pass to the headwaters of the Yukon River. The one-thousand-pound minimum was required by Canadian authorities as a prerequisite to ensure that greenhorn travelers carried enough food and supplies to sustain themselves in the Yukon for twelve months. Once across the border, stampeders proceeded to the shores of lakes Lindeman and Bennett, where they built boats (or hired someone else to build them) in which they would float downstream the remaining 350 miles to Dawson.

The most difficult and least expensive routes took travelers overland through the Canadian interior. One overland route headed north from Edmonton on the northern edge of the Canadian plains, over the Athabasca Landing Trail, traveling north to the shores of Great Slave Lake, along the Mackenzie River, and across the interior mountains in the Yukon. The second trail headed overland from British Columbia's coast to its northern interior, then up the Stikine River valley and through the Glenora mining district, joining the Yukon River at the mouth of the Teslin. Any way you read the map, it was a long, long way to Dawson City.

When they arrived in Dawson, they found a city that quickly grew to twenty thousand souls, all of them intent on making their fortunes before the sun could set on the "last great gold rush" of the nineteenth century. Like other gold rushes throughout the North American West, the Klondike lured people with the promise of easy fortunes, vast wealth, and unlimited opportunity. But the Klondike rush resembled the California rush more than it did most of those rushes in between. While cities like Cripple Creek and Central City, Colorado, and Grass Valley, California, were composed overwhelmingly of American-born populations, the Klondike gold rush society was cosmopolitan. The majority of the Alaska Argonauts came from Canada, the United States, and Great Britain, yet fully 20 percent reported other countries of origin. And while some observers reported Dawson City, Yukon, to be a "community of men," it was always home to a significant number of women and children.[3] Family life was a permanent and important feature of Klondike life from the outset.

In older communities, individuals drew upon long-standing familial and occupational connections for their business and social networks. In gold rush communities like Dawson City, where nearly everyone was a newcomer, family networks existed, but they were often limited to one or two individuals: a brother, a father, a sister, or a spouse. Thus, residents of Dawson City and its surrounds created new networks based on ethnicity, occupation, and place of origin. Like the California rush, the Klondike was host to a wide variety of ethnic groups, including many French Canadians and Scandinavians, as well as smaller groups of Japanese, Chinese, and African Americans. These groups formed formal and informal networks that provided social, economic, and cultural support for one another. French Canadians, for example, through a system set up at a local hotel, offered services to newly arrived Francophones that included assistance in finding food, lodging, and employment, as well as translation services.[4]

Klondikers, then, often established new networks based on family, ethnicity, and place of origin. In a locale where communication was sporadic and difficult, people depended on newcomers to bring information from the outside world. News brought by an individual from his or her hometown or village was often the starting point for a friendship, business partnership, or employment contract. In this way, a common place of origin—even when the individuals had not been acquainted back home—became a basis for friendship and mutual aid. Moreover, whether that place of origin had been another gold rush town like Cripple Creek or a port city like San Francisco, Klondikers often maintained close links with family and friends left behind.

Klondikers had frequently grown up with stories of California's days of '49. Indeed, many had older relatives who had been a part of that early mining excitement, and they carried the myth and legend of the California rush with them when they made the long pilgrimage north in 1898. Documentary evidence from the Klondike points toward the connections to be found among and between participants in other major gold rushes, from California to the Yukon and beyond. Although legend had it that doctors, lawyers, clerks, and housewives made their fortunes in the gold fields of the North American West, many Klondikers were veterans of other mining rushes, some even part of a second and third generation of mining families who could trace their wanderings from one gold field to another back to California and the days of '49.

One famous California Klondiker was George Washington Carmack, born in 1860 in Contra Costa County, across the bay from San Francisco. His parents, like so many other forty-niners, failed to make their fortunes in the gold fields, but Hannah and Perry Carmack had supported their young family by ranching. After the untimely deaths of their parents, George and his sister continued the family traditions: Rose married and spent her life ranching in California while George followed in his father's footsteps, wandering up and down the Northwest Coast, trying (and failing) to find a cure for his gold fever.

In 1885 George Carmack's wanderings led him to the south coast of Alaska. Near present-day Skagway he met a young Tagish Indian man named Keish, and the two became constant companions. Soon they were partners, trapping, hunting, prospecting, even occasionally packing other prospectors' supplies for a fee over the coast mountains to the Yukon interior. In the Tagish tradition, Carmack solidified the bonds of partnership by marrying one of Keish's sisters. When this woman died of influenza in 1888, Carmack followed local custom and married another sister, a woman he called Kate, although her family knew her as Shaaw Tlàa. These unions made the two men brothers, and the bond between the family members was a strong one.

Carmack and Keish, with the aid and companionship of Shaaw Tlàa, spent the next several years working together in a lifestyle that offered them a bare subsistence, seasonally mining, hunting, and trapping. Then one morning in August 1896 this trio, along with Shaaw Tlàa's nephew Kàa Goox, discovered the gold that started the Klondike gold rush. Together the family staked four claims on the creek they dubbed Bonanza. Over the next few years these claims brought the family approximately $500,000 in gold dust and nuggets.[5]

Despite close attachment to his Yukon family (he and Kate had a three year-old daughter named Graphie by 1896), George Carmack also maintained California ties. He regularly wrote to his sister, Rose, in California, sending her money and giving her news about his Yukon activities. A few months after his big discovery, he wrote to say that things were going so well, with the mines paying so richly, that it was almost as if "it was the days of '49 all over again." He referred specifically to his father and to Rose's husband, who had both participated in that great event.[6]

In the summer of 1898, since Rose and her husband were unable to make the trip north, Carmack journeyed south with his new family, Keish, Kate, Graphie, and two nephews. After a much publicized spate of partying and shopping in Seattle and San Francisco, they arrived at the Watson ranch near Hollister, California. Grateful to his sister and her husband for the many years of support, Carmack paid the balance on their ranch mortgage before heading back to the Klondike with his wife and daughter. After this visit, Carmack sent Kate and Graphie back to Rose's ranch occasionally, attempting to resolve the couple's marital and alcohol-related problems. Eventually, Carmack and Kate's marriage dissolved, and Carmack settled with a new wife in Seattle, but he maintained a close relationship with his sister in Hollister until his death in 1922.

Other notable Californians who made the long journey north to Dawson City included Clarence and Ethel Berry, who became two of the wealthiest young Klondikers. Clarence Berry, also the son of a forty-niner, was a fruit farmer from Fresno who arrived in the Yukon in 1894. A year later he returned to California, where he married Ethel Bush, his childhood sweetheart. Together the couple returned over the famed Chilkoot Pass and headed for the Fortymile gold camp in the northern Yukon. There they struggled. Clarence made more money tending bar in the local saloon than from prospecting, while Ethel cooked and mended clothes for the camp's womanless miners.

While working that bar in a Fortymile saloon, Clarence Berry became one of a handful of men to hear George Washington Carmack share the news of his fabulous discovery in the Klondike mining district in August 1896. Like so many prospectors, Berry was a gambler at heart. Within hours he had shucked his apron, kissed his wife goodbye, and begun the 150-mile journey to the new gold mecca. A few days later Clarence Berry staked what proved to be one of the richest claims in the Klondike. While Ethel cooked, cleaned, and laundered for the men, Clarence and his partners extracted over one hundred thousand dollars in placer gold the first season. It did seem, indeed, like the days of '49 all over again.

Ethel soon convinced her sister, Edna, to join them, while Clarence's brother, Henry, also arrived to help with the family's mining operations in 1898. Almost immediately Edna and Henry fell in love and married, keeping the fabulous Klondike fortune within the family. The two couples, known to their friends as the "Bushes and the Berrys" remained in the Yukon until 1900, when they followed the gold rush to Fairbanks, Alaska. Later they all returned to California, where they shrewdly invested their wealth in the newly emerging oil industry.[7]

While some Californians experienced the Klondike as a family affair, others experienced it in separation. Perhaps typical of these were the Goodwins. Charles Goodwin left his wife, Jennie, and their two young children in Los Angeles in May 1897 to join in the Klondike stampede.

Charlie, his brother Phil, and several other Los Angeles men spent the better part of three years in the Yukon seeking their fortune, a goal that eluded them, as it did so many others. Charlie's communication with his family was sporadic, seeming to consist of an irregular few letters written only when could send a little money homeward.

The first installment came nearly a year after his departure. In a brief letter accompanied by a bank draft for one hundred dollars, Charlie wrote that while "I have very little money on hand . . . you said you were short of funds." He confided that his hope had not been fully realized in Dawson City, and he apologized to Jennie for that fact that "it is not one hundred thousand."[8]

A few months later he sent another letter with some gold nuggets. It read: "I send you 8 nuggets by Mr. Hazelett. The small one with the string in it Phil sends to mother. The large one which weighs $21 even money at $16 to the ounce is for you and you will please give one to your mother, one to Jessie. Keep the one that is the longest and have a pin made for yourself. This is written in haste. Yours with Tender love, Charlie. Kisses to little folks and you. Love to all."[9]

While Jennie was perhaps relieved to hear from her absentee husband, the small amounts of money and nuggets must have made it difficult for her to believe in Charlie's dream.

He managed to scrape enough money together to make a visit home the following spring, but as soon as he could borrow the funds to do so, he returned again to Dawson City. Four months later, in July 1899, he finally wrote: "Dear Jennie, I feel as if I could not make any excuse for not writing and will not try. I hoped to be able to send you money before this but could not." After a few lines of explanation about his optimism for his latest mining ventures, he became apologetic for the circumstances in which he had left his family: "Dearest enclosed you will find Draft for $225. I can not send more today but will send more in a very few days. I think if you pay Mrs. Field the interest it will be all right for a few days and I hope to be able to send you plenty from this on. You do not know how I love you Jennie and I feel that I am not worthy of you. I have so many faults."[10]

From fragmented letters like these, we discover some of the tragedy that gold rushes could mean for those left behind. While Charlie was again sending money homeward, his letters make clear that the family was in dire straits indeed. Jennie, who experienced none of the adventure and excitement of the Klondike gold rush first hand, instead tried to hold the family together and keep the creditors at bay. Charlie, carrying his guilt like a leaden weight, moved from one failed venture to the next, trying to make ends meet.

While California sent many of her restless sons northward, with or without their families, the state also relived some of its gold rush era prosperity during the Klondike boom. Steamship companies, wholesale outfitters, dry-goods merchants, and many other entrepreneurial businesses quickly moved to take advantage of San Francisco's railway terminus and waylaid would-be Klondikers on their way to the docks. Five steamers per week left Pacific ports in 1898 bound for Alaska. By the following summer five ships were leaving from each port on a weekly basis as the Alaska Commercial Company scrambled to keep enough ocean-worthy vessels coming in and out of San Francisco. In Seattle and Vancouver BC, the North American Transportation and Trading company did likewise. Businesses that had all but failed in the depression of the early 1890s dusted off their stored merchandise and capitalized on the opportunity to outfit the gold rushers with everything from bicycles to rubber boots and cans of caviar.

Will Purdy, a clerk for the Rock Island Railway, was one of thousands of would-be Klondikers who landed in San Francisco in the winter of 1897–1898. While taking care of last minute plans for his trip to Dawson City, Purdy developed a severe case of cold feet. Soon he wired his wife that he had changed his mind. In San Francisco he had met several people who all told him, with great authority, about the hardships of travel and the inclement weather in the Yukon. Furthermore, Purdy also heard rumors that the Klondike was a hoax—that the stories of fabulous wealth were mere fabrications.

Will's wife of ten years, Martha Munger Purdy, had meanwhile made elaborate arrangements to be able to join her husband and his partners on their Klondike adventure. Leaving her home in Chicago, she journeyed to Kansas to settle her two sons with family members, then traveled on to Denver, where she purchased a large cargo of provisions and supplies. Along with her brother and his friend, Mrs. Purdy now waited for her husband in Seattle, tickets in hand. Back in San Francisco, Will Purdy could not be persuaded to change his mind. He ordered his wife (she had vowed to obey him, had she not?) to return to Chicago while he sorted things out.

Martha, after seeing countless other Klondikers embark from the Seattle wharf, became furious with Will for changing his mind. She undertook to end their union on the spot, writing to inform Purdy that the marriage was over. She told him that she was bound for the Klondike with him or without. If it was to be without him, she added, then she wanted no more to do with him. The couple separated, Martha heading north while Will fearfully remained in San Francisco. Eventually Martha secured a divorce from Purdy, later marrying a Canadian lawyer named George Black, who became Yukon Commissioner and later the territory's first member of Parliament in Ottawa. Purdy, waylaid by other promoters in San Francisco, was pulled in a different direction, choosing to hazard his new business ventures in the warmer climes of Hawaii. There he remained until his death years later in Honolulu.

Besides waylaying prospective Klondikers and heading them in different directions, San Francisco was also the place where many future Klondikers were bitten by the gold bug. Nellie Cashman was fifteen years old in 1860 when she sailed from Ireland to Boston with her mother, her sister, and thousands of other desperate Irish Catholic immigrants. From Boston, the Cashman women moved west. By 1869 they were living in San Francisco, where Nellie caught mining fever.[11] After hearing fabulous stories of the days of '49, she headed for the silver camps of Nevada in 1872, just as the Comstock Lode discovery was starting a new series of mining booms. She decided her fortune would be made in Pioche; there she and her mother, Fanny Cashman, opened the Miner's Boarding House. This business provided the two women needed income while Nellie learned the basics of prospecting.[12]

In 1873, traveling with an otherwise all-male party of two hundred Nevada prospectors, Nellie Cashman headed for the Cassiar mining district of northwestern British Columbia. There, as she later told reporters, she "alternately mined and kept a boarding house for miners" that she operated throughout the summer of 1873.[13] In the fall she relocated to Victoria, where she intended to spend the winter.

While Nellie sat out the winter in the milder climate of the coast, news arrived of a supply shortage and an outbreak of scurvy in the Cassiar district. Cashman rushed into action, persuading six men to accompany her on a supply run against all odds. For seventy-seven days the group trudged and traipsed through the deep snow of the northern British Columbia wilderness with food and supplies, surviving avalanches, extreme temperatures, and all manners of winter storms. Upon her arrival, Cashman set about nursing the mining camp's scurvy victims and distributing food and supplies. Her heroic journey earned Cashman the permanent sobriquet "Miner's Angel."[14]

After spending two more years in the Cassiar district, Cashman left in 1876 to travel around the mining camps of the American West. For a time she stopped in Tucson and Tombstone. In Arizona, "Irish Nellie" continued her life-long habit of combining mercantile enterprise with prospecting, opening a series of businesses that included the Nevada Boot and Shoe Store, a grocery store, the Arcade Restaurant and Chop House, the Russ House, and the American Hotel.[15]

In 1898, at age fifty-three, she could not resist the call of the Klondike. Like most others, Cashman arrived too late to stake a claim on the richest ground, but she managed to purchase both a "fraction" and a regular claim.[16] Cashman mined her own claims side-by-side with her male colleagues, and like them she had no regrets. "I took out over one hundred thousand dollars from that [fractional] claim—and I spent every red cent of it buying other claims and prospecting the country. I went out with my dog team or on snow shoes all over that district looking for rich claims."[17] To support her mining habit during her seven-year residence in the Klondike, Cashman operated first a short-order restaurant and later a grocery store.

From Dawson, Nellie Cashman's permanent love affair with mining led her to Fairbanks and Koyukuk, Alaska. There in the spring of 1924 she contracted double pneumonia. She was hospitalized first in Fairbanks, then in Saint Joseph's Hospital in Victoria, where she died in January 1925. She is buried in the Ross Bay Cemetery in Victoria, British Columbia.[18]

California also sent many professional miners Klondike-bound to represent corporate interests. San Francisco mining engineer George Coffey, for example, journeyed to the Yukon in the employ of a commercial mining company to oversee its Klondike operations in 1898. Like most tourists even today, Coffey often compared his new surroundings to more familiar scenes back home. When he arrived at Lake Bennett in the spring of 1898, for example, he saw so many tents pitched by stampeders waiting for the ice to thaw that the tent city looked "as large as San Francisco from a distance."[19] After recording with disgust that the mounted police confiscated his brandy and cigars at the border, Coffey and his companions arrived in Dawson at the height of the Klondike stampede in the summer of 1898. Here they set about buying, selling, and operating numerous mining properties over the next several months, returning to the company's head office in August of the same year and avoiding having to spend the long winter in the north. Back in San Francisco, Coffey's company administered its Klondike claims from a distance, Coffey making an annual trip to oversee the workings and to buy and sell other mining properties.

By the time the Klondike gold rush played itself out in 1905, the placer gold rushes in the North American West had become a thing of the past. The Klondike excitement, indeed, was the last of the great gold rushes of the nineteenth century. Smaller gold and silver discoveries would continue to lure a few hundred, even a few thousand miners, business owners, and gamblers to new Eldorados in Alaska, Nevada, British Columbia, and Colorado. For decades, Klondike stampeders toiled in western mines in Nome, Fairbanks, Aspen, Cripple Creek, and Leadville. They were part of a North American tradition that was a half-century old, yet the heyday of the gold and silver rushes had passed. Never again would 100,000 men, women, and children leave homes in the four corners of the world bound for far-distant, hazily defined gold fields, confident that they would strike it rich. Two world wars and an international depression would change the world, reorient national economies, and shift public attention. Gone forever were the days when large numbers of speculative spirits believed that somewhere in the western part of the North American continent any individual might make a quick fortune with nothing more than a pick, a shovel, and a gold pan.

Notes

1. See Pierre Berton, *Klondike: The Last Great Gold Rush* (Toronto: McClelland & Stewart, 1972).

2. National Archives of Canada, Canada Census, 1901.

3. James Wheppler, *Yukon Territory: A Community of Men National Historic Sites Manuscript Report* (Ottawa: Department of Indian and Northern Affairs, 1969).

4. Transcript of oral interview, MG 29 C27, Joseph Charles Dubé Papers, National Archives of Canada (hereafter NAC); Ella Lung Martinson, *Trail to North Star Gold: A True Story of the Alaska-Klondike Gold Rush* (Portland OR: Binford & Mort, 1984), 113; McLellan to Maggie Electa, September 8, 1905, MS 82/32 F-1, part 2, file 4, Winifred McLellan Papers, Yukon Archive.

5. Julie Cruikshank, *Reading Voices: Oral and Written Interpretations of the Yukon's Past* (Vancouver BC: Douglas & McIntyre, 1991), 132.

6. George Carmack to Rose Watson, February 16, 1897, cited in James Johnson, *Carmack of the Klondike* (Seattle: Epicenter, 1990), 92; my emphasis.

7. Edna Berry, *The Bushes and the Berrys* (San Francisco: C. J. Bennett, 1941). See also Charlene L. Porsild, *Gamblers and Dreamers: Women, Men, and Community in the Klondike* (Vancouver: University of British Columbia Press, 1988), 78.

8. Charlie to Jennie Goodwin, March 3, 1898, MG 29 C6, Charles Goodwin Papers, NAC.

9. Charlie to Jennie Goodwin, August 10, 1898, MG 29 C6, Charles Goodwin Papers, NAC.

10. Charlie to Jennie Goodwin, 3 July 1899, MG 29 C6, Charles Goodwin Papers, NAC.

11. San Francisco *City Directory*, 1869. See also Sally Zanjani, *A Mine of Her Own: Women Prospectors in the American West* (University of Nebraska Press, 1997); and Suzann Ledbetter, *Nellie Cashman: Prospector and Trailblazer* (El Paso: University of Texas Press, 1993).

12. *Pioche (Nevada) Ely Record*, September 4, 1872.

13. *Victoria (BC) Daily Colonist*, February 15, 1898.

14. *Victoria (BC) Daily Colonist*, February 15, 1898. See also Mary Anderson, "They called her the Angel," *Tombstone Epitaph*, November 1990, 11.

15. Suzann Ledbetter, *Nellie Cashman*, 7; Zanjani, *Mine of Her Own*, 35–36.

16. A fraction was a sliver of ground or a partial claim. A fraction was created when the Canadian government surveyor measured a group of claims and found one to have been staked on the wrong dimensions, thus throwing off all the other claims. Rather than restaking all the other claims—and stirring up controversy— the surveyor usually marked off the fraction, reported it to the mining recorder, and opened it for staking. Ledbetter, *Nellie Cashman,* 13–15; Zanjani, *Mine of Her Own*, 37–39.

17. Porsild, *Gamblers and Dreamers*, 84.

18. Ledbetter, *Nellie Cashman*, 47; John Adams, *Historic Guide to Ross Bay Cemetery* (Victoria: Sono Nis Press, 1998), 41; Ledbetter, *Nellie Cashman*, 61.

19. Diary entry, May 22, 1898, MG 29 C46, George Coffey Papers, NAC.

14

Begun by Gold

Sacramento and the Gold Rush Legacy after 150 Years

Kenneth N. Owens

Gold, as everyone knows, began the city of Sacramento. Of course, the location that would become Sacramento had a prior history, eventful and interesting, before the discovery of gold nearby in January 1848. But until the early reports from Sutter's mill and the Mormon Island diggings on the American River began to attract hundreds, then thousands upon thousands of hopeful, eager gold hunters to the area, it had remained an isolated frontier district: commercially marginal and culturally a border region where a few score whites lived in large part by their skill in exploiting the labor of Native peoples. Despite John Sutter's vigorous efforts to attract settlers to his New Helvetia colony, at the beginning of 1848 this land was still all but unknown to the world outside of northern California. The possibilities here had not even claimed the attention of such an optimistic, speculatively minded, would-be city builder as Samuel Brannan, the ambitious leader of Mormon colonization in California, who twice passed through the area in 1847.[1]

Nature had not fashioned here a place that appeared suitable for urban life. If seen through the cultural spectacles of any outsider before the gold rush began, the area's natural disadvantages easily outweighed its advantages. First, though the site was defined geographically by the junction of the American River with the Sacramento River, neither of these rivers led anywhere that was inviting or likely to become profitable. Heading upstream eastward on the American River, as Jedediah Smith had discovered, the adventurous traveler soon came up against the steep, forbidding, snow-topped ramparts of the Sierra Nevada; and if the adventurer pressed on and found a passageway across that mighty wall, the bleak, water-shy high desert country of the Great Basin posed a further barrier to travel and trade.[2] The outcome was no more promising for those who followed the Sacramento River northward. The Sacramento Valley itself was a frequently flooded basin, lacking timber, with marshlands and natural pastures that went yellow and dry during the hot summer months while the waterways dwindled or disappeared. Ship navigation, never possible on the American River, was also normally barred on the Sacramento above the mouth of the Feather River. At the valley's upper end, the massive cliffs and convoluted, narrow canyons of the Siskiyou and Klamath Mountains formed another great barricade, blocking the way to the fertile Willamette Valley two hundred fifty miles farther north.[3]

To complete the isolation of the Sacramento region, downstream the tule-choked sloughs and deceptive channels of the Sacramento–San Joaquin Delta cut off easy access by either land or water to the San Francisco Bay region.[4] By foot or horseback the trip required a great detour to the south, with river crossings that might halt the traveler indefinitely during periods of high water. Experienced boatmen in small craft could navigate through the delta's maze of channels, but these waterways lacked the leeway for efficient wind-powered sailing, making the voyage tedious and wearing. In the 1840s it required under the best conditions an uncomfortable week or more to travel between the American River and the small trading town of Yerba Buena at the site renamed San Francisco in early 1847. In short, the Sacramento area before the gold rush was halfway to nowhere.

Nature endowed Sacramento's location with other, still more severe handicaps for future urban growth. The extreme heat of summer, with extended periods of one-hundred-degree-plus temperatures, was a climatic constant that discouraged settlement. And, as long-time residents hasten to explain to newcomers, it's a dry heat. The prevalence of a Mediterranean-type climate, rainless from late spring through very late fall, meant disaster for would-be farmers untrained in irrigation. No city could flourish, so Americans thought in the mid-nineteenth century, without an extensive, productive farming hinterland. John Sutter's repeated failures as a farmer drove home the lesson: agriculture could not succeed here. No one in the 1840s could be so demented as to suppose that this area would ever become the center for the nation's richest region of commercial agriculture.

A further problem—then as now this area's most extreme environmental problem—was flooding. Every so often, powerful Pacific storms created flooding episodes that sent the rivers over their natural levees and swept everything before their high, surging flows. Then as now, no one could predict exactly when the floods would come, but only the most naively ignorant or the most willfully blind could fail to know that, at some not-too-distant date, come they would. For good reason, Sutter's native Maidu workers had built the adobe walls of his fort on the highest piece of land convenient to the American River.[5] Their own homes were quite different. Shrewdly, the region's Native peoples built sturdy temporary structures at long-established village sites atop the natural levees of the rivers, planning to move to higher ground when the waters began to rise.[6] All the necessary evidence was clearly in front of the new arrivals of 1848 and 1849. Who, then, would be foolish enough to attempt to plant a city on a flood plain?

One additional set of circumstances argued against the building of an urban center at this site. River cities were notoriously unhealthy in the mid-nineteenth century. In that pre-Pasteur age, a time before the discovery of the microorganisms that cause human disease, medical practitioners would customarily blame widespread health problems on various combinations of environmental, genetic, and psychic or spiritual causes that today may seem quite bizarre. But experience had taught everyone that serious illness was quite prevalent in those towns and cities situated alongside rivers. We should not wonder why. In river cities, residents customarily drew their drinking water downstream from other people's sewage and waste disposal sites. Floods and seasonal overflows readily contaminated shallow wells. Riverside sloughs and low-lying, swampy areas were breeding grounds for disease-carrying insects. Without regulation, public streets and vacant lots became dumping sites for all kinds of waste, including dead animals and household garbage, which frequently was left to rot in the summer heat or to molder on walkways that turned into putrid, muddy bogs during the rainy season.

In the eastern states and especially in the Midwest, inhabitants of river towns were conditioned to seasonal episodes of the ague, a severe, often fatal disease marked by high fever alternating with chills, shaking, and delirium. This disease we identify today as malaria. As we now can document in detail, malaria first reached the Sacramento Valley in 1832–1833, coming south from the lower Columbia River basin with a Hudson's Bay Company fur-trapping brigade. With mosquitoes of the necessary species already here in abundance, the arrival of a few infected individuals set off an epidemic that fatally struck down an estimated 70 percent of the native Indian people in the Sacramento Valley and the delta, perhaps as many as eighty thousand individuals.[7] Following this immense demographic and cultural disaster, malaria became endemic to the Sacramento region, always present, always a danger, especially to newcomers previously not infected and to the young. Moreover, that danger magnified with each group of immigrants that arrived, in particular those already infected who came overland from the river towns of the Midwest, bringing unwittingly in their blood the protozoa that would set off new cycles of infection.

Worldwide, great cities in the nineteenth century were enormous killing machines. City conditions everywhere destroyed far more lives than could be replaced by births among the inhabitants. To survive and grow, every city depended on a constant recruitment of newcomers, whether coming from the adjacent countryside or from distant places. The severe disease death toll in river cities, whether Paris, Vienna, London, Saint Petersburg, Canton, Cincinnati, or Saint Louis, meant this type of site especially had to attract great numbers of immigrants year after year if it was to prosper.[8]

Only one thing anywhere near Sutter's Fort, history tells us, had such a strong attractive power. Sacramento was begun by gold, and it created here in an amazingly short time a prosperous urban center on the far edge of the known, civilized world. Within a few months after the excitement began, Sacramento became the prime commercial and social capital of the gold country. Now its location was a natural advantage, the foundation for swift growth and rapid prosperity. The city's early promoters made it a central outfitting and supply depot, a transportation hub, and a key location for managing the business of the northern Mother Lode mining towns. Not least important, Sacramento became the rowdy, raucous center of sinful recreation for all who passed this way. While San Francisco developed into the great emporium of the Pacific, Sacramento—California's second city— emerged as the prototypical example, the poster child of the gold rush boom towns.

In its role as a mining capital, Sacramento was at first unique in its own time. Nothing like this sudden, booming rise of a major mercantile center from nothing had ever been seen before. America's eastern and midwestern cities, like those in other countries, were all the result of a slower growth, and they all displayed a notably less mixed, less international, less culturally and socially diverse population. An instant city, filled with people who were strangers to one another, coming from every quarter of the globe, Sacramento defined a new type of urban experience. Moreover, in the earliest period of its growth, Sacramento was almost entirely a male city. That, too, was a unique trait, and it gave to this town a few striking features that persisted for many years—perhaps even to the present.[9]

Later mining rushes created similar cities: first, Stockton and Marysville; then Denver, Virginia City, and Helena, and then Rapid City during the Black Hills gold rush. Something comparable happened to give rise to Vancouver BC, Sydney, Australia, and Christchurch, New Zealand, as Pacific

Rim mining capitals. At the end of the century, the Alaskan gold rush brought to life Dawson City and Fairbanks and Nome, replicating in many ways the Sacramento experience. Closer to our own time, the founding era of oil boom towns like Tulsa, Oklahoma, and Dallas, Texas, among others, demonstrated characteristics reminiscent of Sacramento during the gold rush.

To examine these characteristics where they originally appeared, consider first the physical city. By the fall of 1848 the riverfront south of the confluence of the American and Sacramento Rivers had become the site of a lively trade, some of it conducted aboard ships tied to the bank, some in frame buildings and tents that crowded the area, some of it simply conducted in the open, on the river levee. Legally, this location was part of the Mexican land grant that John Sutter had received eight years earlier, before the American conquest, from Governor Alvarado. Sutter, however, had become heavily entangled in debt and increasingly less capable of managing his own business affairs. His oldest son, John A. Sutter, Jr., had just arrived recently from Switzerland. To escape his creditors and, he must have hoped, to put his finances in better order, the elder Sutter signed a power of attorney and transferred his landholdings to young Sutter— although the son spoke awkward English, had little experience in business, and possessed only a rudimentary knowledge of American ways.[10]

In short order Sutter junior entered into a partnership with Sam Brannan, who by now had turned away from promoting Mormon colonization and resolved to build his wealth by gold rush trade and real estate speculation. Anxious to get the Sutter lands onto the market, in December 1848 Brannan and young Sutter hired an Army engineer, Captain William Warner, to survey and lay out a city plan aligned with the riverfront. Captain Warner and his assistant, Lieutenant William Tecumseh Sherman, finished the job quickly. Within a month another of young Sutter's partners, Peter Burnett, began selling the hastily surveyed town lots.

The result of this hurried work Sacramentans still live with today, for Warner and Sherman created a city without a center. They imposed on the terrain the simplest, most mathematically rigid, least imaginative urban design possible, "the standardized grid town *par excellence*" according to urban design historian John Reps.[11] Every resident can describe the original plan's rectangular grid of evenly spaced blocks. The north-south streets are consecutively numbered from the Sacramento River eastward, the east-west streets identified by letters of the alphabet from the American River southward. Utterly simple, instantly self-evident, this plan is remarkably convenient for newcomers. Everyone can find his or her way around downtown Sacramento with only a moment's orientation. But this convenience has always been offset by the lack of a central physical focus for the city. The expedient product of speculative mania in 1848 and 1849, Sacramento's design set aside no land for a civic plaza or courthouse square; it provided no public space that could be identified as the geographical core of Sacramento's official life; it gave the town no commercial or social center.

Over the years Sacramentans have often attempted to compensate for the featureless design of their city. Before he fled Sacramento for Central America, filled with anger toward his former business colleagues, Sutter junior made the city a gift of twelve square blocks dispersed evenly within the undeveloped survey grid.[12] This generous benefaction included what would later become the site of the state capitol, and it included also a block now called Cesar Chavez Park, in front of City Hall. Though pleasant as urban amenities, whether as small urban parks or later as sites for public elementary schools, these blocks did little to bring Sacramentans together. For a few years a tall oak tree on K Street near Sixth became a convenient civic gathering place. As one resident described it, the site served as the commercial exchange, board of trade, and chamber of commerce, all in one. It was an open-air horse market and a place of public debate. Here occurred Sacramento's best-known public lynching in 1851, with the oak tree serving as an improvised substitute for a gallows.[13]

At the edge of the downtown area, construction of the state capitol building with its adjacent capitol park in the 1880s was the first project to modify the mathematical rigidities of Captain Warner's plan. Closer to our own time, Sacramento officials allowed the state highway department to route the Interstate-5 freeway north and south near the riverfront, rather than on the west side of the Sacramento River, where it more properly belonged. This misguided attempt at city improvement, meant in its own way to solve problems based in the Warner survey, destroyed long-established ethnic neighborhoods and accelerated the demise of downtown businesses in the 1960s and 1970s.[14] All the modern city-guided efforts to invigorate business and bring the middle-class public back downtown—building the K Street Mall and Downtown Plaza, developing the convention center and civil auditorium, new hotel construction, the summertime Thursday-night markets, and including the recent discussions of siting a major league ballpark in the former Southern Pacific Railroad yards—all these initiatives have been played out against the background of Captain Warner's remarkably rudimentary, ungraceful, straight-edged exercise in city design.

The social composition and character of Sacramento during the gold rush era has even greater relevance to the modern city. During the gold rush years, to repeat J. H. Holliday's memorable phrase, the world rushed in. Judging by the early census records—a federal census in 1850, a state census in 1852, both produced by imperfect administrative procedures in chaotic times—Sacramento's founding population included quite diverse American populations—New England Yankees, New Yorkers and Pennsylvanians, Virginia cavaliers, backcountry Celts, African Americans from both slave and free states, small-town clerks and work-hardened refugees from rural hardship in the upper Midwest, the Middle Border, and frontier Missouri. What is more, the lure of gold mixed and merged these American types within a context of immigration from many other parts of the world—Mexicans from the Sonora gold country, Chilean miners and merchants, British adventurers, Irish fleeing the potato famine, Germans and French leaving behind the revolutionary turmoil of 1848, villagers from the south of China, where natural disasters and political upheavals were sending tens of thousands abroad.[15]

Sacramento, even more than San Francisco, became an instant city, filled with diverse peoples who were strangers to each other. Each newcomer, as the journalists, diary keepers, and letter writers among them uniformly attested, gained an instant education in cultural diversity if not in social tolerance. According to Sacramento's first historian, Dr. John Morse, during this early period "the whole fabric of society was little less than chaos, and still there was a oneness and harmony in its movements which can scarcely be paralleled in the annals of the world. . . . There was no moral restraint, and yet for months there never was a community more perfectly exempt from violence and immorality."[16] Luzena Stanley Wilson, another eyewitness to Sacramento's first months of existence, in retrospect offered an even more complimentary testimonial to the city's founding population: "They were, as a rule, upright, energetic, and hard-working, many of them men of education and culture whom the misfortune of poverty had forced into the ranks of labor in this strange country. The rough days which earned for California its name for recklessness had not begun. There was no shooting, little gambling, and less theft in those first months. The necessities of hard work left no leisure for the indulgence of one's temper, and the 'rough' element which comes to every mining country with the first flush times had not yet begun to crowd the West."[17]

But as the world rushed in, we should add, with scarcely a pause most of the world rushed right out again. Luzena Wilson also summed up the transient quality of Sacramento's life in 1849: "The population in

Sacramento was largely a floating one. Today there might be ten thousand people in the town, and tomorrow four thousand of them might be on their way to the gold fields. The immigrants came pouring in every day from the plains, and the schooners from San Francisco brought a living freight, eager to be away to the mountains."[18]

A small cadre of merchants, along with other business people and service workers, positioned themselves to turn a profit from the thousands of people that floated through. But these early figures in the city's history themselves seldom stayed long. It is an amazing experience to go through the historical records of gold rush Sacramento, to look at documents of land ownership, to view the first city directories, to read the newspaper stories and advertisements, to scan the minutes of city government meetings, and to see in all these materials scarcely one name that would be familiar in later times. The city was then largely a population of sojourners, some who stayed for a day or two, some who remained a week or a month, and others who found it worth their while to remain here for a short span of years, making their fortune. Although we lack exact statistics, Sacramento's rate of population turnover was huge. Especially striking if compared to other western cities of the same era like Portland or Salt Lake City, where the founding generation established long-lived dynasties that remained prominent and influential decade after decade, most of Sacramento's leading figures seemed to change virtually from season to season.

Some major reasons can be identified quickly, for they were inherent in the city's situation. Floods and fires repeatedly destroyed property, wiped out businesses and personal savings, and encouraged impoverished, shocked residents to move elsewhere. Luzena Wilson and her husband, for example, were operating a rooming house and restaurant close to the riverfront embarcadero in late 1849. They invested their gains in sacks of seed barley, which they stacked up alongside the small frame building they had leased. Then in January 1850 the entire area was submerged by the first great flood in the city's history. When the water finally receded, the Wilsons had to face the worst. "Our little fortune was gone," Luzena later recalled, "the sacks had burst and the barley sprouted—and ruin stared us again in the face. We were terrified at the awful termination of winter, and I felt that I should never again be safe unless high in the Sierra."[19] She and her husband departed the city for the new boom mining town of Auburn, later returned briefly to Sacramento, then established themselves for the rest of their lives in drier, safer ranch lands north of the delta near modern Vacaville.

In a hastily built city of tents and frame structures covered by canvas, fire was the greatest, most persistently worrisome danger to property and lives. The city's bustling business district went up in flames the first time in September 1849. A smaller conflagration in April 1850 destroyed one block along Front Street. In October another fire spread widely through Sacramento's commercial district adjacent to the embarcadero. These disasters, foreseeable but unpreventable under the circumstances, encouraged a few property owners to erect substantial buildings of stone or brick; yet the speculative, transient character of the city's booming business life argued against such long-term capital investment. In early November 1852 Sacramento experienced its most devastating fire, an outbreak fanned by north winds that spread through the entire business section of town, the flames raging so fiercely that the glow at night could be seen in San Francisco, a hundred miles away. Fifty-five blocks were left in ashes.

Business people who remained after the 1852 disaster quickly began to rebuild, this time making brick the construction material of choice. During the next few years Sacramento gained a measure of protection with the organization of volunteer fire companies. The city government also constructed a crudely built water system for fire-fighting emergencies throughout the business district, with the water carried in underground wooden pipes from a reservoir atop a newly built brick city hall at the foot of I Street. Another fire, however, leveled twelve business blocks in 1854, proving that Sacramento was still vulnerable to this danger.[20]

Along with floods and fires, Sacramento's weather, summer and winter, persuaded many to look for more pleasant surroundings. Mary Crocker, a recent arrival in March 1853, succinctly described her impressions of the spring weather in a letter home. "Storms arise, the rain comes down, the wind blows, the mud is deep, yes, deeper than you ever saw."[21] Because men and women alike tended then to dress in layers of heavy fabric, in an age before mechanical refrigeration the extreme heat of the summer months brought its own distinctive forms of suffering. Some enterprising souls made it a successful business to cut ice in the high Sierra lakes and freight it into town, protected by layers of sawdust.[22] In time moderately affluent families founded a virtual Sacramento summer colony by the ocean in Santa Cruz, where wives and children could enjoy the sea breezes—and avoid Sacramento's summertime disease dangers—while husbands and brothers remained at work in the hot, hazardous interior.

For many whose personal correspondence has been preserved, the disease problems in Sacramento were an ever-present worry. The story of the cholera epidemic that struck in October 1850 has frequently been told.[23] Spreading in ways that no one then understood, though we now know that contaminated water sources carried the disease organism, this outbreak killed an officially reported 364 people. (Some estimates ran as high as 600 deaths.) A disease with horrifying symptoms, cholera struck and killed quickly, often within twelve to twenty-four hours. Its appearance created panic, causing Sacramento's residents to abandon the town in great numbers until the danger passed. More than a few never returned.

Among other disease problems, malaria was the most persistent, the most dangerous over the long run, and the most likely to discourage newcomers from making Sacramento their permanent home. Everyone was exposed; virtually everyone went through disease attacks of greater or lesser severity, which could recur again and again. As a precaution after repeated episodes, to take one example, the prominent banker D. O. Mills began to spend part of his summers living with a congenial family on their farm near San Jose, far from the algae-covered, mosquito-breeding sloughs and backwaters of the Sacramento area. As soon as he could reasonably afford it, no one should be surprised to learn, Mills took his Sacramento-created fortune and built a red sandstone mansion on East 57th Street in New York City.[24]

The shortcomings of Sacramento society during the gold rush era, particularly as perceived by the small number of women who arrived here, became another reason for the high population turnover. Respectable women, few in numbers, found themselves accorded the utmost consideration. "It was a motley crowd that gathered every day at my table," Luzena Wilson declared, "but always at my coming the loud voices were hushed, the swearing ceased, the quarrels stopped, and deference and respect were as readily and as heartily rendered to me as if I had been a queen. I was a queen," she recalled. "Any woman who had a womanly heart, who spoke a kindly, sympathetic word to the lonely, homesick men, was a queen, and lacked no honor which a subject could bestow."[25]

Yet this honor did not fully compensate for the absence of female society and for the hard labor it took for women to survive. Even more than San Francisco, during the earliest period of its growth Sacramento was almost entirely a male city. Armies marched to war during the nineteenth century with a larger contingent of female camp followers, cooks, washerwomen, and prostitutes than appeared in Sacramento in 1849. "Women were scarce in those days," Mrs. Wilson remarked. "I lived six months in Sacramento and saw only two. There may be been others, but I never saw them. There was no time for visiting or gossiping; it was hard work from daylight until dark, and sometimes long after, and I nodded to my neighbor and called out 'Good morning' as each of us hung the clothes out to dry on the lines. Yes, we worked; we did things that our high-toned servants would now look at aghast, and say it was impossible for a woman to do. But the one who did not work in '49 went to the wall. It was a hand to hand fight with starvation at the first."[26]

Four years later, well after Luzena Wilson had departed, the output from the mines had brought flush times to the city, and Sacramento contained more women—though the population remained preponderantly male. The work of these female newcomers may have been less arduous than in 1849, but one of them, Mary Crocker, thought the lack of society a heavy emotional burden. "I have found it almost impossible," she wrote home, "for a perfect stranger to make acquaintances. Several that I have met say they have been here a year or two & only know two or three families." Neither the social life nor the living conditions, she believed, made Sacramento an attractive place to settle. "Any person had better take what [money] they can get for three or four years hard work," she advised one of her friends, "& go to the 'States' to enjoy it. Money slips away here about as fast as it is made if one indulges in the common comforts of life; what would last years at home would here disappear in as many months [if one were] living here as they would there. I have not given up the hope of having my final home somewhere East. The wish grows stronger," she concluded, "the more I think of it & the more I become familiar with this country."[27]

The fairy-tale mythology of frontier towns, the sort of story that well-meaning boosters everywhere make up about their civic past, would have us believe that after every major disaster—fire, flood, tornado, or earthquake—the brave, resourceful, wonderfully plucky citizens quickly rushed to rebuild and improve their fair city. The same mythology assures us that the pioneer generation at once become devoted to their new home country, determined to settle, and quickly began to organize institutions of community permanency: churches, schools, hospitals, orphanages, debating and literary societies, and other forms of voluntary association that would provide for the general needs of society. But this Pollyanna-like version of history, however attractive to the sentimental among us, does not fit the facts in Sacramento's case. Natural disasters and dangers, the constant disease problems, and a substantial degree of social fragmentation all contributed to a high population turnover. And with this turnover, Sacramentans—particularly the overwhelmingly male part of society—were too preoccupied with making money to invest substantial time and energy in projects of cultural and social improvement.

It is understandable, if a bit astounding, that so few prominent figures in Sacramento's early history remained here long. John Sutter soon left, of course, relocating first to his Hock Farm property, then to the Swiss-German community in Lititz, Pennsylvania. John Sutter, Jr., declaring that he never wanted to see Sacramento again, moved to Acapulco, Mexico, married happily, began raising a large family, started a successful mercantile business, and in time became both the American consular representative and a highly respected figure among Acapulco's community leaders.[28] Among many others, John Bidwell, Pierson Reading, Samuel Hensley, and Sam Brannan each soon moved on, along with virtually all their business colleagues of 1848 and 1849. The January 1850 flood that drove away Luzena Wilson also sent fleeing Sacramento's first acting troupe, the Atwater company, which had opened the Eagle Theater in the fall of 1849.[29] Hardin Bigelow, the city's first mayor, died in San Francisco after being badly wounded in Sacramento's violent squatters riot, a civil disturbance in August 1850 that also resulted in the death of the city assessor, the county sheriff, and six others.[30] The cholera epidemic that same year killed seventeen members of the pioneer medical profession. Fire convinced the artist Charles C. Nahl to relocate in San Francisco, where he would later paint his immense, romantically idealized depictions of gold rush scenes.[31] Rosanna Hughes, the most prosperous of Sacramento's early brothel owners, had begun to relocate her business interests to Vancouver BC, during the Fraser River gold rush, when she lost her life in the shipwreck of the *Brother Jonathan* off the northern California coast.[32] Mary Crocker was still here in 1860 with her husband, Charles, who had become a successful Sacramento merchant; so too was James McClatchy, a newspaperman prominent in the 1850 squatter's rebellion and by 1860 the owner and editor of the *Sacramento Bee*.[33] Also still here was Dr. John Morse, a leader among Sacramento's medical doctors and the city's first historian.[34]

One obvious consequence of Sacramento's high rate of population turnover was that the town and its society were not shaped by the tens of thousands who came here but rather by the few thousand who stayed. Although we lack the data for a full-scale statistical study, census records, property records, business directories, and detailed biographical information for some residents suggest a general pattern, a few common traits to explain the shaping of Sacramento's pioneer society. Those who preserved their health and made a stake, stayed. Those who did not, those who suffered excessively from disease, or were wiped out and lacked the capital or confidence to rebuild after fire or flood, those whose businesses failed to prosper—these people moved on. Either they returned to their old home country, ready to admit that California had brought them no great fortune, or they searched for further places where fortune might be found. Not only miners but merchants and professional men with California experience, often Sacramento experience, were among the first to open new mining frontiers in southern Oregon, British Columbia, and throughout the Rocky Mountain West.

One other group also departed without fail: those who hit it big, those whose financial success allowed them to live wherever they might like. In case after case, Sacramento's newly rich abandoned the city—its heat, its recurring illnesses, its fire and flood dangers, its limited social and cultural life—and took their wealth elsewhere. As a result, Sacramento's disadvantages for urban living skewed the social order toward the predominance of a reasonably prosperous, not wealthy, middle class. Almost unnoticed, the gold rush established here a stronghold of middle-class values and a bastion of the middle-class lifestyle.

As a few scholars have recently suggested, the connection between the California gold rush and the development of the American middle class in the mid-nineteenth century may be more than tangential. Urban, middle-class life was just beginning to reshape society and popular culture by the 1840s. Like no other event prior to the Civil War, the California gold rush disrupted older communities and older, tradition-bound styles of life tied to the farm and the farming village. Culturally and emotionally as well as economically, the gold rush speeded the transformation of society toward an emerging model of middle-class life that placed personal independence and individual achievement above the habit-fixed constraints of small communities.[35] In Sacramento, this instant city, circumstances strained out a large proportion alike of the unsuccessful and the very successful. Here the traits of personal independence and individual achievement were the admission tickets to an assured social standing.

Throughout the eastern states of the United States and in many other world regions, men and women who headed for California were indulging an ambition for wealth that was significantly new in the world. They were hoping for security and comfort made possible by quick, substantial riches, rather than the dreary, prolonged, slow round of labor that wealth-building had always required for ordinary people. Not everyone did succeed. Indeed, much recent popular history, including especially the Western history TV specials put together by Ken Burns and his talented crew, emphasizes the element of failure that attended the gold rush and other great frontier enterprises of the nineteenth century. But Sacramento's very existence—and the continuing vital life of this city today—provides clear proof that quite a few of these adventurous gold seekers did prosper at least well enough to sustain themselves, and well enough also to finance in time the addition of wives and husbands, children, and mayhap younger brothers and sisters to this society far away from their places of origin. Under U.S. sovereignty, the gold rush rapidly established the basis for a thoroughly middle-class society in northern California, diverse in ethnicity though mainly Euro-American in speech, fashions, and legal institutions. Sacramento was the very model, the ideal case that represented this development.

While the Sacramento region became a living paradigm for evolving Anglo-American middle-class social aspirations, it proved also a locality with strong attractions for immigrating refugees from distressed societies elsewhere in the wider world. The most prominent examples during the gold rush era were the large numbers of immigrants from Ireland, from the German states, and from the Portuguese Azores. Also among the immigrants was a small but influential contingent of Jews from the German states and the Austro-Hungarian Empire who would achieve early success in commerce and banking. These newcomers came mostly in multigenerational family units, men, women, and children—though with young adults in the majority. They were refugees from natural disasters and famine, from political upheavals and repression, from social distress and economic hardships of many types. Cut off from their homelands, most planned to resettle here from the start. Though certainly not every Irish or German or Portuguese or Jewish family that arrived in Sacramento remained for all time, these groups constituted quite distinctive elements in the pioneer population. Without exception they established here many familiar, ethnically based cultural institutions that mediated the stress of migration and the problems of raising a new generation in northern California, isolated from the parents' overseas homeland. To document their presence, one only needs to look at Sacramento's religious history, at the churches they founded—where some of their descendants are worshipers yet today—and at church-related organizations.[36]

Chinese immigrant gold seekers, a preponderantly male population, were another critically important group that reached northern California in large numbers during the gold rush era. But through the 1850s most Chinese were dispersed in the placer mining camps throughout the gold country. San Francisco, their port of entry, quickly became the metropolitan center for Chinese business and social affairs. Sacramento and other interior towns served only as staging areas and service centers for Chinese working in the mining regions. A few Chinese boarding houses, small-scale groceries, and herb shops in Sacramento operated as satellite enterprises, often linked to the great Chinese merchant houses of San Francisco. Federal census takers in 1860, recording another service industry, counted nearly one hundred Chinese women residents in Sacramento, apparently all located in one or another of the small Chinese brothels clustered close to the embarcadero in the West End.[37] By 1870 these women were gone, another sign of the continued concentration of Chinese urban enterprise and social life in San Francisco, a tendency encouraged by growing anti-Chinese agitation throughout northern California. Only after passage of the federal Chinese Exclusion Act in 1882 did demographic patterns begin to shift among the California Chinese, leading toward the twentieth-century development of family-centered communities and fixed, long-term settlement in Sacramento and other localities outside San Francisco.[38]

As with the Chinese, all foreign-born immigrant groups in the Sacramento region would measure their success in time by their acculturation to the middle-class lifestyle that was coming increasingly to typify Anglo-American society in the last half of the nineteenth century. The massive transfer of population from rural villages and small towns to urban centers, with the accompanying transformation in lifestyles, family patterns, cultural horizons, and generational ambitions, was the central demographic and social phenomenon of this age—termed by historian Eric Hobsbawm "The Age of Capital."[39] This dual process of demographic transfer and social transformation had a worldwide sweep, as seen in the immigration history of all the western United States and nowhere more clearly than in northern California during the gold rush era. Sacramento's heritage of racial, ethnic, and cultural diversity, still strongly evident at the turn of the twenty-first century, has been accompanied throughout the city's history by a commitment to the commonplace, an embrace of middle-class, bourgeois joys as a basis for the good life.

The city's leadership, dominated from the start by merchants and professional men, showed a high degree of entrepreneurial energy decade after decade, with efforts to make Sacramento attractive to newcomers—excepting for many years Chinese, Japanese, and other Asian-born immigrants—and to keep it prosperous and growing.[40] After a disastrous flood in early 1850, construction of a rudimentary flood protection levee on the American River was the city government's first and most important project. City officials and private property owners cooperated a few years later, after more floods, in an ingenious, hugely ambitious scheme to haul in landfill and raise the level of the downtown streets a full nine feet, converting the first floor of older buildings into basements.[41] As the gold rush was ending, Sacramento's middle-class leaders put together a political deal that gave their city the permanent state capital—and with it, in modern times, a population of state workers that strongly reinforces the city's middle-class ethos.[42] Four ambitious Sacramento merchants in the late 1850s launched the enterprise that became the Central Pacific-Southern Pacific railroad. Their risk-taking and shrewd political dealing made the city the western terminus of the first transcontinental rail line, ensuring Sacramento's survival and expanding its role as a regional transportation and business hub.[43]

Over the years the city's leaders, mostly through the use of public authority and public funds, have taken many other steps to overcome the problems of location. Sacramento can now boast, for example, highly effective municipal systems for waste disposal, for supplying low-cost, high-quality water, and for mosquito eradication as well as other public health measures.[44] Late in the nineteenth century the *Sacramento Bee*, the city's popular morning newspaper, began a tree-planting campaign that helped immensely to beautify city neighborhoods and moderate the harsh impact of the summer climate. A group of local entrepreneurs made Sacramento the first West Coast urban center to be electrified by hydroelectric power, transmitting electricity long distance from a generating plant on the American River at Folsom.[45] Today a long-established municipal utility district provides residents with the cheapest energy rates in northern California. Two federally funded transportation projects during the 1930s ultimately ended the region's physical isolation: constructing the Yolo causeway to provide a major interstate highway connection between Sacramento and the Bay area and dredging a deep water channel from San Francisco Bay that makes Sacramento a port for ocean-going freighters.

Among other public efforts, the city and county governments have cooperated to set off and maintain the American River Parkway. This twenty-three-mile-long public parkway borders the river inside the levee boundaries. Complete with biking, jogging, and bridle paths as well as access for boaters and fishers, the parkway protects the riverside setting from commercial encroachment. No longer a liability, the river has become a prime urban amenity, although issues of adequate flood protection continue to concern public officials throughout the region.[46]

A few continuing consequences of Sacramento's middle-class birth deserve attention. For one thing, the flight of great fortunes from Sacramento, a process that continued apace during successive eras, has meant that very little old money has stayed in the community. As a result, for better or worse, the city has few monuments to wealth of the type that add distinction to some western towns. Sacramento-created money built magnificent mansions—but they are mostly found in New York City, in Mill Valley, on Nob Hill in San Francisco, and in other more interesting, cooler, less disease-ridden places, not in Sacramento. Sacramento-created money founded a distinguished private institution of higher education—but it is located in Palo Alto, not in Sacramento. Sacramento-created money has endowed a magnificent church in San Francisco, bred champion race horses in Kentucky, hired workers to excavate the ancient ruins of Troy, and established in Rome a foundation meant to benefit rural farm populations all over the world. Recently a Sacramento-based fortune has acquired a major league baseball franchise—but it is located in Pittsburgh, Pennsylvania, not in Sacramento.

As a result of the absence of old money in the community, private philanthropy lags. Elsewhere, in San Francisco or Portland, for example, it is mostly old money that keeps symphony orchestras and local ballet troupes alive. Elsewhere, old money frequently finances lecture series, art museums, history museums, and similar community-oriented cultural enterprises. Sacramento middle-class society provides no consistently generous private support for such ventures, and the community is poorer for it.

Lacking old money and major private investment in community institutions, Sacramento's middle class has tended to rely on government at all levels to underwrite and sustain its cultural and recreational institutions. The cooperative management of the American River Parkway by city and county authorities is a leading case in point. The city and the county maintain an outstanding system of public parks that includes golf courses, tennis courts, swimming pools, and even bocci ball courts. The city and the county have also cooperated in maintaining such popular attractions as the Sacramento Zoo, a children's fairy-tale town, and the Crocker Art Museum, notable as the first professionally run art museum established in western America. In partnership with the state park system and private business people, local authorities have taken a leading part in fostering the development of the Old Sacramento Historic District, with its museums, stores, and family-centered recreational attractions.

Through abundant use of public authority, the Sacramento environment has been thoroughly reengineered and refashioned from the natural region found here before the beginning of European American settlement. What we may read as natural in today's Sacramento is a work of human art, marked by the elimination or drastic reduction of many native species and the introduction of hundreds upon hundreds of newcomer species—plants, mammals, birds, and fish—both by design and by accident. Today Sacramentans enjoy the shade of Australian eucalyptus trees, Dutch elms,

Chinese pistachio, and Japanese plums, among other exotic trees. They wade through weedy thickets of Russian yellow star thistle along the levees. In addition to the California quail, they may catch sight of Chinese pheasants and English starlings. Fishing enthusiasts take striped bass and American shad in the region's rivers, introduced from the East Coast more than a century ago. These and countless other exotics have changed the face of nature.

Meanwhile, Sacramentans have rebuilt the underlying structure. Engineering ingenuity has refashioned the land and redirected the waters. Generations of effort have raised Sacramento's downtown street levels, filled in sloughs and bogs, channeled and redirected the rivers, changed the course of creeks and streams, and dammed and diked and dredged from one end of the county to the other. They have planted and built, cut and constructed, nipped and tucked, to alter the area's whole appearance. What we perceive as nature in Sacramento today, in short, is to the original natural environment about what Pamela Lee of Baywatch fame is to the natural woman.

The gold rush era, with its mostly male society, established a largely male-oriented popular culture that became another enduring legacy of Sacramento's formative period. By the choice of Sacramento's earliest policymakers, the town was wide open. Its entertainment business, catering to a transient male population, helped in no small way to define the character of the infant metropolis. Even after the gender balance began to shift toward parity, a male saloon and brothel subculture long remained embedded in the city's social life, a subculture geographically concentrated in the West End district near the Sacramento River. Urged by U.S. military officials, Sacramento's city government adopted a red-light abatement ordinance to abolish brothels after World War I, following an exceedingly divisive public controversy.[47] Yet some will argue that this subculture still thrives, only slightly altered, close to the state capitol complex.

To some extent, Chinese, Irish, German, and other immigrant males found work during the gold rush era in domestic service occupations normally taken by women in Anglo-American society. They became cooks and waiters, laundrymen, house servants, hotel attendants, and boardinghouse keepers. But the educational and humanitarian roles also customarily filled by women in providing schools, orphanages, and health care generally suffered neglect in Sacramento even after the demographics began to change somewhat during the 1860s. It remained, for instance, for the Sisters of Mercy, a contingent of Roman Catholic nuns from Ireland, to open Sacramento's first school and first orphanage after their arrival in

1857. The creation of the Mercy hospital system, one of the region's major health institutions today, is the outgrowth of the sisters' devoted work over generations.[48] Other women led the struggle for public-funded common school education in Sacramento through the decades of slow growth that succeeded the gold rush.[49] While Sacramento's voters have elected two women mayors in the twentieth century and a third in the election of 2000, issues like the public funding of male professional sports illustrate a persistent cultural divide along gender lines.

Today Sacramento appears greatly changed from the gold rush city. Indeed, the region is now in the midst of a new kind of gold rush. Thanks to improvements such as air conditioning, cheap hydroelectric power, and the flood control benefits of Folsom Dam and levees built by the Army Corps of Engineers, most of the extreme hazards and inconveniences of life in the gold rush era are now abated. New businesses are starting here, and old firms are transferring headquarters or branch offices to the area. Every day refugees from the Los Angeles basin and the San Francisco Bay region appear in Sacramento real estate offices, equity rich from the sale of their former homes in areas now too pricey and too crowded, too impacted by urban growth for them to remain. Quality of life is still an issue, but this issue now favors growth and makes new fortunes for those investing in real estate development and construction. Downtown redevelopment is proceeding with great expectations; north, west, east, and southeast of the city, the hills—and flatlands—are alive with the sound of hammers.

With all this activity, newer immigrant groups are again finding Sacramento a choice location for beginning their American experience. Once again the city is undergoing an urban frontier movement that brings here distressed, dispossessed expatriates and hopeful transcultural adventurers from many lands, replicating in their own lives the historical dual processes of demographic relocation and social transformation. Most recently, significant numbers of new residents have arrived in Sacramento from Southeast Asia and mainland China, Mexico, Columbia and Guatemala, the former Soviet Union (especially the Ukraine), the former Yugoslavia, Iran, Palestine, Uganda, Ethiopia, and other countries in sub-Saharan Africa. Once again adult immigrants find themselves to some degree bewildered. Their needs strain the resources of underfunded social support facilities; their presence is not always warmly welcomed by older residents. They often remain self-segregated in ethnic ghettoes, attempting to hold onto familiar ways of their homeland—especially traditional foods and religious practices—only to see their children and grandchildren becoming pizza-eaters, bilingual and bicultural experts, avid to hip-hop their way into mainstream American life.

The mid-nineteenth-century gold discoveries in northern California along with those in Australia, Friedrich Engels remarked ruefully to Karl Marx, created large new markets "out of nothing," a development the two socialist theorists had not anticipated when writing the *Communist Manifesto*.[50] In Sacramento and similarly situated places adjacent to gold country, gold also created large new cities out of nothing, another unanticipated consequence of worldwide European expansion and the invasion of once peripheral regions by capitalist commerce and industry. These gold rush cities and the societies they fostered were significantly different than any previously known. Formed by voluntary mass migration and settlement, built on the energy and ambitions of speculative, adventurous men and women, they were unique in cultural diversity, a singular dedication to commercial profit, and the resolutely middle-class character of their commercial and social leaders. These cities did not become centers for class conflict; the circumstances of their birth and growth gave them a destiny that avoided the revolutionary struggle prophesied by Marx and Engels in 1848.

Edward Gould Buffum, a New York journalist who happened to be traveling in California at the time of the gold discovery, hazarded in 1850 his own shrewd yet idealistic assessment of what the worldwide consequences of the gold rush might prove to be. In his volume *Six Months in the Gold Mines*, Buffum imagined the widespread benefits that could arise from the wealth being uncovered daily in the Golden State. "The starving millions of Europe," he wrote, "will find in the mountain gorges of California a home with profitable labour at their very door-sills, and the labouring men of our own country will find it to their interest to settle among the auriferous hills." Not only in the Mother Lode backcountry but throughout the length and breadth of the state, Buffum declared, California's resources could provide a permanent increase in the wealth and well-being for those who came there—and for those others, as well, who made them welcome. "Never in the world's history," he asserted, "was there a better opportunity for a great, free, and republican nation like ours to offer to the oppressed and down-trodden of the whole world an asylum and a place where by honest industry, which will contribute as much to our wealth as their prosperity, they can build themselves happy homes and live like freemen."[51]

Now looking back 150 years, we may see that Sacramento and its environs represent in substantial degree the fulfillment of Buffum's social and moral vision. Sacramentans should think themselves fortunate to have such a gold rush heritage. For here is a place where ordinary people, frequently refugees from hardship, have succeeded in finding productive work and a decent income; they have found it possible to create homes for themselves under conditions of assured political liberty and personal freedom. We should not erase from historical memory the episodes of ethnic and racial intolerance that in Sacramento, as elsewhere, mark the efforts of diverse peoples to live together, nor should we fail to recognize the social frictions that persist in our own time. But there is something else to be understood about the region's past that might occasion pride or at least a sense of civic satisfaction. During the gold rush era, the people of Sacramento usually survived and prospered by shaping an open-minded middle-class consensus on divisive issues, prompted by no ideology except pragmatic good sense. With good fortune, this part of the gold rush heritage can also continue to be a historical model and a valuable guide for Sacramento's future well into a prosperous new millennium.

Notes

1. For the activities of John Sutter and his compatriots in the region prior to 1848, see Dillon, *Fool's Gold*; and Owens, ed., *John Sutter and a Wider West*. Samuel Brannan's visits to Sutter's Fort are recorded in Bagley, ed., *Scoundrel's Tale*, 197–203, 223–24. The standard overview for the history of the region is Joseph McGowan, *History of the Sacramento Valley*, 3 vols. (Chicago: Lewis Historical Publishing Company, 1961).

2. Jedediah Smith's visits to the region are recounted in Dale Morgan, *Jedediah Smith and the Opening of the West* (Indianapolis: Bobbs-Merrill, 1953), 207–8, 258–60. Smith's journal record of his unsuccessful attempt in May 1827 to cross the Sierra Nevada by following the American River upstream can be found in George R. Brooks, ed., *The Southwest Expedition of Jedediah S. Smith: His Personal Account of the Journey to California, 1826–1827* (Glendale CA: Arthur H. Clark, 1977), 154–62.

3. Jedediah Smith's attempt to find a way from the Sacramento Valley across the Siskiyou range in 1828 ended in frustration, climaxed in July by a Native assault on his unguarded Umpqua River camp that left only Smith and three others alive. A Hudson's Bay Company expedition led by John Work first opened a route to connect the Columbia River and the Sacramento River in 1832–1833, staying east of the Siskiyous, skirting Mount Lassen, and entering the Sacramento Valley by way of Cow Creek. Morgan, *Jedediah Smith*, 261–69; Alice Bay Maloney, ed., *Fur Brigade to the Bonaventura: John Work's California Expedition, 1832–1833, for the Hudson's Bay Company* (San Francisco: California Historical Society, 1945).

4. On the natural environment of the Sacramento Valley and the delta, see Elna

S. Bakker, *An Island Called California: An Ecological Introduction to Its Natural Communities* (Berkeley: University of California Press, 1972), 123–43; and John C. Williams and Howard C. Monroe, *Natural History of Northern California* (Dubuque IA: Kendall/Hunt Publishing Company, 1976), 135–63, 173–208.

5. The Sutter's Fort site was later substantially graded down by workers reconstructing the fort building as a historical monument in the 1880s and early 1890s. See Charles L. Gebhardt, *Final Report, Archeological Investigations of Sutter's Fort State Historical Monument by Sacramento State College, Spring of 1955 and by Charles L. Gebhardt, Fall of 1957 and Spring of 1958* (mimeographed, Sacramento: author, 1958); William H. Olson, *Archeological Investigations at Sutter's Fort State Historical Monument* (Sacramento: State of California Division of Beaches and Parks, Interpretive Services, 1961); Kenneth N. Owens, *Final Report on Cultural Resources within the K-L-28–29 and K-L-29–30 Blocks, Sacramento, California* (Cultural Resources Management Report for Sutter Community Hospitals and Sacramento City Planning Office, 1984), all on file at the Sacramento Archives and Museum Collection Center; Frank Lortie, "Sutter's Fort," *American West* 17, no. 3 (1980): 12–15.

6. Norman L. Wilson and Arlean H. Towne, "Nisenan," in *California,* ed. Robert F. Heizer, 387–97, vol. 8 of *Handbook of North American Indians,* ed. William C. Sturtevant, ed. (Washington DC: Smithsonian Institution, 1978).

7. Bonita Louise Boles, "The Advent of Malaria in California and Oregon in the 1830s," *Golden Notes* 36, no. 4 (winter 1990); Joseph A. McGowan, "Miasma in Sacramento, 1860–1950," *Golden Notes* 24, no. 3 (fall 1978); Sherburne F. Cook, *The Epidemic of 1830–1833 in California and Oregon* (Berkeley: University of California Press, 1955).

8. On the disease dangers of city life, see William H. McNeill, *Plagues and Peoples* (Garden City NY: Anchor Press/Doubleday, 1976); Arno Karlen, *Man and Microbes: Disease and Plagues in History and Modern Times* (New York: G. P. Putnam's Sons, 1995), 47–63; Sir MacFarlane Burnet and David O. White, *Natural History of Infectious Disease,* 4th ed. (Cambridge, England: University Press, 1972), 13–14.

9. Thor Severson, *Sacramento, An Illustrated History: 1839 to 1875—From Sutter's Fort to Capital City* (San Francisco: California Historical Society, 1973) provides an outstanding description of Sacramento's early years, accompanied by a wealth of illustrations. Another well-crafted general account is Edward H. Howes, "The World's Gateway to Gold, 1848–1860s," in John F. Burns, ed., *Sacramento: Gold Rush Legacy, Metropolitan Destiny* (Carlsbad CA: Heritage Media Corp., 1999).

10. A detailed description of the circumstances appears in John A. Sutter, Jr., *Statement Regarding Early California Experiences,* ed. Allan R. Ottley (Sacramento: Sacramento Books Collector's Club, 1943). Written for his lawyer in 1855 as the younger Sutter sought in some fashion to salvage a remnant of his father's

Sacramento real estate fortune for the family and to justify his own earlier actions, this account states the particulars in one of the greatest, most successful land frauds ever to be perpetrated in western America. Young Sutter, as he came to realize far too late, was poisoned and drugged by his trusted business partners, a rapacious set of unscrupulous scoundrels, who induced him to sign over most of his father's Sacramento property and to pay them exorbitant fees for their time and trouble as they defrauded him shamelessly.

11. John Reps, *The Making of Urban America: A History of City Planning in the United States* (Princeton: Princeton University Press, 1965), 308.

12. The grants are recorded in the Sacramento City Tax Assessment Rolls, book A, housed in the city archives at the Sacramento Archives and Museum Collection Center. An appreciative volume, prepared by the students of McClatchy Senior High School in 1948, describes the status of the park blocks at that date: *Park Grants of John A. Sutter, Junior* (Sacramento: Nugget Press, 1948).

13. Dorothea J. Theodoratus and Kathleen McBride, *History of the Sacramento City Block 6th and 7th, K and L Streets, 1848–1920* (Sacramento: Redevelopment Agency of the City of Sacramento, 1978); Luzena Stanley Wilson, *Forty-niner: Memories Recalled Years Later for her Daughter Correnah Wilson Wright* (Oakland CA: Eucalyptus Press, 1937), 17–18.

14. Ken Lastufka, "Redevelopment of Sacramento's West End, 1959–1970: A Historical Overview with an Analysis of the Impact of Relocation" (master's thesis, California State University, Sacramento, 1985); Thomas Dean Norris, "Metropolitan Growth in the Sacramento Area during World War II and the Post-War Period" (master's thesis, California State University, Sacramento, 1982). For the impact on adjacent neighborhoods, see Kenneth N. Owens, *Oak Park Historical Overview* (Cultural Resources Management Report for the Sacramento Redevelopment Agency, 1980); and by the same author, *Alkali Flat Historical Overview* (Cultural Resources Management Report for the Sacramento City Redevelopment Agency, 1979).

15. An excellent summary of population movement into northern California during the gold rush era appears in the prize-winning study by Walter Nugent, *Into the West: The Story of Its People* (New York: Alfred A. Knopf, 1999), 54–65.

16. John Morse, *The First History of Sacramento City, Written in 1853, With a Historical Note on the Life of Dr. Morse by Caroline Wenzel* (Sacramento: Sacramento Book Collector's Club, 1945).

17. Wilson, *Forty-Niner*, 17.

18. Wilson, *Forty-Niner*, 18.

19. Wilson, *Forty-Niner*, 24–25.

20. Accounts of Sacramento's early experiences with fires can be found in Howes, "Gateway to Gold," 36–37; Severson, *Sacramento*, 106–7; and Charles E. Nagel, "A Fight for Survival: Floods, Riots and Disease in Sacramento, 1850" (master's thesis, California State University, Sacramento, 1965).

21. Mary Crocker to Mrs. Lydia Seymour, March 25, 1853, typescript transcription, Special Collections, California State Library, Sacramento.

22. Eugene M. Itogawa, "The Natural Ice Industry in California" (master's thesis, California State University, Sacramento, 1974).

23. Morse, *First History*, 50; Charles E. Nagel, "Sacramento Cholera Epidemic of 1850," *Golden Notes* 4, no. 1 (October 1967); Mitchel Roth, "Cholera, Community, and Public Health in Gold Rush Sacramento and San Francisco," *Pacific Historical Review* 66, no. 4 (1997): 527–51. A colorful description appears in Groh, *Gold Fever*, 215–23. For the circumstances that brought cholera to the western United States in 1849 and 1850, see Charles S. Rosenberg, *The Cholera Years: The United States in 1832, 1849, and 1866* (Chicago: Chicago University Press, 1962).

24. Darius Ogden Mills, "Biography of Darius Ogden Mills," Bancroft Library, University of California, Berkeley; Burelle Press Clipping Service, "In Memoriam Darius Ogden Mills," Special Collections, California State Library; Willard Thompson, "D. O. Mills," *Golden Notes* 30, no. 4 (winter 1984).

25. Wilson, *Forty-niner*, 14.

26. Wilson, *Forty-niner*, 15–16.

27. Mary Crocker to Mrs. Lydia Seymour, March 25, 1853, Special Collections, California State Library.

28. John A. Sutter, Jr., *Statement Regarding Early California Experiences*.

29. Charles V. Hume, "The Sacramento Theater, 1849–1885" (Ph.D. diss., Stanford University, 1955); and by the same author "The Eagle Theater, 1849," *Golden Notes* 19, no. 3 (August 1973); and "First of the Gold Rush Theaters," *California Historical Society Quarterly* 46, no. 4 (1967): 337–44.

30. Literature on Sacramento's squatters' riot includes Dennis M. Dart, "Sacramento Squatter Riot of August 14, 1850," *Pacific Historian* 24, no. 2 (1980): 156–67; Mickey Knapp, "The Squatter's Riot, A Dramatic Episode in Sacramento's History," *Golden Notes* 38, nos. 3, 4 (fall/winter 1992); Mark Anthony Eifler, "Crossroads City: Culture and Community in Gold Rush Sacramento, 1849–1850" (Ph.D. diss., University of California, Berkeley, 1992); Donald J. Pisani, "Squatter Law in California, 1850–1858," *Western Historical Quarterly* 25, no. 3 (1994): 277–310; and Nicolai Laquaglia, "Hardin Bigelow, The First Mayor of Sacramento" (master's thesis, California State University, Sacramento, 1968).

31. Charles Christian Nahl Letters to his Family, 1846–1854, Bancroft Library; Nahl Family Letters, 1842–1867, Bancroft Library.

32. On Rosanna Hughes, see Carol Radovich and Kira Russo Bauer, "The Prostitute as Business Woman: Sacramento, 1850–1880," graduate seminar paper, January 1992, on file, Special Collections, California State University, Sacramento.

33. K. D. Kurutz, "Sacramento's Pioneer Patrons of Art: The Edwin Bryant Crocker Family," ed. John F. Wilhelm, *Golden Notes* 31, no. 2 (summer 1985).

34. See the biographical sketch of Dr. Morse by Caroline Wenzel in her edition of his *Early History of Sacramento*, cited in note 18 above.

35. The major work that advances this analysis is Brian Roberts, *American Alchemy: The California Gold Rush and Middle-Class Culture* (Chapel Hill: University of North Carolina Press, 2000); see also Goldman, *Gold-Seeking*.

36. The Sacramento Museum and History Division, with funding from the California Council for the Humanities, sponsored a series of Sacramento ethnic community studies during the 1980s. The narratives for these studies are on file at the Sacramento Archives and Museum Collection Center. Particularly relevant are the following works in this collection: The Chinese, by Sylvia Sun Minnick; the Portuguese, by Joseph d'Allesandro; the Irish, by Elizabeth McKee; the African Americans, by Clarence Caesar; the Italians, by Bruce Pierini; the Germans, by Thomas D. Norris; and the Jews, by Alice Kingsnorth. Other pertinent works include Lapp, *Blacks in Gold Rush California*; Caesar, "Historical Demographics of Sacramento's Black Community, 1848–1900," 198–213; Bragg, "Knowledge is Power," 214–21; Marlene S. Gaines, "The Early Sacramento Jewish Community," *Western States Jewish Historical Quarterly* 3, no. 2 (1971): 65–85; Gottard Deutsch, "David Lubin: A Remarkable Jew," *Western States Jewish Historical Quarterly* 14, no. 4 (1982): 316–201; Willard Thompson, "David Lubin: Sacramento's Pioneer Merchant-Philosopher," *Golden Notes,* 32, no. 1 (spring 1986); Bernard M. Kaplan, "An Historical Outline of the Jews of Sacramento in the Nineteenth Century," *Western States Jewish Historical Quarterly* 23, no. 3 (1991): 256–67; John Francis Dulury, "Irish Nationalism in Sacramento, 1850–1890," *Golden Notes* 36, no. 2 (summer 1990). On the religious history of pioneer Sacramento, see especially Steven M. Avella, "Phelan's Cemetery: Religion in the Urbanizing West, 1950–1869, in Los Angeles, San Francisco, and Sacramento," in *Rooted in Barbarous Soil,* 250–315.

37. Cindy Baker, "Sacramento's Sophisticated Ladies: Prostitution in 1860," *Golden Notes* 41, no. 2 (summer 1995).

38. In addition to the narrative by Sylvia Sun Minnick cited in note 36, substantial information will be found in Chinn, Lai, and Choy, eds., *History of the Chinese*

in California. The history of Chinese agricultural workers in the Sacramento–San Joaquin Delta is brilliantly explored in Chan, *This Bittersweet Soil*. General accounts include Sucheng Chan, *Asian Californians* (San Francisco: MTL/Boyd Fraser, 1991); Barth, *Bitter Strength*; and Daniels, *Asian America*.

39. Hobsbawm, *The Age of Capital, 1848–1875*.

40. While most published research on anti-Chinese and anti-Japanese agitation in northern California has centered on San Francisco, Sacramento was also a focal point for propaganda efforts directed toward the restriction of immigration from eastern Asia. James McClatchy, an Irish immigrant who became publisher and editor of the *Sacramento Bee*, was prominent in the anti-Chinese cause. His son Valentine McClatchy became a leading propagandist in the anti-Japanese movement at the beginning of the twentieth century.

41. Barbara Lagomarsino, "Early Attempts to Save Sacramento by Raising its Business District" (master's thesis, California State University, Sacramento, 1969); Justin Turner, "The Sacramento Floods in the 1850s," *Pacific Historian* 8, no. 3 (1964): 129–33; Marvin Brienes, "Sacramento Defies the Rivers, 1850–1878," *California History* 58, no. 1 (1979): 2–19.

42. Joseph A. McGowan, "California's Capitol, 1849–1854," *Golden Notes* 14, no. 3 (April 1968); Severson, *Sacramento*, 185–91.

43. Severson, *Sacramento*, 171–82; Walter P. Gray III, "The Railroad Era in Sacramento, 1860–1880s," in *Sacramento*, ed. John F. Burns, 46–56.

44. Joseph A. McGowan, "Miasma in Sacramento, 1860–1950," *Golden Notes* 24, no. 3 (fall 1978); Joseph A. McGowan, "Clear, Clean Water, 1850–1923," *Golden Notes* 24, no. 4 (winter 1978); Cedrik R. Zemitis, "Garbage in Sacramento, The Transition from Private Enterprise to Municipal Control, 1892–1922" (master's thesis, California State University, Sacramento, 1998).

45. Robert D. Livingston, "Illuminating Sacramento, 1853–1874," *Golden Notes* 27, no. 4 (winter 1981); Rowena Wise Day, "Carnival of Lights: The Story of Electric Power in Sacramento, 1879 to 1985," *Golden Notes* 16, nos. 2–3 (July 1970).

46. Lucinda Woodward and Jesse M. Smith, *A History of the Lower American River* (Sacramento: American River Natural History Association, 1977).

47. This controversy is best followed in the pages of the *Sacramento Bee,* whose editor, C. K. McClatchy, was a vehement opponent of the measure. Charles M. Goethe, the son of Sacramento's first German Lutheran minister, became a leading advocate and activist on behalf of the measure. Goethe's role is inadequately documented in the C. M. Goethe Papers housed in the University Archives at California State University, Sacramento.

48. Mary Evangelist Morgan, *Mercy, Generation to Generation: History of the First Century of the Sisters of Mercy, Diocese of Sacramento, California* (San Francisco: Fearon Publishers, 1957).

49. On the history of Sacramento women, see, among other items, Allan R. Ottley, "Angels Without Wings: The Scarcity of Women in Pioneer Sacramento," *Golden Notes* 37/38, no. 4 (winter 1991); Terry R. Willis, "Sacramento Women in 1872" (master's thesis, California State University, Sacramento, 1979); Wendy Welles Franklin, "The Capital and Women's Rights, 1850–1911," *Golden Notes* 34, no. 4 (winter 1988); Irma West, *Walking Tour of Medical Pioneer Gravesites* [Sacramento Pioneer Cemetery] (Sacramento: Sacramento-El Dorado Medical Society Historical Committee, n.d.); Elaine Connolly and Dian Self, *Capital Women: An Interpretive History of Women in Sacramento, 1850–1920* (Sacramento: Capital Women's History Project, 1995). The role of women in education is described in Jane L. Jensen, "The Development of Sacramento Public Schools, 1854 to 1900" (master's thesis, California State University Sacramento, 1954); and Bragg, "Knowledge is Power," 214–21.

50. Engels to Marx, August 24, 1853, quoted in Hobsbawm, *Age of Capital*, 62.

51. Buffum, *Six Months in the Gold Mines*, 85. A summary of Buffum's career by John W. Caughey appears in the introduction of the 1959 reprint of this work published by the Ward Ritchie Press.

Contributors

Michael J. Gonzalez teaches U.S. history, California history, and Chicano history at the University of San Diego. He was a contributor to *Contested Eden: California before the Gold Rush*, edited by Richard Orsi and Ramón A. Gutiérrezm (University of California Press, 1998), and is currently completing a history of nineteenth-century Los Angeles.

Albert L. Hurtado is Travis Professor of Modern American History at the University of Oklahoma. He received the Ray Allen Billington Award of the Organization of American Historians for his volume *Indian Survival on the California Frontier* (Yale University Press, 1988). His most recent work is *Intimate Frontiers: Sex, Gender, and Culture in Old California* (University of New Mexico Press, 1999).

Elizabeth Jameson holds the Imperial Oil and Lincoln McKay Chair in American Studies at the University of Calgary. Her publications include *All That Glitters: Class, Conflict, and Community in Cripple Creek* (University of Illinois Press, 1998), which received the Rodman W. Paul Award for Outstanding Contributions to Mining History from the Mining History Association. She is also the coeditor of *The Women's West* (University of Oklahoma Press, 1987) and *Writing the Range: Race, Class, and Culture in the Women's West* (University of Oklahoma Press, 1997).

Susan L. Johnson is associate professor of history at the University of Colorado, Boulder. A recent research fellow at the Huntington Library, she is the author of *Roaring Camp: The Social World of the California Gold Rush* (W. W. Norton, 2000).

Sylvia Sun Minnick, of Chinese American descent, was raised in Malaysia and San Francisco's Chinatown. She is a frequent lecturer and writer on Chinese American culture and international business etiquette. She is the author of *samfow: The San Joaquin Chinese Legacy* (Panorama West, 1988) and served as deputy assistant director of the California States Parks Department for state sesquicentennial planning.

Shirley Ann Wilson Moore is professor of history at California State University, Sacramento. She is the author of *To Place Our Deeds: The African American Community in Richmond, California, 1910–1963* (University of California Press, 2000). Her most recent book is *Above the Rockies of Prejudice: African American Women in the West* (University of Oklahoma Press, forthcoming, coedited with Quintard Taylor).

Jeremy Mouat is associate professor of history at Athabasca University in Alberta, Canada. He has written widely on mining history and in 1997 received the Mining History Association's Rodman W. Paul Award for Outstanding Contributions to Mining History. His most recent book, *Metal Mining in Canada, 1840–1950*, was published in 2000 by the National Museum of Science and Technology in Ottawa.

Kenneth N. Owens is professor emeritus of history and ethnic studies at California State University, Sacramento, where he founded the Capital Campus Public History Program. His previously edited works include *John Sutter and a Wider West* (University of Nebraska Press, 1985). He is now completing a documentary history of Mormons in the California gold rush.

Charlene Porsild, a native of the Yukon and a former Fulbright Fellow, has taught at the University of Nebraska–Lincoln and is now director of the Montana Historical Library and Archives. Her book *Gamblers and Dreamers: Women, Men, and Community in the Klondike* (University of British Columbia Press, 1998) won the Western History Association's W. Turrentine Jackson Award and the Canadian Historical Association's Clio Prize in 1999.

Martin Ridge, a former editor of the *Journal of American History*, is a senior research associate in the Huntington Library and past president of the Western History Association. He is the coauthor of *The American West* (Indiana University Press, 1999) and the forthcoming sixth edition of *Westward Expansion* (University of New Mexico Press, 2001).

Brian Roberts is assistant professor of history at California State University, Sacramento. He is the author of *American Alchemy: The California Gold Rush and Middle Class Culture* (University of North Carolina Press, 2000).

Malcolm J. Rohrbough is professor of history at the University of Iowa. He received the Caughey Western History Association Prize and was cowinner of the Ray Allen Billington Award of the Organization of American Historians for his book *Days of Gold: The California Gold Rush and the American Nation* (University of California Press, 1996). His other publications include

Aspen: The History of a Silver Mining Town, 1879–1893 (University Press of Colorado, 1986).

Clark C. Spence is professor emeritus at the University of Illinois. He is a past president of both the Western History Association and the Mining History Association. His many books deal with Western development and with the mineral industry. Included among these works is the prize-winning *Mining Engineers and the American West: The Lace-Boot Brigade, 1849–1933* (Yale University Press, 1970).

Index